TOKYO

GUIDE

BE A TRAVELER - NOT A TOURIST!

OPEN ROAD TRAVEL GUIDES SHOW YOU
HOW TO BE A TRAVELER – NOT A TOURIST!

*Whether you're going abroad or planning a trip in the United States, take Open Road along on your journey. Our books have been praised by **Travel & Leisure, The Los Angeles Times, Newsday, Booklist, US News & World Report, Endless Vacation, American Bookseller, Coast to Coast**, and many other magazines and newspapers!*

Don't just see the world – experience it with Open Road!

ABOUT THE AUTHORS

Patrice Fusillo has just returned from Japan after more than ten years of living in Tokyo, where she ran the Institute of Foreign Bankers in Tokyo and was active in cultural exchange. Patrice now makes her home in Oakland, California. Noriko Araki, a lifelong Tokyo resident, is a freelance writer. Trained as an anthropologist, Noriko enjoys looking at her culture and society from both inside and out. Both avid travelers, Noriko and Patrice have written monographs on Japanese culture.

BE A TRAVELER, NOT A TOURIST - WITH OPEN ROAD TRAVEL GUIDES!

Open Road Publishing has guide books to exciting, fun destinations on four continents. As veteran travelers, our goal is to bring you the best travel guides available anywhere!

No small task, but here's what we offer:

• All Open Road travel guides are written by authors with a distinct, opinionated point of view – not some sterile committee or team of writers. Our authors are experts in the areas covered and are polished writers.

• Our guides are geared to people who want to make their own travel choices. We'll show you how to discover the real destination – not just see some place from a tour bus window.

• We're strong on the basics, but we also provide terrific choices for those looking to get off the beaten path and *experience* the country or city - not just *see* it or pass through it.

• We give you the best, but we also tell you about the worst and what to avoid. Nobody should waste their time and money on their hard-earned vacation because of bad or inadequate travel advice.

• Our guides assume nothing. We tell you everything you need to know to have the trip of a lifetime – presented in a fun, literate, no-nonsense style.

• And, above all, we welcome your input, ideas, and suggestions to help us put out the best travel guides possible.

TOKYO

GUIDE

BE A TRAVELER - NOT A TOURIST!

Patrice Fusillo & Noriko Araki

OPEN ROAD PUBLISHING

1st Edition
Text Copyright ©1999 by Patrice Fusillo & Noriko Araki
Maps Copyright ©1999 by Open Road Publishing
- All Rights Reserved -
Library of Congress Catalog Card No. 98-66338
ISBN 1-883323-89-4

ACKNOWLEDGEMENTS

We thank the many people who helped us capture the energy and vitality of Japan. Many of the maps appear courtesy of the Japan National Tourist Organization and we thank JNTO's Isao Yoshiike, Kaneyuki Ono and Marian Goldberg for their assistance. Judith T. Smith tirelessly assisted with editing. Big thanks to our publisher, Jonathan Stein, for giving us the opportunity to write this book.

Thanks also go to Nancy Berry, Sandy Berry, Rosemary and Glen Bonderud, Steve Butler, Jane Faller, Takeshi Hasegawa, Nagako Hiyoshi, Steve and Chikako Hytha, Takashi Katano, Pat Langan, Rose Eng Lee, Milagros Louise, Yin-wah Ma, Jane Singer Mizuguchi, Cesare Monti, Sue Muroga, Shigeko Nishiyama, Hideko Sakurai, Keiko Sakurai, Anne Torige, Yumi Yamazaki, Jan Wessel, Patty Goodman, Reiko Kuribayashi, Namiko Sakamoto, Nancy Wilson and Jack and Lina Wood. Last, but not least, we thank our husbands, Tadashi Araki and David Hytha, and our children, Naoko and Nobuyuki Araki and Renee and Allison Hytha.

TABLE OF CONTENTS

CONTENTS

CONTENTS

14. SEEING THE SIGHTS   209

15. NIGHTLIFE & ENTERTAINMENT   279

16. SPORTS & RECREATION   289

CONTENTS

CONTENTS

CONTENTS

SIDEBARS

1. INTRODUCTION

Tokyo thrives as one of the most dynamic and exhilarating capitals in the world. The city's energy and excitement are as electric as the neon lighting up the Ginza, Shinjuku and Shibuya.

The heart of modern Japan, Tokyo is home to the national government, the financial industry, the arts, fashion and retailing. While Japan remains firmly anchored in the 21st century, it still reveres age-old traditions. Japan has been more successful than most countries in maintaining a balance between old and new. Craftsmen spend months creating a perfect lacquer bowl while hundreds of Walkmen roll off a production line every hour. High atop a 50-storied steel and glass skyscraper, a small wooden Shinto shrine receives daily offerings of rice and sake wine.

Some people avoid Tokyo, assuming it's not exotic enough — they picture only skyscrapers and businessmen dressed in dark suits. Others avoid it because they have heard stories of $150 melons and $300-a-pound beef and assume the place is way over budget for them. Still others fear traveling where they can't read the signs. Set aside these worries. Temples, virtual reality game centers, dramatic Kabuki dance, state-of-the-art factories, serene gardens, glittering urban centers, meditative tea ceremony, postmodern architecture, a zillion stores and restaurants and much more awaits you. We detail highlights of the best-known sights, but also recommend off-the-beaten-path alternatives.

Are you worried about going outside your hotel to try other restaurants? We get you into restaurants where locals go and prepare you to order like a pro in no time. Afraid you won't know how to act at a Japanese inn? We explain the etiquette, including when to take off your shoes and how to use a Japanese bath. Not sure what temples and shrines are all about? We give you enough background information to help you understand what you see and, more importantly, how to enjoy it.

We tell you how to find the best prices on international tickets and how to travel economically within Japan. Yes, we detail Japanese inns and hotels where you'll be pampered in a style to which you'd like to become accustomed, but we also tell you about places where it costs less to stay than at a Holiday Inn in the US. So pack you bags, get set, and come visit one of the world's great cities — Tokyo!

2. EXCITING TOKYO!
- OVERVIEW

Japan might be the most overanalyzed country in the world. Entire forests have been sacrificed to produce books explaining Japan to Westerners. So it's no surprise that everyone visits Japan with expectations. Some people romantically picture Japan as the *Teahouse of the August Moon,* a nation where the entire population dresses in kimono and lives a rarefied life in quaint buildings, writing *haiku* poetry and performing tea ceremony as delicate *koto* melodies waft through the air.

Others see Japan as a vision of the future, out of control: huge faceless sprawling cities with millions of people crowding into subways, living in cramped apartments, racing to keep up with the pace of robots next to them on the assembly line.

A third group, the road warriors who fill the business class seats of planes crossing the Pacific, interact with aggressive businessmen driving hard bargains around the world and see Japan as just plain hard work.

In reality, Japan contains aspects of all three, but much more. The country of 125 million people working hard and playing hard also offers beautiful scenery, exceptional monuments, a fascinating history and an endless numbers of unique experiences:

- Stand in Shinjuku Station, the world's busiest train station.
- Climb to an isolated mountain temple in a dense forest an hour away from the same train station.
- Marvel at a sea of neon signs so dense you can read a newspaper at night on the street.
- Visit a war museum perennially at the center of controversy over Japan's past.
- Bathe in a steaming outdoor hot spring bath catching snowflakes on your tongue.
- Watch your car, TV or Walkman come off its production line.
- Join an entire nation in celebrating cherry blossoms.
- See meditative tea ceremonies performed in rustic huts.

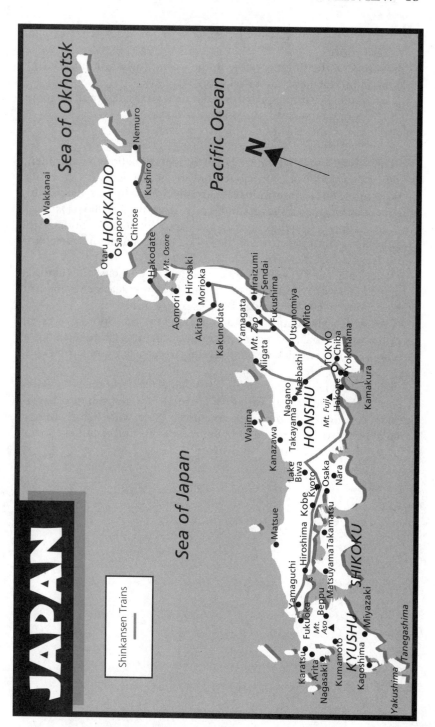

- Exchange toasts with fun-loving Japanese in a raucous bar under the railway tracks.
- Enjoy some of the finest cooking in the world, some of it uncooked.
- Ski on an indoor slope on a sweltering 90° day.
- Marvel at unbelievably high prices — but then go to a discount store and buy a camera that's still unavailable overseas.
- Gaze in awe at the world's largest bronze Buddha.

Tokyo is the pulse of modern Japan. Seat of the national government, the city isn't a stodgy place inhabited only by bureaucrats. It's the center of the fashion and retailing industries, the big trading houses, the banking and financial industries, the arts and music. Home to 150,000 restaurants and bars, people crowd the entertainment areas into the wee hours of the morning. Once the castle town of the Tokugawa shoguns, some neighborhoods still evoke a memory of the feudal past.

Near Tokyo lies **Yokohama**, a cosmopolitan port city; **Kamakura**, a former capital with a multitude of temples in a quiet seaside setting; and **Hakone** and the **Izu Peninsula**, Tokyo's playgrounds.

Fascinating places match fascinating experiences. Sports lovers can revel in *sumo*, baseball, soccer and a host of martial arts. Crafts aficionados can choose from ceramics, weaving, dyeing, papermaking and woodworking to name just a few.

Experience Japanese hospitality by staying at a traditional inn. Bathe at a hot spring resort. Try a variety of Japanese cuisine from *sushi* bars to noodles to *kaiseki*, elaborate haute cuisine. Sing your heart out at a karaoke bar. Browse through temple flea markets and antique stores.

Take the plunge. Tokyo awaits you.

3. LAND & PEOPLE

Japan perches on the ring of fire encircling the Pacific Ocean. The crush of plates formed dramatic mountains and enormous volcanoes. The resulting four main islands – **Hokkaido**, **Honshu**, **Shikoku** and **Kyushu** – and over one thousand smaller islands stretch 1200 kilometers.

Mountains define Japan. They created the archipelago by rising from the floor of the Pacific Ocean to form its backbone. Mountains cover the interior of the four main islands and often run down to the water's edge. Venerated **Mount Fuji** at 3776 meters is Japan's tallest, but the **Japan Alps**, named after their European cousins, have more than 20 peaks over 3000 meters. Volcanoes – 188 in all – dot Japan. More than 40 are still active, but eruptions are hardly daily events.

The island chain is crescent shaped; Tokyo and Kyoto are actually east/west of each other, rather than north/south. Tokyo shares the same latitude as Los Angeles and Raleigh, North Carolina. Sendai is even with New York and Wakkanai, the northern tip of Hokkaido, with Montreal.

Japan's forests cover 67% of the country compared to only 10% of Great Britain. Why does everyone think of Great Britain as a green nation and Japan as an overpopulated megalopolis? Japan has very little flat land. Most of the narrow country's interior is mountainous and offers great off-the-beaten track getaways – you are never more than 100 kilometers from the sea in any point in Japan.

The islands of Japan are at the meeting point of major geological plates – this means lots of seismic activity. They average about 7500 earthquakes a year – that's 20 a day – but before you scratch Japan off the visit list, know that the vast majority are too weak to be felt except by sensitive seismographs. The big ones come along only once every 70 to 100 years.

The few plains support the vast majority of Japan's population. While Japan's overall population density is only 331 per square kilometer, the greater Tokyo area and the Kobe-Osaka-Kyoto region crowd in over 10,000 people per square kilometer. And the Tokyo-Yokohama area supports 25 million people, the largest urban center in the world. But take an hour-long train ride to the mountains and you're hard pressed to find a soul. Japan is about the same size as California but if you take the amount of habitable land and subtract the amount used for agriculture and industry, the entire country, all 125 million people, ends up living in a space the size of Connecticut. Seventy percent of the population lives along the Pacific coast from Tokyo to northern Kyushu.

Although the sea surrounds Japan, it has used the seas to keep the world at arms' length for most of its history. Japan was not a major ocean-going nation. The oceans served as Japan's defense against invasion; other than a disastrous attempt to conquer Korea in the late 16th century and the expansionism in Asia leading to World War II, Japan focused inward.

FUN FACTS

California is larger than the whole of Japan.

Japan's land is 1/25 the size of the US. The population is 1/2 of the US.

Japan's gross domestic product (GDP) is over 60% of the size of the US GDP. Per person GDP is $40,897 (in 1995) versus $27,799 for the US. Japan's economy is nine times larger than China's.

About 14% of Japan is agricultural land; 67% is forest and woodland. Population density per square kilometer: 331. How does this compare? Hong Kong: 5481; Singapore: 4741; Bangladesh: 818; India: 279; Germany: 228; China: 124; US: 28; Russia: 9; Canada: 3; Australia: 2.

Japanese have the world's longest life expectancy: in 1995 it was 82.8 years for women, 76.3 years for men. US life expectancy: 79.1 for women and 72.3 for men.

WEATHER

Extending over twenty degrees of latitude from the chilly northern tip of Hokkaido to subtropical Okinawa, Japan has many different climatic zones. Hokkaido is very cold in winter and cool in summer. Northern Honshu has a cold winter and a hot summer. Tokyo, Kyoto and western Japan have fairly mild winters and hot, steamy summers. The Japan Sea coast gets harsh and snowy winters. Okinawa is subtropical. All of Japan except Hokkaido experiences a month-long rainy season early June to mid-July.

We feel sorry for Japanese weather forecasters. Because islands comprise the country, the weather patterns are unstable, so the day to day weather is unpredictable. It's not unusual for tomorrow's weather to be opposite of this morning's newspaper report.

All of Japan, except Okinawa, supports four distinct seasons. Japanese culture exalts in celebrating the seasons. Cherry blossoms in spring, foliage in autumn, the heat of summer and snowfall in winter mark major milestones of the year.

Geography and climate patterns have blessed Japan with copious amounts of usable water from rain, melting snowcaps and large lakes. The climate lent itself to rice cultivation. Rice growing demands cooperation among farmers to distribute water. Some argue this fact is the basis for the emphasis on cooperation in Japanese society and culture.

SOCIETY & PEOPLE

Japan is almost always characterized as a society where social harmony is valued higher than individuality. In a country of 125 million people, the reality is much more complex.

Certainly Japan has a strong group orientation. At any tourist sight around the world, bus loads of Japanese travelers follow flag toting guides. Pins with company logos adorn employees' lapels as if they were Gucci jewelry. From a young age, children in both public and private schools wear military-looking uniforms.

But many don't fit the mold. Japan has more than its share of eccentrics from computer designers to novelists, from craftsmen devoting their lives to reviving a dying art to corporate executives writing poetry in their leisure time.

But the average Japanese also doesn't fit this mold. People assert their individuality although it may be in different and less dramatic ways than in the West. More Japanese than ever opt to travel individually. Children who have lived overseas were once shunned when they returned to Japan; now special schools and programs help them maintain their second language proficiency and cross-cultural skills. Company employees bail out to run a new venture or a bed and breakfast in a ski resort or climb the world's great peaks.

Many people assume that the large corporations, which produce the cars, electronics, steel and toys known around the world, employ the vast majority of Japanese workers, but it is not true. More people work for small companies and mom-and-pop operations that do not provide the cradle-to-grave safety nets. But not all large companies are lean manufacturing machines. Banks and financial institutions still operate as if they were in the stone age. Cashing a simple traveler's check can take 20 minutes and involve a half-dozen bank clerks.

The company has assumed many of the functions once provided by the extended family. While lifetime employment is no longer an undeniable right in the large corporations (and it never was in smaller companies), the company often provides housing, commuting passes, vacation hostels and even matchmaking services. Companies function hierarchically. Salaries and promotion are based on age, not skills. Workers endure more than many of their counterparts in the West: two hour commutes on packed trains, cramped living conditions and long hours in the office. Employees often arrive home late in the evening following after-hours socializing with colleagues and customers. The subways and commuter trains are as crowded at 10pm as they are at 6pm. Wives almost never participate in business entertainment.

Although contemporary society developed from a feudal system, Japan is remarkably egalitarian. World War II effectively destroyed most of the wealth of the old families; postwar land reform finished the process. Aristocratic titles were abolished after the war. The imperial family lineage is restricted to a small group; princes marry commoners and princesses born into the imperial family lose their titles upon marriage.

Education defines Japan's elite today. Graduates of top universities enter the prestigious government ministries and large corporations. Scions of aristocratic families figure prominently among the elite, but so do people from average families.

Japan is overwhelmingly middle class. One amazing fact about Japanese corporations is the range in salary between the company president and the lowest paid employee is among the lowest in the world.

The countryside has emptied out as people migrated to urban centers for good jobs. Farmers are fairly affluent today thanks to generous government subsidies. But the sons who stay behind to work the family farm are hard-pressed to find Japanese women willing to marry into the hardworking lifestyle. Some marry Philippinas and Thai women.

The Role of Women

The role of women is a highly complex subject. Until the mid-1980s, most women worked only in clerical positions (called OLs for Office Ladies). Then a labor shortage and an equal opportunity employment law strengthened women's positions in the workplace. This law has no teeth; it doesn't carry penalties for companies who did not comply. Companies have established a professional track for women, but many women have been disappointed by the limited opportunities; only 1.5% of senior managers and just over 7% of lower level managers are female.

Being a housewife and a mother still carry a lot of respect in Japan. Women often quit their jobs either when they marry or when they give birth to their first child. But to maintain a high standard of living, many will work part-time. Women run the household, handle the finances and take chief responsibility for the children and their education. With many husbands away until late in the evening, they live fairly independent lives. Despite the reputation for fathers being absent, you will see lots of families together on weekend excursions from zoos to ski slopes.

Japanese women are quite picky about whom they marry. Their social status is largely dependent on their husband's employment. If they do not find someone with the right credentials, they prefer to remain unmarried, a path taken by an estimated 14% of young women today. Many live with their parents and spend their considerable income on clothing, entertainment and travel. Women who did not marry by the age of 25 used to be branded "Christmas cakes," out of date after the 25th. Now the average age of marriage is in the late 20s.

Weddings

Weddings are large, formal and expensive affairs, usually taking place at hotels. Traditionally, wedding ceremonies were Shinto and held at shrines or hotels, attended only by immediate family members, and followed by a large reception. More people now opt for Christian weddings so their friends can attend the ceremony itself, and in Japan you don't have to be a Christian to have a church wedding. On weekends, the lobbies of large hotels see an endless parade of wedding parties dressed in kimono and other finery.

Most people find their own mates (80% marry for love) or friends and family may introduce them to appropriate partners. No matter how they meet, brides and grooms usually ask an older couple to serve as their ceremonial "go-between" at the wedding ceremony. At the reception, the go-betweens sit with the couple on the dais while the parents sit at the back of the hall.

Speeches by bosses, colleagues and friends punctuate wedding receptions. The bride, queen for a day, starts off wearing a traditional wedding kimono or a white wedding gown and changes into one or two other Western-style ball gowns during the reception. As a counter to this formal affair, a second, more informal party for friends at a restaurant or disco usually follows the main reception. Most Japanese travel overseas on honeymoons. Hawaii and Australia are two popular destinations.

All of this does not come cheap. The average marriage in Tokyo, including reception, honeymoon and finding a new apartment, costs ¥6.5 million (roughly $60,000). The reception expenses average ¥2.7 million (about $20,000) although gifts of money offset about half that expense.

The groom bears the greatest expense, then the bride, the parents of the bride and the parents of the groom.

Japan has one of the lowest divorce rates among developed nations. Laws discourage divorce, but social pressure plays an equally large role. Divorce has become more common in the last few years and remarriage has also increased.

Kids & School

Japan's birthrate has hit an all time low of 1.43 births per woman, not enough to sustain the current population levels. Women rarely bear more than two children. Cramped living conditions and the expense of a first-class education deter most from having larger families.

Since college education is the greatest determinant of a child's career success, education competition begins in preschool, and even before. Upwardly mobile parents press their children to get into the "right" kindergartens so they are on track for admission to the top universities. Some three and four year olds even go to cram school to prepare for admission to kindergarten.

Cram schools supplement the normal education to get an edge in taking exams. Japanese school children go through examination hell to get into the better middle and high schools as well as into universities. If a student fails to gain admission to a good university, rather than attending a second-rate one, he or she may choose to spend a year of intensive study at a test preparation school and retake the exams the following year.

There are some cries to change the entrance exam system, but little reform appears forthcoming. About 40% of high school graduates go on to colleges, universities and junior colleges. While it's very difficult to gain admission to top Japanese universities, once admitted, most Japanese say that university life is considerably less rigorous than high school. Many students consider the four years a respite between examination hell and a lifetime of work.

The Security Net

The government and Japanese pundits worry about who will support an increasingly aging population. In 1997, for the first time the number of people over age 65 exceeded the number of children under 14. Retirement age is between 57 and 60, but many workers take on a new job and work another five to ten years usually at reduced pay. Most security guards appear to be over 60. For many, retirement means time for a more active cultural life and travel.

Most people retire with a pension equal to two years' salary, woefully inadequate to support themselves. Thus in the postwar period, Japanese have salted away 15 to 20% of their annual income in preparation for old age. Health care is from cradle to grave, but with some twists. In many hospitals, you must provide your own meals and linens. Traditionally, aging parents lived with the oldest son, but with small urban apartments, longer life spans and smaller families, this custom has changed too.

Government

Japan is a democratic country with a two-house parliament called the **Diet** that's led by a prime minister elected by the majority party. The emperor comes from the longest continuously reigning dynasty in the world but today has only ceremonial duties. Japan is divided into 47 **prefectures**, each with its own governor and assembly. Each city, town and village also has its own government.

Politics in the postwar period have been dominated by one party, the conservative **Liberal Democratic Party** (LDP) – the joke is that it's neither liberal nor democratic. However, the last several years have witnessed major political upheaval with the LDP dividing into several conservative parties; the main opposition, the Socialists, self-destructing; and a host of political finance scandals. Most of the recent political divisions are based on personality, not on ideology.

Different from US politics, the national bureaucracy wields enormous power by writing as well as implementing the laws the Diet passes. Japan's best and brightest go into an alphabet soup of ministries. The country runs on the often touted "Iron Triangle" of the LDP, the bureaucracy and industry. Although some change is afoot, political stability has fostered the economic growth of postwar Japan.

The postwar Constitution renounces war. Japan's commitment of troops to United Nations' peacekeeping efforts is a constant source of debate in the government. Japan's armed forces, named the Self-Defense Forces, receive the third largest defense budget in the world.

THE JAPANESE YEAR

While modern Japan seems high tech and urbanized, by and large the Japanese year still revolves around the traditional agrarian calendar. Here are the highlights of the year:

New Year's Day is January 1. Japan switched from the Chinese lunar calendar to the Western calendar in the late 19th century, but until after World War II family holidays revolved around the old calendar.

The New Year's celebration, the most important holiday in the year, spreads over several days. Everything stops. Offices close December 28 or 29 until January 3 or 4. Although museums and even some temples close, it's one of the best times of the year to get a sense of traditional culture.

Preparations for New Year's holiday begin right after Christmas. Houses are decorated with pine, bamboo and plum — all auspicious symbols. Just as Christmas decorations in the West stay up for some time, Japanese keep their New Year's decorations up until January 7.

The New Year's holiday is a family time. They gather together to eat special meals and spend the time playing traditional games such as guessing poems, spinning tops and flying kites. Before midnight, people begin to visit Shinto shrines to pray for prosperity in the coming year. It's called *hatsumode*, first visit of the year. Some of the most popular shrines have several million visitors during the first few days of January. If you happen to be in Japan during the New Year's celebrations, go to a Shinto shrine to share the excitement and enthusiasm of people optimistically welcoming the new year.

NEW YEAR'S DECORATIONS

*Shimekazari (Shinto Straw Festoons) are made with rope, string and folded **washi** paper, and placed at the front entrance, tokonoma alcove and other locations at New Year's to keep evil spirits from entering the home. Some people also adorn the fronts of their cars with them during the New Year's season.*

***Kadomatsu** are pine branches and bamboo arranged in a stand and placed at either side of the entrance. They welcome the good spirits. People also put pounded rice cakes in the **tokonoma** and cook **oseichi**, special food to welcome the gods.*

Coming of Age Day is January 15. All those who turn twenty between January 16 of the previous year and January 15 of the new year become adults. They then can vote and buy alcohol and tobacco. Many of these new adults go to Shinto shrines to pray for good fortune — on auspicious occasions, Japanese pray to Shinto gods — and throw parties to celebrate. The young women and a few young men dress in formal kimono, so remember to take your camera to the shrines.

Setsubun, February 3, marks the passing of winter although we think it is more wishful thinking than anything else. Japanese buy special soy beans at supermarkets and throw them in every room of the house declaring: "Luck come in, devils go out!" Some Shinto shrines perform dances where beans are thrown to expel the demons in the coming year.

Valentine's Day, February 14, was a cultural transplant during the Occupation after World War II. It's widely celebrated by young people, but there's a twist. We don't know if the Allied Powers were trying to be

SCHOOL STARTS WHEN?

Japan is one of the few developed countries where the school year starts in April. Recently some people have begun to advocate starting the school year in September to bring it in line with international practice. Believe it or not, one of the main reasons it hasn't changed is the emotional tie with cherry blossoms. Most Japanese associate the first day at school with seeing cherry blossoms in full bloom.

funny or the soldiers wanted to receive lots of sweets, but from the beginning, women gave chocolate to men. Today, they give chocolate not only to their special honeys, but to all the men at their offices. Men are supposed to give a return gift on March 14, White Day.

Girls' Day (Hina Matsuri) is celebrated on March 3. The tradition started with families going on outings to view peach blossoms. Girls would throw paper dolls into the river to cast off illness and misfortune. Eventually, the dolls became more elegant and elaborate and no one threw them into the water any more. Instead these dolls came to represent the imperial court and were set up on stands. Today, maternal grandparents usually give a set of dolls for a child's first girls' day. Set up about a month before the actual day and taken down on March 3rd, superstition says if the dolls aren't taken down on Girls' Day, the girl won't get married.

White Day, March 14. This holiday dates back only to the 1980s. Men are supposed to give white chocolate to women as repayment for Valentine's chocolate. To us this holiday always seems to be manufactured by the candy companies.

Vernal Equinox Day, March 20 or 21. On the first day of spring, like the first day of autumn, Japanese clean the graves of their ancestors.

Ohanami, Cherry Blossom Viewing. Late March through mid-April. Cherry blossoms are so much a part of Japanese society that the weather forecast, in what meteorologists call the "flower front," reports on cherry blossoms and estimates peak viewing times. Incredibly, the predictions are almost always correct.

Japanese love cherry blossoms, their brief bloom a simile for the impermanence of life itself. Cherry blossom viewing goes back hundreds of years. Woodblook prints and screen paintings show splendid viewing parties. A generation or two ago, families would gather under the trees with a picnic and enjoy the flowers. Today, companies plan elaborate outings, sending the newest recruits to save space in prime spots. In the evening, when everyone gathers, beer and *sake* flow freely and are consumed with large quantities of food. In the latest twist, some groups bring video monitors to view tapes of cherry blossoms. What could be more Japanese?

Beginning of School Year, April 1. There's a summer break mid-July through September 1, and a two-week break at the end of March.

Golden Week, April 29 through May 5. Within this period, there are four national holidays: April 29, May 3, 4 and 5, so many people take off the entire time. It's a really bad time to travel anywhere in Japan because everything is so jammed; *shinkansen* trains run at 160% of capacity and expressways (what a misnomer) sport 70-kilometer backups. But Golden Week is a lovely time to visit big cities; they are like ghost towns even though museums, temples, department stores and most restaurants stay open.

Children's Day, May 5. This holiday used to be called Boys' Day, but after World War II, in the spirit of equality, it changed to Children's Day. But to this day, it's mainly families with sons who fly *koinobori*, large carp streamers. Just as carp swim upstream, children are urged to work hard, hard enough to go against the currents to achieve success.

O-chugen Gift Giving Season. Gifts are exchanged in June and early July.

GIFT GIVING SEASONS

Gift giving is an important custom in Japan. There are two formal gift-giving seasons, at the end of the first half of the year and at year's end. Japanese love to give presents. The gesture is more important than the present itself. Japanese are almost obsessed with the idea that if they don't give presents, they have not expressed their gratitude, pleasure or other feelings. So gift giving helps society function smoothly.

Most people give practical presents such as food items, fruit or whiskey. We love to go to department stores to check out the elaborate gift displays; seeing ten cans of Budweiser beer or fruit cocktail expensively packaged in a box cracks us up. Presents do get recycled, but most people won't admit it.

Japanese also take time and pride in gift wrapping – the form is often more important than the substance. Formal calligraphy announces the gift giver's name on special paper on top of the glossy wrapping paper.

Foreign visitors are usually exempt from this gift-giving frenzy, but bring a small present from your country if you are going to visit a Japanese home.

Summer Fireworks *(hanabi)* displays have been held in July since the Edo period as a psychological relief from summer's oppressive heat and humidity.

O-Bon, August 13 to 16, is the Buddhist festival of the dead. During this time, spirits of the deceased return to their hometowns. City dwellers also return to their hometowns to visit their ancestors' graveyards. Nowadays, most people go as an excuse to see family, or travel elsewhere. There are a lot of summer festivals around this time. People dress in cotton *yukata* robes, eat at open air stalls and perform *bon odori* dances. If you are traveling in Japan during this period, be sure you make reservations well in advance — because trains, airplanes and highways are crowded. We like to stay in the cities because they empty out but museums, department stores and most restaurants remain open.

Autumnal Equinox, September 23 or 24, the first day of autumn. Traditionally this day is the one when Japanese clean the graves of their ancestors. Lots of Shinto shrines have harvest festivals, and local shrines have children parade *mikoshi* (portable shrines) around the neighborhood.

Autumn Foliage Viewing takes place in October and November. Like cherry blossom viewing, it has taken on almost cult status. Famous viewing sites such as Nikko and Kyoto become impossibly crowded.

Shichi-go-san Festival (Seven-Five-Three), November 15, is one of the most photogenic events of the year. Bring lots of film when you visit shrines. Girls age seven and three and boys age five go to a shrine to pray for good health. In the old days, these ages were considered to be dangerous years for children. Most of the girls dress in fancy kimono and some boys wear the traditional *hakama* outfit. Families celebrate the festival anytime during the week or two around November 15, not only on that one day.

Christmas, December 25. Japan is not a Christian country; only a minuscule portion of the population is Christian, but you would never know it looking at department stores. On November 1, as soon as the Halloween decorations are put away, Christmas decorations appear. Many Japanese exchange Christmas presents with family members or close friends, but there is no element of religion involved. Christmas cakes with white frosting are eaten on Christmas day. Christmas Eve, incidentally, is the year's biggest date night, similar to New Year's Eve in the US.

End of Year Preparations. The end of the year is so busy, it is called *shiwasu*, "even the master teacher runs" because the usually sedate teacher must also run to finish all the chores. Houses must be cleaned, all debts must be settled and any outstanding matters taken care of so that you can start the new year with a clean slate. Japanese give end-of-year presents called *oseibo* to anyone for whom they feel obligation such as doctors, companies and individuals. Companies hold *Bonenkai* "let's forget the bad luck in the year" parties. On New Year's Eve, Japanese eat *soba* noodles — the length of the noodles suggests longevity.

Matsuri Festivals

The roots of Japan's many festivals lay in the agrarian nature of society. Many of the festivals occur in the spring when farmers would pray for successful harvests and in the autumn to give thanks to the gods. At Shinto festivals, *mikoshi* (portable shrines) parade through the streets, pulled or carried by eager townspeople.

The **Gion Festival** in Kyoto in July, Takayama's spring and autumn festivals and the big summer festivals in Akita, Aomori and Hirosaki in northern Honshu rank among Japan's most popular.

JAPANESE RELIGION

Ask most Japanese whether or not they are believers in Shintoism or Buddhism and the answer is "Yes." Many small Shinto shrines are found on Buddhist temple grounds. The tolerance and symbiotic relationship between the two religions in Japan often bewilder Westerners.

Unlike Christianity or Islam, in Japan religion is not exclusive. Most Japanese have Shinto marriages, birth and coming-of-age celebrations. They go to Shinto shrines at New Year's to pray for prosperity and before examinations to pray for success. But Shintoism doesn't do well with death, which is considered polluting, so Japanese turn to Buddhism for funerals and the afterlife.

Shinto

The original Japanese religion is Shinto, an animist religion. Shintoists worship natural objects such as mountains, the sun and animals for their supernatural powers. The most important aspect of Shintoism is that ancestors are also worshipped. Lively legends set forth the origins of Japan. The Yamato clan, from whom the current imperial line traces its heritage, claims to have descended from the Sun Goddess, Amaterasu. Shinto gods, called *kami*, number in the thousands.

Most Shinto shrines are simple wooden structures with little adornment. Representing the sacred space inhabited by *kami*, shrines aren't cluttered with statues. A simple *torii* gate, traditionally made of wood but sometimes constructed of cement or metal, marks the entrance. Near the gate there is a basin of water to cleanse your hands and mouth as ritual purification before entering the precincts.

The main hall contains a small area where believers sit while rites are performed. In front of the main building sits a money box. Japanese throw some coins in the box, clap two times, bow and pray. Some shrines have a gong or bell on a long rope; pulling the rope helps get the gods' attention. Sacred dances called *kagura* are performed on the small covered platforms in front of the main hall of some shrines. The shrine sells amulets and fortunes.

You may notice strips of white paper tied to trees and fences. These are *omikuji*, fortunes which you can purchase for ¥100. When the fortune is very good, Japanese post it to make sure the gods take note; when it's very bad, they post it to pray for the gods to change it. If it's okay, they take it home. The fortunes are almost always in Japanese, but a few shrines, such as Kasuga Shrine in Nara, have ones in English.

You may also notice small wooden plaques hanging on posts on the shrine's grounds. These plaques are called *ema*, literally horse pictures. In ancient days, people donated horses to the shrine, but when it became too expensive, not to mention cumbersome, they donated pictures of horses. This custom evolved into a shrine producing small plaques usually with pictures of the shrine or the year's zodiac animal. Japanese purchase these plaques, write their prayers on the back and hang them so the gods can help them achieve their goals. Our highly unofficial survey reveals most have to do with passing entrance exams, having luck in love or recovering from an illness.

Buddhism

In the 5th and 6th centuries, Buddhism was introduced to Japan by Koreans. Prince Shotoku adopted Buddhism as a state religion for the ruling class, but the religion did not supplant Shintoism; the two existed side by side.

Prince Shotoku set up a system of building a Buddhist temple in each of the 64 provinces with Todai-ji Temple in Nara as the head. The close relationship between Buddhism and the state placed too much political power in the hands of the monks. This meddling became so annoying that in the late 8th century, Emperor Kammu moved the capital from Nara to Kyoto.

The early days of the Kyoto Heian period saw new forms of Buddhism. The priest Kukai (Kobo Daishi) went to China to study Buddhism and established esoteric Shingon Buddhism, centered at Mt. Koya outside of Osaka. The esoteric sect relied on ritual and mystic experiences to achieve enlightenment, and their temples were located in mountain settings. Enryaku-ji Temple on Mt. Hiei, under the priest Saicho, became the center for the Tendai sect that emphasized the belief in Amida, a benevolent intermediary to the Buddha.

Pure Land Buddhism decreed that anyone could gain salvation by sincere chanting of the Amida Buddha's name. This belief had enormous

WHICH ANIMAL ARE YOU?

Just as Zodiac signs in the West symbolize particular traits of those people who were born under a particular sign, the animal of the year, eto in Japanese, has meanings in Japanese culture. Twelve animals make a twelve-year cycle. The original concept must have come from ancient China like so many other things in Japan.

Japanese legend goes something like this. In the old days, a god or a Buddha wanted to test the loyalty of the animals, so he sent a quick message to each to visit him ASAP. As soon as the message arrived, the Ox began its trek, knowing he wasn't a fast mover. Amazingly, he thought he'd made the trip in record time. But, lo and behold, just as the Ox arrived, a smart Mouse jumped off his back, and voila, the mouse was first to greet the god! So the Mouse is first and then the Ox followed by Tiger, Rabbit, Dragon (the only imaginary animal), Snake, Horse, Sheep, Chicken, Monkey, Dog and Wild Boar.

Japanese enjoy associating various personal characteristics of those born in a certain animal's year – a Mouse is known to be hard working; an Ox, patient; a Tiger, short tempered. Knowing a person's animal gives a good hint a person's age without being too direct. Perhaps, you can deceive another's eyes by six years, but to look 12 years younger or older than you actually are needs more than a special technique!

Toward the end of each year, many varieties of the animal of the next year begin to appear in craft shops and department stores. Made from Japanese paper or from clay, people display their animals for fun and possibly for protection. The year of the Tiger, 1998, will be followed by the year of the Rabbit, 1999. Tiger women are supposed to be domineering types but so are tiger men, don't you think? We find the animal of the year makes a special present at baby showers. By the way, a cat chose to enjoy a nap rather than going to greet a god, so we don't have anyone officially born in the year of Cat. Interestingly in Vietnam there's a Cat instead of a Rabbit. Which animal are you?

appeal to aristocrats who saw chaos and collapse of social order everywhere. It also made Buddhism accessible to the masses; up to this point, Buddhism was the domain of the aristocratic upper classes only.

In the Kamakura period (12th to 14th century), Buddhism brought from China became more Japanized. The priest Shinran founded the populist True Pure Land Sect. The charismatic priest Nichiren founded a Buddhist sect bearing his name in the 13th century. His nationalistic ideology derided other sects for being foreign.

Zen Buddhism also caught hold in Japan in the early years of the Kamakura period. Zen relied on *zazen* (meditation) and *koan* (philosophical riddles) to achieve enlightenment. A believer would constantly think of the riddle until all other thoughts left his head. Only then could he achieve enlightenment. These self-discipline aspects made Zen popular with the warrior class.

During the Edo period, the Tokugawa shogunate regulated nearly every aspect of life, including the freedom to travel. Going on a pilgrimage was one of the few legitimate excuses to hit the road. People traveled great distances to visit temples and shrines. Naturally when they got there, they also wanted to enjoy themselves. Small towns and entertainment districts grew up around the temples' gates.

When you visit a Buddhist temple, the first thing you'll notice is a large free-standing wooden entrance gate, frequently a two-storied affair. *Nio* (fierce guardian statues) often stand watch inside the gate, ready to repel evil spirits. Buddhist temples have no standard configuration. The main hall, usually called *hondo* or *kondo*, will have a Buddha figure of worship, but it may not be visible. There's often a lecture hall called *kodo*, a bell tower, sometimes a multistoried pagoda and usually the abbot's quarters. Zen temples have *shukubo* (dormitories) and kitchens since their priests live communally. If the kitchen is open to the public, be sure you go in to see the huge stoves where priests prepare vegetarian meals for hundreds of monks.

At the main hall, believers put money in a box and bow and say their prayers. You can buy incense and candles and offer them with a prayer, quite similar to the Roman Catholic Church. At some temples you'll see people waving incense smoke over their bodies, believing that the incense will heal their ailments and protect them from illness.

Christianity

St. Francis Xavier brought Christianity to Japan in 1549 when he landed in Kyushu. Some feudal lords were converted but the religion never made major inroads. In 1597 the ruler Hideyoshi ordered the death of 26 priests and converts, ushering in an era of persecution. The Shimabara Rebellion in 1637 was the last stand of the Christians who gathered in a castle outside of Nagasaki. Over 37,000 Christians were killed in the siege. The remaining Christians went underground and were called Hidden Christians.

In the late 19th century when Japan ended its long period of isolation, Western missionaries came and started churches and schools. But Christianity has never attracted more than a small percentage of the Japanese population.

Religion in the Modern Period

Until the beginning of the Meiji period (1868), respect for Shinto *kami*, adoration of Buddha, and the practice of ancestor worship all existed side by side. To accompany the "restoration" of imperial power, the Meiji government found moral justification in "State Shintoism." Buddhism, branded as a foreign religion that subverted Japanese Shintoism, was persecuted and many temples and treasures destroyed. The emperor, as a descendant of the Sun Goddess, provided the link between the gods and the state.

The new Constitution, written during the Occupation following World War II, guarantees religious freedom. New religions as well as Christianity have their adherents. **Soka Gakkai**, derived from Nichiren Buddhism, appeals to the disaffected lower middle class and formed a political party called Komeito. **Aum**, a fringe cult-religion, catapulted into the headlines with its deadly sarin gas attack in the Tokyo subways in 1995. Most people remain with Shintoism and Buddhism for their daily lives.

Are Japanese religious? Each year more than half the Japanese population go to a Shinto shrine at New Year's to pray for prosperity, but just as many Westerners go to church on Christmas, it doesn't necessarily indicate a high degree of religious involvement. Many people maintain altars in their homes to pray for their ancestors. Some people have Buddhist altars, some have Shinto and some have both. In this way, religion is part of Japan's cultural life.

JAPANESE ARCHITECTURE

Traditional Japanese houses emphasize a harmony with nature much more than their Western counterparts. Wood is the main building material and the rooms are designed to look out onto gardens. The entire side of the house opens to become part of the natural environment. To Japanese, staying cool during the sizzling hot and humid summer has been more important than keeping warm in the cold winter. While traditional houses are still built in rural areas, in the cities new houses are overwhelmingly Western style, but most have at least one Japanese room.

What is a Japanese room? *Tatami* straw mats cover the floor and a *tokonoma* alcove displays art and flower arrangements. *Shoji*, sliding doors with paper panels, divide the room from a veranda that overlooks a garden. Diffused light coming through the *shoji* adds a wonderful softness to the interior. *Fusuma*, heavy sliding doors often decorated with paintings, divide rooms. Wooden sliding doors on the exterior of the building protect the veranda and room. Natural wooden beams, posts and ceilings are complemented by plaster or earthen walls.

The history of Japanese architecture as we know it begins in the 6th and 7th centuries, when court buildings and temples imitated Chinese and Korean forms.

Gradually, the Japanese changed the Chinese architectural forms to a more indigenous residential architecture for the aristocracy called *shinden-zukuri*. Japanese elements were incorporated into Chinese layout and construction techniques: using unfinished wood, putting in gravel gardens and raising the floor. *Shinden* is the main hall of the complex. Partitions, not walls, divided rooms. Buildings connected to each other by covered walkways. A large pond reached by a covered walkway was nearby.

By the Momoyama period, *shoin* architecture developed, evolving from Zen priests' studies that looked out onto a garden. The style eventually became the audience halls for feudal lords. Much of what we think of as traditional Japanese: *tatami* mats, *tokonoma* alcoves, *shoji* screens, and decorative door paintings came from this style.

The simplicity of tea ceremony influenced Japanese architecture beyond the rustic tea hut; it led to the development of a more natural style of *shoin* called *sukiya* architecture. It is airy, less ornate and doesn't have boldly decorated door panels. *Sukiya* uses only the best natural materials.

The Momoyama period was also the golden age of castle building. The new style of gun warfare necessitated defensive castles. The prototype built by Oda Nobunaga at Azuchi on the shores of Lake Biwa was destroyed just a few years after completion. Castles had massive stone walls and were often surrounded by moats. Plaster covers the wooden structure and the remaining exposed wood was lacquered for fire resistance. Castles had windows designed for firing muskets and shooting arrows as well as openings for dropping stones and hot oil on invaders. Warriors did not live in the multistoried castle keeps but rather in residences on the grounds.

Commoners, of course, did not live on a grand scale. They had modest wooden dwellings called *minka* (people's houses). Many different styles of *minka* reflect climatic conditions. In the snowy mountains of central Japan, farmers built structures with steep thatched roofs so the snow would slide off. Other areas used tile roofs. **Minka-en**, an open air museum near Tokyo, features about twenty farmhouses moved from all over Japan.

In the Meiji period, Western architecture became very fashionable, as did buildings combining Western and Japanese styles. Western architects like British Josiah Condor came to Japan to design monumental buildings and train Japanese. **Tokyo Station** and the **Bank of Japan Building** are outstanding examples.

Today, Japan has an active contemporary architecture scene. Architect Tange Kenzo brought modern Japanese architecture into the international limelight with the **National Gymnasiums** in Yoyogi Park in Tokyo, built for the 1964 Olympics. Today Ando Tadao and Isozaki Arata are two of the most prominent names among the considerable number of innovative architects transforming Japanese and foreign cities with their postmodern architecture.

JAPANESE GARDENS

Gardens with bushes pruned to strange shapes, gardens of only rock, moss and gravel, gardens the size of postage stamps, plants hundreds of years old, but Lilliputian sized. What are these Japanese gardens all about?

Japanese gardens are carefully designed and cultivated works of art, but there is little that's natural about them except the materials. Throughout Japan's history, the garden has gone through several transformations.

Heian Period *(8th to 12th century)*

The aristocracy of the Heian period built gardens with large ponds for boating. Designed to be viewed from the water or from the adjacent buildings, these gardens were not meant for strolling. Aristocrats held poetry and music parties in these natural landscapes. In the later part of the Heian period, many aristocrats turned to faith in the Amida Buddha who promised a peaceful heaven to all believers. This Western Paradise was often depicted in gardens filled with flowering trees and plants.

Kamakura Period *(12th to mid-14th century)*

In medieval times, gardens became places to stroll. Walking along the path, each step brought a new view in the exploration of the garden. Dry landscapes appeared as parts of the larger garden: large rocks were used to represent mountain scenery, waterfalls and streams.

Muromachi Period *(mid-14th to mid-16th century)*

Zen Buddhism took hold in the turbulent times of the medieval period when central authority collapsed. Zen gardens took the dry landscape design, which was one element of the larger gardens, and used it to build small gardens. These gardens usually surrounded the priests' quarters and were used for meditation. The rocks, gravel, moss and small bushes are abstracts. Maintenance of a garden — raking gravel, removing falling leaves — became a religious exercise for Zen priests.

Momoyama Period *(late 16th century)*

Japan was unified under three successive warlords and an era of prosperity began. These warlords' gardens, like their castles and residences, were designed to impress. Momoyama gardens had lots of rocks and exotic plants brought by Portuguese traders from Southeast Asia, and were masculine symbols of authority. The gardens were designed to be viewed from the veranda so most did not have paths for strolling.

Tea Gardens

The cult of tea ceremony, which took off in the Momoyama period, led to a very different type of garden. The tea garden transports the visitor from the mundane outside world to the ethereal environment of the teahouse. Walking along the dewy path, a visitor makes a transition, setting aside all earthly cares and getting into a serene state. The goal is to create a walk in the woods but does not mean the garden is wild. The carefully groomed garden has local species of plants and trees, but not flowering trees or flowers. Tea gardens use stepping stones, stone lanterns and stone water basins. Water basins placed near the ground mean visitors have to crouch to use them, putting them closer to nature.

Tea gardens came to have inner and outer areas, divided by a gate. In the outer, the visitor could change clothes in a small shed and wait on a bench for the host. The inner garden contains a covered bench, a water basin and the teahouse itself. Since tea gardens were usually designed into existing space in urban areas, they are quite small.

Edo & Meiji Eras

By the Edo period (17th to 19th century), large gardens were built for aristocrats and warriors. Used for strolling, these gardens had a variety of vistas you would notice as you walked along a path. Many gardens used "borrowed scenery," incorporating the vista of a distant mountain or another scene into the garden itself.

In the Meiji era, Japanese landscape designers began incorporating Western design. **Shinjuku Gyoen Garden** and **Furukawa Garden**, both in Tokyo, combine Japanese and European garden design.

TEA CEREMONY

Tea ceremony isn't just having a cup of tea in the afternoon. Amazingly, much of what the world associates with Japanese aesthetics derives from the tea ceremony.

Tea, originally used as a medicine, came from China and became popular among Zen Buddhists in the 12th and 13th centuries. Tea drinking gradually evolved into a formal and ritualistic aesthetic experience. Tea ceremony came to be conducted in a rustic tea hut set in a small garden. Tea ceremony became an art form.

Today, the highly stylized tea ceremony is still practiced by men and women. Hot water is added to powdered green tea and whipped until it's frothy. Before you drink your tea, you must admire not only the setting of the room, but also your tea bowl, the flowers in the *tokonoma* alcove and the tea itself. A small sweet is served to counter the tea's bitter taste.

Experience a tea ceremony at one of the special schools for tea ceremony or at a large hotel.

FLOWER ARRANGING

Japanese flower arranging is the antithesis of Western arranging where every space is filled. The Japanese asymmetrical and often sparse arrangement dates back to the medieval Muromachi period. Flowers, arranged in a variety of containers, are placed in the *tokonoma* alcove of homes, inns and temples. There are many different schools of flower arranging, some very classical like Ikenobo and Koryu while others like Sogetsu are quite avant-garde. Many of the larger schools offer instruction in English, and visitors are welcome.

JAPANESE ART

Utilitarian pottery and ritual clay objects, made during the **Jomon Period** (10,000 B.C.–300 B.C.) comprise the earliest Japanese art. In the subsequent **Yayoi Period** (300 B.C.–A.D. 300) pottery thrown on a wheel and bronze ritual objects such as mirrors and bells appeared. The **Kofun Period** (A.D. 300–700) produced elaborate *haniwa*, clay figures of people and animals that were placed on the large keyhole-shaped burial mounds.

Religious art flourished in Japan after the introduction of Buddhism in the 6th century. Originally the art copied Korean and Chinese objects, but developed a Japanese style within a short period of time. Most Japanese art in the Heian period was religious art, with the exception of handscrolls called *Yamato-e* (literally Japanese paintings), an indigenous style of painting.

For all its political chaos, the Kamakura era was a dynamic time for sculpture. The sculptors Kokei, Unkei and Kaikei made dramatic and realistic sculptures.

Strongly influenced by Chinese Sung Dynasty landscape paintings, Zen ink paintings dominated the arts during the Muromachi period. While the early works by Zen monks imitated the Chinese, the great monk-artist Sesshu changed all that by putting his personal imprint on monochrome landscape painting.

The brief **Momoyama Period** saw an explosion in the arts. The great age of castle building led to dramatic screen paintings on gold leaf to embellish the dark castles and the residences. The Kano school painters were commissioned to make bold, larger-than-life compositions to glorify the military leaders. Genre painting also came into its own during the

TREASURING NATIONAL TREASURES

*Japan takes great pride in its history and traditions. Early in this century it enacted laws protecting works of art and other cultural assets. The most important buildings and works of art were designated **National Treasures** and those less important but also worthy of preservation were named **Important Cultural Properties**. About 1000 objects and buildings are National Treasures; some 11,000 are Important Cultural Properties. The government provides financial assistance to museums, temples and other owners for the preservation of these valuable assets.*

*After World War II, the Japanese government recognized endangered traditions also needed preservation. Craftsmen, artisans and performing artists who have reached the pinnacles of their fields are designated **Intangible Cultural Assets**, but are more commonly called **Living National Treasures**. About 150 people currently hold Living National Treasure status, masters in fields as divergent as ceramics and weaving, swordmaking and noh chanting. Japan is the only country that so honors the people who preserve traditional culture.*

Momoyama period. The merchant class amassed wealth and wanted paintings of everyday life. Other paintings depicted Portuguese who came to Japan and were called *Nanban* (Southern Barbarian) paintings, so named because the Portuguese sailed into Japan from the south. These paintings illustrate the Japanese fascination with the exotic foreigners.

The **Kano School** became the official painters to the Tokugawa shogunate, and Kano Tanyu moved to Edo with the shogun. The Kano School looked to China for inspiration. A more indigenous school of painting was the **Rimpa School**, which took inspiration from the Japanese Yamato-e paintings. Their works were decorative and abstract and have enormous appeal even today.

In the Edo Period Japan entered a long period of isolation. Cut off from other cultures, it looked inward. Feudal lords had to make periodic trips to Edo, the seat of the Tokugawa shogunate, and needed to present gifts. Each province worked hard to develop unique high quality art. The Nabeshima domain in Kyushu produced exquisite porcelain exclusively used as gifts to the shogun and other feudal lords.

For wealthy merchants at the other end of the social spectrum, *ukiyo-e,* pictures of the floating world, caught their fancy. The early paintings gave way to woodblock prints by the early 18th century. These prints used courtesans and *kabuki* actors as their themes and were distributed widely at low cost. Frowned upon by the Edo elite, *ukiyo-e* received little attention until the paintings reached Europe where they had a profound effect upon the Impressionists including Van Gogh and Cezanne.

With the Meiji Restoration in 1868, Japan began incorporating Western perspective in a type of painting called *nihon-ga*. Many Japanese went to Paris to study and painted totally in the Western style.

Today, we find that traditional Japanese aesthetics are expressed best not in contemporary art but in the fashion designs of Issey Miyake and Yohji Yamamoto and architectural accomplishments of Ando Tadao and Isozaki Arata.

TRADITIONAL CRAFTS

Japan's craft movement thrives today. Unlike many other countries, Japan continues to appreciate its crafts traditions even in the face of modern industrialization. Japanese relish their products and have the money and willingness to pay the high cost of these labor intensive objects.

Part of the credit for maintaining craft traditions goes to the "Mingei Movement" of the 1920s and 1930s. A dedicated band of artisans including Yanagi Soetsu, Yamada Shoji and Kawai Kanjiro along with the British potter Bernard Leach, saw beauty in the everyday objects made by unknown craftsmen. This influential group of people saved many a craft from extinction.

For a good overview of Japanese crafts, visit the **Japan Traditional Crafts Center** in Tokyo. While they sell all the objects they display, the center also functions like a museum and has video tapes demonstrating the processes. A few of the major crafts follow.

Ceramics

Few countries have Japan's reverence and love of pottery. We are sure one of the reasons Japanese serve food on individual plates is to have an excuse to surround themselves with beautiful ceramic dishes. Pottery making goes back to prehistoric times, but in the 16th century Momoyama period, rustic local pottery got a big boost when it became the favored choice for tea ceremony. In the 17th century, porcelain production burgeoned in Kyushu and Kyoto. Today, some artisans continue producing pottery based on traditional techniques and patterns while others are making innovative contemporary ware, more an art than a craft.

Some of the major pottery production centers are **Arita**, **Echizen**, **Imbe**, **Kagoshima**, **Kanazawa**, **Karatsu**, **Kyoto**, **Mashiko**, **Seto**, **Shigaraki**, **Tajimi** and **Tokoname**.

Textiles

Japan's textile traditions stretch from the banana fiber fabrics of Okinawa to the heavy fibers of northern Japan. Cotton, silk and linen are the most commonly used fibers. In the Edo era, the shogunate prohibited the merchant class from wearing silk, so to subvert this rule they wore subdued cotton kimono lined with silk. Indigo-dyed cotton was the uniform for the peasant while the upper classes luxuriated in silk.

Kimono are no longer worn daily and are mostly worn at formal occasions, similar to Westerners wearing evening gowns. Some women are willing to pay huge sums of money for hand-dyed kimono. Young women take courses to learn how to wear a kimono.

Among the many different textile designs is *yuzen*, a process popular in **Kanazawa** and **Kyoto**, painting designs on silk. *Shibori* is a tie-dying technique, but nothing like the tee shirts popular in the US in the 1970s. *Kasuri*, or ikat, dyes patterns on the threads before weaving them to create a design. Elaborately woven brocades are made in **Kyoto**. Other kimono have stenciled or embroidered designs. **Okinawa** produces brightly colored *bingata* fabrics, some stenciled while others are painted freehand.

Old kimono and other textiles are some of the great bargains in Japan. Go to a shrine flea market for a wide selection.

Lacquer

Japan produces so much lacquer ware that in Europe the term "japan" means lacquer, just like "china" means ceramics. The sap of the lacquer tree is applied again and again over a wooden base to create a lacquered object. Sometimes the natural grain of the wood shows through while other times the lacquer forms an opaque surface. Lacquer should be kept in a humid environment to prevent the wood from cracking, so it may not be the ideal gift to take home. Less expensive lacquer pieces may have a core made of composite wood or plastic.

Sometimes Westerners have a difficult time telling the difference between real lacquer and plastic, but after picking up a few pieces the differences are apparent.

The main lacquer producing areas are **Aizu Wakamatsu, Hirosaki, Kamakura, Kyoto, Wajima, Takayama**, the **Kiso district (Hirasawa** and **Narai)** and **Yamanaka** near Kanazawa.

Wood & Bamboo

Japan's abundant forests means lots of wood is available for furniture making. *Tansu*, Japanese chests, are used for storage in traditional Japanese houses. Mountainous areas such as **northern Honshu, Matsumoto, Takayama** and **Niigata** excel in furniture making. Bamboo baskets are found throughout Japan but the **Okayama** and **Beppu** areas are particularly famous production sites still utilizing traditional weaving patterns.

Metalwork

Iwate Prefecture in northern Honshu is known especially for cast iron tea kettles called *nambu tetsubin*.

Washi Paper

Japanese *washi* paper, often called rice paper in the West, has nothing to do with rice. Paper is made from the fibers of the mulberry plant. Some *washi* paper has large fibers with attractive textured patterns while other paper is painted or stenciled. Many different objects are made from *washi* paper: lampshades, screens, luncheon mats, wallets, umbrellas and, naturally, stationery. **Mino** and **Echizen** are two of the largest *washi* production centers.

PERFORMING ARTS

Japanese traditional performing arts, although holdovers from the Edo Period, find large and appreciative audiences throughout the country. *Kabuki, bunraku* and *noh* are the big three.

Kabuki

Kabuki is the most accessible of traditional Japan's performing arts for non-Japanese and Japanese. We urge you to make time to see *kabuki* not only to enjoy the highly stylized performance but also to take in the festive ambiance. The brief English synopsis will give you the plot, but just like Shakespearean plays, the plot is only one aspect of the entire experience: you can't help but be dazzled by the sumptuous costumes, the acting, the music and the stylized movements. Each time we go, we notice something we haven't found before. *Kabuki* is for entertainment, so enjoy.

Okuni, a female dancer from Izumo Grand Shrine, started *kabuki* when she went to Kyoto to raise funds for the shrine in the early 16th century. She led a troupe of dancers who performed spirited and lusty dances on the banks of the Kamo River in Kyoto. Screen paintings show the excitement people felt watching these women dance in striking costumes. Okuni soon incorporated plots in her dances and used *noh* drums and flutes. *Kabuki's* popularity grew.

Many of the dancers were prostitutes; and some brothel owners would have women dance *kabuki* to entice customers. Because of this lewd image, the Tokugawa shogunate banned women from dancing *kabuki* in 1629. Young boys then played the women's roles, but eventually they were also prohibited from dancing. By mid-Edo period all the parts were played by adult men.

The merchant class in Edo took to *kabuki*. It had almost everything the merchant class, the lowest social class, yet the wealthiest, enjoyed most — beautiful "women," tales of love, vengeance, adultery, war, ghosts and death.

Kabuki actors specialize in male or female roles. Watch carefully how the *onnagata* (the male actors who play female roles) conveys femininity through the movements of his hands, eyes and hips.

The musicians are off to the side of the stage, behind a curtain. Dramatic music indicates an actor is about to appear on the stage via the *hanamichi*, literally the "flower path," the long entrance walkway through the audience to the left side of the stage.

Feel the excitement of the audience as the plot reaches its climax. At a most untimely moment, you may suddenly notice your neighbor is eating oranges or chocolate right in middle of the climax. Don't let it bother you. In the old days people went to *kabuki* theater the same way they went for a picnic, carrying lunch, supper, tea and snacks. It's not considered rude to eat and drink your way through a *kabuki* performance although the rustling of papers and *bento* boxes can get annoying. Since performances last several hours, you are welcome to come and go as you please. You can take your own meal or buy a *bento* box or sandwich in the theater.

In *kabuki* there's a real intimacy between the actors and the audience. You might be surprised to suddenly hear a member of the audience shout out something incomprehensible. He is probably screaming the actor's name. It's like saying "Bravo," but is usually done by a member of the actor's fan club.

The major theaters in Tokyo are **Kabuki-za** and the **National Theater** in Tokyo. They offer two programs a day, each lasting about four hours: the first program begins at around 11am and the second at 4:30pm. At the Kabuki-za, *kabuki* is performed every month from the 1st until the 26th. Get the English guidephone; it really helps you understand what is going on.

To be on the safe side you should reserve your seats in advance. If you only want to see *kabuki* for a short time, Kabuki-za in Tokyo offers one-act tickets called *makumi-seki*. Buy them 15 minutes before the act begins. These are nose-bleed seats, high up in the back of the theater, and although you can't rent English earphones, you still can have a delightful introduction to *kabuki*.

Bunraku

Japan's traditional **puppet theater** evolved into popular entertainment for all classes, but especially for the common people, at roughly the same time as *kabuki* — in the early 17th century. *Bunraku* combines three elements — texts narrated by the chanters, the *shamisen* music introduced to Japan around 1570 from the Ryukyu Islands (Okinawa), and three-quarter size puppets — which make *bunraku* so intriguing. The great playwright **Chikamatsu Monzaemon** authored 130 plays in the 17th century. One of his most famous works, *Love Suicide of Sonezaki* (Sonezaki is now in central Osaka) was made into a *bunraku* play just a few weeks after the true love tragedy occurred.

When we first start watching *bunraku*, it's hard to ignore the three puppeteers dressed in black manipulating each puppet. As the plot gets more and more complex we cease noticing these men and simply enjoy watching the dolls come alive.

Hand-made, the puppet's head is an art itself. Special craftsmen produce these dolls using techniques handed down from generation to generation. We love to watch the facial expressions of the puppets, changing delicately by the puppeteer's manipulation. Watch the master puppeteer (who usually appears unmasked in formal kimono) as he takes on the puppet's persona while simultaneously keeping his distance. Also enjoy the puppets' strikingly colorful and elegant costumes.

Pay attention to the narrator who sits next to the *shamisen* musician. Watching him narrate the story exhausts us. Listen to the deep piercing notes of *shamisen*. The music, the chanting and the puppets themselves combine to provide a riveting theatrical experience.

Bunraku is based in Osaka but performs several months a year in Tokyo. If it's in town when you are, do your best to see it. The English language earphones are worth their small rental price.

Noh

Unlike *kabuki* and *bunraku*, *noh* never had mass appeal. It's the art for cultured individuals, not unlike opera in the West. *Noh* originated with the Shinto religion when priests danced at shrines to ensure a good harvest. Later troupes of roaming actors performed on behalf of the priests.

During the Muromachi period (14th to 15th century), under the patronage of the shogun, *noh's* distinctive drama form developed. **Ze-ami Motokiyo** (1363–1443) not only wrote most of the major plays but also established the aesthetic of *yugen*, the elegant, the profound and the mysterious, which *noh* expresses. Ze-ami also established the stage, costumes, masks and acting conventions.

Noh is a masked dance drama performed by men dressed in sumptuous costumes of elaborate silk brocade. The costumes are works of art by themselves and are often displayed in museums.

Musicians, playing drums and flutes, and the chorus sit on the stage, a smallish square with an entrance passageway at the left. There's little movement in *noh*. Actors take slow steps and their voices are garbled by the masks. Most plays express psychological tension between the main actor *(shite)* and a bystander *(waki)* and usually involve spirits and demons interacting with mortals.

Noh is a beautiful art form but is difficult to appreciate. If you go expecting understatement, you won't be disappointed. Some plays have been translated in English and it helps if you know the play before you attend the performance. Occasionally, a *noh* theater will have a performance with an English introduction. Jump at the chance to attend it.

Kyogen

Kyogen is a comic interlude performed between *noh* plays to give the audience time to relax (apart from sleeping during the *noh* performance). This farcical theater deals with every day human relationships. The major characters are feudal lords, servants, priests, novices, farmers and merchants, all who want to enjoy the good life. Kyogen is light and accessible and is increasingly performed on its own. Occasionally *kyogen* plays are performed in English.

Japanese Traditional Music

Hogaku, traditional Japanese music, came from China and Korea. Traditional instruments are used in *kabuki, noh* and *bunraku* theaters, but the music is also performed for music's sake. *Gagaku* is the court music from the Heian times and is sometimes still performed, either to accompany dance or songs or solely as instrumental music.

The main instruments in the Japanese classical repertory are drums, *shakuhachi* and other flutes, *koto* (zither), *biwa* (lute) and *shamisen* (stringed instrument).

Classical performances are common in the large cities. The Nihon Ongaku Shudan (Pro Musica Nipponica) plays modern music using Japanese instruments.

Buyoh

Buyoh is classical Japanese dance derived from *kabuki* but performed for dance's sake, not as part of a dance drama. Unlike *kabuki,* both women and men participate in performing abstract and narrative dances.

Butoh

Butoh is avant-garde dance, popularized by the Sankai Juku troupe in the 1970s. The stark dance from usually features nearly naked performers with shaven heads and bodies painted white.

Taiko

Taiko, drumming on instruments of many different sizes, derived from Shinto festival drumming. Several troupes including Kodo and Za Ondekoza raised it to an art form and have gained world-wide attention for their creative and expressive use of percussion. Kodo holds a big "Earth Celebration" every August on Sado Island. If there's a *taiko* performance when you're in Japan, by all means attend.

LANGUAGE & KEY PHRASES

Japanese don't widely speak English, but don't let the language barrier deter you from traveling in Japan. People are friendly and will go out of their way to make sure you are okay.

Although Japanese study English in junior high school, high school and college, the emphasis is on passing exams, not on comprehension and speaking. Say "hello" to high school students and it's unlikely that they can carry the conversation any further. But in the big cities, a surprising number of people speak English, especially people who work in the tourist trade.

Prepare to be illiterate. Japanese does not use the Western alphabet. Unlike traveling in Europe, you won't be able to read signs. But don't be shy about asking people to help you. Speak slowly and clearly.

In the big cities, lots of signs are in English including in subway and train stations. Although it's fashionable for beauty shops, restaurants, bars, bakeries and boutiques to have signs in English, it doesn't mean there is an English-speaking staff inside.

Should you take a Japanese language course before coming to Japan? If you are spending one week in Tokyo or Kyoto, don't bother. If you are going to be spending an extended period in remote rural areas, then it's worth the effort. But make sure you take a Japanese-for-Travelers course rather than an introductory class in Japanese.

We find that a good phrase book goes a long way. We like Berlitz' *Japanese for Travelers* because you can point to the written Japanese.

Japanese didn't have a written language so around the 6th century they adopted Chinese characters called *kanji*. Since these characters didn't mesh well with spoken Japanese, they developed two syllabic alphabets to use with the *kanji*.

The vowels in Japanese are very clear (like Italian) and always pronounced the same way:

a as in f**a**ther
e as in r**e**d
i as in pol**i**ce
o as in m**o**re
u as in f**oo**d

If you learn only one word in Japanese, the most useful word is *sumimasen*. It technically means "I'm sorry" and "excuse me." You can use it to get someone's attention, to request a favor and to say thank you.
Here are some basic phrases to get you on your way.

O-hayo gozaimasu	Good Morning (use until mid-morning)
Kon-nichi wa	Good Day (use mid-morning until evening)
Konban wa	Good Evening
O-yasumi nasai	Good Night (use before going to bed)
Sayonara	Good-bye
Domo arigato	Thank you
Doo Itashimashite	You are welcome
Sumimasen	I am sorry, Excuse me
Wakarimasen	I don't understand
Hai	Yes
Iie	No
Moshi-moshi	Hello (on telephone)
Hajime mashite	How do you do? (When first meeting someone)
O-genki desu ka?	How are you?
Hai, okagesama de	Fine, thank you.
Chotto matte kudasai	Please wait a minute.
Onegai shimasu	Please (said when requesting a favor or service)
Tasukete!	Help!
Kaji	Fire
Nan desu ka?	What is it?
Nanji desu ka?	What time is it?
Doko desu ka?	Where is it?
Dare desu ka?	Who is it?
Ikura desu ka?	How much does it cost?
Yasui	Inexpensive
Takai	Expensive
Migi	Right
Hidari	Left
Massugu	Straight

TWO COUNTRIES DIVIDED
BY A COMMON LANGUAGE

Japan uses a lot of English loan words, pronouncing them in a Japanese way. Bus is basu, taxi is takushi, computer is compuuta, television is terebi, all fairly straightforward. But some loan words in Japanese do not relate to their English primary meaning and sometimes they are shortened so they are unrecognizable. A native speaker could be completely confused. Here's a sampling:

Smart *(sumaatto)* – *Stylish*

Family con *(fami con)* – *Computer games played on TV (short for family computer)*

Wa-pro – *Word processor*

Body con *(bodi con)* – *A short, form fitting dress (short for body conform)*

Creap – *A brand name for non-dairy coffee creamer*

Salaryman *(sarariman)* – *A male company employee*

OL or **Office Lady** *(Ofisu redii)* – *A female clerical worker*

Skin *(sukin)* – *A condom*

Seku hara – *Sexual harassment*

Wet *(wetto)* – *Emotional*

Dry *(dorai)* – *Unemotional, realistic*

Talent *(tarento)* – *Television personality*

Trainer *(toraina)* – *Sweatshirt*

Mansion *(manshon)* – *Apartment building*

Depaato – *Department Store*

Free size *(furi saizu)* – *One size fits all*

Tomatte	Stop
Ichi	One
Ni	Two
San	Three
Shi (Yon)	Four
Go	Five
Roku	Six
Shichi (Nana)	Seven
Hachi	Eight
Kyu	Nine
Ju	Ten
Hyaku	Hundred
Sen	Thousand
Man	Ten Thousand

Form teens by putting the number after *ju* (10): 15 = *ju-go*

Form hundreds by putting the number before *hyaku* (100): 500 = *go-hyaku*

Form thousands by putting the number before *sen* (1000): 2000 = *ni-sen*

Form ten thousands by putting the number before *man* (10,000): 30,000 = *san-man*

ETIQUETTE

Here are a few points of Japanese etiquette that will make your trip go more smoothly. For etiquette in Japanese restaurants, inns and baths, see the Food & Drink and Planning Your Trip chapters.

Bowing: Japanese don't shake hands, they bow. The angle of the bow depends on the relationship between the two people. Friends may merely nod their heads while greeting the emperor necessitates a deep bow with your head down to your knees. Unless you plan to have an audience with the emperor, don't worry about it too much. Japanese who have some knowledge of the West will often put out their hands to shake. The best advice is to follow the lead of the person you are greeting.

Name Cards: Everyone in Japan has a name card called *meishi* and business people exchange them as soon as they meet. You won't need them while traveling for pleasure but they are mandatory for business. However, if you plan on meeting a lot of people, for instance, if you're a member of an exchange program, have a card made up with your home address.

Names: Japanese traditionally write the family name first, followed by the given name. We have used this same order for names in this book. Usually Japanese are addressed by their family name, followed by *san*, an all-purpose honorific meaning Mr., Mrs., or Ms. Don't call Japanese by their given names unless they specifically request you to.

Footwear: Japanese exchange shoes for slippers when they enter houses and remove the slippers when walking on *tatami* (straw) mats. Workers often wear slippers in offices, but guests do not. You also have to remove your footwear when entering a Buddhist temple. Wearing slip-on shoes will make your life easier.

4. A SHORT HISTORY

THE EARLIEST YEARS

Archaeological finds show there have been people hanging around Japan for a long time, maybe more than 30,000 years. Apparently, hunters crossed land bridges that once connected Japan with the Asian continent. Archaeologists have found remains of their early stone tools.

JOMON PERIOD

(ca. 10,000–300 B.C.)

At the end of the ice age, global warming melted ice caps, and the rising sea level cut Japan off from the continent. The period takes its name from earthenware decorated with *jomon* (cord marking). People used earthenware and lacquered containers, so lacquering – "japanning" – is a very old process. By the end of the era, villagers had extensive contact with neighboring areas as well as with the Korean peninsula.

The Japanese diet today is healthy provided you avoid fast food, but in Jomon times, it was even better balanced. People ate the meat of animals hunted in the forest and gathered roots, nuts and saltwater shellfish. The semipermanent villages had huts with thatched roofs sunken into the earth. Jomon settlements have been found throughout the Japanese islands.

The Japanese language, which most linguists connect to Korean and other Altaic (Turkic and Mongolian) languages, developed during the Jomon period.

YAYOI PERIOD

(ca. 300 B.C.–A.D. 300)

During the Yayoi period, Japanese learned rice cultivation, metal-working, pottery making and textile weaving from the Asian continent. The actual name, Yayoi, comes from an area in Tokyo where advanced earthenware was discovered.

IN THE BEGINNING...

*In the beginning were two deities, **Izanagi** and **Izanami**, an exceedingly fertile couple who were brother and sister. They gave birth to the islands of Japan as well as to other gods. Izanami died while giving birth to the God of Fire. Izanagi tried to follow her to the land of the dead but couldn't stand the putrid smell. He continued to give birth to deities including **Amaterasu**, the Sun Goddess, and her brother **Susa-no-o**, the God of Storms.*

Susa-no-o angered Amaterasu by destroying her palace and rice fields so she retreated to a cave, which plunged the world into darkness. To lure her out, one god performed a lewd dance. As she listened to other gods howling with laughter, Amaterasu's curiosity was aroused and she asked what was going on. The gods told her the most powerful god had appeared. Amaterasu stuck her head out to see who it could possibly be and saw her own reflection in a mirror. The gods took advantage of this opportunity to pull her from the cave. Susa-no-o was exiled and eventually ended up in Izumo, near present-day Matsue.

*Amaterasu sent her grandson, Ninigi, to earth to rule over Japan. He arrived in southern Kyushu with imperial regalia: a mirror, a sword and a jewel. Ninigi's grandson, **Emperor Jimmu**, fought his way east conquering his enemies, including the gods at Izumo, and became the first emperor of Japan thus establishing the imperial line.*

Wet-rice cultivation was introduced into Kyushu from the Korean peninsula and spread rapidly throughout western Japan and then to northern Japan. Becoming a rice-growing culture meant villagers had to cooperate closely to irrigate rice paddies, leading to the development of a more sophisticated social organization. Villagers cultivated fields with iron implements.

While iron was used for utilitarian objects, bronze was the metal of choice for rituals and rulers. Elaborately decorated ceremonial bronze mirrors, bells, swords and spears were also produced.

Towards the latter part of the Yayoi period, loosely organized political entities emerged. The first written account of Japan appears in Chinese chronicles around A.D. 57 and refers to the "Land of Wa," composed of several small states. *Wa* meant petty, but over time the Japanese changed it to a homonym meaning harmony.

Himiko, a shaman queen, ruled an area that scholars believe was in northern Kyushu. In A.D. 237, Himiko sent an envoy to the Kingdom of Wei (China). Yes, it's hard to believe it in Japan's male-dominated political world today, but a woman is the first ruler of Japan mentioned in a written history.

KOFUN PERIOD

(ca. A.D. 300-593)

By the mid-4th century, the **Yamato** clan had increased its power until it controlled most of the central regions and established the Yamato court. Its base was the Yamato plain in present-day Nara Prefecture. Although the first 15 emperors of Japan are shrouded in myth and legend, the Yamato rulers were the first emperors of Japan and set up a colony in Korea.

This age is known for its large *kofun* — keyhole shaped burial mounds — built for the emperors and other members of the imperial family. Many of the tombs were ringed with *haniwa*, clay figures and objects that might have been substitutes for live burials. The largest *kofun* is **Emperor Nintoku's** (early 5th century) in Osaka Prefecture. Located on an 80-acre site, it is 500 meters long, 35 meters high and surrounded by three moats; it rivals the pyramids in size.

As Buddhism was introduced from the Asian continent by mid-6th century, the ruling class devoted its wealth to the creation of temples, thus ending the Kofun period.

ASUKA PERIOD

(593-710)

The Asuka Period is generally regarded as the beginning of the historic era in Japan. The **Empress Suiko** was crowned in 593 and designated Asuka, in present-day Nara Prefecture, as the capital of Yamato.

This era was strongly influenced by Buddhism, which arrived from China via Korean immigrants. They also brought the Chinese writing system and Chinese Confucian principles. During roughly the same period that Christianity transported Mediterranean culture to northern Europe, Buddhism served as the vehicle to carry Chinese culture from the mainland to Japan. By the end of the 6th century, Buddhism was firmly established as the religion of the ruling classes.

In 604, the Seventeen Article Constitution was set forth by **Prince Shotoku**, a devout Buddhist and regent for Empress Suiko, his aunt. The constitution established Buddhism as the state religion and strengthened the unity of the state, using the Chinese administrative system as a model. Prince Shotoku founded **Horyu-ji Temple** in 607 and encouraged scholars to spread Buddhism among the ruling class. He sent a series of diplomatic missions to China. In a letter from the emperor of China written in 607, Japan was referred to as the Land of the Rising Sun for the first time. Missions to China continued for the next 200 years despite the great expense and dangers of crossing the treacherous South China Sea.

After Prince Shotoku's death in 622, the Soga clan assassinated Shotoku's son and usurped power. In 645 a coup d'etat deposed the empress who was succeeded by her younger brother. **Prince Naka-no-Oe**, who led the coup with **Nakatomi-no-Kamatari**, became the crown prince and later ruled under the name of **Emperor Tenchi**. Given the name Fujiwara as a reward, the Nakatomi clan remained powerful regents to emperors for the next 500 years.

In 645 Emperor Tenchi instituted the **Taika Reforms**. Based on Tang China, the reforms abolished private land ownership, placing all land under imperial control; rival clans were stripped of their land but, in return, were given aristocratic titles. The reforms also established the principle of a permanent capital. Prior to these reforms, the capital moved every time a new emperor or empress came to power.

PRINCE SHOTOKU

Prince Shotoku (574-622) figures prominently in any Who's Who of Japanese history. He set in motion the changes that would lead to the Taika Reforms which altered Japan's political landscape. Born into the Soga clan, the ruling family of the time, he became regent for his aunt Empress Suiko. A devout Buddhist, he founded Horyu-ji and many other temples. At the same time, he recognized the political impact of Buddhism, setting up a hierarchy under central control. In 604 the Seventeen Article Constitution, which established Confucian ethical and political principles, was proclaimed to the people. The first article, "Harmony is to be valued," shows the concept of harmony has been central to Japanese society for a long time.

NARA PERIOD
(710–794)

Heijo-kyo, present-day Nara, was designated as the permanent capital by the emperor in 710. Its layout was based on the grid system of Tang China's capital city Chang-an, now known as Xian. In present-day Nara the actual site is a park on the outskirts of the city.

The Nara court was closely modeled after the Chinese system and included a central bureaucracy. Buddhism prospered. This golden age of temple building resulted in 361 new temples including **Kofuku-ji** and **Todai-ji**, which houses an immense bronze Buddha in the world's largest wooden building.

PILLOW TALK

During the Asuka and Nara periods, Japan imported Chinese culture in a big way. But in the Heian period, it slowly digested and transformed these imports until they became uniquely Japanese.

*The most notable example is the writing system. Since Japan didn't have its own written language, it borrowed Chinese ideographs in the 6th century. Grafting onto a written language was cumbersome, so in the early Heian period, the Japanese introduced two **kana** alphabets spelling out Japanese words. Formal documents were written in Chinese characters, but private letters, including love letters, were written in the new kana. Aristocratic women learned to write; until this era, only men learned to read and write. Although men continued to use Chinese ideographs, women were free to write in kana.*

*Two of Japan's most well-known works of literature are "The Tale of Genji" by **Murasaki Shikibu** and "The Pillow Book" by **Sei Shonagon**. Written by court women in the Heian period, they give riveting insights to the intrigue, love and politics of court life.*

The court at Nara spent such large amounts of money that it found itself in dire financial straits. The Buddhist monks became so powerful that they began to undermine the power of the emperor. During the last 10 years of the period, the capital moved to Nagaoka replacing Heijo-kyo as the permanent capital. In 794 the capital moved again — this time to Kyoto.

Japanese began using Chinese ideographs in the 6th century. In 712 the *Kojiki*, the oldest Japanese record of ancient Japan, was compiled, and in 720 the *Nihon Shoki*, Chronicles of Japan, were completed. Up to that time, Japan had neither a written record of its history nor a written language of its own. The two chronicles are heavily based on the mythological origins of Japan and use these myths to firmly establish the emperor as a descendent of the Sun Goddess, Amaterasu.

HEIAN PERIOD
(794–1185)

In 794 **Emperor Kammu** established the capital called Heian-kyo, Capital of Peace, in present-day Kyoto. He desperately wanted to get away from the powerful Buddhist temples in Nara that undermined his authority. Like Nara's Heijo-kyo, the city layout copied China's capital, Chang-an.

Emperor Kammu allowed only two temples within the city's precincts, Sai-ji and To-ji, both at Kyoto's southern perimeter. Enryaku-ji Temple was built on Mt. Hiei, northeast of the city, to protect it from the evil spirits residing in that direction. Kammu had hoped to limit the power of the Buddhist temples, but within a few generations, they were firmly enmeshed in the ruling structure.

The Heian period was the golden age of Japan's aristocratic culture. Under the emperor, the nobility lived a life of leisure indulging in poetry, music and other cultural pastimes. Art and architecture flourished and Japanese artistry came into its own, breaking free from the Chinese dominated aesthetic of the earlier ages. By the middle of the Heian period, the court stopped sending embassies to China, and Japan became isolated from the Asian continent. Unfortunately, few monuments of the Heian period remain.

For a while the emperors kept control of the government and the land. But in time, their functions became more centered on ritual and culture. The **Fujiwara** family gained strength as regents, the highest ranking ministers who ran the state. The Fujiwara married their daughters to emperors so their grandsons would be emperors. The emperors retired early, sometimes after reigning just a few years.

In the 11th century, the Fujiwara women stopped producing heirs. Emperor Go-sanjo (reigned 1069-1072) was the first emperor in a hundred years who did not have a Fujiwara mother. Political power passed to retired emperors, called cloistered emperors, who competed with the Fujiwara for the acquisition of land. The aristocrats and monks appointed local families to administer their land, greatly increasing the power of these provincial officers.

The aristocracy was having too good a time to notice that trouble was brewing in the provinces. Law and order broke down; provincial families started small armies that gave birth to the *samurai* (warrior) class. Soon there were two powerful regional warlords. The emperor used one of these clans, the **Taira** (also known as the Heike clan), to rid himself of the Fujiwara regents.

But the Taira were soon enmeshed in a power struggle with their rivals, the **Minamoto** (also known as the Genji clan), and a struggle over imperial succession ushered in a period of civil war. The Taira imprisoned the emperor and put the emperor's grandson, whose mother was a Taira, on the throne. The Minamoto fought back and, in the sea battle of Dan-no-ura in 1185, annihilated the Taira. The Heian era, the "era of peace" went down in flames.

HISTORIC COMPARISONS

In Japan & Asia	In Europe & America
794: Capital of Japan established at Kyoto	*800:* Charlemagne crowned emperor of Holy Roman Empire
1069-1072: Reign of Emperor Go-sanjo	*1066:* William the Conqueror crowned king of England
1185: Establishment of the first shogunate(government by warriors) in Japan	*1215:* King John of England issues Magna Carta
1271: Marco Polo begins his journey to the court of Kublai Khan in China	
1274: Kublai Khan invades Japan for the first time	
1281: Second invasion of Japan by Kublai Khan	
1333: Ashikaga Shogunate established in Japan	*1337:* One hundred years of war begins between England and France
1467: Onin War begins in Japan, ushering in one hundred years of war and chaos.	*1492:* Columbus lands in America
1639: Japan begins 200 year period of isolation	*1620:* The Mayflower lands at Plymouth Rock
	1776: US Declaration of Independence
	1789: French Revolution
	1804: Napoleon crowns himself emperor of France
	1837: Victoria becomes the queen of England, ruling until 1901
1839–42: Opium Wars in China	
1853: Commodore Perry sails his black ships into Tokyo Bay	*1861–65:* Civil War in the US
1867: Tokugawa shogun is overthrown	

KAMAKURA PERIOD

(1185-1333)

When the Minamoto defeated the Taira, **Minamoto Yoritomo** established a military government centered at **Kamakura**, close to present-day Tokyo. He wanted to get away from the intrigues of the court and shelter his warriors from the easy life of Kyoto. Yoritomo asked the emperor to name him shogun; reluctantly he complied in 1192. For the first time political power shifted into the hands of the warrior class where basically it remained until 1868.

The emperor and his court remained in Kyoto but were powerless. The court allowed the shogun to appoint vassals to run the provincial estates, which led to the establishment of a feudal system. The samurai code solidified, stressing loyalty and obedience to their superiors above all else.

After only three generations, there was no heir to the Minamoto shogun and power shifted to the Hojo clan, the family of the first shogun Yoritomo's powerful wife, **Hojo Masako**.

Under **Kublai Khan**, the Mongols invaded Kyushu in 1274 and 1281 in attempts to control Japan. On both occasions, the Mongol fleets were damaged by mighty typhoons while the whole country could do nothing but pray frantically for victory. That's why the Japanese called these typhoons *kamikaze* – divine wind. No foreign force ever occupied Japan until the end of World War II in 1945.

While the Mongol invasions brought national unity against an external threat, it also planted the seeds for decline. Resentment grew from the other samurai: the Hojo, who monopolized the top positions, did not adequately reward the samurai who fought the Mongols. **Emperor Godaigo**, with the support of disaffected warriors, overthrew the shogunate in 1333.

Despite all the turbulence, the Kamakura era was one of great artistic flowering. A dynamic style of sculpture blossomed under priest-artists such as **Unkei** and **Kaikei**. Zen Buddhism, with its tenets of strict mental discipline and meditation, appealed to the warrior class and also found favor with emperors and aristocrats.

MUROMACHI PERIOD

(1333- 1573)

Emperor Godaigo's success in returning power to the throne was short-lived. **Ashikaga Takauji**, the samurai leader who helped Godaigo overthrow the Kamakura shogun, turned against the emperor, attacked Kyoto, and forced Godaigo to retreat to **Yoshino**. Takauji installed another emperor and had himself appointed shogun, ruling from Kyoto.

In the meantime, Godaigo set up a separate, competing court in Yoshino in 1333. This dual system meant the emperors lost the last vestiges of power and the government was firmly in the hands of the shogun.

The Ashikaga shogunate could never control Japan. The regional warlords increased their power, fighting among themselves and sometimes even taking on the central government. The **Onin War** broke out in Kyoto in 1467; what began as a battle for shogun succession lasted for ten years and destroyed Kyoto in the process. When the Onin War was over, there was no clear winner, just weaker armies. Law and order had broken down completely and the **Warring States** era began. The shogun, who was the central authority, had no power over the regional *daimyo* (feudal lords) who constantly battled with each other. As *daimyo* were able to expand the territory under their control, regional political and economic centers emerged. One *daimyo* could not unify the country. Instead, chaos reigned.

In 1543 a Portuguese ship, blown off course, landed on the small island of Tanegashima, just south of Kyushu. This seemingly insignificant event was to change the course of Japanese history: the Portuguese had firearms. Japan mastered this new technology and was soon producing its own guns. The feudal lords who mastered gun warfare suddenly had the upper hand. Christianity was also introduced; **St. Francis Xavier** landed in Kyushu in 1549. Although he was allowed to spread his good tidings, Christianity never became a major force in Japanese spiritual life.

The Ashikaga shoguns were more interested in the arts than governing. Much of what we think of as traditional Japanese culture has its roots in this era: *noh* theater, tea ceremony, flower arranging and brush painting.

MOMOYAMA PERIOD
(1573-1603)

Through a brilliant strategy of firearm warfare, **Oda Nobunaga**, the feudal lord of an area near Nagoya, gained control of large sections of Japan. He was absolutely brutal, destroying all that stood in his way. His troops overran the temple-fortress of Mt. Hiei, northeast of Kyoto, killing thousands of monks and leaving nothing standing. It wasn't as though he had slain passive monks deep in meditation; they, too, were a heavily armed force. In 1573, Nobunaga deposed the last Ashikaga shogun and continued to unify the country. While attending a tea ceremony in Kyoto, Nobunaga was assassinated by one of his vassals.

Toyotomi Hideyoshi, Nobunaga's most trusted general, and, incidentally, a person who rose from the lowly position of foot soldier, continued Nobunaga's campaign. By 1590, the seemingly impossible happened: Japan was united. Hideyoshi then turned outward and attacked Korea, but these campaigns ultimately ended in failure.

After unifying Japan, Hideyoshi did much to centralize power. He ordered a census and froze movement between the warrior and farmer classes. Until then, the lines between lower-ranking samurai and farmer had been fluid. Hideyoshi conducted a sword hunt, confiscating swords from the farmers and monks; only samurai could be armed. Taxes had to be paid in rice. Hideyoshi began moving the feudal lords to different fiefdoms to reward or punish them, in effect making the *daimyo* regional administrative officials.

Hideyoshi was brilliant at all things except one: producing an heir. Late in his life, his favored consort gave birth to two sons, but one died as an infant. When Hideyoshi died in 1598, his only son was still young. Hideyoshi set up a group of five councilors, the most powerful feudal lords, to oversee the affairs of state, hoping that they would keep each other in check. But before long, **Tokugawa Ieyasu** saw his opportunity. Ieyasu's dramatic victory at the **Battle of Sekigahara**, fought in 1600 on the plains outside of Nagoya, ensured his dominance by defeating the feudal lords loyal to Hideyoshi's heir. In 1603, Ieyasu had the emperor name him shogun.

This short-lived era was one of the most dynamic in Japan's history, not only militarily but also in art and architecture. Feudal lords built huge castles to protect their fiefdoms against the new forms of firearm warfare. They stood as tangible symbols of power and authority.

With peace came prosperity, and the feudal lords sumptuously decorated their castles and residences with golden screens, paintings and gardens. Nobunaga's Azuchi Castle set the standard although it was destroyed only a few years after its completion. Hideyoshi built dazzling castles in Fushimi (south of Kyoto) and Osaka. **Himeji Castle** in Himeji City and **Nijo Castle** (Nijo is actually a palace) in Kyoto are the best surviving examples of the grand architectural style of the Momoyama era.

The tea ceremony came into its own and elevated Japanese ceramics to an art. Tea ceremony also popularized more rustic forms of architecture since the ideal place to perform the ceremony is in a simple hut. New kinds of performing arts, *kabuki* and *bunraku* puppet theater, began during this time.

JAPAN'S RULING PERSONALITIES

A famous poem illustrates the different personalities of the three successive unifiers – Oda Nobunaga, Toyotomi Hideyoshi and Tokugawa Ieyasu. Imagine each man's reaction as he is given a nightingale or cuckoo bird.

Nobunaga says ruthlessly: "If the cuckoo will not sing, I will kill it."
Hideyoshi shows his ingenuity: "If the cuckoo will not sing, I will make it sing.
And Ieyasu shows his patience: "If the cuckoo will not sing, I will wait for it."

A famous anecdote tells how the three men made an omelet together: Nobunaga broke the eggs, Hideyoshi beat them, and Ieyasu ate the omelet.

TOKUGAWA (EDO) PERIOD

(1603-1868)

Tokugawa Ieyasu's rule ushered in a long period of peace and prosperity; Tokugawa shoguns ruled for the next 15 generations. Ieyasu moved his administration to a small castle town called **Edo** (present-day Tokyo). Using Hideyoshi's social system as a foundation, he created four classes: warrior, farmer, artisan and merchant. Controls were put into effect on all aspects of life but, within the framework, townspeople prospered and cities grew. In the 18th century, Edo had one million residents and may have been the largest city in the world.

The Tokugawa shogunate viewed the spread of Christianity as a threat. In the 1630s, the shogunate expelled all foreigners and banned Christianity. Japan closed its ports; foreigners could not enter and Japanese could not leave. The only exceptions were two small enclaves that remained in Nagasaki — one for Chinese and one for Dutch.

In order to control the feudal lords, their families were obligated to reside in Edo when the lords were in their own domains. Through a system called *sankin kotai*, the shogunate required the feudal lords to come to Edo every year. Naturally, they didn't travel alone but were accompanied by retainers and servants, often numbering hundreds of people. Such massive endeavors siphoned off a lot of funds; even if they'd wanted to revolt, feudal lords couldn't have afforded it. To accommodate these feudal entourages, small post towns and roads developed to Edo from all corners of the country. The same transportation network was used for the distribution of goods.

Merchants were on the lowest rung of society. Consumption laws restricted almost every aspect of their lives from what clothes they could wear to how many stories high their houses could be. But they flourished under the burgeoning commercial system. They amassed commercial wealth and become the moneylenders to the increasingly impoverished feudal lords and samurai, who were forbidden to engage in commercial activity. Some of the merchant families have gone on to create large corporations with names that are familiar today: Mitsui, Sumitomo and Yasuda. Mitsukoshi, Japan's oldest department store, started as a kimono shop during the Edo period.

As the commoners prospered, so did their arts. *Kabuki* theater flourished as did *ukiyo-e*, woodblock prints. Licensed by the shogunate, large pleasure quarters appeared where music, dance and poetry became intertwined with the skin trade.

But in time, cracks appeared in the system. The shogunate and feudal lords raised their rice taxes to cover growing expenditures. The gap widened between merchant/landowners and peasants, and the peasants began to revolt.

On the international front in the 19th century, Western powers were colonizing China and demanded Japan reopen its borders. In 1853 **Commodore Matthew Perry's** black ships sailed to Tokyo Bay and forced the government to accept a friendship treaty. Soon trade treaties were signed with the US and other Western powers. But the Tokugawa shogunate was ill equipped to handle these crises, and lower ranking samurai toppled the shogun in 1867. The movement solidified over returning the emperor to power. In 1868, the **Meiji Restoration** installed the **Meiji Emperor** as head of government.

MEIJI PERIOD THROUGH WORLD WAR II
(1868-1945)

For the next few decades, massive changes swept the country. The capital and the emperor moved to Edo, renamed **Tokyo**.

When the Meiji era started, Japan was a weak, undeveloped country emerging from more than two hundred years of isolation. Suddenly it was exposed to the international stage. By the end of Meiji, less than fifty years later, Japan had made major changes in its social, economic and political systems to catch up with the West, and had become a military power by defeating China and Russia.

The new constitutional government consisted of parliament (called the Diet) and an executive branch. The dismantled feudal domains gave way to a system of prefectures, and feudal lords assumed titles based on European peerage systems. The government, modeled after the West, established banking, rail and ship networks, and communication, legal and educational systems. Government and private companies worked together to build a strong industrial base.

Urban Japanese had a love affair with all things Western. People donned Western clothing, began to eat meat and foods favored in the West, and built Western-style buildings.

JAPAN'S GREAT LEAP FORWARD

*In the middle of the 19th century when Japan opened to the rest of the world, Japanese were shocked to discover how over two centuries of isolation left them ignorant of Western developments in science, medicine and engineering. So one of the first things the Meiji government decided was to bring in, at substantial cost, the leading overseas experts. Over 4000 **oyatoi** (literally honorable employees) came to advise the government on the construction of the new state and to educate the next generation of leaders. The Japanese government considered this a temporary measure to make up for lost time. By the mid-1870s the government began to cut back on the number of oyatoi because of the huge expense and because the quality of the advisors varied widely.*

More then half of these advisors were British. They concentrated on public works – construction of the railways and shipping industry. The French were bureaucrats, the Germans doctors and policemen and the Americans teachers and agricultural specialists. All left an impact on the Japanese society, some which are still seen today in ways big and small: the genesis of today's excellent rail system, the uniforms schoolchildren still wear, the legacy of beer making.

But learning wasn't only one way. Some of the foreign experts became fascinated by traditional Japanese art and culture and made efforts to preserve the traditional artifacts of Japanese society just when Japan wanted to throw it all away. Ernest Fenollosa, an American professor of philosophy and art played an important role saving from destruction traditional Japanese Buddhist artifacts and art; his collection is in the Museum of Fine Arts in Boston.

The government began to assert itself on the international scene, trying to revise the unequal treaties the Tokugawa shogunate signed. Japan went to war with China in 1894–95; the victorious Japan received Taiwan as a colony. In 1904–5, Japan challenged and defeated Russia, which was the first time an Asian nation defeated a European power. The defeat gave a strong boost to the Japanese military. In 1910, Japan annexed Korea, the trophy Hideyoshi wanted three hundred years earlier.

During World War I, Japan sided with the Allied Powers of Britain and France and attacked German territories in China. After the war, some of these colonies came under Japanese control.

Industrial growth led to the increasing polarization of Japanese society. Large numbers of people flocked to the cities to work in factories. Poor working conditions led to dissent and Marxist labor movements took hold. At the same time, ultranationalists demanded territorial expansion. The worldwide panic of 1929 led to fewer markets for Japan's exports.

The feeble government could not cope with all these problems and became dominated by military extremists. Japan annexed Manchuria in 1932 and invaded Beijing in 1937. Britain, Holland and the US responded to Japanese expansion in China by imposing a series of economic sanctions including an oil embargo. Negotiations between Japan and America to settle the dispute were inconclusive.

In December 1941, the Japanese military attacked Pearl Harbor in a preemptive strike to break the embargo and eliminate US naval forces from blocking its expansion in Asia. The US immediately declared war on Japan. Japan was initially successful in gaining control of much of Asia, including Southeast Asia and the lion's share of China, but the tide turned against the Japanese military as early as June 1942. By mid-1943, Japan was losing the war.

By the end of the war, Allied bombing had reduced almost every city in Japan to rubble. Dropping the atomic bombs on **Hiroshima** and **Nagasaki** in early August 1945 led to the Japanese surrender on August 15. **Emperor Hirohito**, who ruled from 1926–89, addressed the Japanese people by radio for the first time in history. He urged Japanese to "Endure the unendurable and suffer what is insufferable," a famous line indelibly etched in the memory of all Japanese born before the war.

POSTWAR PERIOD
(1945-Present)

Under the command of **General Douglas MacArthur**, American Allied Forces occupied Japan for six and a half years after the end of World War II. The Japanese government, put in power by MacArthur and the Occupation forces, restructured Japanese society. A new constitution drafted in 1947 renounced war and gave broad civil rights such as freedom of speech and religion. Women received the vote. Land reform was carried out and the *zaibatsu*, large industrial conglomerates (the original military industrial complexes), were broken up. The new government was based on a parliamentary system. The emperor remained as the symbol of the state and implicitly relinquished any divine right to rule.

In September 1951, Japan signed the **San Francisco Treaty**, which allowed Japan to conduct foreign policy. Economic development became the government's top priority. The Korean War in the 1950s gave Japan the impetus to reconstruct its economy and by the 1960s, Japan was competing in the world market. Hosting the Olympics in 1964 was Japan's coming-out party.

The postwar government has been overwhelmingly dominated by the Liberal Democratic Party (LDP). With the triangle of a strong party, strong bureaucracy and strong industry, the LDP shepherded Japan through its economic redevelopment. Japan's well-educated and hard-working population rose to the challenge at great personal sacrifice. Often overlooked is the role of women, so-called shadow workers, who contributed to economic growth by freeing men from all domestic responsibility. Japan now has the world's highest per capita income and is the second largest economy on the planet.

In the late 1980s, protracted economic growth and cheap credit led to frenzied increases in the price of land, in the stock market and in other valuations. The cost of land in major cities skyrocketed and middle class families found themselves shut out of the real estate market like never before. Japanese companies were so flush with cash, they bought up large chunks of Hawaii and other prime US properties at highly inflated prices. All of this came crashing down in 1992 with a recession that stymied the Japanese economy for the next half-dozen years.

Rapid economic development has come at a high price. A growth policy based on exports causes friction with Japan's trading partners. Rapid redevelopment at any cost means high levels of pollution and environmental damage. Urban dwellers sacrifice high standards of living and a rapidly aging population is increasingly expensive to support. Prohibited by the Constitution from maintaining an army, the Japanese "Self-defense Force" actually constitutes one of the 9th or 10th largest military forces in the world and is under pressure to participate in peacekeeping missions around the globe. The Japanese government is under pressure to play a role in international affairs commensurate with its economic power. All these issues pose challenges in the coming decades.

When Emperor Hirohito died in January 1989, his son **Akihito** ascended the throne ending 63 years known as the Showa era and ushering in the current **Heisei** period.

TOKYO'S HISTORY

Tokyo began as **Edo**, a fishing village where the *daimyo* (feudal lord) **Ota Dokan** built his castle in the 15th century. It remained a backwater until 1590 when Toyotomi Hideyoshi awarded the fiefdom to **Tokugawa**

Ieyasu. After Hideyoshi's death, Ieyasu consolidated power and had himself named shogun in 1603. He found Edo to be the perfect place to rule Japan — far from Kyoto, home of the imperial court, and on the large and fertile Kanto plain. Ieyasu built his castle on the site of Ota's.

In the Tokugawa era, Japan closed its doors to the outside world. Edo grew rapidly in this peaceful and prosperous milieu. As a means of control, all of Tokugawa's samurai lived in Edo as did the families of the feudal lords. The feudal lords themselves alternated between their domains and Edo. When you include the retainers of the feudal lords, some half-a-million samurai spent at least a part of the year in Edo. Naturally, the number of merchants, artisans and laborers grew in order to provide services for the population. By the 18th century, Edo had over one million residents and ranked among the largest cities in the world.

The Tokugawa's castle was the grandest in Japan. The city itself is set up as a typical castle town. The labyrinth of dead end roads was designed to confuse an attacking army. Unfortunately, to this day, it confuses residents and visitors alike. The residences of the feudal lords and samurai were to the northwest, west and south of the castle in a belt ringing the hills called **Yamanote**. The commoners lived on reclaimed land east of the castle that became known as *shitamachi,* literally, low city.

As the Edo period went on, the samurai class grew more and more impoverished and dependent on the increasingly wealthy, but still bottom-of-the-social-ladder, merchants. Although the Tokugawa shogunate issued many decrees in an effort to control the merchant class, ways were found around them. For instance, merchants were forbidden to wear silk so they wore clothing with rough cotton on the outside but lined with fine silk. Merchants had restrictions on the number of stories in their houses, but the interior didn't always match the exterior. Because of these restrictions, the aesthetic that blossomed had a veneer of restraint.

Perhaps because of the restrictions, an exuberant popular culture flourished and people flocked to *kabuki* theater and the pleasure quarters where they were entertained by *geisha* trained in music and dance as well as worldly pleasures. Woodblock prints, *ukiyo-e*, literally pictures of the floating world, captured the excitement of the scene.

By the middle of the 19th century, the Tokugawa shogunate had run out of steam. **Commodore Matthew Perry** sailed his black ships into Tokyo Bay and demanded that Japan open its doors. The shogunate eventually complied but couldn't take the stress of the new era. A movement of lower-ranking samurai from far-off western Honshu and Kyushu toppled the government; and in 1868 the Meiji Emperor was restored to power. The new capital, renamed Tokyo (Eastern Capital), became the residence of the emperor ending Kyoto's 1100 year tenure as the capital.

Rapid modernization and industrialization followed. New Western-style buildings became fashionable — some wooden, others brick. One particularly famous building, the Rokumeikan, was the scene of many balls where Japanese dressed in formal Western attire. At this time, *haikara* (high collar) came to mean anything Western and intellectual — Western shirts with high collars were such a contrast to open-collared kimono. People poured in from the countryside to work in the new factories, and Tokyo's population grew.

But there were setbacks along the way. The **Great Kanto Earthquake** in 1923 struck at mid-day while lunch was being cooked on charcoal braziers. Huge conflagrations destroyed neighborhoods of dense wooden houses, and when the smoke cleared, 140,000 people had perished and half the city was in ruins. Tokyo rebuilt and within a decade was back to its prequake levels. Again, during World War II, Tokyo was nearly flattened by American air raids. On one night over 100,000 people died. After the war, the city sprang up again.

Tokyo is the pulse of modern Japan. Not only are the Diet and government ministries based here, but it's also the center for the banking and financial industry, the big trading houses, the fashion and retailing industry, music and the arts and on and on. Because the government plays a central role in industrial planning, even corporations based in Osaka and Kyushu feel the necessity to maintain large offices in Tokyo. Rural Japanese have gravitated to the cities in search of a better life.

As the population has increased, Tokyoites have been forced to live further and further from the city center. Many have long commutes on packed trains; one and a half hours each way is not uncommon. The national government continues to discuss decentralization and moving all or part of its offices to another city, but we'll believe it when we see it.

The emperor lives on the Tokugawa's castle grounds in what is now called the Imperial Palace. While Tokyo is no longer a castle town, it has some remnants. Tokyo's convoluted road system, a holdover from the castle era, makes the city difficult to navigate. One of the major Japanese newspapers, the *Asahi Shimbun*, divides its metro news coverage into Jonan, Johoku, Josai and Joto — literally, south, north, west and east of the castle.

THE ROLE OF THE JAPANESE EMPEROR

The **imperial family** is a source of fascination to the Japanese public and many regard its members as celebrities. Nearly every week women's magazines feature imperial family members in color photographs. But the imperial family lives privately behind the "chrysanthemum curtain" (the 16-petal chrysanthemum is the imperial symbol). This distance only makes the media and the public clamor for more information.

The Japanese emperor descends from one of the world's longest continuing lineages. The first written histories of Japan, compiled under the auspices of the emperor in the 8th century, take great pains to trace the roots of the ruling family to the Shinto Sun Goddess **Amaterasu**. Some of the earliest emperors actually practiced a dual system: the celibate older brother took care of Shinto religious rituals while the younger brother had political control and produced heirs to continue the line.

Soon after the introduction of Buddhism in the 6th century, the emperors realized the powerful centralizing force of the religion and became avid believers. Shintoism and Buddhism existed side by side. More often than not, emperors became Buddhist monks after they abdicated. And abdicate they did. Perhaps it was the stress of the office, but few emperors spent more than a handful of years in the top position. Emperors came to have little political power, either forceful regents or shoguns ruled in their behalf from the 10th century on.

This system continued until 1868. Low-ranking samurai, who master-minded the overthrow of the Tokugawa shogunate, coalesced around "returning" the emperor to power. The Meiji Emperor moved from Kyoto to Tokyo and the capital moved with him — powerful symbols that he was head of the nation. Even so, the emperor had little real political power; the constitutional government ruled in his name.

The fledgling government found it convenient to push the concept of "State Shinto," a national religion, with the emperor at its head. This idea provided the basic symbol for continuity of the imperial lineage, which was needed by the new government to achieve modernization with the least resistance. After all, who could be against the emperor? The emperor, as the connection between the gods and the state, was beyond reproach. Although historically many emperors built magnificent Buddhist temples and became monks after abdication, Buddhism was now discredited and many temples were destroyed. There was a frenzy of Shinto shrine building including a national system of state shrines headed by Yasukuni Shrine in Tokyo.

During the Meiji period, the emperor system changed in important ways. The emperor now ruled for life and could only be succeeded by a male heir, (although previously there had been female emperors — empress is a title reserved for the wife of the emperor.) The Meiji Emperor fathered 14 children before one male lived. This system has meant great stability; since 1868 Japan has only had four emperors.

Elements of the extreme loyalty and fealty of the warrior class transferred to the emperor: when Emperor Meiji died in 1912, General Nogi, a hero of the 1905 Russo-Japanese War, committed suicide. **Meiji Shrine**, deifying the emperor and empress, was built in Tokyo with funds collected from citizens all over Japan. The right wing militarism of the

1930s and 1940s, which culminated in Japan's involvement in World War II, was carried out in the name of Emperor Hirohito. How much he really knew and approved is a hotly debated topic among historians.

After the end of the World War II, American experts on Japanese culture and language convinced General Douglas MacArthur the emperor was a valuable asset in maintaining control of the Japanese. If the emperor proclaimed Japan would be a democracy, people would follow. MacArthur realized that trying the emperor as a war criminal would make the maintenance of law and order almost impossible, and he didn't want to lose lives of American soldiers keeping peace in occupied Japan.

The first chapter of the Constitution, which came into effect on May 3, 1947, proclaims "sovereignty resides in the people" and "the emperor is the symbol of the state and of the unity of the people."

The emperor lost his divine status. The aristocratic classes lost their titles; titled royalty became restricted to the immediate male family members of the emperor. The current empress, **Michiko**, is the first commoner to marry into the imperial line; she has been joined by Princess Masako, wife of the crown prince; Princess Kiko, wife of the emperor's second son, and the wives of other princes. Female members of the imperial family lose their imperial status when they marry, which is why some speculate that Princess Nori, the only daughter of the current emperor, isn't in any rush to find a mate.

JAPAN'S HISTORICAL PERIODS

Jomon Period: ca. 10,000–300 BC
Yayoi Period: ca. 300 BC–AD 300
Kofun Period: ca. AD 300–593
Asuka Period: 593–710
Nara Period: 710–794
Heian Period: 794–1185
Kamakura Period: 1185–1333
Muromachi Period: 1333–1573
Momoyama Period: 1573–1603
Edo Period: 1603–1868
Meiji Period: 1868–1912
Taisho Period: 1912–1926
Showa Period: 1926–1989
Heisei Period: 1989–present

5. PLANNING YOUR TRIP

BEFORE YOU GO

WHEN TO VISIT - CLIMATE

Tokyo has four distinct seasons offering travelers a range of choices. For us, autumn is the best time to visit, although Tokyo's autumn begins later than in Europe or North America. Tokyo's autumn begins in mid-September and lasts until the end of November. Fall foliage is spectacular in places close to Tokyo, such as Nikko and Hakone.

Spring is another popular travel time. Cherry blossoms are spectacular in late March and early April, but the weather is usually unstable. A glorious spring day can be followed by several cold and rainy ones. From the end of April until early June, the weather is clear and sunny, and many flowers are in bloom.

Rainy season begins in early June and lasts a little over a month. The season is unpredictable — some years it rains heavily and other years there's almost none. But the weather is always cloudy and humid with fairly large variations in temperature.

About mid-July, the hot, steamy summer follows the rainy season. Usually, there are about two months of high temperatures and humidity, making touring almost unbearable. If you have to travel in the summer, we recommend you choose the rainy season over the muggy summer months. Typhoons are in-season during August and September; the summer heat finally dissipates in mid-September when there's a little rain, and the air is crisp and clear.

Tips for Winter Travel

When you travel in Japan's mountains in the winter, you need to dress as warmly as you would in mountains anywhere during the winter. But in the Tokyo area, where there are great temperature variations, even from day to day, here are some tips to help you enjoy winter touring.

- Layer your clothing. Scarves are good for regulating your body temperature. Over your street clothes, wear a sweater and a jacket, preferably windproof. It's much more practical than wearing one heavy coat. Make sure you have gloves and a hat.
- Bring heavy socks or bootie-type slippers. Since you must remove your shoes to enter most temples, your feet freeze rapidly without an extra layer.
- Buy hot packs, *hokaron,* at any drug store. There's a brand called Mycoal that has its name in English. Some types come with adhesive backing to stick on clothes. For your own protection, never put a hot pack directly on your skin. They stay warm for hours and are great to put in your pockets and at the back of your neck. We'd never survive winter without them.
- Most vending machines sell warm drinks including canned coffee, tea, cocoa, corn soup and Japanese tea. The cans are so hot when they come out of the machine that they can double as good hand warmers.

When to Travel — Avoiding Peak Times

Most Japanese travel at the same time because it's the only time they can get time off from work without feeling guilty. Try to avoid traveling during these peak times, although it's a good time to be in Tokyo, Osaka and other large cities. They empty out. If you do travel during these peak times, be sure to make your reservations well in advance. The newspapers often report 70 kilometer tie-ups on the expressways, and *shinkansen* trains run at 150% of capacity. Some peak periods:

- **New Year's**, *December 27 through January 4*
- **Golden Week**, *April 29 through May 5*
- **O-Bon Holiday**, *August 13-16*

Other busy times are April-May and October-November. Make your reservations in advance.

TOKYO'S AVERAGE TEMPERATURE & RAIN

	Jan	Feb	Mar	Apr	May	June
Temp °C	3	4	7	13	17	21
Temp °F	37	39	45	54	62	70
Rain, inches	4.3	6.1	9	10	9.6	12

	July	Aug	Sept	Oct	Nov	Dec
Temp °C	25	26	23	17	11	5
Temp °F	77	79	73	62	51	41
Rain, inches	10	8	11	9	6.4	3.8

WHAT TO PACK

First of all, what not to pack. Pack lightly! Taxis from the international airports are expensive. In most train stations, porters are scarce as are escalators and elevators. You'll have to struggle with your luggage up and down steps. Coin lockers big enough for large suitcases are difficult to come by and only the largest train stations will have baggage storerooms. The less you have with you, the easier your trip.

For touring, pack comfortable clothes. Japanese tend to dress quite well so you'll probably feel out-of-place in sloppy jeans. That doesn't mean you have to dress up for sightseeing, but you don't want to look sloppy.

We find it best to layer clothing. Except in the heat of August, when it's always hot and muggy, the temperature is unpredictable. In spring and fall, you'll need a jacket or sweater. In the June-July rainy season, it can be cool and rainy or warm and rainy, so make sure you have a light jacket and a folding umbrella. Summer is hot and humid, but you may need a light jacket to prevent yourself from freezing in air-conditioned hotels and restaurants. You'll need a fairly heavy coat in winter since it can snow in Tokyo.

Comfortable walking shoes are a must. Japan is a country best discovered on foot. Most likely, you'll be using mass transportation a lot and that means going up and down a lot of stairs. Our friends visiting from overseas tell us they have never walked so much in their lives.

Don't forget your slip-on shoes. Shoes come off when you enter Japanese houses and restaurants with *tatami* mats. Shoes come off when you enter most temples. They even come off at many museums. So shoes come off and on a lot. And you'll be glad when you don't have to stop to untie and tie them time and again. Reminder: to avoid embarrassment, make sure your socks don't have holes.

Hotels and inns nearly always supply *yukata* (cotton kimono robes), tooth brushes and hair dryers, so lighten your bag by a few ounces. If you are staying at inexpensive accommodations, bring a towel.

You should also always carry pocket tissues and/or a handkerchief to use as a hand towel or napkin. Public toilets usually do not have hand towels, but most have toilet paper.

A small folding umbrella is essential. It can rain any time of the year. Make sure you have one extra pair of shoes and socks in case your feet get soaked. During the rainy season, take waterproof shoes and a light raincoat.

Make sure you pack drugs, both prescription and over-the-counter. You won't find many familiar brand names such as Tylenol, and it will be difficult, if not impossible, to fill your medical prescriptions. If you wear glasses, have a copy of your prescription in case you lose or break your glasses.

North American appliances generally work in Japan without a converter or adapter so you can leave the extra equipment at home.

While you can generally buy almost anything you need in Japan, you may not like the price. Double the US price is average, sometimes it's more. And worse yet, clothes are styled for petite Japanese — a sweater sleeve might be halfway up your arm or pants may fit more like shorts. If you are a large person or wear large shoes, you could have real difficulties. So it's best to be self-sufficient.

Camera film purchased at a discount electronics shop is one of the few things cheaper in Tokyo than New York. But film at tourist sights is expensive. Throw away cameras are readily available.

COST OF TRAVEL

Japan always heads the list of the most expensive travel destinations. And there's good reason. At a deluxe hotel, room rates start at ¥20,000 (about $175-200 at today's exchange rate, but check the paper – recent rates have fluctuated between ¥80 and ¥130 to the dollar) and are often twice as much for two. Hotel food is expensive. Breakfast can cost ¥3000 — imagine freshly squeezed orange juice for ¥1500, lunch for ¥6000 and dinner ¥10,000 and up. If you stay at a deluxe *ryokan* (Japanese inn), dinner and breakfast are included although the rate can be ¥30,000 per person or higher. Expenses of ¥50,000 per day are common for top-of-the-line travel.

These costs are comparable to staying in similar accommodations in European capitals. These expenses may be okay for the businessman on expense accounts or for the traveler who's willing to pay for the best accommodations; for the average traveler, Japan can cost quite a bit less.

A rail pass, which is bought in your home country and validated after arrival, and advance-purchase domestic air tickets minimize transportation costs. The Welcome Inn Reservation Center and Japan Inn Group can arrange accommodations for you at between ¥4000 and ¥8000 per person. At rock bottom; youth hostels are ¥3000 or under per night.

Frugal travelers should plan on spending about ¥10,000 per person per day excluding transportation — this includes hotel, meals, subways and admission charges. A moderate budget is about ¥20,000 a day. Top-of-the-line can cost from ¥30,000 per person.

If you budget about ¥1000 for breakfast, ¥700 to ¥3000 for lunch — lunchtime specials are one of Japan's best kept secrets — and ¥3000 to ¥5000 for dinner, you'll eat quite well. Dinner and breakfast are included in the cost of most Japanese inns.

Temple and museum admissions are extremely reasonable — ¥300 to ¥1000 — but can add up when you are visiting several a day.

PASSPORTS & VISAS

Yes, you must have a valid passport to travel to Japan. Americans can apply for one at regional post offices or go directly to a district office. But don't procrastinate because sometimes it can take several months to work its way through the passport agency.

Visas depend on your nationality. Currently, citizens of the United States, Canada, New Zealand, France, Italy and a host of other countries need not apply for a visa in advance if they are staying in Japan for less than three months for business or leisure. To be sure, check with the Japanese Embassy in your country. You can come for business meetings but can't draw salary from a company in Japan. The Japanese government does not allow you to extend your stay. To do so, you must leave the country and return. Hint: if you are desperate, you can fly to a nearby foreign city such as Seoul, return immediately and stay another three months. But if you do this more than twice in a row, immigration may give you a hard time. If you want to change from a temporary visitor visa to a working visa, the immigration bureau requires you to leave the country to obtain the new visa. Again, Seoul is the closest place.

Citizens of Austria, Germany, Ireland, Liechtenstein, Mexico, Switzerland and the United Kingdom can stay for six months without applying for a visa in advance.

If you will be earning money in Japan or want to stay for a longer period, you have to get a visa before you travel.

In the US, the Japanese Government maintains visa sections in Consulate Generals in Atlanta, Anchorage, Boston, Chicago, Detroit, Honolulu, Houston, Kansas City, Los Angeles, Miami, New Orleans, New York, Portland and Seattle.
- **New York**: *Consulate General of Japan, 299 Park Avenue, New York, NY 10171. Tel. 212/888-0889*
- **Washington**, **DC**: *Embassy of Japan, 2520 Massachusetts Avenue, Washington, DC 20008. Tel. 202/939-6900*
- **San Francisco**: *Consulate General of Japan, 50 Fremont Street, San Francisco, CA 94104. Tel. 415/777-3533*

Be sure you call to check their hours before you go; these guys make bankers' hours look like overtime.

CUSTOMS & HEALTH
Arriving

On the airplane you will be given an immigration form and a customs declaration. You need not fill out the customs declaration unless you are over the allowances; see below.

If your plane arrives from a third-world country, you may have to fill out a yellow health form reporting your whereabouts for the last 14 days and informing the health authorities if you have symptoms such as diarrhea, vomiting or fever. If you come from the US or Western Europe, you just walk through the barrier without turning in a form. We had friends who marked "yes" to one of the symptoms; the next day the Health Service came to their house to quarantine them and spray everything with antiseptic.

You shouldn't have much problem clearing customs. The Japanese government allows you to bring reasonable amounts of personal effects and equipment. You can also bring in duty-free gifts totaling ¥200,000, three bottles of liquor, 400 cigarettes, and 2 ounces of perfume. Persons 19 and under cannot bring in liquor or cigarettes. If you don't exceed the allowances, go to a counter marked Duty Free. If you're over, go to a counter marked Dutiable Goods. When you are carrying fruit, fresh flowers or other agricultural products, you need to stop at the quarantine desk for an inspection before you clear customs; there are restrictions on some items.

If you arrive from a country known for drug trafficking, Customs might give your bags more than a once-over. Sometimes they x-ray sealed boxes. Naturally, drugs and firearms are a no-no. Customs agents may actually ask you if you are carrying drugs or guns.

Returning to America

On your return trip to the US, the airline will give you a US customs declaration form. You need to fill out one per family. The US allows you to bring in one liter of alcohol and 200 cigarettes duty free. US residents can take in $400 of goods duty-free per person; nonresidents are allowed $100. On amounts over $400, Customs assesses a flat-rate duty of 10% on the next $1000. Above that, the duty varies with each item. Also, be sure to declare it if you are carrying more than $10,000 in currency.

If you are traveling with high-priced foreign-made goods like fur coats or expensive jewelry, register them with the US Customs at the airport in the US before you depart to ensure there is no question of being charged duty on your return. You won't have any problem with a laptop computer.

TOURS & TRAVEL AGENTS

Large operators offer tours as well as package deals that include airfare and hotels, but your time is your own. Unless it is a special-interest one, we don't recommend tours; tour operators tend to take people to standard sights only. But you might find it economical to use some of the package tours the large operators organize. Their buying power can get you air and hotel rates you cannot get on your own. Here are a few

operators that offer tours, package deals, discount air tickets, discount hotel rates and the Japan Rail Pass.
- **Japan Travel Bureau** (JTB). Japan's largest travel agency. The New York office is at *810 7th Avenue, 34th floor, New York, NY, 10019. Tel. 212/ 698-4900, Fax 212/586-9686. Web site: http://www.jtbi.com.* JTB has offices all over the world.
- **Kintetsu International Express.** *1325 Avenue of the Americas, Suite 2001, New York, NY, 10019. Tel. 212/259-9510, Fax 212/259-9505. Web site: http://www.kintetsu.com/index.html.*
- **Tokyu Travel America.** *21221 S. Western Avenue, Torrance, CA, 90501. Tel. 310/783-6560, Fax 310/782-7347. Web site: http:// www.tokyutravel.com.*

A few smaller agencies offering economical packages are:
- **Airport Travel.** *5959 W. City Boulevard, Suite 1407, Los Angeles, CA, 90045. Tel. 310/410-0656; 800/310/5549, Fax 310/410-1954. Web site: http://www.airporttravel.com.* They offer low-cost packages and homestays.
- **Singapore Airlines.** They offer a 7-day air and hotel package from Los Angeles for $999. This package is available through travel agents.

Consolidators
Travel agents who issue consolidator or other low-cost tickets advertise in the Sunday travel sections of *The New York Times, The Los Angeles Times* and other major newspapers. Several that we have used are:
- **Japan Budget Travel**, *9 East 38th Street, New York, NY. Tel. 212/686-8855*
- **Euro-Asia Holidays**, *47 West 34th Street, New York, NY. Tel. 212/279-8528, Fax 212/279-8539*
- **Express Fun Travel Service**, *330 Tenth Street, San Francisco, CA 94103. Tel. 415-864-8005; 800/722-0872, Fax 415-863-9523*

Special Tours & Opportunities
While none of these tours is exclusively confined to Tokyo, check them out for travel with a different twist:
- **Walking Tours of Japan** (they aren't all walking tours) has to be one of the best-kept tour secrets. Run by Steve Beimel and Michael Kuranoff who know Japan inside and out; their tours give you an insider's perspective at a moderate price. *Espirit Travel, 2101 Wilshire Boulevard, Suite 101, Santa Monica, CA, 90403. Tel. 800/377-7481; 310/829-6060.*

CYBERTRAVEL

You can practically travel to Japan without leaving your computer chair. Here's some of our favorite websites:

Japan National Tourist Organization: *www.jnto.go.jp. Every cybertrip to Japan should begin at JNTO's website for good introductory information on travel to Japan and in-depth information on regions. It's also especially good for listings of events.*

Narita Airport: *www.narita-airport.or.jp/airport-e. Everything you need to know about Narita Airport from flight departures and arrivals, services, restaurants and stores and extensive ground transportation schedules. Unfortunately having all this info doesn't make the airport any closer to Tokyo. For additional ground transportation info, try the Narita Airport Access Guide: www.sfc.keio.ac.jp/~bbq/NARITA/index.en.html.*

Tokyo Subway Navigator: *metro.jussieu.fr:10001/bin/select/english/japan/tokyo. Need to get from point A to point B? Plug in the areas and the navigator will tell you which train(s) to take, a list of the train's stops and how long it takes.*

Tokyo Food Pages: *www/twics.com/~robbs/tokyofood.html. A foodies' dream. An exceptionally comprehensive resource on food from where to buy it, how to cook it and where to eat it.*

Tokyo Q Magazine: *www.so-net.or.jp/tokyoq. A weekly online magazine with feature articles and nightlife listings.*

Tokyo Journal: *www.tokyo.to. The print version is Tokyo's popular monthly magazine with the most extensive listings in town. Unfortunately, the online version seems to have only limited nightlife listings.*

Tokyo Meltdown: *www.twics.com/~robbs/tleisure/htm. A useful guide to Tokyo's entertainment, art, architecture and much more. For the person who has everything, you can download icons of Tokyo's trains.*

Currency Converter: *www.bloomberg.com/markets.wei.html or www.oanda.com.cgi-bin/ncc. Can't figure out how much it really costs in your home currency? This site could be a shopper's best friend.*

Hotel HotLine: *jgl.biglobe.ne.jp/english. Offers discounts off the full rate at some of Japan's larger hotels.*

Yokohama: *www.CITY.YOKOHAMA.jp/indexE.html. Make sure you leave time for Tokyo's sister-city just down the road.*

Realtime Tokyo: *www.nttls.co.jp/tower/tower.html. Every cyber-trip to Tokyo should end with this photograph of the skyscrapers of Shinjuku, updated frequently.*

- **Koto Associates'** tour is almost private; they take only six people on their explorations of the Japanese countryside. They run four tours a year: two in the spring and two in the fall, each on a theme such as festivals or architecture. *Koto Associates, 2900 Smith Grade, Santa Cruz, CA 95060. Tel. 408/427-1034. Email: ibabambu@cruzio.com.*
- **Journeys East's** tours emphasize experiencing Japanese culture. Participants stay in traditional inns and meet local people. *Journeys East, PO Box 1161-B, Middletown, CA, 95461. Tel. 800/527-2612; 707/279-9539, Fax 707/279-9403. Email: JEinUSA@aol.com.*
- **Seniors Abroad** runs homestay trips for persons over 50. *Seniors Abroad, 12533 Pacato Circle North, San Diego, CA, 92128. Tel. 619/485-1696, Fax 619/487-1492.*

Hands-on Experiences

Japan has so many craft and art traditions, you may want to augment a trip to Tokyo by participating in a workshop outside the city:
- **Papermaking Workshop.** A three-day workshop is held monthly in a traditional farmhouse in the countryside near Mino, a papermaking town in Gifu Prefecture, near Nagoya. Run by a group of foreigners interested in preserving this dying art, the workshop is a hands-on introduction to Japanese papermaking. The workshop is run in English, Japanese and other languages as needed. *Washi Survival School, 2485 Warabi Yatsubo, Mino-shi, Gifu, 501. Tel. (0575)34-8335, Fax (0575)34-8355.*
- **Ceramic Workshop and Homestay.** A five-week workshop is held each summer for ceramic artists to work with the potters of Tokoname, a ceramic center with a 900-year heritage. Apply by February 28. *International Workshop of Ceramic Art in Tokoname (IWCAT), c/o Tokoname Chamber of Commerce and Industry, 5-58 Shinkai-cho, Tokoname, Aichi, 479, Fax (0569)34-3223. Email iwcat@japan-net.or.jp. Web site: http://www.japan-net.or.jp/~iwcat.*
- **Niijima International Glass Art Festival** is held every November at Niijima, a small island 10 hours by boat from Tokyo. International glass artists participate in the nine-day workshop. *Niijima Glass Art Center, Mamashita Kaigan Street, Niijima-mura, Tokyo, 100-04. Tel. (04992)5-1540, Fax (04992)5-1240.*
- **Art Camp Hakushu** is a camp and festival held each summer on a farm in Yamanashi Prefecture in central Japan. Tanaka Min, one of the leaders of the avant-garde Butoh dance, leads a dance/body workshop. Other workshops include architecture, visual arts, children's, farming and music. *Art Camp Hakushu, Body Weather Farm, 81 Daibo Hakushu, Kitakoma-gun, Yamanashi, 408/03. Tel. (0551)35-2465, Fax (0551)35-3130.*

- **International Zen Center**, near Kyoto, welcomes international visitors who would like to experience Zen meditation and temple life. Stays can be as short as one day or several months. *Kyoto International Zen Center (Rinzai sect), Jotoku-ji, Inukai Sogabe-cho, Kameoka, Kyoto, 621. Tel. (0771)24-0152, Fax: (0771)24-0378, e-mail: kyotozen@zen.or.jp.*
- **Earth Celebration** is organized by the world famous Kodo Drummers. The festival on Sado Island in late August features percussion artists from all over the world. *148-1 Kaneda Shinden, Ogimachi, Sado-gun, Niigata, 952-06. Tel. (0259)86-3630, Fax (0259)86-3631.*
- **Toga International Arts Festival** draws drama lovers from all over the world to its traditional and avant-garde performances. The 10-day festival is held in early August in Toga, a small mountain village near Toyama. The renowned architect Isozaki Arata designed the festival's amphitheater. *2-14-19-302 Shimoochiai, Shinjuku-ku, Tokyo, 161. Tel. (03)3951-4843 or (0763)68-2216.*
- **Taiko Drumming Weekends** are organized periodically by Wanderlust Adventures. *Contact Cathy Bernatt, Apt. 801, 1555 Finch Avenue, E. Willowdale, Ontario M2J4X9 Canada. Tel. 416/495-9555.*
- **Home Visit System**. In about a dozen cities, the Japan National Tourist Office (JNTO) has established a program to visit a Japanese family in their home. There's no charge and you can spend a few hours, usually in the evening, talking with the family. Be sure to take a small gift such as flowers, cookies or something from your home country. Telephone contact numbers are given either in the home visit system or practical information section of the cities where it operates.

Further Information

For other opportunities from study tours to cooking schools, the Shaw Guides are an excellent source of information. Access them at *http://www.shawguides.com.*

The **National Registration Center for Study Abroad** (NRCSA), a consortium of universities and language schools, has information on language and cultural programs. *823 North 2nd Street, Milwaukee, WI, 53203. Tel. 414/278-0631. Web site: http://www.nrcsa.com.*

TRAVEL FOR THE DISABLED

Traveling with disabilities is a challenge in Japan. Superficially, it appears that Japan has done so much. Subways and many thoroughfares have sidewalks with raised lines and dots ("street Braille" a friend calls them) to guide the blind. Many traffic lights chirp to assist them. Trains and buses have "Silver Seats" for the disabled and the elderly. But when we look around, we realize it's rare to see a blind person or someone in a wheelchair.

Japan tends to keep its disabled hidden in institutions and behind walls. Sometimes you'll see physically or mentally handicapped people on an outing to a zoo or park, but most of the time they are out of view.

It's almost impossible to get from the street to a train platform without climbing stairs. A few stations have wheelchair lifts on the stairs, and the number will probably increase. Elevators in train stations are practically unheard of. Train companies protest it's too expensive to build elevators for so few people. Their position is that they will provide personnel to carry people in wheelchairs up and down stairs as long as they know in advance. To demonstrate the indignity of such a system, activists occasionally organize a protest by having 20 or 30 wheelchairs converge on a station at the same time.

We're not trying to discourage disabled people from visiting Japan. Just be prepared and remember that it's not easy to get around.

The Japan Red Cross has put out a bilingual book called *Accessible Tokyo*; it's a must for the disabled traveler. The book gives detailed information on facilities at hotels, shopping areas, museums, theaters, parks and zoos. Get a copy by sending five international postal coupons (or within Japan ¥390 in stamps) to **The Japanese Red Cross Language Service Volunteers**, *c/o Volunteers Division, Japanese Red Cross Society, 1-1-3 Shiba-daimon, Minato-ku, Tokyo, 105, Fax (03)3432-5507.*

Large hotels often have rooms outfitted for wheelchair use. The **Japanese Society for Rehabilitation of the Disabled** is involved with the Toyama Sunrise Hotel in Tokyo. Single rooms cost only ¥3900 to ¥5200 and twins ¥5600 to ¥10,000. Contact them at: *1-22-1 Toyama, Shinjuku-ku, Tokyo, 162. Tel. (03)3204-3611, Fax (03)3232-3621.*

ACCOMMODATIONS

Japan has a wide range of accommodations from deluxe hotels to small family-run inns. Picking the right place goes a long way toward making or breaking your trip. It depends on your pocketbook and what type of accommodation you feel comfortable with. In large cities, accommodations are almost exclusively Western hotels while in remote villages, there may be nothing but small Japanese inns.

JAPANESE INNS

Staying in a Japanese inn is one of the best ways to experience Japanese culture. We recommend you do it at least once during your trip. The inns are keepers of a tradition that has all but disappeared from the daily lives of Japanese. Perhaps that's why Japanese enjoy staying at **ryokan**, traditional Japanese inns. They take great pride in their food, their personal service, their facilities and gardens, however small, and their interior design.

There are many types of *ryokan*, from small wooden inns to large cement buildings with hundreds of rooms. We prefer the smaller inns. Most inns with over 30 or 40 rooms give you cookie-cutter service. The rate for most *ryokan* includes two meals, dinner and breakfast.

Your room will be a sparsely furnished traditional Japanese room with *tatami* mats on the floor, a *tokonoma* alcove where flower arrangements and art are displayed and sliding *shoji* doors with paper panels. If it isn't a multistoried building, your room will probably look out on a small garden. In older inns, there may not be a private toilet, which, we must complain, is a pain in the middle of the night. Larger inns may have a communal bath in addition to the private bath. Don't be shy. Enjoy this opportunity to take a bath in a spacious tub looking out at nature.

Dinner will most likely be served in your room. As a matter of fact, your room is all-purpose: living room, dining room and bedroom. As you enter the room, you'll notice a low table with cushions where you sit to drink tea. The maid sets up your dinner on this table. After dinner, the maid moves the table and sets up *futon* bedding on the floor. In the morning, the maid returns to fold up the bedding and set up breakfast on the table. In larger inns, breakfast may be served in a communal dining hall, often as a buffet. In this case, there will probably be some Japanized Western food items such as ham, bread and coffee.

There are some drawbacks to Japanese inns. They are fairly rigid in their meal times, and you are often out of luck if you want to have a late dinner, say anything after 7pm. They also have rigid check-in and out times, usually check-in is from 3pm and check-out at 10am. Often the maid will be knocking on the door at five after ten if you are still in the room. The inns, however, are happy to hold your luggage.

Another drawback is the attendant frequently comes in and out of your room, bringing tea and meals, and clearing dishes. She does leave you alone after she sets up the *futon* bedding after dinner, but if you want a high level of privacy, the whole procedure is intrusive. And some inns wake you up in the morning with music over the loudspeakers.

In *ryokan*, the price is based per person. If there are more than two people in your group, you may get a slightly lower price. Japanese inns prefer to have a party of four stay in the same room. *Ryokan* prices begin at about ¥8000 per person with two meals and can go as high as ¥70,000 for a deluxe room in a top inn. The average rate is about ¥15,000 per person.

How to Behave at a Japanese Inn

Staying at a Japanese inn is a unique experience. Don't be surprised if you feel like a VIP. At the front door, the staff is usually waiting to greet you and give you your slippers. Take off your shoes and leave them at the entrance. In some larger inns, you'll wear your shoes to your own room. You may be asked to fill out a registration card in the lobby, but often you complete it in your own room. The staff will accompany you to your room and help you to get settled. Be sure to remove your slippers before entering the *tatami* mat room.

You'll get a lot of personal attention from your room attendant; probably she'll only be taking care of two or three rooms in total. She will serve you Japanese tea and sweets in your room, and, while you have tea, will explain the inn's facilities and arrange a time for your dinner and breakfast — it sounds flexible, but your choice is usually within fairly narrow parameters. She may ask if you would like to order beer or *sake* (rice wine) with dinner.

Japanese think it's a luxury to take a bath before dinner and will usually indulge themselves at a *ryokan*, either in the communal bath or a private bath. After a bath, Japanese don a *yukata* (cotton robe) provided by the inn and may stroll around garden before dinner. They will wear their *yukata* until they dress in the morning. It's okay to wear them to eat dinner and to walk outside in a small resort town, but not in a large city.

Yukata come in several sizes and if you are tall, the room attendant may automatically bring you a larger one so you don't have to go around with your knees showing. If she doesn't, ask for XL. Make sure you wear the *yukata* with the left side over the right, and tied with the belt provided. The deceased are dressed in kimono with the right over the left, so make sure everyone knows you're still alive and kicking. Sometimes *yukata* have so much starch, they practically stand up by themselves.

You'll find special slippers in the toilet room. It's a real no-no to wear them out of that room because they are considered unclean.

Ryokan serve dinner on the early side, about 6pm, and it can be a drawn-out affair with a procession of courses. If you're going to arrive after 6pm, make sure the inn knows ahead of time. You may not be able to get dinner after a certain time unless prior arrangements have been made. Some inns will allow you to stay without eating dinner. After dinner, the maid clears away your dishes and sets up the *futon* bedding. We often enjoy a walk while she tidies up the room for the night. At the entrance, inns have *geta* (wooden sandals) so you won't have to put your street shoes back on; if you wear a size 13, you may have to reclaim your own shoes.

Ryokan may lock their doors at a certain hour, such as 11pm. Check with the inn if you plan to stay out late.

In the morning, the maid will put away your bedding and set up your breakfast. If breakfast is in a communal room, the bedding will disappear while you're out of the room. Check-out is quite early, usually 10am, and you are expected to clear your room by that time.

You don't need to tip a maid unless she provides you with exceptional service such as washing your clothes or making special arrangements. If you would like to tip her, wrap the money in paper or an envelope and slip it to her after she serves tea or after picking up the breakfast dishes. ¥1000 to ¥2000 is sufficient.

Japanese *onsen* inns (hot springs) basically operate the same way except guests take a lot of baths.

A few tips:
• If sitting on the floor is painful, pile up several seat cushions to make a modified chair if your room doesn't have a chair and table — usually there's a small Western-style seating area next to the window.
• If you can't live without coffee or English tea, take instant with you. Boiling water is always available.
• Japanese pillows can be a pain in the neck. Traditional pillows are filled with barley and sometimes are really hard. If it's too uncomfortable to sleep on, we put our pillows under the *futon*. If that's still too hard, we give it up all together and use a towel or sweater.
• If the idea of eating fish and rice in the morning sends your stomach into tailspins, ask if they will prepare a Western breakfast: *"yoshoku."*

Onsen

Onsen are hot spring areas. Japanese go to get away, and take baths for therapeutic purposes or for relaxation. They have become extremely popular in the last decade or so with all segments of society: families, young singles and senior citizens.

Onsen inns run the same way a *ryokan* runs, but *onsen* will have large communal indoor baths (divided by sex) and often outdoor baths, *rotemburo,* where you may bathe among rocks and lush greenery. In remote areas, some inns have mixed bathing.

Minshuku

Minshuku are small family-run inns, usually less expensive than *ryokan*. You do not have the high level of service of a *ryokan* but it is replaced by the personal attention of the proprietor. The two meals are home-cooked fare and are usually served in a communal dining room.

As a *minshuku* guest you will have to make up your *futon* bedding and put it away. The mattresses are stacked in the closet. To make the bed, first put down the foam mattress and then the cotton mattress. If there isn't a foam mattress, you can put down two cotton mattresses. Next, put the

BATHING ETIQUETTE

Over the centuries, Japanese have developed a deep love of bathing and a unique way of enjoying it. A bathtub is used only for soaking, never for cleaning. Before you get into the tub, wash yourself. Small stools and basins are provided: sit down, lather up and then rinse thoroughly. Only then are you ready to enter the bath.

Warning! Be extremely careful; the water may be scalding. You can cool down a small bath by adding some cold water, but there's little you can do to cool down a large one. If there's an outdoor bath, its temperature is almost always lower than an indoor bath's.

Don't pull the plug when you finish.

Japanese use small white towels that they sometimes put on their heads when they sit in the tub. They are not washcloths, and Japanese are horrified if you dip them in the bath water.

sheet on the mattress and tuck it in. The quilt and top sheet are together as one unit, and you place it on top of the bottom sheet. In the morning, fold everything and put it away except for the dirty sheets and *yukata* robes. Towels may not be provided at *minshuku* so it's best to take one. Toilets and baths are usually down the hall.

In rural areas, *minshuku* may have only space heaters and can get quite cold at night. At some places in the mountains, the proprietor will give you a little charcoal warmer to put in bed to keep your feet warm.

Minshuku run between ¥5000 and ¥9000 per person with two meals.

PUBLIC LODGES & PUBLIC VACATION VILLAGES

Kokumin shukusha, public lodges, and *Kokumin kyukamura*, public vacation villages, are run by local governments to provide low-cost accommodations in parks and vacation areas. They are inexpensive, functional and clean. The rooms, usually Japanese style, are comfortable although architecturally unexciting. The lodges have a lounge area for coffee and a choice of meals. Public lodges are popular in season, so you may need to make reservations well in advance. Most lodges are equipped with heating and air-conditioning systems.

With two meals, public lodges cost between ¥7000 and ¥12,000 per person.

WESTERN-STYLE HOTELS

Western hotels are a good choice for someone on business who needs all the services as well as travelers in large cities who want the comforts, service and flexibility of a Western hotel.

Deluxe: The top deluxe hotels compare with the best worldwide. They provide all the comforts you expect: a high level of service, a choice of restaurants, 24-hour room service, a concierge to help you with any request, business centers, shopping arcades, health centers and travel service. They are very similar to their cousins in the US or Europe except that the rooms may be smaller than comparable ones in an American hotel. The international chains like Hilton and Hyatt have hotels in Japan, but there are also some excellent hotels that are independent or part of a Japanese chain. Within the rarefied top class of hotels, there is little to differentiate them except for location. Expect to pay ¥20,000 and up for a single in a deluxe hotel in a large city.

Next come the medium-priced Western hotels. They are not as flashy as the deluxe and may not offer all the services; for example, there may be only one or two restaurants. Although the rooms are usually smaller and their carpets not as new, they do have private baths. Medium priced hotels start at about ¥10,000 for a single.

Business Hotels offer Western-style accommodations and are geared to the Japanese businessman on a limited expense account. The rooms are small, functional and almost always have a small bathroom attached. They offer limited services – no room service and sometimes no restaurant, but most will serve breakfast for a modest additional charge, usually between ¥700 and ¥1000. Business hotels sell drinks and cigarettes from vending machines.

The rooms can be very small, but business hotels are good choices for inexpensive accommodations in convenient locations – often close to the train station. Just remember they're not the Ritz. Business hotels vary in price from about ¥6000 to ¥12,000 for a single.

Pensions are usually small, Western-style accommodations in resort areas, especially in the mountains. They often pride themselves on their Western cuisine. Prices at pensions vary from ¥6000 to ¥15,000 and usually include two meals.

Youth Hostels are inexpensive accommodations open to people of any age. You do not need to be a member of the International Youth Hostel Federation. Service and facilities have been improving in recent years as the hostels have been trying to attract families and adult groups.

Youth hostels cost between ¥1500 and ¥4000 per person per night; meals are extra.

UNIQUE EXPERIENCES

Love Hotels

Eminently practical, the Japanese designed love hotels for private time. You'll spot them by their whimsical design, lots of neon, small or no windows and names like Hotel Princess and Hotel Charming. Built to ensure privacy, the entrances have gates where the couple is out-of-sight immediately after entering, and covers are provided for automobile license plates. The check-in process is completely impersonalized: choose a room from the pictures on the wall and pay a cashier who is behind a screen.

They say the majority of people who use love hotels are married — to each other. Couples lack privacy in a small apartment where children tend to sleep with their parents and grandma may be just a paper wall away. We're still skeptical. Can you imagine exiting a love hotel and someone sticking a clipboard in your face and asking "Are you two married?" What would you say?

You can rent a love hotel room for two hours ("Rest") or overnight ("Stay"). They are cheaper than staying at a business hotel, and the beds are bigger, but the drawback is you can't check in for the night until about 9pm. But the rooms are clean and they all have private baths. And where else could you sleep in a Tarzan room? You must be a hetero couple to stay at love hotels. A two-hour "rest" costs about ¥4000; and it's ¥8000 for an overnight "stay." Prices are clearly posted outside and you'll often find weekday afternoon specials.

Love hotels tend to be clustered in districts, not only in large cities but also in rural areas and around expressway interchanges. If you are stuck at Narita Airport, there's a group of love hotels at Tomisato, a small town about 10 kilometers from the airport.

Capsule Hotels

Only in Japan where land is so valuable and drinking so widespread, would capsule hotels develop. They cater to businessmen who are out working or drinking past the last train. It's cheaper to spend the night at a capsule hotel than take a taxi home.

Capsule hotels give you a space similar to a train berth — about the size of a coffin — with a *futon* mattress and television. Baths are communal. Most capsule hotels are open only to men and cost about ¥4000 per person to stay overnight.

MAKING HOTEL RESERVATIONS

Travel agents can make hotel reservations at hotels and larger inns. If you book through the overseas offices of the large Japanese travel agencies (JTB, Kintetsu, etc.), the rate is often cheaper than the full-price rack rate that we list. Contact numbers for these agencies are under organized tours. Ask for the seasonal specials when you use large travel agencies in Japan.

There are also several services to assist the individual traveler:

Welcome Inn Reservation Center

This service, organized by the International Tourism Center of Japan, makes reservations for overseas visitors at small inns and inexpensive hotels throughout Japan. Obtain a brochure from JNTO overseas offices. From outside Japan, you can request reservations by mail, fax or email: *Welcome Inn Reservation Center, c/o International Tourism Center of Japan, B1. Tokyo International Forum, 3-5-1 Marunouchi, Chiyoda-ku, Tokyo, 100. Tel. (03)3211-4201, Fax (03)3211-9009. Email: wirc@www.jnto.go.jp.* You can also access information through the JNTO home page: http://www.jnto.go.jp.

Once you arrive in Japan, you must go in person to their reservations counter at the Tourist Information Center in Tokyo or Kyoto to book rooms:

• **Tokyo Tourist Information Center**: *B1, Tokyo International Forum, 3-5-1 Marunouchi, Chiyoda-ku, Tokyo, 100. Open 9:15am to 4:45pm, Monday through Friday.*

• **Kyoto Tourist Information Center**: *1st floor, Kyoto Tower Building, Higashi-Shiokoji-cho, Shimogyo-ku, Kyoto, 600. Open 9am to 4:30pm, Monday through Friday.*

Japanese Inn Group

This association of inexpensive small inns and *minshuku* goes out of its way to welcome foreign tourists. The association issues a brochure that is available at overseas JNTO offices or from the association itself. The brochure has a photo and map for each inn and lists its facilities. You are not required to eat meals at the inn. You can book a room by mailing or faxing the reservation form directly to the inn; you'll receive a confirmation. These accommodations tend to be basic but friendly, clean and comfortable.

Write to or call: **Japanese Inn Group Head Office**, *c/o Sawanoya Ryokan, 2-3-11 Yanaka, Taito-ku, Tokyo, 110. Tel. (03)3822-2251, Fax (03)3822-2252. JNTO has information on the Japanese Inn Group on its home page: http://www.jnto.go.jp.*

Japan Minshuku Center

They book reservations for minshuku throughout Japan, but you can also make reservations directly with the inn. *B1, Tokyu Kotsu Kaikan Building, 2-10-1 Yurakucho, Chiyoda-ku, Tokyo. Tel. (03)3216-6556. English is spoken. Open 10am to 7pm. Closed Sunday.*

Youth Hostels

National Office: *Suidobashi Nishiguchi Kaikan, 2-20-7 Misaki-cho, Chiyoda-ku, Tokyo 101. Tel. (03)3288-1417.*
Reservations can be made on the internet: *http://www.999.com/JYH/ JYH+ENGLISH/jyh.html.*

FOR MORE INFORMATION

JNTO – the **Japan National Tourist Organization** – has offices throughout the world. They have brochures and maps and are helpful in answering your questions.
The North American offices are:
- **New York**: *One Rockefeller Plaza, Suite 1250, New York, NY 10020. Tel. 212/ 757-5640*
- **Chicago**: *401 N. Michigan Avenue, Suite 770, Chicago, IL 60611. Tel. 312/ 222-0874*
- **San Francisco**: *360 Post Street, Suite 601, San Francisco, CA 94108. Tel. 415/989-7140*
- **Los Angeles**: *624 S. Grand Avenue, Suite 1611, Los Angeles, CA. Tel. 213/ 623-1954*
- **Toronto**: *165 University Avenue, Toronto, Ont. M5H 3B8. Tel. 416/366-7140*

JNTO also maintains offices in Sao Paolo, London, Paris, Geneva, Frankfurt, Bangkok, Hong Kong, Seoul and Sydney.

6. ARRIVALS & DEPARTURES

The lion's share of international flights arrive at **Narita Airport** (NRT), officially the New Tokyo International Airport, outside Tokyo or at **Kansai International Airport** (KIX), near Osaka. There are some international flights into regional airports such as Sapporo, Nagoya and Fukuoka, but they are almost exclusively intra-Asia flights. If you are heading to the Osaka/Kyoto/Kobe area or points west, investigate flying into Kansai International Airport. It will save you the hassle of getting there from Narita.

China Airlines, the Taiwan airline, flies into Haneda Airport, which is otherwise used for domestic flights. Haneda is more convenient to Tokyo than Narita. You can fly China Airlines from Taipei and from Honolulu to Haneda.

BY AIR

Traveling from North America, American Airlines, ANA (All Nippon Airways), Canadian Airlines, Delta Air Lines , Japan Airlines, Korean Air, Malaysia Airlines, Northwest Airlines, Singapore Airlines and United Airlines provide direct service. The major gateway cities are Atlanta, Chicago, Dallas, Detroit, Honolulu, Los Angeles, Minneapolis, New York, Portland (Oregon), San Francisco, San Jose (California), Seattle, Toronto, Vancouver, and Washington, DC. Since the flight is so long, do yourself a favor and choose a flight with an easy connection.

All major European carriers serve Japan from their countries.

Most airlines offer three classes of service: First, Business and Coach. So many business people travel to Japan that on some flights business class takes up most of the plane. A number of airlines, including American, Canadian, Delta and United have nonsmoking flights to Japan. If you are allergic to smoke, avoid Japanese carriers. We have friends who discovered too late that they had the only two nonsmoking seats in their section.

Making Air Reservations

Any travel agent can issue tickets to Japan. Ticket prices are all over the map. In coach, it's possible a passenger could pay three or four times more than the person sitting next to him. If you phone the airline asking for fares, they will have a standard fare and some lower APEX (advance purchase) fares. But you can get less-expensive fares by going through travel agents who deal with consolidators — the airlines' way of selling wholesale seats. Our advice is to shop around and decide whether it's worth the savings to have more restrictions. Actually, consolidator tickets often have fewer restrictions than APEX tickets.

If you are planning to travel elsewhere in Asia, it's almost always less expensive to have the destination included in your ticket rather than buying a separate ticket in Japan, You can get some fairly cheap discount tickets in Japan, but they give you little flexibility.

The big Japanese travel agencies such as Japan Travel Bureau, Kintetsu Travel, and Tokyu Travel offer discount tickets as well as packages. See their addresses above under *Tours & Travel Agents*.

Surviving the Flight

No matter how you look at it, the flight is going to be long. Flying time is 13 1/2 hours from New York, 13 from Chicago and 10 1/2 from San Francisco. Because you cross the international date line traveling from North America, you arrive the day following your departure. Returning to North America, you arrive the same day you leave Japan. Flying west actually takes longer than flying east because the Pacific jet stream runs west to east.

There is almost no way to make the trip bearable. Some friends knock themselves out; others sleep naturally. We just endure. Good books — occasionally a good movie, but don't count on it — help pass the time. A friend uses this time to catch up on her letter writing.

Not eating airline food helps; request fruit plates and other special meals in advance. We find heavy airline food tends to make us feel worse, so we bring fruit and snacks. Drink lots of liquids — about one cup of water an hour; the airline cabin is almost humidity free. Avoid alcoholic drinks because they lead to further dehydration. Don't be tempted just because they're free. If you get up periodically and walk around the cabin, you can improve your circulation as well as your state of mind.

On most airlines, once the plane's door is locked, you are free to change seats within your class. If you see several unoccupied seats, move immediately before some savvier traveler takes them. It helps to stretch out if you have extra seats, but be careful about the bulkhead seats — you can't raise the armrests. The same applies to some three-in-a-row business class seats.

JET LAG

Unless you are coming from Asia or Australia, jet lag is an inescapable part of traveling to Japan. There are jet-lag diets, but we've never had the discipline to follow them – who wants to drink coffee only at strange times? To minimize jet lag, eat lightly on the plane, avoid alcoholic beverages, drink plenty of water and walk around to keep your blood flowing. When traveling west from the US, Patrice's husband, who's flown enough miles on airplanes to be awarded a free trip to the moon, swears by sleeping for several hours immediately after take-off and then staying awake for the rest of the flight. This system puts him closer to the Japanese schedule. Easy to say, but since flights leave North America around noon, how can we sleep then?

After arriving in Japan, go to your hotel, have dinner and stay up as late as you can, 9 or 10pm if you can manage it. We find taking melatonin or Tylenol PM helps before going to bed; we still wake up at 2am but can get back to sleep fairly easily. And if you are wide awake at 5am, rather than grumbling, get an early start on the day by going to the fish market or checking your e-mail.

The day after your arrival, try to spend some time outdoors because sunshine helps your body reset its clock. Late afternoon, around 4 or 5pm, is usually the worst time; you can hardly keep your eyes open. Rather than giving in, take a walk or do exercises to wake yourself up.

It will take a few days to get over jet lag. If your trip is for just a few days, it may not be worth the effort to try. We have come to the conclusion that the more exhausted we are before a trip, the easier it is to get over jet lag.

Be sure to ask for a seat assignment when you make your reservations or else you might find yourself right next to the bathroom or wedged in a center seat. If smoke bothers you, ask for a seat as far away from the smoking section as possible; it won't help you if the smoking section starts in the row behind you.

Some airlines do not assign seats in the exit rows until the day of the flight. If you'd like extra leg-room, inquire when you check in.

People have individual preferences about window or aisle seats. You can lean against windows to rest and won't have people climbing over you to get to the aisle. But then, it's troublesome to get up and out. Aisles offer stretching room and easy access to bathrooms, but you have to put up with people climbing over you. It's up to you.

If two people are traveling together, some airlines will allow you to reserve a window and an aisle seat with an empty seat in-between. If the flight is full and someone is assigned that seat, that passenger is almost always grateful to trade for an aisle or window.

Don't get discouraged. It's a long flight, but it's well worth it.

FROM THE AIRPORT TO THE CITY
NARITA AIRPORT (NRT)

When you arrive at **Narita Airport**, dog-tired after umpteen hours on the road, don't be surprised to find that you still have a 60-kilometer trek into Tokyo! Don't despair, train service makes it almost bearable.

Who knows why the airport is so far away from the city? It's something to do with noise and land rights, and since the government is still fighting with radical farmers over land, great big Narita has only one runway.

Narita is **New Tokyo International Airport** as opposed to Haneda, Tokyo International Airport. Haneda handles domestic flights almost exclusively.

Narita has two terminals imaginatively named Terminal 1 and Terminal 2. Terminal 2 opened several years ago and has helped ease the severe congestion, but it does not make using the airport a pleasure. A free shuttle bus connects the terminals: at Terminal 1, use bus stop 0; at Terminal 2, use bus stops 8 and 18.

Between 2 and 6pm, the peak arrival time, foreigners may stand in line for an hour at the Immigration counters. If you are a non-Japanese resident of Japan, use the Japanese lines; if you are a visitor, you have to wait. Congestion continues into the baggage area: the carousels, even in Terminal 2, are quite close together. The good news is there are usually plenty of free baggage carts, and you can use them on the escalators.

As you exit the baggage and customs area, there are counters for money exchange, hotel reservations, limousine bus tickets, delivery services to send suitcases, and a Japan Rail counter to validate rail passes. An airline information counter has basic tourist information and can help you with ground transportation. For info on all of Japan, go to the Tourist Information Office in Terminal 2.

Domestic transfers: Narita has only a few domestic flights. To connect with domestic flights, you'll probably have to trek to Haneda Airport, which is two hours away by bus.

Money Exchange

Money exchange counters are in the arrival area. They are open from 6:30am to 11pm in Terminal 1 and 7am to 10pm in Terminal 2. They stay open until the last flight arrives. The Bank of Tokyo-Mitsubishi has full banking services in both terminals between 9am and 3pm, Monday through Friday.

Amenities

Terminal 2 has a free playroom for children. On the 3rd floor, it also has day rooms, showers, a business center and a video room. There are a number of stores in each terminal, but most are outside the transit area. Duty free shops are inside the transit areas. The selection in the Duty Free shop in Terminal 1 is limited mainly to alcoholic drinks and cosmetics so don't wait until the last moment to do your shopping. Terminal 2's Duty Free shops have a more extensive selection.

Delivery Services

Send your luggage to your hotel and travel unencumbered. Go to the ABC counter outside customs. Charge is ¥1860 per bag for the greater Tokyo area, and luggage is delivered the next day. You can also send luggage anywhere else in Japan.

When returning to Narita, you can send your bag ahead. Several days ahead of your departure, call **Sky Partners**, *Tel. (03)3545-1131*, to arrange pick-up or ask your hotel to arrange it for you. Sending bags to Narita costs ¥2100 each. You travel hassle-free to Narita by train and pick up your luggage at the ABC counter at the airport.

GROUND TRANSPORTATION FROM NARITA

There's no end to the number of ways you can get into Tokyo from Narita. Which one you choose depends on your budget, the amount of luggage and time you want to spend.

Taxi

If money is no object, taxi is the easiest way to get to Tokyo although it's not always the fastest. The fare to central Tokyo averages about ¥25,000, including expressway tolls. The drawback is that if the expressway traffic is moving at a snail's pace, so are you. Taxi trunks house a large LP gas tank, which means you can't put in as many suitcases in there as you think, but station wagon taxis are often available at the airport.

Trains

The most dependable way into Tokyo is by train. By connecting to the subway and/or other travel lines, you can get practically anywhere. The shortcoming is that trains are difficult to navigate with heavy luggage. It's not too bad at Narita where you can take your luggage cart almost to the train. At the other end, you have to carry everything up and down stairs to get to a taxi or connect to another train, and porters are rare. An alternative is to send your luggage from the airport to your downtown hotel (see Delivery Services above); it will arrive the following day. That way, all you'll have to worry about is your carry on bag. We love the train if we're traveling light or have sent our bags ahead.

Narita Express (NEX): JR runs this comfortable, reserved-seat express train several times an hour to Tokyo Station (¥2890) with some trains continuing on to Shinjuku (¥3050), Ikebukuro (¥3050), Shinagawa (¥3050) and Yokohama stations (¥4100). NEX takes 55 minutes to Tokyo Station. The spacious seats offer ample leg room, and each car has a large luggage storage place. During peak travel times, the trains fill up, but standing is allowed. You can buy your tickets at the JR booth on the first floor or on the basement level near the train platforms.

A less-expensive alternative is to take the regular **JR express train** on the same line. It's an ordinary train without reserved seating or special luggage areas; it takes about 90 minutes to reach Tokyo Station. The fare is ¥1260.

Keisei Railway Skyliner: Fares are cheaper than NEX, but Ueno, the terminal station, is not as central as Tokyo Station. The Skyliner is an all reserved-seat train that stops at Nishi Nippori and Ueno Stations – either station ¥1880. The trip takes just under one hour. Note: Nishi Nippori is the more convenient transfer point to the JR Yamanote line, Tokyo's loop line. The Skyliner is not as popular as NEX and usually has seats available when NEX is sold out.

Keisei offers the cheapest fare to Tokyo via its limited express train *(tokkyu)*. For ¥1000, the train takes about 70 minutes to Nishi Nippori and a few minutes more to Ueno.

Limousine Bus

Limo buses have the advantage of whisking you away from terminal exit to hotels and other points around Tokyo. If they do not stop at the hotel where you are staying, you can take a short taxi ride to your final destination. They accept two pieces of luggage per person, and their personnel load and unload your baggage. Sounds great? Here's the bad news: Tokyo traffic can be pretty horrendous, and the trip can take more than two hours at peak times. We take the bus when we want to have our luggage with us and want a fairly hassle-free ride.

The Limousine Bus counter – you can't miss its big orange sign – has a bilingual computer screen that lists departure times. Select your destination and buy a ticket for the appropriate bus; be aware of your departure time and go outside to wait at the location number marked on your ticket and on a sign outside the terminal. The bus company accepts credit card payments at its Tokyo City Air Terminal (TCAT), Shinjuku Station, Yokohama City Air Terminal (YCAT) and Narita Airport counters. If you board a bus at a hotel to return to Narita Airport, you'll have to pay cash for your ticket.

If we have a lot of luggage and don't want to risk spending time sitting in traffic, we take a bus to TCAT on the eastern side of the city which avoids downtown traffic. Usually the trip doesn't take more than an hour. At TCAT, we pick up a taxi, either a normal one or a station wagon taxi. A fairly efficient way to get into the city, this way is much cheaper than taking a taxi all the way from Narita to center city.

To return to Narita Airport by limo bus, it's best to have a reservation made at least one day in advance. Hotels can make it for you or call *Tel. (03)3665-7232.*

Buses run to and from the areas listed below. The times are best-case scenarios; during rush hours, it could take much longer. The limo bus counter staff should be able to give you fairly accurate running times.
- **Tokyo City Air Terminal**: ¥2700, 55 minutes
- **Tokyo Station, Yaesu Exit**: ¥2800, 70 minutes
- **Haneda Airport**: ¥2,900, 75 minutes
- **Shinjuku Station and Hotels**: ¥2900, 85 minutes
- **Ginza Area Hotels**: ¥2800, 80 minutes
- **Akasaka Area Hotels**: ¥2900, 85 minutes
- **Shinagawa and Ebisu Area Hotels**: ¥2900, 85 minutes
- **Shiba Park Area Hotels**: ¥2900, 80 minutes
- **Kudanshita Area Hotels**: ¥2900, 90 minutes
- **Maihama Hotels and Disneyland**: ¥2200, 60 minutes

Car Rental
Toyota, Nippon and Nissan have counters at both Terminal 1 and 2; do yourself a favor and let someone else get you into Tokyo.

Tokyo City Air Terminal (TCAT)
Departing passengers should know about TCAT at Hakozaki, which is at the Suitengu-mae subway stop on the Hanzomon line. From TCAT, you can get on a limo bus to Narita. Because the bus doesn't need to go through the most congested sections of Tokyo, it usually takes under one hour to reach the airport.

Ask your airline whether or not you can check in at TCAT and find out the minimum check-in time. Several airlines have check-in counters where you can get your boarding pass, check your luggage, buy your departure tax ticket and, best of all, clear immigration. Keep your departure tax receipt in a safe place because you'll need to show it at the airport.

During peak travel times at the airport, you may wait more than 30 minutes in immigration lines, but at TCAT you rarely wait more than five. Immigration authorities give you a pass that allows you to by-pass the airport immigration counter altogether. Just surrender your pass at the glass window along the wall of Narita's immigration area.

Departure Tax

The departure tax for Narita (technically called the Passenger Service Facility Charge) is ¥2040 for adults and ¥1020 for children age 2-11. You can buy the ticket at the bright green machines before you enter the immigration area. To pay by credit card, stop at the JCB credit card counter; there's one in each terminal.

If you arrive and depart Narita the same day and if you decide to leave the transit lounge, you do not have to pay the departure tax. Should you decide to leave the lounge, make sure you take your ticket, boarding pass and passport with you.

Security

When we enter Narita Airport, we always feel that there must be a war going on that we don't know about. Security is very tight and guards in battlewagons hang around looking serious. You'll need to show your passport to enter the airport. What's this all about? Militant farmers blew up part of the airport when it first opened in 1978. Can you guess where your Passenger Service Facility Charge goes?

Contact Numbers

Reminder: if you are calling Tokyo from Narita, you must use the (03) area code.
- **Flight information**: *Tel. (0476)34-5000*
- **Narita Customs**: *Tel. (0476)34-2128*
- **Tokyo City Air Terminal**: *Tel. (03)3665-7111*
- **Tourist Information Center**: *Tel. (0476)34-6253*

Layover Suggestions

You have a five-hour layover at Narita Airport. "Great," you think, "I'll go into Tokyo for a meal." Think again. Narita is in the boondocks so don't even consider going into Tokyo unless you have at least a 9- or 10-hour layover.

There are a handful of short excursions you can take to see a little of the "real Japan," both old and new.

Narita City, home of Narita-san Shinsho-ji Temple, a huge complex visited by millions of Japanese each year. It's one of the most popular temples to visit during New Year's. From JR Airport Station, take the local train to JR Narita Station (¥230, 10 minutes). Walk the kilometer down **Omotesando**, Pilgrim's Path; it takes about 15 minutes if you don't stop, but how can anyone not stop?

On the right side of Omotesando, close to the station, is Ramen Bayashi, an inexpensive Chinese noodle shop with large portions. Lion's Den, a little further down on the left, serves Western-style food. The proprietor speaks fluent English. Fujikura Shoten, two blocks further down on the left, is a wonderful bamboo shop selling all sorts of goods: their bamboo radish grater is famous. Just past the bamboo shop is **Narita Tourist Pavilion** (Narita Kankokan). Open 9am to 5pm. Closed Monday and December 29-31. Free admission. The Pavilion gives a good history of the temple and displays some of its festival floats and woodblock prints of Narita in the Edo Period. On Thursday mornings, the hall welcomes you to participate in Japan's meditative tea ceremony.

Continue down Omotesando until you enter **Shinso-ji Temple**. The temple was founded in 940. It's difficult not to be impressed with the imposing gate and buildings. You'll see many amulets for sale. Narita-san, as the Japanese affectionately call the temple, is willing to be responsible for your traffic safety. Buy one of the charms and you'll be protected against traffic accidents. When you're in a taxi, look for a synthetic brocade square hanging from the side of the front window — the traffic safety charm. We bet more than half come from Narita-san.

Narita Koen Park, a lovely strolling garden, is behind the main temple buildings. All in all, a few relaxing hours spent in Narita City should help you cope with your airport experience.

National Museum of Japanese History, **Sakura** (Kokuritsu Rekishi Minzoku Hakubutsukan, "Reki-haku"). This huge museum — 35,000 square meters of floor space — has excellent exhibits using both artifacts and excellent replicas covering Japanese history and culture including archaeology, folklore and history. It's a good introduction to Japan's traditional society and culture. English earphones are available. The museum is located in Sakura Park, which was once the castle grounds of a powerful feudal lord. *Take the Keisei local train from Keisei Airport Station to Keisei Sakura Station (¥420, 20 minutes). From the station, it's a 20-minute walk or 7-minute taxi ride. Open 9:30am to 4:30pm. Closed Monday (Tuesday if Monday is a holiday) and December 27 through January 4. ¥400.*

Tokyo Disneyland. If the kids are with you, what better way to entertain them than at Mickey's Kingdom? Airport limo bus takes one hour. *Adults: ¥3600 general admission, ¥5100 for unlimited rides. Children age 4-11, ¥3570; children age 12 through 17, ¥4590. Tel. (047)354-0001.*

GETTING AROUND JAPAN BY TRAIN

Japan is a train-lover's dream. Rail lines connect the far corners of the four main islands. You can find steam engines as well as some of the fastest trains in the world. Millions of Japanese ride trains every day. Japan is ninth in the world in total rail mileage but is first in actual passenger miles — no easy feat given countries like India and China have more than ten times Japan's population.

In 1889, a train from Osaka to Tokyo took 19 hours; today it takes 2 1/2 on the super express *Nozomi shinkansen*. **JR – Japan Rail** – is currently experimenting with mag-lev trains, but don't expect to ride above the rails for a while.

At the center of all this activity is a handful of companies called Japan Rail Group, more commonly known as JR. Spun off from the government-operated Japan National Railways in the 1980s, companies known as JR East, JR Central, JR West, JR Kyushu, JR Hokkaido, et al., work together to provide seamless service so you probably won't realize as you travel around the country that these are different companies. In addition to JR, private companies provide train service, usually in the larger cities and usually at lower cost than JR.

Shinkansen Trains

Coming on the scene in 1964 and signaling the end of the postwar period with Japan achieving the state-of-the-art high-speed service, the *shinkansen* (high-speed) train is still a symbol of Japanese technology. Today, France's TGV is faster. English speakers call Japan's *shinkansen* trains **bullet trains**, but since Japanese don't know that term, we use *shinkansen*. If you ask a conductor how to get to a bullet train, he'd just scratch his head.

Japan has a network of *shinkansen* lines. The **Tokaido-Sanyo line** runs from Tokyo through Yokohama, Nagoya, Kyoto, Osaka, Kobe, Hiroshima and terminates in Fukuoka at Hakata Station. The **Joetsu line** runs from Tokyo to Niigata on the Japan Sea. The **Tohoku line** runs from Tokyo via Sendai to Morioka. The **Akita line** runs from Tokyo to Akita City; **Yamagata line** from Tokyo to Yamagata City; **Nagano line** from Tokyo to Nagano City. If you immediately notice a common thread, it is that they all start or end in Tokyo — a dramatic example of what being the center of power means.

In Tokyo, the *shinkansen* trains all depart and arrive at **Tokyo Station**, with the exception of the Tohoku *shinkansen* that departs from both

TRANSPORTATION INFORMATION

The best source for train information is the JR English Information Line, open Monday through Friday, 10am to 6pm, Tel. (03)3423-0111. Or call the Japan Travel Phone toll free between 9am and 5pm daily: 0088-22-4800 or 0120-44-4800. These numbers don't work in Tokyo or Kyoto. In Tokyo call (03)3201-3331 and in Kyoto (075)371-5649.

Tokyo and Ueno Stations. *Shinkansen* stations often have "Shin" in their name, such as Shin-Osaka or Shin-Yokohama. Shin means new and these stations were newly built for the *shinkansen* and are usually away from the center of the city.

Shinkansen have two classes of service, **ordinary** *(futsu-sha)* and **superior** (Green Car — *guriin sha*). For most people, ordinary class is, well, ordinary but adequate. If you are very large, the seats might be tight. Green Car offers larger seats, more leg room and a more exclusive environment. Usually, Japanese corporations only provide Green Car for their top executives.

Shinkansen trains usually run like clockwork, but nature can wreak havoc with their schedules. Snow slows them down as does the flooding that accompanies typhoons. And if there's an earthquake, service is at a standstill until the entire track is checked for damage. If your train is more than two hours late without notice when you boarded it, you are entitled to a refund upon your arrival. The refund consists of the express surcharge, but not the basic fare.

Reserved (*shitei seki*) and unreserved (*jiyu seki*) seats are available. Reservations cost ¥500 and are worthwhile for your peace of mind. If you have a rail pass, there is no additional charge for a reservation. During peak travel seasons and heavy travel times like Friday evening, if you don't have a reservation, you may end up standing for the better part of the trip. About one-half of the train is reserved. The platform signs, in English, will tell you which cars are which. If you are traveling without reservations, line up as soon as you can at the place marked on the platform; it may make the difference between sitting and standing. On a mid-day train mid-week, you can usually get a seat in the unreserved section.

Speed has its price. *Shinkansen* trains have a substantial surcharge over the basic fare. To gain access to the trains, you must cross an additional ticket barrier inside the JR station. You must show your ticket at the *shinkansen* gate and when exiting give the agent your surcharge ticket or seat reservation ticket (but not the main ticket). It's quite confusing.

Sometimes a *shinkansen* ticket is in two parts, one for the regular fare and one for the surcharge or the seat reservation. If you have two tickets, you surrender the surcharge ticket at the *shinkansen* barrier and the other one as you exit the station. If you only have one, hold on to it; show it at the *shinkansen* barrier but do not surrender it until you reach the second barrier.

If you are utterly confused, just show your tickets to the person at the gate; he will take the correct one. Just be careful not to give your entire ticket away at the *shinkansen* barrier because you'll have to do some explaining at the main station barrier. If this happens, just say *"shinkansen"* and the staff person will probably figure it out.

SHINKANSEN TRAVEL

Travel by **shinkansen**, *zinging along the rails at 200 kilometers an hour, is an experience not be missed, but most of your fellow passengers will be almost blasé. After settling in your seat, you'll notice that a lot of riders (except children) have started to nod off regardless of the time of day. For many Japanese, the shinkansen is the place to catch up on sleep.*

You'll never starve on the train. Through the aisles, attendants push carts laden with coffee, juice, beer, whiskey, sandwiches, bento box meals and ice cream. They even offer boxes of sweets for sale as souvenirs. If you can't find anything to eat on the cart, there's usually a small canteen in one of the cars; and some trains have dining cars too.

When we first used our laptop computer on the train, people would watch with curiosity, but today laptops are more common place. And in the age of the cellular phone, the train is a traveling office to many businessmen – the few who aren't napping, that is. JR requests passengers use the cellular phones only at the ends of the cars so other travelers aren't disturbed; most people comply.

If you're feeling left out because you don't have a cellular phone, you can make a call from public phones on the train. You can buy telephone cards from the vending machine next to the phone. Even telephones are hungry on a train; you'll see how quickly they eat up your card.

Stops are announced in English. Make sure you gather up your belongings and head for the exit before the train pulls into the station. Stops are brief and you don't want to get stuck on the train. If you don't get to the exit quickly, you may end up at the next station. Believe it or not, it happened to a friend of ours.

Also, remember to keep your ticket; you'll have to surrender it at the station.

Limited Express, Express, & Local Trains

   Limited express *(tokubetsu kyuko)* trains are the fastest next to the *shinkansen*. Yes, we know that limited express sounds slower than express. But in this case, a limited express makes a more limited number of stops than an express train. Confused? Just remember that limited express is faster than express. They run on normal tracks and don't make as many stops, so they get there faster than express trains.

   You must pay a limited-express surcharge *(tokkyu ken)*. There are reserved and unreserved seats and, just like the *shinkansen*, reservations cost ¥500. You are allowed to change the reservation once at no charge. Most limited express trains have Green Cars for an additional fee.

   Express *(kyuko)* trains stop at only at the larger stations. You pay a surcharge, but not as high as the limited express fee. Express trains have reserved and unreserved cars.

   Rapid *(kaisoku)* trains make more stops than express. You do not pay a surcharge, and they do not have reserved seats.

   Local *(kaku eki teisha)* are the slowest trains and stop at every station. They do not have reserved seats.

Purchasing Tickets

   You can buy JR tickets at any JR train station. Limited express and *shinkansen* tickets are sold at the *midori no madoguchi* (Green Window) sales counter. At smaller stations, they may not have a *midori no madoguchi;* then the clerk in the office can sell you a ticket. At very small stations in rural areas, *shinkansen* tickets are unavailable.

   You can buy local and express tickets from **vending machines**. The fares are shown on a chart above the machines. In big cities, the larger JR stations will have a fare map in English. If you don't know the fare, you can go to the ticket window and tell the staff person your destination or buy a ticket for the minimum fare and pay the rest on the train or when you get off. If you buy a regular ticket, but end up on a limited express, you can pay the surcharge on the train. Some of the vending machines will take ¥1000, ¥5000 and ¥10,000 notes. Look for the symbol on the top of the machine. Generally you can buy a ticket at a vending machine up to about ¥1800. After that, you have to buy it at a counter.

   Even though the ticket you buy may cost the equivalent of the average annual income in many a third-world country, JR deals almost exclusively in cash. If you want to pay by **credit card**, in Tokyo you have to go to the Tokyo Station's Travel Service Center near the Yaesu central exit or to Shinjuku Station's Travel Service Centers; one is near the South exit, another near the East exit. There are other JR Travel Service Centers, but these are the only three that accept credit cards. In Osaka Station, the Travel Service Center will accept credit cards. Another way to pay by plastic is to buy your JR ticket from one of the large travel agencies such as JTB. They usually accept credit cards.

The trains fares we list under *Arrivals & Departures* for each city are one-way fares.

Making Reservations

JR's ticketing staff speak very little English – what were they doing in school during their six years of English classes? To make it easier, write down the date, your destination, the number of tickets and the time of the train you want. Also write down if you want smoking or nonsmoking. If you know the specific train number and/or time, write it down too. Show this information to the ticket agent. It's much easier to have it all in front of you than to try to communicate orally.

The JNTO puts out a booklet in English called *Railway Time Table* listing schedules of the *shinkansen* trains and other popular routes and the fine points of train fares. You can obtain a copy at any JNTO office. See *For More Information* at the end of this chapter.

If you want to do some investigative work, JR publishes a comprehensive **train schedule** as big as a telephone book and entirely in Japanese. A copy is usually near station ticket counters. If you have a good bilingual map, you can decipher the schedule. This process is cumbersome and time consuming, but at least you can get some information. In the front of the book are full-color maps of Japan. Use your bilingual map to match up the Japanese names of cities. You'll notice there's a number next to the train line on the map. That's the page number of the schedule. Turn to that page and try to match up the Japanese writing of your points of departure and arrival to figure out the train times. One drawback is not all the trains listed run daily; some run only on holidays or weekends.

Japan Rail Pass

The **Japan Rail Pass** is an economical way for you to travel on JR trains, buses and ferries if you are doing a lot of moving around. If you are simply traveling round-trip from Tokyo to Kyoto, it is less expensive to buy an individual ticket. Generally, if you start in Tokyo and are going beyond the Kyoto/Osaka/Kobe area, it's cost effective to buy a 7-day pass.

The catch is that rail passes can be used only by foreign visitors who are here on short-term visits for sightseeing. You must have "temporary visitor" stamped into your passport. If you've come for business, you can use it as long as you are listed as a temporary visitor. If you are traveling under any other kind of visa such as an entertainment visa, you are ineligible. Foreigners living and working in Japan are ineligible. JR is strict and will not issue a rail pass if they deem you are ineligible.

JAPAN RAIL PASS FARES, IN YEN			
	Ordinary Class		*Green (First) Class*	
	Adult	*Child (6 -11)*	*Adult*	*Child (6-11)*
7-day pass	*28,300*	*13,900*	*37,800*	*18,900*
14-day pass	*45,100*	*22,250*	*61,200*	*30,600*
21-day pass	*57,700*	*29,800*	*79,600*	*39,800*

You must purchase your rail pass exchange order outside Japan. Most travel agencies can obtain one, but if you have difficulty, contact an overseas JNTO office for names of agencies. You have to present the exchange order to a JR office in Japan to receive the actual rail pass, and you must show your passport. If you validate your rail pass at Narita or Kansai International airports, you can use it to take a JR train to the city. You can also wait and validate it at a JR Travel Service Center in any major city. You'll receive a list of places with your exchange order. When you validate your pass, specify the date you wish to begin travel. It does not have to begin on the day you validate your pass.

Should you get a rail pass? It depends on your itinerary. Yes, if you will travel a lot in a short time. It may be cheaper to buy point-to-point tickets if you plan to spend longer periods in a limited number of places. This decision is something you make ahead of time because it is absolutely impossible to buy the exchange order in Japan.

One nice thing about the rail pass is it saves a lot of the hassle of buying tickets at the train station. You have absolute flexibility, jumping on and off trains whenever you want. And if you want seat reservations, you can get them at no extra charge. We recommend that you get seat reservations so you don't have to worry about standing.

The fine print: The rail pass is not valid for travel on the *Nozomi shinkansen*, the fastest train between Tokyo and Fukuoka. And it's good on JR trains, buses and ferries, but not on private train lines or any other buses or ferries. If you want to take an overnight train, you have to pay a supplemental charge. And take good care of your pass; if you lose it, you're out of luck.

You can buy more than one rail pass; they do not need to run consecutively. For instance, if you are staying in Japan for two months, you can get one for the first part of the trip, and another for the latter part.

JR East Pass

JR East, the rail company which serves a large area from the northern tip of Honshu Island, Japan's main island, to Nagano in central Japan, recently introduced the **JR East Pass**. If you are heading north or east from Tokyo, it may save you money. The pass is limited to JR East's service areas and to people who have short-term tourist visas.

The pass offers two features which the JR Rail Pass doesn't: a discounted fare for "youths" aged 12 through 25 (in ordinary class only), and a flexible four-day pass which can be used on any four days within a 30 day period. In addition to the flexible four-day pass, JR East offers passes for five and ten consecutive days.

You must buy an **Exchange Order** before traveling to Japan; present the order in Japan to receive the actual pass. Most travel agents can issue exchange orders; if you have difficulty, try the overseas offices of Japan Airlines or of the large Japanese travel agents such as JTB, or contact the Japan National Tourist Organization.

The price of a **five-consecutive-day pass** in ordinary class is ¥20,000 for adults (above age 25), ¥16,000 for youths (age 12-25) and ¥10,000 for children (age 6-11). The fare for green car (first class) is ¥28,000 for people age 12 and over and ¥14,000 for children age six through 11. Children under six travel free but do not get their own seat.

A **ten-consecutive-day pass** in ordinary class runs ¥32,000 for adults, ¥25,000 for youths and ¥16,000 for children. The fares for green car run ¥44,800 for adults and ¥22,400 for children.

The **flexible four day pass** in ordinary class costs ¥20,000 for adults, ¥16,000 for youths and ¥10,000 for children. For green car, ¥28,000 for adults and ¥14,000 for children.

Special Fares

JR runs some special fares that you may want to consider. Note: Most of these discount tickets are not valid during Golden Week, the mid-August Obon season and New Year's.

Full Moon Pass. Isn't it a great name? This pass gives unlimited travel by Green Car on all JR trains except *Nozomi* (superfast *shinkansen*) to a couple whose combined ages are 88 and over. You're also eligible for a 20% car discount by Eki Rent-a-car. The cost is ¥79,000 for a 5-day pass, ¥98,000 for 7-day pass and ¥122,000 for 12-day pass; these prices are for two people. This pass can be worthwhile if you do a lot of traveling, not just round-trip to one city or if you are traveling to a distant city, e.g. Tokyo to Fukuoka. But when you compare this cost with the cost of a Green Car rail pass, it shows what a good deal the rail pass is.

Nice Middy Pass. Who makes up these names up? This pass is for two or more women over 30 traveling together. It's available only in the spring and autumn. Three days unlimited travel in ordinary class costs ¥56,000 for two women and ¥84,000 for three.

JR Shuyuken (Area pass). The area passes include train fare from a major city to the destination area plus unlimited travel within the zone. They are usually valid from 8 to 14 days. The drawbacks are you still have to pay an additional *shinkansen* or limited express surcharge and unless you are doing extensive traveling within the zone for a long period of time, you can usually do better with a regular ticket. Wide Shuyuken is for a large area such as Hokkaido or Kyushu while Mini Shuyuken is for a smaller area.

Series Ticket (Kaisuken) on the shinkansen. This set of six one-way tickets carries you between two points. The tickets must be used within three months but not necessarily by the same person. It's worthwhile if you are three or more or need to make repeat trips. You don't realize great savings, but every little bit helps. For instance, Tokyo-Kyoto *kaisuken* costs ¥71,880 or ¥11,980 each way. The regular *shinkansen* fare is ¥12,970.

Q Kippu. These tickets are discounted round-trip tickets good on limited express trains and some *shinkansen* trains. They are good for unreserved seats only.

JR Rent-a-car. JR offers train and car rental combination tickets, 20% off train fare and 20% off car rental. Most large stations have JR's Eki Rent-a-car. JR usually has a special deal: if you travel more than 200 kilometers on a JR ticket, you receive specially reduced prices for car rental.

Travel Agents

Some of the large travel agents such as JTB issue JR train tickets and make *shinkansen* and limited express train reservations. Look for the JR symbol outside. Many of the larger agencies accept credit cards.

Children

JR and other train companies are kind to parents. Children under six ride free although they don't get their own seat. If you want to guarantee a seat, you have to buy a child's ticket. Children ages six through eleven pay half-fare, rounded off to the higher ¥10. Twelve and over pay the full adult fare. On JR ticket machines, there's a button for children's tickets. Press this button and the children's price is displayed.

English Information

JR Information Line can give you information in English on schedules, fares, best routings, discount tickets, etc. The staff is really excellent. They're open Monday through Friday, 10am to 6pm, *Tel. (03)3423-0111.*

ESSENTIAL TRAIN VOCABULARY

eki	train station
kisha	long distance train
densha	regional train
shinkansen	bullet train
tokkyu	limited express train
kyuko	express train
futsu sha	local train
jiyu seki	unreserved seat
shitei seki	reserved seat
kin'en seki	nonsmoking
kippu	ticket
katamichi	one way
ofuku	round trip
ichi mai	one ticket
ni mai	two tickets
san mai	three tickets
yon mai	four tickets
kodomo ichi mai	one child's ticket (age 6-11)
kodomo ni mai	two child's tickets (age 6-11)
josha ken	basic ticket
tokkyu ken	limited express surcharge
guriin sha	green car (premium class)
guriin sha ken	green car surcharge
tsugi no densha	next train
(place) ma-de no kippu	ticket to (place)

Useful Questions:

ikura desu ka?	what's the fare?
(place) ma-de nan ban homu desu ka?	The train to (place) leaves from what platform?
kono densha wa (place) ma-de ikimasu ka?	Does this train go to (place)?

7. GETTING AROUND TOKYO

Subways and trains are the most efficient ways of getting around town because you don't get stuck in traffic. A good map is essential, and the one put out by the **Japan National Tourist Organization** (JNTO) is one of the best. In addition to covering the central city, there is a subway map and a suburban train map. For more detail, *Tokyo: A Bilingual Atlas,* is excellent and available in hotel bookstores and stores stocking English books.

BY FOOT

Tokyo is best seen on foot. If you race from place to place, it's really difficult to get a good feel for the city. Instead, choose a specific area, take the subway to it and explore on foot to your heart's content. Just make sure your shoes are comfortable.

BY SUBWAY & TRAIN

A great rail system whisks you around town. The trains and subways are clean, fast, inexpensive, run every few minutes and are unbelievably reliable. It's true that you can practically set your watch by them, and, incredibly, the transit authority even posts a schedule. Trains start running about 5:30am and continue till around midnight. You'll find the times of the first and last trains posted outside entrances to the stations.

Tokyo subways and trains are a source of disbelief to jaded New Yorkers. Upholstered seats, overhead racks for packages, signs alerting you the train is arriving, markers on the platform floor indicating where the doors will open, arrival announcements, and graffiti-free trains and stations are taken for granted by the Japanese. On the other hand, the crowded rush-hour trains, especially between 8 and 9:30am, can really get your day off to a miserable start.

PACKED LIKE SARDINES

*The Japanese expression **sushi zume**, the equivalent of "packed like sardines," means made like sushi. A sushi chef slaps rice and fish together without a millimeter of air between them. To a passenger aboard a packed rush-hour train, a can of sardines looks positively spacious. Men have been known to arrive at their offices with lipstick stains on their suit jackets – souvenirs from poor female commuters pushed up against their backs.*

Each subway line has an identifying color; it's painted as a stripe on the train and the signs have a circle of that color. By following these colors, it's easy to make connections.

Several different transit systems serve Tokyo. The subway itself, called *chikatetsu* (literally underground train), has two systems: **Eidan** and **Toei**. You can ride within each system on one ticket, but you must pay a double fare to connect. You can buy a special ticket that allows you to transfer between the two systems for a slight savings. At the ticket machine counter, there's a fare map for these connections, but it is almost never translated into English.

Then there are JR trains that run above ground. The **JR Yamanote** is a loop line that circles central Tokyo. Other JR lines run east/west, radiating out of central Tokyo like spokes of a wheel. Subways and JR lines require two different fares.

Additionally, there are private lines that run from the suburbs to Tokyo. They usually terminate at a station on the Yamanote line but, to make things really confusing, sometimes they continue into Tokyo as subways. If you connect from private lines to subways or JR, you must pay two fares but the fares can be put together on the same ticket.

All the trains run on a zone system and fares are based on distance. For the subway, ¥160 is the minimum fare and will usually carry you four or five stops. The fare rises to ¥190 for five to about nine stops and ¥230 for ten to about 15 stops.

Purchase your ticket at the ticket machines. Both subways and JR trains have two kinds of machines; the older machines flat against the wall, and the new machines that protrude at an angle. The angled machines are bilingual, so it's easier to use them. They accept ¥1000, ¥5000 and ¥10,000 bills. If the station has only the older machines, look at the top to see if they take large bills. The station attendant will break a large bill.

A fare map in Japanese is posted on the wall above the machines. Most of the subway stations and some of the JR stations have English-language fare maps, usually beside the machines. If you cannot figure out the fare, buy a ticket for the minimum amount and pay the difference to the clerk at the gate when you get off.

Before you go onto the platform, insert your ticket in a computerized gate; make sure you remember to pick up your ticket; keep it in a safe place because you have to present it when you exit.

The subway sells a stored-value card called **SF Metro Card** that is available in denominations of ¥1000, ¥3000 and ¥5000. JR has a similar card called IO (pronounced e-o) for ¥3000 and ¥5000. Make sure you don't buy a JR Orange Card — they are good only for buying tickets from a machine.

The stored-value cards are really handy for visitors because you don't have to figure the fare; you just put the card in the ticket gate machines both entering and exiting, and the correct fare is automatically deducted. If you forget to take your ticket out of the machine, a bell will ring to remind you. You can also use these stored-value cards to buy individual tickets from the machines.

There are also passes for unlimited travel, but unless you are going to do a lot of moving around Tokyo in one day on the trains, it's less expensive to buy point-to-point tickets.

The different plans are as follows:

- **Tokyo Free Kippu Ticket**. ¥1580. Good for one-day travel on the JR trains, Toei subway trains, Toei buses and Eidan subway trains. Buy the pass at JR stations and major subway stations. You can't use it on JR express trains. You must buy the pass at a ticket booth.
- **Tokunai Free Kippu Ticket**. ¥730. Good for one-day travel on the JR trains within Tokyo's 23 wards — generally within the JR Yamanote line loop and a few stations farther out.
- **Toei One-day Economy Pass** *(Ichi nichi joshaken)*. ¥700. Good for one-day travel on the Toei subway line, Toei buses and Toei streetcar. Available at subway stations. The Toei subway has only a few lines, so this pass isn't useful to most visitors.
- **TRTA (Eidan) Subway One-day Open Ticket** *(Ichi nichi joshaken)*. ¥710. Good for one-day travel on TRTA subways. Buy the pass at subway vending machines that accept the Metro card. If it's one of the machines that's angled out from the wall, the button for the pass is marked in English.

Private lines tend not to have fare maps in English, so buy the minimum fare and pay the difference when you exit. Even though most stations are computerized, there's always an attendant.

Children under six ride the trains free of charge; ages six through eleven are half-price, rounded up to the nearest ¥10. Some fare machines have a button marked *kodomo* and "children," others have the half-price

LOOPING AROUND TOKYO

The JR Yamanote line circles central Tokyo. A complete loop takes one hour. There are two lines – one running clockwise, the other counterclockwise. Eventually you'll arrive at your destination even if you get on the wrong one.

The Yamanote is not the fastest way around town. It makes 29 stops, but it is convenient because every station except three connects with at least one subway or train line. Since the Yamanote runs above ground, some suggest taking it all the way around to get a feel for the city. But, frankly, you won't see much of the city because of all the buildings near the tracks.

You'll rarely wait more than a few minutes for a train. Cars get so crowded during the rush hour that some trains have cars with folding seats. During the morning rush hour, you're not allowed to sit, which makes it easier to pack in more people.

buttons below in red, behind a clear plastic protector. Lift the plastic to buy a ticket.

BY BUS

Tokyo's extensive bus network is not very user friendly. The routes are pretty convoluted and traffic conditions can make the ride slow going. Route maps are almost never in English. Generally we recommend that you stick to trains and subways.

But if you do take a bus, the fare costs ¥200 – deposit your money in the clear plastic fare box as you enter. The fare machine gives change for ¥500 coins and ¥1000 bills if you put your money in the appropriate slots, not in the plastic box.

BY TAXI

Getting around Tokyo by taxi is convenient for relatively short trips, but it's much faster to take a train to get across town. The meter usually starts at ¥660 for two kilometers, but with recent deregulation, companies offer slightly different fares. A small number of taxis offer a fare of ¥320 to ¥340 for one kilometer to entice customers who are going only a short distance. There's no additional fee for luggage. Between 11pm and 5am, you pay a 30% surcharge that is reflected in the meter. Remember, no tipping.

Most taxis will take a maximum of four passengers; they'll take five if they don't have bucket seats in the front. Japanese taxi drivers are about

ESSENTIAL TAXI JAPANESE

(place) ma-de onegai shimasu	*Please take me to (place)*
Tomatte kudasai	*Stop*
Migi magatte	*Turn right*
Hidari magatte	*Turn left*
Massugu	*Go straight*
Reshito onegai shimasu	*Please give me a receipt*

as honest as you can get, but they speak almost no English. They turn on the meter automatically, and if they take a roundabout route, it's usually out of ignorance.

Taxis cruise so you only have to raise your arm to hail one. Empty taxis have red lights on the passenger side of the dashboard and at night a roof light is lit. Technically, you are not supposed to hail taxis in crosswalks, but they will stop. Hotels and train stations have taxi queues. If you're having difficulty getting a taxi, go to the nearest large hotel.

Given Tokyo's traffic congestion, most drivers are fairly considerate, so we don't have the cacophony of horns you hear New York. And, you don't have to fear for your life when you step into a taxi.

Make sure you have a map to your destination to give the driver unless you are going to a very famous landmark like Wako Department Store in Ginza for example. And make sure you have your hotel's address card for your return trip. Usually the name of the hotel is the same in Japanese and English, but there are exceptions. If you say, "Imperial Hotel," to a taxi driver, most likely you'll get a blank stare; Japanese call it, *"Teikoku Hoteru."*

BY CAR

You may not be able to live without your car back home, but you really do not want to drive in Japan. Train and air transportation are fast and efficient. Urban traffic is a nightmare; car rentals, parking and gas are exorbitant and the highway tolls between cities often are as much as the train fare. And, Japan drives on the left side of the road, opposite the US, Canada and continental Europe. British and Australian drivers can breathe one sigh of relief.

All airports have car rental counters. The large train stations have them as do the larger towns and cities. The main car rental companies are: **Nippon Rent-a-Car**, **Toyota Rent-a-Car**, **Mazda Rent-a-Car**, **Japaren** and **Eki Rent-a-Car**. Hertz also has operations here, but doesn't have as many outlets as the others. The advantage with Hertz is it's easy to make reservations in North America. Nippon Rent-a-Car has a relationship with National Car Rental so you can book through them in North America.

The car rental companies have nearly identical rates. For ¥300 you can get a "Member's Card" that gives you 20% discounts on all but the smallest car. It's worthwhile getting one.

Car rentals for the first 24-hour period run from ¥8800 for a subcompact to ¥28,000 for a luxury sedan. Prices for subsequent days decrease about 30%. You can rent a car for as short as 6 hours.

Reservations numbers:
- **Japaren**: *Tel. (03)5397-8911*
- **Mazda**: *toll free: Tel. 0120-17-5656*
- **Nissan**: *Tel. (03)5424-4123*
- **Toyota**: *Tel. (03)3264-0100*
- **Nippon**: *Tel. (03)3469-0910*
- **Hertz**: *toll free: Tel. 0120-38-8002*
- **Eki Rent-a-Car**: *make reservations through Japan Rail*

DRIVING IN JAPAN

To rent a car, you must have an **international driver's license**. In the US, get it at the American Automobile Association. If you are going to drive, a good bilingual road map is essential. We like **Road Atlas Japan** published by Shobunsha and available in English language book stores. Its maps have helpful information such as "this road closed in winter" or "this road extremely congested in fall." These are the things you really need to know.

The main roads in rural areas are remarkably well marked in English. The expressways have bilingual signs as do many of the national and prefectural roads. If the signs aren't in English, these roads have route numbers that are posted fairly regularly.

Alcohol and driving do not mix. Japanese law does not allow any alcohol in the blood so you can't even have one drink and drive. The police routinely stop cars for breath tests. Penalties for drinking while intoxicated are high.

The stop sign is a red triangular sign pointing downwards. Japan uses international traffic signs.

The Japan Auto Federation has a reciprocal relationship with the American Automobile Association and other auto associations. If you are a member, you can use their services.

Remember, Japan drives on the left side of the road.

TOURIST INFORMATION

• **Tourist Information Center (TIC)**: *B1, Tokyo International Forum near Yurakucho Station, 3-5-1 Marunouchi, Chiyoda-ku, 100. Open 9am to 5pm, Monday through Friday; 9am to 12 noon Saturday. Closed December 29 through January 3. Tel. (03)3201-3331.* Make sure you pick up TIC's excellent map of Tokyo; you have to ask for it. The office has extensive travel information on all of Japan. They tend to give out standard brochures, but if you ask them specific questions, they'll get the information for you. TIC has a Welcome Inn Reservation Center where, once in Japan, you must go in person to request reservations at moderately priced accommodations all over Japan. The reservation center doesn't operate on Saturday mornings.

• **Teletourist Service**: 24-hour tape recording in English of events in Tokyo: *Tel. (03)3201-2911.*

• **Shinjuku Station**: Information Bureau of Tokyo is located near the East Exit and another one is near the West Exit. *Open 9am to 6pm. Closed Sunday.*

• **Tokyo Station**: Information Bureau of Tokyo is near the Yaesu Exit. *Open 9am to 6pm. Closed Sunday.*

• **Home Visit System**: Call the Tourist Information Center, *Tel. (03)3201-3331.*

• **Goodwill Guides**: Tokyo Metropolitan SGG Club, *Tel. (03)3842-5566.*

JAPANESE ADDRESSES

*Addresses are a world unto themselves and maps are an absolute necessity. Tokyo has 23 wards called **ku**. The wards are divided into districts. Large districts are divided into two or more sections called **chome**. Blocks each have a number and buildings within the block have a number.*

Addresses are written 4-3-2 Roppongi or 3-2 Roppongi, 4-chome. What this means is the building is in the 4th chome of Roppongi, on block three and in building two. Good luck finding it. Even cab drivers have difficulty finding places. Always ask your host or a restaurant to fax a map to you at your hotel or else you may wander indefinitely. Ask for a landmark building. If you are really desperate, go to the closest police box. Neighborhoods often have maps posted showing every block in the district.

8. BASIC INFORMATION

BUSINESS HOURS

Standard business hours are 9am to 5pm, Monday through Friday. Banks are open 9am to 3pm. Department stores are open 10am to 7 or 8pm. Most department stores close one weekday, but all are open on Saturday and Sunday.

CLOTHING SIZES

You'll notice immediately that Japanese are smaller than Americans or Europeans, so buying clothes may be a problem. Even if you are slender, garments, even Western designer labels, are designed to fit the shorter limbs of the Japanese.

Japan has a unique sizing system:

Women's Clothing

Japanese	9	11	13	15	17
American	6	8	10	12	14
English	8	10	12	14	16
Continental	34	36	38	40	42

Men's Clothing

Japanese	S	M	L	LL	LLL
American	34	36	38	40, 42	44, 46
English	34	36	38	40, 42	44, 46
Continental	44	46	48	50, 52	54, 56

Men's Shirts

Japanese	36	37	38	39, 40	41, 42
American	14	14 1/2	15	15 1/2, 16	16 1/2, 17
English	14	14 1/2	15	15 1/2, 16	16 1/2, 17
Continental	36	37	38	39, 40	41, 42

Women's Shoes

Japanese	23	23 1/2	24	24 1/2	25	25 1/2	26
American	6	6 1/2	7	7 1/2	8	8 1/2	9
English	4 1/2	5	5 1/2	6	6 1/2	7	7 1/2
Continental	36	37	38	39	40	41	42

Men's Shoes

Japanese	25	25.5	26	26.5	27.5	27.5	28	29
American	6	6 1/2	7 1/2	8	9	9 1/2	10	11
English	5	6	7	8	9	9 1/2	10	11
Con'l	39	40	41	42	42 1/2	43	44	45

Children's Clothing

Japanese size	Height/Inches	Weight/Kilos	Weight/Lb.
60 cm	to 26"	to 7 kg	to 16 lb.
70 cm	26 - 30"	6 - 9 kg	14 - 21 lb.
80 cm	30 - 34"	9 - 12 kg	20 - 28 lb.
90 cm	34 - 38"	12 - 15 kg	26 - 33 lb.
100 cm	38 - 42"	14 - 18 kg	31 - 40 lb.
110 cm	42 - 46"	17 - 21 kg	37 - 48 lb.
120 cm	46 - 50"	20 - 24 kg	44 - 55 lb.
130 cm	50 - 53"	23 - 29 kg	52 - 64 lb.
140 cm	53 - 57"	28 - 36 kg	62 - 80 lb.
150 cm	57 - 61"	57 - 61 kg	75 - 95 lb.

DELIVERY SERVICES

Japan has private package delivery services called *takkyubin*. Parcels are sent from one part of Japan to another quickly and efficiently. These services are great and make traveling in Japan easier. Japanese usually ship their skis, golf clubs, and suitcases to their destinations ahead of time so they can travel unencumbered. We send our suitcases ahead to Narita Airport to avoid the hassle of carrying them. Cost varies by weight and destination but usually runs between ¥1000 and ¥2000.

Take advantage of this system by shipping your purchases and unneeded items to the hotel at your final destination in Japan so you don't have to carry everything with you. Hotels can provide boxes and arrange the delivery service, or you can take your parcel to practically any convenience store. There are several delivery companies, each recognizable by its logo displayed in front of stores: cat, pelican, kangaroo, etc.

Some of the big companies offering international courier services are **United Parcel Service**, *Tel. (03)3639-5441;* **Federal Express**, *Tel. toll free 0120-003-200;* and **DHL**, *Tel. (03)5479-2580.* The post office's international express mail is called **EMS**; it's less expensive than the courier services but does not guarantee a delivery date.

ELECTRICITY

Japan's electricity is 100 volts. Eastern Japan is 50 cycles while western Japan is 60. In the late 19th century, Germans engineered the western electrical system while Americans designed the eastern; the result is this schizophrenic system.

Since 100 volts is so close to America's 120, appliances run without converters although they run more slowly. American plugs (two vertical prongs) are standard in Japan. Electric clocks and other very sensitive machinery go out of kilter because they run more slowly, but there's no problem with computers and most electronic equipment. American hair dryers work but run slightly slower.

You'll need plug adapters as well as converters for any 220 volt appliances. Top hotels will provide them upon request.

EMBASSIES
- **Australia**: *2-1-14 Mita, Minato-ku, Tokyo. Tel. (03)5232-4111*
- **Canada**: *7-3-38 Akasaka, Minato-ku, Tokyo. Tel. (03)3408-2101*
- **New Zealand**: *20-40 Kamiyama-cho, Shibuya-ku, Tokyo. Tel. (03)3467-2271*
- **United Kingdom**: *1 Ichibancho, Chiyoda-ku, Tokyo. Tel. (03)3265-6340*
- **United States**: *1-10-15 Akasaka, Minato-ku, Tokyo. Tel. (03)3224-5000*

EMERGENCY TELEPHONE NUMBERS

To report a fire or call an ambulance, dial 119. Large cities have English-speaking personnel. Remember to speak slowly. On a pay phone, press the red button and dial 119. No money is needed. Ambulance is *kyukyu sha;* fire is *kaji.*

To call the Police, dial 110; use these three digits anywhere in Japan. On a pay phone, press the red button and then dial 110. No money is needed.
- **Japan Helpline**: *24-hour assistance with any matter. Toll free: 0120-461-997.*
- **Tokyo English Lifeline (TELL)**: *Tel. (03)3264-4347. 9am to 4pm; 7pm to 11pm. If you are having a personal crisis.*

ENGLISH LANGUAGE PUBLICATIONS

Japan has four English-language newspapers. None rivals *The New York Times*, but there is a lot of emphasis on international news using wire service stories. The *Japan Times* has the largest circulation and is the only one of the four that is not published by a vernacular Japanese newspaper.

The *Japan Times, Mainichi Daily News* and *Daily Yomiuri* are morning papers while the *Asahi Evening News* comes out in the afternoon.

The *Nikkei Weekly*, the English edition of the *Nikkei Shimbun*, Japan's *Wall Street Journal*, gives a good summary of business news and trends.

The *International Herald Tribune* and *Asian Wall Street Journal* are widely available at hotel shops.

International editions of *Time, Newsweek, Business Week, Fortune*, and other publications are available at hotel shops and bookstores with English-language sections.

MEDICAL FACILITIES

Japan's national health insurance system does not cover visitors. Make sure your insurance covers you in Japan. If it doesn't, take out an overseas travel policy in your own country.

In an emergency, ask hotel personnel to phone for a doctor or an ambulance. If you are not at your hotel, dial 119 for an ambulance (*kyukyu sha*). The operator will ask your address. Remember to speak slowly. The ambulance staff provides little assistance other than transportation. They are not paramedics and may have only oxygen. The ambulance will take you to the closest hospital that has space and can treat you for your ailment. They do their best to take foreigners to an international hospital.

Emergency rooms in Japanese hospitals do not run the same way as in American hospitals. If there isn't a bed, you may not be accepted. It's best to have a doctor make arrangements or the ambulance will find you a hospital. In a medical emergency, the **Japan Helpline** can assist you by finding the closest English-speaking doctor or hospital. Call toll free, 24 hours a day, *Tel. 0120-461-997*.

Most doctors work on a clinic system: you go in and wait your turn. Japanese doctors tend to prescribe a lot of drugs and are their own pharmacists. They also tend to give you only enough medication for a few days so you have to come back. (National health reimburses doctors by the number of visits, therefore they try to stretch them out.) Japanese doctors tend to give their patients little information about their conditions; there's a feeling that it's a "burden" on a patient. If this information is not volunteered, you may need to ask a lot of questions, especially about what kind of medication or treatment you are given. Doctors in international clinics and hospitals work in a more international style.

In Tokyo the largest international clinic is **Tokyo Medical and Surgical Clinic**, *Mori #32 Building, 3-4-30 Shiba Koen, Minato-ku, Tokyo. (Across from Tokyo Tower). Tel. (03)3436-3028. Hours are 9am to 5pm Monday through Friday and 9am to 12 noon Saturday.* A doctor is on call 24 hours.

St. Luke's International Hospital, located in the Tsukiji area of Tokyo, has a long history of experience with international patients. Its

Japanese name is Sei Roka Byoin. *9-1 Akashi-cho, Chuo-ku, Tokyo. Tel. (03)3541-5151.*

Oriental Medicine is popular in Japan. Based on Chinese medical theories, acupuncture, moxibustion and acupressure *(shiatsu)* are used to treat various conditions. If you would like to try it, **Edward Acupuncture Clinic** in Tokyo is run by a Japan-trained British doctor, Edward Obaidley. *Coop Sangenjaya 301, 2-17-12 Sangenjaya, Setagaya-ku. Tel. (03)3418-8989.*

MONEY & BANKING

The dollar-yen exchange rate fluctuates daily. In the last several years, **the rate for US dollars has varied between ¥110 and ¥145.** Check the business page of your newspaper for current rates.

Japanese currency is called **yen** (¥). Coins come in denominations of 1, 5, 10, 50, 100 and 500 yen. The one-yen coin is small, lightweight and silver colored; it feels about as insignificant as it is. The 5-yen coin is copper colored with a hole in the center. It's unique as it's the one coin that has its denomination written only in Japanese. The 10-yen coin is copper colored and is slightly larger than the 5. The 50-yen coin is silver with a center hole. The 100-yen coin is silver, slightly larger than the 50-yen piece and has no hole. The 500-yen coin, incidentally the most valuable coin in general circulation in the world, can really weigh you down. These large silver-colored coins are as substantial as they are valuable.

Bank notes come in ¥1000, ¥5000 and ¥10,000 varieties and are all clearly marked.

Don't underestimate your cash needs. Japan is an expensive country and money goes quickly. It's also a cash-based country. Credit cards are accepted at more and more places in cities but not in rural areas. You'll be fine using credit cards if you stick to large hotels, the larger Japanese inns, and some of the more expensive restaurants, but you don't want to be held hostage by your credit card. Sometimes we find a place that says it accepts Visa or MasterCard but will only honor cards issued by Japanese financial institutions.

Foreign currency is not accepted. You can purchase yen-denominated traveler's checks overseas, but we don't think it's worth the effort; most establishments won't accept them so you have to cash them at banks or hotels anyway. US-dollar traveler's checks are the most convenient. Members of the American Automobile Association can buy traveler's checks without charge, and even if you pay a 1% fee, it's offset by the more favorable exchange rate.

WHO ARE THESE GUYS ON THE MONEY?

When you pull out the bills in your pocket, don't expect to find Emperor Akihito. Who are these guys adorning your paper money? Japan is one of the few countries that doesn't put portraits of the emperor or politicians on its notes.

Natsume Soseki (1869-1916) graces the ¥1000 note. Japanese consider him one of the greatest writers of the modern era and his books, "Botchan" and "I am a Cat," are translated into English.

Nitobe Inazo (1862-1933) embellishes the ¥5000 note. He was one of Japan's most international statesmen. In late 19th century Nitobe studied in the US and in Germany. He married an American woman, wrote "Bushido (The Way of the Samurai)," served as the first president of Tokyo Women's Christian College, a prestigious women's college, and was Assistant General Secretary of the League of Nations.

Fukuzawa Yukichi (1835-1901) is pictured on ¥10,000 note. Fukuzawa went to the US on the first ship to cross the Pacific in 1860 after the long period of isolation. He is best known as the founder of Tokyo's Keio University, the oldest private university in Japan. Fukuzawa strongly advocated equality between social classes and between the sexes.

Changing Money

Money can be changed at the airport after you clear customs formalities at international arrivals. The exchange counters stay open until the last flight arrives. Most banks exchange money during operating hours from 9am to 3pm, Monday through Friday (a few small ones may not have facilities). Banks close on holidays. You can exchange cash or traveler's checks for Japanese currency, but you must show your passport.

Some travelers buy foreign currency in their home countries before going abroad. The exchange rate isn't usually that good and money exchange is fairly painless at Japanese airports. If you want to buy some yen for your peace of mind, purchase just enough for the first few days.

At the bank or money exchange counter, you'll notice several different rates posted. Some are for buying yen, others for selling. Remember, if you are changing dollars, you look under the buying column, because you are buying yen. Traveler's checks have a more favorable rate of exchange than cash, usually about one yen difference. This difference often compensates for the 1% fee you may have paid for traveler's checks.

The myth of Japanese efficiency evaporates at the foreign exchange counter of a bank. After you fill in the form and hand over your funds, the transaction goes through about a half-dozen hands as everyone checks to make sure no mistakes have been made. The entire procedure often takes 10 or 15 minutes or even longer. Airport counters are much more efficient.

Hotels and department stores also exchange money although the rate is not as favorable as a bank offers.

Citibank is our bank of choice for exchanging money. The staff speaks English; the rate is good, and business is conducted efficiently. Naturally, the branch network is not as extensive as Japanese banks, but there are several branches in Tokyo as well as in Yokohama, Osaka and Kobe. Some branches are open Saturday from 10am to 2pm. Call their toll free, 24-hour information line: *Tel. 0120-50-4189*. Citibank's ATMs are open 24 hours and accept Plus and Cirrus system cards.

Cash, ATM, & Credit Cards

Japanese carry a lot of cash. In Japan, with crime low, theft isn't a major concern, but being careful goes without saying. Even if you use credit cards for most of your hotels and meals, you'll need cash for transportation, lunches and small purchases. Personal checks are not widely used.

If you need cash:

Get cash from an ATM either as an advance against a credit card (you must have a PIN number) or directly from your bank account with an ATM card. This process looks easy since ATM machines are everywhere. But ATMs run by Japanese banks do not accept foreign credit cards. You have to use an ATM run by a nonbank finance company that accepts foreign credit cards. But beware, your bank or company may have a limit as low as $250, which isn't a lot of yen.

Citibank, DC and Mullion ATMs will accept international Visa and MasterCard that are Plus System or Cirrus. JCB ATMs will accept Plus System bank cards. UC ATMs accept Cirrus MasterCards. To take out the guesswork, call your credit card company (they all have English speaking personnel) for the closest machine or office:
- **Visa**: *(toll free) Tel. 0120-133-173*. Visa card holders can also get cash advances at branches of Sumitomo Bank.
- **MasterCard**: *Tel. (03)5350-8051*
- **American Express**: *(toll free) Tel. 0120-376-199*
- **Citibank**: *(toll free) Tel. 0120-50-4189*

American Express offers a check cashing service for its card holders at its Hibiya office in Tokyo, *Tel. (03)3214-0280*.

NATIONAL HOLIDAYS

Banks, post offices, schools, government and private offices are all closed on national holidays. Stores are generally open although mom and pop shops will probably close. Museums and restaurants are usually open. If a holiday falls on a Monday, many museums, which are ordinarily closed, will open and take the following day as a holiday. When a holiday falls on a Sunday, Monday is a holiday.

Japanese travel on holidays so train, air and hotel reservations need to be made well in advance, especially if the holiday forms a long weekend. The peak travel times are around the New Year (December 27 through January 4), Golden Week (April 29 through May 5) and August 13-16.

Holidays include:

• January 1	New Year's Day (banks and post offices usually close until Jan. 4)
• January 15	Coming of Age Day
• February 11	National Foundation Day
• March 20 or 21	Vernal Equinox Day
• April 29	Greenery Day
• May 3	Constitution Day
• May 4	Additional holiday between two holidays
• May 5	Children's Day
• July 20	Marine Day
• September 15	Respect for the Aged Day
• Sept. 23 or 24	Autumnal Equinox Day
• October 10	Health Sports Day
• November 3	Culture Day
• November 23	Labor Thanksgiving Day
• December 23	Emperor's Birthday

NATURAL DISASTERS

Earthquakes

Japan has some of the shakiest real estate on earth. Most of the quakes are too small to be felt, and a "big one" comes along only every 80 years or so. Japan has some of the strongest building codes in the world. If you do experience an earthquake, here are a few basic precautions:

• Stay inside. Unless you are in a rural area, it is safer to be indoors than outside where falling glass and debris can injure.

• If you are in an apartment or house, turn off the gas on the stove.

• Open a door or window so you have an escape route should the shifting building jam an exit.

• Get under a table or desk. If you don't have one, stand under the doorway.

• If you are on the street, stay away from any high walls; take cover in the nearest building.

• Elevators are equipped with seismic detectors and will stop at the nearest floor. Do not stay in the elevator.

• Every neighborhood has a designated evacuation point, usually a park or school. Do not evacuate unless the building is unstable or threatened by fire.

• In an emergency, NHK radio and television and FEN radio (US military radio, 810 AM) will broadcast reports in English.

Tidal Waves

Tsunami, or tidal waves, can strike the coast after an earthquake. Low-lying areas have warning sirens. If you are on the seacoast and feel an earthquake or hear the sirens, immediately head for higher land.

Typhoons

Typhoons are generally more an annoyance than anything else. During the August-to-October season, Japan may experience a half-dozen typhoons, but they are fairly localized. A typhoon that hits Kyushu usually does not have any effect on Tokyo. They are not as strong as the ones that hit the more tropical countries and usually bring only heavy rain and wind, sometimes causing landslides in mountainous areas.

Typhoons do create uncomfortable sightseeing, and the heavy rains can cause air, train and bus delays. Usually a typhoon will blow over within a day.

PERSONAL SAFETY

Japan is one of the safest countries in the world. There's very little violent crime (in 1996 only 17 people were killed by firearms — sounds like a bad weekend in New York). Don't let this low crime rate fool you. That suitcase you leave alone at a train station will probably be there when you return in five minutes, but then again, what if it isn't? Petty crimes such as pick-pocketing and purse-snatching occur, so keep your eyes open and be careful.

People love to tell amazing stories of how taxi drivers tracked them down to return forgotten items. We don't want to pooh-pooh them because it does happens, but you can't count on it. Patrice left a camera (with her name and address on it) in a taxi and never saw it again. We know a foreign resident who was upset because the camera he left in the lobby of his own apartment building was gone when he returned 30 minutes later. "I thought it would be safe; this is Japan," he said. Don't take any chances.

In most places, it's safe for a woman to walk alone at night although we avoid some of the sleazier entertainment districts. Taking trains and buses alone are no problem.

YOUR LOCAL NEIGHBORHOOD POLICE BOX

The police in Japan have a system of neighborhood police boxes, called **koban**. *They're staffed by a few policemen who use the box as a center. From it, they ride around the neighborhood on bicycles and get to know the residents and merchants.*

Since Japan has a fairly low crime rate, the police aren't very busy catching criminals. Their main task, at least in urban areas, is to give directions to bewildered souls who can't find their destinations. The police boxes are equipped with excellent maps showing the area building by building; stop in if you ever get lost. The police seldom speak more than a few words of English, but they can point out things on a map.

If you lose your wallet and don't have any money to get to your hotel, the police can lend you the funds. If you lose anything, report it; the police will do their best to track it down.

POST OFFICES

Post offices are distinguished by a red symbol that resembles a T with an extra horizontal line on top. Post offices offer both postal and banking services, so there are two sets of counters. In urban post offices, the postage counter is usually marked in English. If it isn't, the staff will direct you to the right place.

Post offices are open 9am to 5pm, Monday through Friday. Major post offices in large cities will also have Saturday and sometimes Sunday hours, and the biggest will have a 24-hour counter.

Sending a letter under 25 grams within Japan costs ¥80; ¥90 for up to 50 grams. If it's over 12 x 23.5 cm (slightly smaller than an American business envelope), the cost is ¥120 for up to 50 grams. Postcards sent within Japan cost ¥50.

Postcards sent by airmail anywhere in the world cost ¥70 and aerograms are ¥90. Letters sent within Asia cost ¥90 for the first 25 grams and ¥50 for each additional 25 grams. Letters to North America, Europe, Middle East and Oceania cost ¥110 for the first 25 grams and ¥80 for each additional 25. Mail to Africa and South America costs ¥130 for the first 25 grams and ¥100 for each additional 25.

The post office staff automatically shows you the cost on a calculator, so communication is rarely a problem.

The post office has an international express service called **EMS**. It is less expensive than using international delivery services such as Federal Express and DHL although it may not be quite as fast.

Inexpensive boxes are sold at post offices. You can mail boxes overseas if they weigh under 20 kilos (44 lb.).

Japan recently implemented a seven digit postal code, three digits followed by a dash and four more digits.

Convenience and other stores displaying the postal T sign sell stamps as do larger hotels. Postal boxes, usually red, are in front of post offices and at many other locations on the sidewalk. You cannot mail a letter by putting it in a residential mailbox; they are for delivery only.

Stamp collectors should ask for commemorative stamps, *kinen kitte*. The Tokyo Central Post Office at Tokyo Station has a large philatelic section.

ESSENTIAL POSTAL VOCABULARY

kitte	*stamp*
kookuu fusho	*aerogram*
hagaki	*postcard*
kookuu bin	*air mail*
funa bin	*sea or surface mail*
futoo	*envelope*
hako	*box*

SMOKING

Depending on your perspective, Japan is either a smoker's paradise or a nonsmoker's hell. As the only developed country where the number of smokers is increasing, Japan is a tobacco company's dream come true. More than 50% of Japanese men smoke, and women in their twenties are the fastest growing segment of the market. Popular American brands are readily available; cigarettes cost about ¥250 a pack, and vending machines are on nearly every street corner.

If you arrive armed with nonsmoker's rights, you will have to make some adjustments. Don't expect Japanese to be apologetic or polite about their smoking — people feel free to light up almost everywhere. Some taxis are so smoke filled that you can't see through the windows, and the driver keeps on puffing. On the plus side, cigars and pipe smoking are a rarity.

Nonsmoking sections are unavailable in most restaurants, and those that have them tend to be in hotels or Western-style places. You can ask for nonsmoking (both "nonsmoking" and *kin'en seki* are used), but most traditional Japanese restaurants simply aren't familiar with the concept. If cigarette smoke really bothers you, avoid bars and *izakaya* drinking establishments where the air is often blue with smoke.

Smoking is prohibited on commuter trains and subways although train platforms may have designated smoking areas. Long distance trains have cars designated smoking and nonsmoking in both reserved and unreserved cars. If smoke bothers you, be sure you request "*kin'en seki*" when you make your seat reservation. Just walking through some smoking cars on *shinkansen* trains makes us wish we had our aqua lungs.

Occasionally, in fairly remote areas, a limited express train may consist of three cars only: one reserved for smoking and two unreserved, one for smoking and one for nonsmoking. In this situation, we usually make reservations in the smoking car but check for available seats in the nonsmoking, unreserved car. If there aren't any seats in the smokefree atmosphere, our logic is that a smoky seat is better than no seat at all.

TAXES

Japan has a 5% consumption tax added to the price of all goods and services. On some things such as taxi fares and newspapers, the tax is included in the price. But on most items, the tax is added at the cash register. We are forever walking around with pockets full of change; nothing ever costs an even amount.

If your meal in a restaurant costs over ¥7500 per person, an additional tax of 3% is added. And if your accommodations are over ¥15,000 per person per night, there's an additional 3% local tax.

TELEPHONES

You are never far from a telephone in Japan. Public phones are everywhere: in restaurants, hotel lobbies, coffee shops, on the street, in the subway station and on *shinkansen* trains. Some are simple, oversized dial phones that accept only ¥10 coins; others are state-of-the-art public phones with ISDN lines and digital displays.

Calling Japan from Overseas

Japan's country code is **81**, which means when calling Japan from overseas you must dial 81 before the area code. Then you must drop the first (0) of the area code. When we give you phone numbers, the area codes is in parentheses. Area codes are a series of numbers ranging from 2 digits to 6, but they all begin with 0. So if a Tokyo number is listed as (03)1234-5678, from overseas you dial your country's international access number, then 81, then 3: the (03) area code with the initial 0 dropped, then the number 1234-5678. The most frequent mistake is people forget to drop the 0 of the area code.

Calling Within Japan

Long distance within Japan: When you call long distance within Japan, you must use the complete area code. Long distance may not be as far as you think. Even if you're calling the next town, if its area code is different, you must dial it. If you are calling Tokyo from Narita Airport or Osaka from Kansai International Airport, you must dial the area code.

Local calls in Japan: Dialing local calls, omit the area code and dial the number. Local numbers are not standard; they can have anywhere from 5 to 8 digits.

Toll free is called Free Dial. These numbers usually begin with 0120 or 0088. To call from a pay phone, insert ¥10 to make the call; it will be returned.

Old Tokyo numbers. Several year ago, all Tokyo numbers within the (03) area code went to 8 digits. If you have an old number that only has 7 digits, add a 3 between the area code and the number.

Using Pay Phones

Some public telephones accept only coins, others only telephone cards and others take both. A local call costs ¥10 for 90 seconds and will disconnect if you don't deposit more money. You can put in ¥10 and ¥100 coins; unused coins are returned, but the machine doesn't give change. If you insert a ¥100 coin and only talk ¥20 worth, you will not get a refund.

Telephone cards are convenient because you don't have to worry about having change. Cards come in denominations of ¥500 and ¥1000 and are sold nearly everywhere: at hotels, convenience stores, subway kiosks, vending machines, etc. Insert the card, dial the number and the cost of the call is deducted. Cards have message units worth ¥10 each; units are displayed in a window on the phone. If you finish one card, insert another without interrupting your call. Telephone cards are especially convenient for long distance calls as the units click by at a quick pace.

Calling Overseas from Japan

International telephone calls from Japan are expensive. Hotels are notorious for jacking up charges for international calls, so it's usually in your interest to bypass the hotel switchboard whenever you can.

One way is to use the Home Country Direct systems. You dial an access number and then either dial the telephone number or talk to your home country operator. Americans can use AT&T, MCI and Sprint calling cards.

Access numbers:
- **AT&T**: *Tel. 0039-111*
- **MCI**: *Tel. 0039-121*
- **Sprint**: *Tel. 0039-131*

For other home country direct access codes, dial 0051.

Telephone booths marked international will allow you to make overseas calls using telephone cards. Seven-Eleven and other convenience stores sell international telephone cards that can be used at any telephone booth (one is called the "Love Home Card").

KDD is the largest international operator. You can reach their bilingual operators at 0051.

TIME DIFFERENCE

The entire country of Japan is within one time zone, 9 hours ahead of Greenwich Mean Time, and 14 hours ahead of New York (Eastern Standard Time). Japan doesn't use daylight saving time; subtract one hour when figuring the time difference from a country that does have daylight saving time.

TIPPING

Tipping has never caught on in Japan and we hope it never does. We save so much brainpower by not having to figure out correct percentages. You do not tip waiters, taxi drivers, hairdressers, bell boys, bathroom attendants — no one (there's one exception, so keep on reading). We have offered tips for exceptional service only to have them refused. If you leave money on a restaurant table, it's likely the staff will chase after you to give it back, presuming you forgot it.

Large hotels and restaurants will add a 10% service charge to your bill, but most eateries do not.

The one exception is that some people tip when they stay at an expensive Japanese inn, giving ¥1000 or ¥2000 to the room attendant. They tip either after the attendant has poured tea and given an introduction to the inn or in the morning after breakfast. The money can't just be handed over openly, it's considered too crass. It's put in a small envelope and presented surreptitiously.

A highly unofficial survey of our friends found about half tip at Japanese inns. Our recommendation is not to tip unless you want something special such as laundry washed. (In high-class inns, the staff will wash your clothes without an additional charge).

TOILETS

You'll come across two types of toilets in Japan, traditional squat types and Western toilets. To use the squat type, face the hooded side of the toilet and give your leg muscles a good workout. Make sure your clothing doesn't touch the ground.

There are a lot of public bathrooms. Those in department stores, hotels, fast-food shops and restaurants are usually well maintained, but facilities in public parks and subways leave something to be desired; they are not unsafe, just smelly. Toilet paper is usually provided, but paper hand towels are not, so make sure you have tissues or a handkerchief.

Most often, signs for appropriate toilets are indicated by female and male figures. If not, you can ask "*onna?*" for women and "*otoko?*" for men. To ask where the toilet is, say "*toi-re*" or "*o-te-arai*" with a rising intonation.

Toilet seats have gone high tech. In department stores you may encounter a toilet seat that has a control panel resembling a 747's. In reality, it's a built-in electronic bidet with buttons controlling water temperature, strength and aim of stream and air dryer. Actually, it's best to ignore the whole thing and look for the flusher on the tank of the toilet. If you can't find a flusher at the usual place, look around. Sometimes it's on the floor or wall. It may even be activated by an electric eye.

WHEN HIGH TECH MEETS TOILETS IN JAPAN

We were at a party when an American woman came out of the bathroom laughing hysterically. A broad wet stripe was splashed across her dress and face. She had turned around to flush the toilet and hit the bidet button instead giving herself an instant shower.

A British friend lives in an apartment with a state-of-the-art bathroom. Everything has a button, even one to raise and lower the toilet seat. Noriko tried unsuccessfully to lower it manually. "Why can't I move it by hand?" she asked. "Japanese don't want to contaminate themselves by touching toilet seat germs, even in a private residence," was the reply. The door to this same bathroom opens and closes by remote control buttons.

The latest toilets will actually analyze your urine. What's next? Pregnancy tests?

Sometimes small restaurants have only unisex bathrooms. Walking through to the toilet stall, there may be a urinal in the sink area. A woman is supposed to just walk past a man using it as if he isn't there. Often in park facilities, the urinals are visible to people outside.

Recently built rest rooms have wheelchair access stalls.

For some inexplicable reason, certain segments of the Japanese male population, including taxi drivers and those under the influence of alcohol, think the closest wall is their urinal. There's nothing you can do except ignore it.

Many young Japanese women have decided that they do not want anyone to hear their sounds of elimination and flush the toilet to mask the noise. To counter this waste of water, some buildings have installed buttons which when pressed, sound like flushing water. Only in Japan...

TOURIST OFFICES

The Japan National Tourist Office runs **Tourist Information Centers** specially for foreigners at Narita and Kansai International Airports and in Tokyo and Kyoto. Stop by for brochures, maps, travel advice and general information. The Tokyo and Kyoto offices have Welcome Inn Reservation Centers that will book rooms at reasonably priced hotels and inns.

Tokyo

Tokyo International Forum, B1F, 3-5-1 Marunouchi, Chiyoda-ku, Tokyo, 100. Tel. (03)3201-3331. Open 9am to 5pm, Monday through Friday; 9am to 12 noon Saturday. Closed Sunday and holidays.

Narita Airport

Terminal 2, 1st floor. Tel. (0476)34-6251. Open daily 9am to 8pm.

Japan National Tourist Organization Web Site

The JNTO web site address is *http://www.jnto.go.jp*. Extensive information on traveling in Japan and good links.

Prefecture Information

Tokyo has tourist and promotion offices for most prefectures where you can pick up brochures and even buy some local products, but don't expect to find an English-speaking staff. The offices are concentrated in two places near Tokyo Station: the top floors of the Daimaru Department Store at the station's Yaesu exit and at the Kokusai Kanko Kaikan, to the left of the Yaesu exit. Most are open 9am to 5pm, Monday through Friday.

Japan Travel Phone

For travel information and language assistance call the Japan Travel Phone daily between 9am and 5pm. Outside Tokyo and Kyoto, call toll free: *Tel. 0088-22-4800 or 0120-44-4800*. Within Tokyo, call *Tel. (03)3201-3331*. Within Kyoto, the number is *Tel. (075)371-5649*. The Tokyo and Kyoto numbers are not available Saturday afternoon and Sunday.

Local Tourist Bureaus

If you travel outside of Tokyo, you'll see that almost every town or city which gets tourists will have a travel information center at the train station. You can usually get an English map and some basic information and have an agent book a hotel or inn for you. You'll need to give your price range. Larger cities will have English speaking staff, but in smaller places, you'll have to communicate at some basic level. Tourist offices are called *kanko annai-sho.*

WATER

Yes, you can drink the water. You may not like the chloride taste of city water, but it's potable. If you prefer, you can find both imported and domestic mineral water in supermarkets and convenience stores. For a while it was chic to hang around with a bottle of Volvic water, but that fad seems to have passed.

WEIGHTS & MEASURES

Japan is on the metric system. Below are some useful tables for you:

Weight

1 gram	0.035 ounces
1 kilogram	35.27 ounces
	2.2 lb.
1 ounce	28 grams
1 pound	454 grams
	0.454 kilograms

Kilograms to pounds: multiply kilograms by 2.2
Pounds to kilograms: multiply pounds by 0.45

Length

1 centimeter	0.39 inch
1 meter	39 inches
1 kilometer	0.62 miles
1 inch	2.5 centimeters
1 foot	30 centimeters
	0.3 meters
1 mile	1.6 kilometers

Kilometers to miles: multiply kilometers by 0.62
Miles to kilometers: multiply miles by 1.61

Volume

1 liter	1.06 quarts
	0.26 US gallon
1 gallon	3.78 liters

Liters to US gallon: multiply liters by 0.26
US Gallon to liters: multiply gallons by 3.78

Temperature

0°C	32°F
20°C	68°F
100°C	212°F

An easy way to convert roughly from **Celsius to Fahrenheit** is to double the Celsius temperature and add 30. For example: 20°C x 2 + 30 = 70°F. For an exact amount, take 9/5 of the Celsius temperature and add 32.

Fahrenheit to Celsius: subtract 32 from Fahrenheit temperature, multiply by 5 and divide by 9.

9. FOOD & DRINK

THE BASICS

The Japanese love to eat out. The country has literally hundreds of thousands of restaurants from hole-in-the-wall places to elegant tea houses, boisterous beer halls, exclusive bars and much, much more. Prices vary from a few hundred yen for noodles at a stand-up counter to ¥40,000 or ¥50,000 for rarefied *kaiseki*. Restaurants are more than eateries; people go to bond with their colleagues, to relieve the stress of corporate life, to date, and to cement relationships and business deals.

Japanese food is more than raw fish and rice. Noodles in soup or plain; grilled, boiled and stewed meat and fish; deep fried vegetables and fish; curry rice; fried pork cutlets — all are now Japanese. When you add readily available Western food from spaghetti to hamburgers, Southeast Asian and other ethnic food, the culinary choices are nearly limitless.

To entice you out of your hotel, we've compiled lists of the major types of restaurants and the most common menu items to help you decide where and what to eat. As a non-Japanese-speaking visitor, it's really easy to eat only in hotel restaurants, but on the whole, most are overpriced and geared to visitors on expense accounts. Aren't you here to explore Japan? Be adventuresome and eat where Japanese eat. It's a great way to get a glimpse of everyday life and sample all kinds of different food.

Right away, you'll notice plastic food models that are outside many restaurants to tempt prospective diners. These miniature works of art are useful for ordering; beckon to a staff member to accompany you and point to your choice. You might have to swallow your pride, but you'll get the meal you think you want.

If you are counting pennies, and even if you aren't, lunch nearly always costs less than dinner. Restaurants have lunch specials often for a fraction of the nighttime cost. It's a great way to try an expensive restaurant and stretch your travel dollars.

Restaurants often have set fixed meals, *setto* and *teishoku*, and course meals, *kosu*. With set meals or *teishoku*, the entire meal usually comes at the same time, often on a tray. A *teishoku* will usually have the main course plus rice, soup and pickles. A course is similar to a set, but food is served one course after the other. A meal served in courses will always finish with rice, pickles and soup.

Japanese food is traditionally served in individual dishes. We'd hate to be dishwashers since even the simplest meal can generate at least a half-dozen dishes.

Your hotel may advertise a Viking breakfast. Don't be alarmed; Erik the Red is not joining you. Viking simply indicates the meal is a buffet; the term is used to describe any buffet meal — breakfast, lunch and dinner.

We divided restaurants into four categories:
- **Inexpensive**, *Under ¥3000*
- **Moderate**, *¥3000 to ¥6000*
- **Expensive**, *¥6000 to ¥12,000*
- **Very Expensive**, *Over ¥12,000*

RESTAURANT ETIQUETTE

When you walk into a restaurant, a staff member will greet you, *"Irrashaimase"* (welcome). You don't need to answer, just smile. You may be asked how many are in your party: *"Nanme sama...?"* Holding up the correct number of fingers is appropriate. If you are shown to a seat on a *tatami* mat, be sure you remove your shoes before stepping on the straw mat. If you are allergic to smoke, ask for no smoking, *kin'en seki;* no smoking sections are new to Japan and limited almost exclusively to hotel and Western restaurants, but there's no harm in asking.

Japanese have a wonderful custom of providing wet towels, *oshibori*, that are usually hot, but sometimes are chilled in summer. Use the towel to wipe your hands. In most restaurants you keep it for your napkin. If the *oshibori* is taken away, use a handkerchief or tissue instead. Using napkins is not a Japanese custom, which means they aren't usually provided; when you find them, they can be small, waxy and pretty useless.

Japanese eat Japanese food with chopsticks so give it your best try. If you are absolutely unable to get food to your mouth, ask for a fork. Most restaurants have them. When you are not using your chopsticks, lean them on the chopstick rest or put them across your plate. Never leave them sticking out of food. It reminds Japanese of the bowls of rice offered to the deceased at their graves.

It's impolite to use your own chopsticks to pick up food from a communal dish unless you have turned them end-for-end and use the clean part. The exception is with *nabe* stew pots. Never pass food from one set of chopsticks to another. It reminds Japanese of funerals where cremated bones are removed by family members.

The Japanese like to use appropriate tableware. Japanese food is eaten with chopsticks; Western food with a knife and fork; curry rice with a spoon and fork; and *ramen* noodles with a Chinese ceramic spoon. Fingers are okay for *sushi* at a *sushi* bar, but at a table, use chopsticks. Use chopsticks to eat Japanese noodles (*soba* and *udon*) and drink the broth straight from the bowl. Mom may have scolded you for doing it at home, but here it's the custom. Also, remember it's okay to slurp your noodles — sorry, Mom. Notice the Japanese at the next table; obviously, at least among men, slurping is perfectly acceptable. It's supposed to enhance the flavor.

Most of the time, you pay after your meal. But, at cheap stand-up noodle shops, museum canteens and other public places, you may have to buy a ticket for your food up front. Sometimes tickets are sold by vending machines and other times at the cash register.

Japanese don't usually mix food and money. You'll almost never be asked to pay at the table. (The exceptions are the Parisian cafes and some trendy California-Asian restaurants.) Money is handled at the cash register near the exit. If your bill is presented to your table after you're served, take it to the cash register to pay. If it is not presented to your table, don't worry, it will appear magically when you get to the cash register. At the register you'll usually find a small tray, put your money in this tray, rather than handing it directly to the cashier. Your change will be returned on the same tray. Of course, at fast food shops, pay at the counter when served. In cities more and more restaurants accept credit cards, but small noodle shops and mom and pop places do not.

Best of all, there's never any tipping — ever. Hotels and some upscale restaurants will add a service charge. You will have to pay the 5% consumption tax and, if the bill is over ¥7500 per person, a 3% local tax will be added. What a relief not to worry about how much to tip.

Japanese do not eat food on the street, and it's considered in bad form to do so. No one will reprimand you for an occasional ice cream cone, but you'll notice most Japanese hang around the ice cream parlor until they finish.

ALCOHOLIC DRINKS

Japanese usually drink beer or *sake* with their meals. When they go out with colleagues after work, drinking is usually more important than eating. Restaurants serving traditional Japanese food will have beer, *sake*, whiskey and perhaps *shochu* (a sweet potato liquor) on hand. For other alcoholic beverages, you have to go to a bar.

When you go out for drinks, try following the Japanese custom of pouring drinks for your companions and they, in turn, will pour yours. It's considered gauche to pour your own drink, so hold your glass while it is being filled, and when everyone has a full glass, toast with a rousing *"Kampai!"*

ESSENTIAL FOOD & DRINK VOCABULARY

Here are a few words you might need in a restaurant:

Oyu	*hot water*
Omizu	*cold water*
Ocha	*Japanese tea*
Fooku	*fork*
Supuun	*spoon*
Naifu	*knife*
Ohashi	*chopsticks*
Osara	*plate*
Chawan	*rice bowl*
Gohan	*rice*
Choshoku	*breakfast*
Chushoku	*lunch*
Yushoku	*dinner*
Okanjo	*bill, check*
Biru	*beer*
O bin	*large bottle of beer*
Chu bin	*smaller bottle of beer*
Nama biru	*draft beer (sometimes served in bottles)*
Durafuto biru	*draft beer, always from a keg*
Sake	*Japanese rice wine*
Atsukan	*hot sake*
Hiya	*chilled sake*
Mizu wari	*whiskey and water*
Shochu	*spirits usually made from sweet potato*
Oyu wari	*shochu with hot water*
Ume sawa	*shochu with soda and a plum*
Uron tii (uron cha)	*oolong tea (popular with people who don't want alcohol)*
Koka kora	*Coke*

If you say "Oishikatta" (it was delicious) and "Gochiso sama" (thank you for the meal) as you finish paying the bill, the Japanese will be impressed with your language ability.

SAKE - THE DRINK OF THE GODS

Sake, rice wine, was first brewed more than a thousand years ago as an offering to the gods. Signifying purity, even today small cups of sake are placed on Shinto altars in homes and shrines. When you go to a Shinto shrine, look for casks of sake piled at the entrance. People donate sake to the shrine as a way of requesting the good graces of the gods. Sake is used to toast weddings, births, and just about any celebration. Remember the word **Kampai**, *literally "bottom's up," you can use it to toast any occasion.*

You can drink sake warm or cold. When served chilled, it is often poured into a small square wooden box where there's a little salt in one corner. The texture of the wood gives the sake a real earthy taste. When served warm, sake is poured into tiny ceramic cups that are good for just one or two sips.

Sake is made from rice that is polished to remove all the outer layers. Good quality water and rice are essential for the production of superior sake. That's why Fushimi in Kyoto and Nada in Kobe are famous for their sake. Most rice wine is still produced by local breweries, just like wineries in the European countryside

You can enjoy drinking sake at any time, not only with food. Traditionally, Japanese drink sake when admiring cherry blossoms and autumn foliage, when moon viewing and snow viewing, and merely for sake's sake.

NOODLES - SOBA & UDON

Noodles, along with rice, are a staple of the Japanese diet. It is said that Japanese living overseas often miss their noodles more than anything else.

The history of noodles spans centuries and continents. The noodles Marco Polo brought back to Europe from China have evolved into pasta, a not-so-distant cousin to Japanese *soba* and *udon*. Developed in the kitchens of Zen temples, *soba* appealed to all classes during the Edo period.

Today noodles are available everywhere from cheap stand-up train station shops to rustically decorated restaurants; they're an inexpensive and filling casual meal. Most noodles are machine made today, but some shops still take great pride in making their own noodles by hand. Often a window on the street provides a perfect viewing place for passersby. One afternoon we spent a good half-hour watching the chef kneading *soba* dough and cutting it into thin strips with a huge cleaver. His work-of-art was delicious.

Most noodle shops serve both *soba* and *udon*. *Soba* is a thin, long noodle made of buckwheat flour. Until this century, it was the staple food for people living in mountainous areas where rice couldn't be cultivated. *Udon* is a thicker, white noodle made of wheat flour. *Udon* and *soba* are prepared in similar ways; be sure to tell the restaurant staff which one you want.

Cold noodles are served plain on a straw mat along with a dipping sauce in a cup and a small dish containing leeks and *wasabi* (grated horseradish). Place the leeks and horseradish in the sauce; then put a chopstick's worth of noodles in the sauce and eat them from the cup. When you've finished your noodles, the staff may offer you a pot of milky water in which the noodles were boiled. If you feel adventuresome, pour this water into the dipping-sauce cup and drink it as soup.

Hot noodles are served in a fish-based broth that can include vegetables, seaweed, or meat. If you like spicy food, sprinkle your noodles with *shichimi* (hot red pepper flakes), found on the table and not fiery hot. Eat the noodles with chopsticks and drink the broth directly from the bowl. It's polite to slurp as you eat the noodles, but it's an art we're still striving to perfect. If you down a whole bowl of broth, you'll undoubtedly develop an unquenchable thirst that will last all afternoon. There's no need to drink it all; just take a sip.

Each region prepares broth in a slightly different way. Tokyo's broth is dark and quite salty while Kyoto's is lighter. Regions also have their special noodles: Nagoya prides itself on *kishimen*, a white wheat noodle cut flat, resembling fettuccini.

When you order, specify *soba* or *udon*. If you want an extra large portion, tell the staff *"omori,"* which will cost one or two hundred yen more.

Soba is supposed to be good for your health and helps lower blood pressure. Japanese must eat *soba* on New Year's Eve because the long noodles symbolize longevity and long lasting good luck.

Cold noodles:

Mori soba (udon)	plain cold *soba (udon)* noodles
Zaru soba (udon)	cold *soba (udon)* with dried seaweed sprinkled on top
Tenzaru soba (udon)	cold *soba (udon)* with *tempura* on the side
Hiya mugi	thin white noodles served chilled (only in summer)
Somen	a very thin noodle served in chilled water (only in summer)

Hot noodles:

Kake soba (udon)	soba (udon) in broth with green onions
Sansai soba (udon)	soba (udon) in broth with mountain vegetables
Nameko soba (udon)	soba (udon) in broth with small, slippery mushrooms
Kitsune soba (udon)	soba (udon) in broth with fried thin tofu
Tempura soba (udon)	soba (udon) in broth with a deep fried shrimp
Tororo soba (udon)	soba (udon) in broth with grated mountain potato
Tsukimi soba (udon)	soba (udon) in broth with a raw quail egg
Namban soba (udon)	soba (udon) in broth with duck or chicken
Tanuki soba (udon)	soba (udon) in broth with little fried bits of *tempura* batter
Nabeyaki udon	udon cooked in a ceramic casserole in broth with vegetables, chicken, fried shrimp and fish cake

RAMEN

Ramen, long, thin Chinese-style egg noodles, are served in pork or chicken broth with bean sprouts and a thin slice of pork. *Ramen* shops almost always serve *gyoza,* fragrant Chinese dumplings filled with minced pork, cabbage, ginger and onion. Standard condiments are soy sauce, chili oil, vinegar and white pepper. Concoct your own mixture as a dipping sauce.

Often brightly lit and decorated with Chinese motifs, *ramen* shops provide a place for cheap and fast food and are popular with students. Usually you'll find a counter and a few small tables where you can enjoy your noodles.

The basic *ramen* menu is:

Miso ramen	noodles in fermented bean paste broth
Shoyu ramen	noodles in soy sauce flavored broth
Shio-aji ramen	noodles in salt flavored broth
Gyoza	sautéed pork dumplings, a serving is usually about six dumplings
Yakisoba	sautéed noodles with meat, fish and vegetables

SUSHI

Just say "Japanese food" to most foreigners and they immediately think of *sushi.* Nothing could be more quintessentially Japanese than *sushi* chefs wearing pristine white jackets and *hachimaki,* rolled towels wrapped around the head, solemnly slicing fish behind untarnished wooden counters. *Sushi* has a 400-year history.

Sushi basically refers to anything served with vinegared rice; it doesn't have to be raw fish only. Patrice was in a *sushi* bar when a German tourist sat next to her. This man was a vegetarian but wanted to try *sushi*. It turns out that he could easily fill up on nonfish *sushi*.

Sushi and *sashimi* are both served in *sushi* bars. *Sashimi* is plain slices of raw (and occasionally cooked) fish. (*Sashimi* is also served as a starter as a part of a larger meal in other restaurants.) *Sushi* is fish served on top of a rice patty or rolled in rice and is eaten with thin slices of pink pickled ginger called *gari* and dipped in soy sauce called *murasaki*. (*Sushi* has its own parlance). *Gari* and a cup of piping hot tea are served to refresh your palate so you can appreciate the different flavors.

You can put some horseradish (*wasabi*) in the soy sauce. Some purists prefer to put tiny amounts on the fish instead. Either way is okay. *Sushi* has the horseradish already in the center. If you'd like yours made without horseradish, just say *"sabi nuki"*.

Big hint: Learn from our experience. When dipping your *sushi* in soy sauce, make sure you dip the fish side; if you dip the rice side, the rice patty disintegrates before your eyes.

Sushi comes in two ways, *nigiri* and *chirashi*. *Nigiri* is fish on an individual cake of rice. *Chirashi* is an assortment of fish placed on top of rice in a bowl.

In a *sushi* bar, you can order a la carte just by pointing. Many places offer set menus at lunch, but not too many do in the evening. Set menus usually come in three grades: *nami* or *ume* is regular; *jo* or *take* is special; and *tokujo* or *matsu* is premium. The difference is more in the type of fish rather than quantity. Sometimes the set is only an assortment of *sushi*, other times it includes soup and pickles.

We usually drink beer or *sake* with *sushi* and finish off with tea. We also like to end our feast with a bowl of *miso* soup, *aka dashi*.

One type of inexpensive *sushi* shop is called *kaiten zushi*, revolving *sushi* bar. The guests sit at a circular counter with a conveyor belt running around it. The chefs assemble the *sushi* and put it on the belt. You help yourself to whatever comes around. If you don't see what you want, ask the chef to make it. At the end of the meal, the clerk counts your plates. Different color plates signify different prices, but conveyor belt *sushi* is always cheap, with most dishes going for ¥120 to ¥200. *Sushi* purists turn up their noses, but it's a lot of fun.

You're most likely to find the following items at a *sushi* shop:

Akagai	red clam
Ama-ebi	raw shrimp
Anago	cooked eel with thick sauce
Awabi	abalone (expensive)
Buri	yellowtail, in season in autumn and winter

Ebi	cooked shrimp
Hirame	flounder
Hotate	scallop
Ika	squid
Ikura	salmon roe (expensive)
Katsuo	bonito, in season April through June
Maguro	tuna
Toro	premium cut of tuna, fattier than *maguro*
Chu toro	premium cut of tuna, fattier than *toro*
O toro	most fatty cut of tuna and most expensive
Saba	mackerel
Sake	salmon
Shiromi	white fish, such as flounder and sea bass
Tai	sea bream, in season in spring
Tako	cooked octopus
Uni	sea urchin roe (expensive)
Nori tama	sweet sliced omelet
Maki	generic name for fish or veggies rolled with rice and thin seaweed
Kappa maki	cucumber roll
Tekka maki	tuna *(maguro)* roll
Oshinko maki	pickle roll
Natto maki	fermented soy bean roll
Negi toro maki	leek and fatty tuna roll
Ume shiso maki	pickled plum and beefsteak leaf roll

YAKITORI

Yakitori (literally, grilled chicken) shops are usually casual, neighborhood places where the beer and *sake* flows freely and morsels of chicken and other food are skewered and grilled over a charcoal fire. There are often big red-paper lanterns out front and counters inside where you can sit and watch your food prepared. You may smell a *yakitori-ya* before you see it; the fragrance of grilled charcoal escapes with smoke into the street. Most *yakitori-ya* are open only in the evening. There is a genre of new, upscale *yakitori* restaurants, but most are down home cheap eats. Legend has it a Dutch man in Nagasaki during the Edo period secretly whet the appetite of the Japanese by introducing them to grilled chicken. A well-known *yakitori* restaurant chain in Tokyo has taken its name, Nanbantei (Southern Barbarians, which means any Europeans) from this folklore.

Most *yakitori* costs ¥150 to several hundred yen a stick. In addition to ordering a la carte, many places offer a set, usually about five to seven sticks, all different. *Yakitori* isn't only chicken; vegetables, pork and other foods are also grilled.

Some of the most common types are:

Momo	dark chicken meat
Sasami	white chicken fillet without skin
Tebasaki	chicken wings
Tsukune	chicken meatballs
Shoniku	chicken with skin
Kawa	chicken skin
Reba	liver
Motsu	giblets
Negima	leeks
Ginnan	ginko nuts
Piiman	small green peppers
Negi maki	pork rolled around leeks
Shiso maki	shiso mint rolled with pork
Aspara maki	pork rolled around asparagus

KUSHIAGE

Kushiage is skewered morsels of food similar to *yakitori*, but dipped in batter and deep fried rather than grilled. Usually you order by the set with a certain number of sticks. Some places keep bringing you different sticks until you ask them to stop.

TONKATSU

Tonkatsu is pork breaded and deep fried. Inside the crunchy thick crust, the meat is soft and tender. *Tonkatsu* is always served with a mound of shredded cabbage, to help you digest the oil, and a thick soy sauce. It's a popular lunch for office workers as well as a casual dinner out. Some restaurants will give unlimited servings of cabbage and rice and may come around asking *"Okawari?"* ("refills?"). Say *"Hai"* for yes and *"Ii desu"* for no.

Tonkatsu is one of the first Western style foods to become popular in the late 19th century when Japan ended its period of isolation. The government, trying to reduce the influence of Buddhism, lifted the ban on eating meat. *Tonkatsu* comes in two main forms: *hire* (fillet) and *rosu* (chop). The fillet uses the tenderloin and is soft and nearly fat free. The *rosu* is what we know as pork chops and has a layer of fat around the edge. Purists prefer the *rosu* because the meat is more flavorful. The fillet costs more because it's a premium meat.

The *teishoku* (set meal) comes with soup, rice and pickles. Just add *teishoku* to the end of the following to order:

Hire katsu	pork fillet cutlet
Rosu katsu	pork chop cutlet

Ebi furai	prawns breaded and fried
Kaki furai	oysters breaded and fried (usually available only in winter)
Shogayaki	sauté of thin slices of pork, ginger and onions

TEMPURA

Tempura, fish and vegetables dipped in batter and quickly fried, is popular with foreigners. Japanese learned the cooking technique from the Portuguese when they came to Japan in the 16th century. The shogun Tokugawa Ieyasu loved *tempura* so much that legend says he died at age 74 from overeating it.

Along with *tempura* you're served *tentsuyu*, dipping sauce in a bowl, and a small mound of grated *daikon*, radish. Plop the radish into the sauce and dip the *tempura*. Purists like to sit at the counter of *tempura* shops so the food can go directly from the frying pan to the clean sheet of white paper on the plate. They are right; it tastes better hot. The paper helps to drain any excess oil. We love to watch chefs make ice cream *tempura* for dessert.

Tempura is often served as a set meal, *teishoku*, with rice, soup and pickles but you can also order it a la carte (*ippin*). *Tempura* shops sometimes also sell *tendon*, shrimp *tempura* in a bowl of rice topped with a sauce. Usually sitting at the counter and ordering a la carte is more expensive than ordering a set.

Tempura teishoku	*Tempura* set with a variety of fried fish and vegetables and rice, pickles and soup
Tendon	Fried shrimp on a bowl of rice
Kakiage	*Tempura* cutlet made with shrimp, scallops and vegetables

YAKINIKU

Yakiniku (grilled meat) is a Japanese version of Korean food. Meat is marinated in a soy-garlic, hot-pepper mixture and grilled at the table. Some shops still use charcoal braziers, but most use high-tech, built-in gas grills with an internal fan to whisk away the smoke.

PICKLES & RICE TREATS!

One of our favorite remarks from a visiting friend goes something like this: "If you want my honest opinion, Japanese have a lot to learn about making pickles." Heinz or Vlasic they're not, but Japanese pickles have their own unique taste and charm. Japanese always serve pickles and rice at the end of a meal. Give them a try and you may never eat kosher dills again.

Yakiniku is spicier than Japanese food and has a big following among young people. *Yakiniku* restaurants also serve Korean vegetables and sometimes Korean soups. Some *yakiniku* restaurants offer *teishoku*, especially at lunch. The *teishoku* includes rice, soup, vegetables, and pickles. But usually in the evening you order a la carte. Make sure you order vegetables as well as meat and rice to eat with it.

After you order, the staff will turn on your grill and bring plates of raw food. You can control the temperature of a gas grill, with charcoal you are out of luck. When the food is cooked, put it in the plate of dipping sauce. We like to put the meat and vegetables on top of our rice and eat the two together.

Food for grilling:

Karubi	beef from the rib
Rosu	lean beef
Hire	beef fillet
Reba	beef liver
Tan	beef tongue
Buta rosu	lean pork
Chikin	chicken
Nasu	eggplant
Shiitake	mushrooms
Yasai moriawase	assorted vegetables
Yakiniku teishoku	set meal

Other:

Kimuchi	kimchi, spicy pickled cabbage
Namuru	marinated vegetables such as sprouts and spinach
Kuppa	meat and vegetables in a rice and egg drop broth
Wakame soup	seaweed soup

COFFEE SHOPS & CAFES

For a tea-drinking country, the Japanese love their coffee. Coffee houses are everywhere; many serve an expensive cup of coffee in smoky surroundings, but for the price of one cup, you can spend the entire day; no one will ask you to leave. Some people use coffee shops as their offices and classrooms, conducting business and giving lessons. Coffee shops are warm in winter and cool in summer while people's apartments may not be.

In a classic coffee shop, coffee is expensive, running between ¥400 and ¥800, and there are no refills. Some places have elevated the coffee making process to an art and produce a superb cup. Others are fairly mediocre. There's a new breed of inexpensive coffee-shop chains (Pronto,

Veloce) that produce a decent cup of coffee at a reasonable price (about ¥180). It's fast-food coffee, you order at a counter; there's also a self-serve baked-goods counter. Starbucks has arrived, but it doesn't look like traditional coffee establishments are going out of business.

Most coffee shops serve some food, usually toast, sandwiches, pilaf and curry rice. Coffee shops are a great place to eat breakfast with their **morning service**. No, it has nothing to do with church. In the morning from about 8am until 11am, there's a special deal when you get coffee or tea, toast and salad, and sometimes a hard-boiled egg, all for around ¥500.

Here's some basic coffee shop vocabulary:

Kohi	generic coffee
Burendo kohi	blended coffee, usually the standard
Amerikan kohi	American coffee, usually weaker
Uinnaa kohi	Viennese coffee (with whipped cream)
Moka kohi	Mocha coffee
Kafe ore	cafe au lait
Aisu kohi	iced coffee
Esupuresso	espresso
Kapuchino	cappuccino
Kocha or *tii*	tea such as Lipton's
Miruku tii	tea with milk
Remon tii	tea with lemon
Aisu tii	iced tea
Miruku	milk
Kokoa (hotto, aisu)	cocoa (hot, iced)
Remon sukkashu	lemon squash
Orenji jusu	orange juice
Koka kora	coca cola

Coffe shop food:

Pirafu	pilaf
Kare raisu	curry rice
Hamu sando	ham sandwich
Yasai sando	vegetable sandwich
Mikkusu sando	mixed sandwich: ham, tuna, cucumber, lettuce
Tosuto	toast (often about three slices thick)

NABE, SHABU-SHABU & SUKIYAKI

Nabe is a one-pot stew cooked at your table, usually in a ceramic pot. This winter fare is often eaten at home but available in restaurants also. It's different from a stew in Western cooking because *nabe* uses a thin broth and the food cooks quickly. The simmering broth is brought to the table along with fish or meat and vegetables, tofu and clear noodles. You cook your own food. At the end of the meal, noodles or rice cakes are put into the flavorful broth which you drink as a soup.

Yose-nabe	stew with vegetables and fish or chicken
Dote-nabe	oyster stew
Ishikari-nabe	salmon stew, a Hokkaido specialty
Udon-suki	*udon* noodles stew

Shabu-shabu is a *nabe* variation very popular with foreigners. You cook razor thin slices of beef, vegetables and tofu in a broth in a copper pot and then dip them in a sesame or soy sauce. Many restaurants serve an all-you-can-eat menu *(tabe hodai)* that satisfies the meat cravings of many an international visitor. *Shabu-shabu* is relatively expensive because beef isn't cheap. The price depends on the type of beef: American is cheapest; then generic Japanese beef; then Matsuzaka; then Kobe; the latter two are premium beefs.

Sukiyaki is another beef dish popular with international visitors. *Sukiyaki* evolved as a Japanese dish after eating beef was introduced at the end of the 19th century.

Thin slices of beef, vegetables and tofu are sautéed with a sweet soy sauce in an iron skillet at the table. The waitress cooks *sukiyaki* for you. At Japanese homes, cooking *sukiyaki* is invariably the father's duty.

Chanko-nabe is stew eaten by sumo wrestlers and is also available in special restaurants. Sumo wrestlers eat large quantities to give themselves bulk, but in small servings the food is certainly not fattening. Traditionally the meat of four legged animals like beef or pork wasn't used to make *chanko-nabe* — it reminded the wrestlers of being on their hands and knees, that is, losing a bout.

Sakana-chanko	stew with fish
Toriniku-chanko	stew with chicken

TEPPANYAKI

Teppanyaki is food cooked on a steel grill. It can be very downscale where you cook it yourself (usually at a *okonomiyaki* restaurant) or upscale where chefs cook the meal before your eyes. Benihana of New York raised *teppanyaki* to a theatrical art, but in Japan, it's usually a fairly subdued dining experience. Because *teppanyaki* generally involves beef, it's a fairly expensive meal and can be exorbitant at hotel and other top restaurants.

The chef will usually ask you if you want your meat *wafu* style (soy sauce flavored) or *miso* sauce flavored.

Teppanyaki	usually comes as a set and includes meat and vegetables, rice, soup and pickles and sometimes grilled ice cream.
Saaroin suteiki	sirloin steak

Tendaroin suteiki	tenderloin steak
Hire suteiki	fillet

CURRY

Lovers of Indian curry will not recognize the Japanese version, a thick mild curry sauce with a few specks of meat served with rice and red ginger pickles. It's copied from English curry, which is more sweet than spicy, which fits the Japanese palate. Curry is fast food and a favorite among students looking for a cheap, filling meal. Actually, we have to admit that it grows on you.

Chikin kare	chicken curry
Bifu kare	beef curry
Pooku kare	pork curry
Hayashi kare	hashed beef curry

ODEN

Oden, skewers of fish and vegetables stewed in a broth, is winter fare and a favorite of *yatai*, the night stalls set up in cities. Even convenience stores have pots of *oden* on their counters in winter — it's the ultimate Japanese fast food.

There is some regional variation in ingredients but the main ones are:

Atsu age	blocks of deep fried tofu
Fukuro	fried tofu pouch filled with vegetables
Ganmodoki	tofu patty with bits of vegetables
Konbu	kelp seaweed
Daikon	giant radish
Konnyaku	gelatinous cake made from a tuber
Shirataki	white noodles made from a tuber
Tamago	hard boiled egg
Tsukune	chicken meat balls
Gobo	burdock root
Dango	fish cake in a ball
Satsuma age	fried fish cake, sometimes with bits of vegetables
Hanpen	a white, spongy fish cake
Tako	octopus

UNAGI

Unagi is freshwater eel and the dish is especially popular in the heat of summer because it's supposed to give stamina. Usually the eel is dipped in a heavy soy sauce, barbecued on charcoal and served over rice. Tradition has it that to promote his friend's business, Hiraga Gennai, a weird Edo period scholar, promoted the idea that *unagi* should be eaten on the day of the ox in summer (around July 20) to combat the heat. It's also supposed to improve virility so you may find more men than women eating it.

Una don	Grilled eel served over rice in a bowl
Unaju	Grilled eel grilled served over rice in a lacquer box
Unagi teishoku	Eel over rice, soup and pickles
Unagi no kabayaki	Eel grilled on skewers
Shira yaki	Eel grilled without the thick sauce

DONBURI

Donburi is Japanese fast food eaten by people in a hurry. It's cooked and served over rice in a large bowl. Its low price makes it popular with students. A number of chains, such as Yoshinoya with its bright orange signs, sell it along with some noodle shops and other inexpensive eateries.

Gyu-don	Sautéed beef and onions over rice
Oyako-donburi	Sautéed chicken with a soft omelet and onions over rice
Katsu-don	Breaded and fried pork cutlet on rice with a soft omelet on top
Tendon	Fried shrimp over rice with sweetened soy sauce

YOSHOKU - WESTERN FOOD, JAPANESE STYLE

Yoshoku is Japanized Western food that developed after the Meiji Restoration in 1868 when Japan was fascinated with anything Western, including food. This hybrid cuisine is rather strange to Western visitors. Some of the classic dishes are omelets filled with rice and served with ketchup and gratins that are mostly cream sauce. As a cuisine, *yoshoku* is fading fast, being eclipsed by more authentic Western food. While young people now flock to Italian trattorias and French bistros, older folks still enjoy eating this comfort food.

Some of the offerings are:

Omuraisu	omelet wrapped around rice
Korokke	croquettes

OKONOMIYAKI

Okonomiyaki is often called pizza, but the only thing in common is a round shape. *Okonomiyaki* is most popular in the Osaka to Hiroshima corridor, although restaurants can be found all over Japan. The name literally means "cooked as you like it." You usually cook it on a grill at your table, cooking the bits of meat, seafood and vegetables held together with a thin pancake batter. You can season the finished product with green seaweed powder, bonito flakes, red pickled ginger or mayonnaise. *Okonomiyaki* restaurants usually also serve *yakisoba*, grilled noodles, which you also cook yourself. It's almost always an inexpensive meal, costing around ¥1000.

You order your meal by choosing the ingredients you want:

Gyuniku	beef
Buta	pork
Ika	squid
Tako	octopus
Yasai	vegetables
Mikkusu	mixed (usually all of the above)
Yakisoba	stir fried *soba* noodles (can choose above ingredients)
Yaki-udon	stir fried *udon* noodles (can choose above ingredients)

ROBATAYAKI

Robatayaki restaurants are casual and lively places where guests sit at a counter and the cooks, kneeling in front of a charcoal grill surrounded by platters of vegetables, fish and meat, prepare food as you watch. Ordering is easy – simply point at the food you want and about five minutes later, it will come to you freshly grilled. The waitresses and cooks will shout out your order so the whole experience is noisy and cheerful.

Drinking beer and *sake* are as much of the experience as eating the food. While *robatayaki* restaurants seem like they should be fairly inexpensive, some are very pricey.

KAMAMESHI

On the plastic food displays, you may notice rice cooked in an iron kettle set into a wooden box. This is a *kamameshi* restaurant. Rice is topped with meat, vegetables and/or seafood and steamed until cooked. When you are served, stir the ingredients into the rice until it resembles stir-fried rice.

Gomoku meshi	five ingredients, usually vegetables, shrimp and chicken
Tori meshi	chicken
Sake meshi	salmon
Ebi meshi	shrimp
Takenoko	bamboo

VEGETARIAN CUISINE

Until the mid-19th century, Buddhism prohibited eating meat so the traditional Japanese diet consisted of fish, vegetables and grains. Even today, vegetarians can easily find something to eat in most Japanese restaurants.

Zen Buddhist temples raised vegetarian fare to an art. Called *shojin ryori*, it relies primarily on vegetables, tofu, *miso* bean paste and wheat gluten. Since it's a lot of work to prepare, *shojin ryori* tends to be expensive. One variation is *fucha ryori*, vegetarian temple food with a Chinese influence. Heavier sauces are used and food is served from large platters, rather than in individual portions. Kyoto and Mt. Koya are good places to sample vegetarian temple food although restaurants can be found in Tokyo and other large cities.

KAISEKI

Formal Japanese cuisine served at important occasions is known as *kaiseki*. Originally it was a meal served after the tea ceremony, which helps explain why quantity has never been of prime importance. The emphasis is on using seasonal foods and the freshest ingredients available. Beautifully arranged on individual ceramic dishes that are chosen to reflect the nature of the food, the meal is as much a feast for the eyes as it is for the stomach. Eating *kaiseki* is similar to eating one appetizer after another. Although the amounts are small, you realize how full you are by the 8th or 9th course. *Kaiseki* tends to be expensive because of its labor-intensive preparation and the high cost of ingredients. Try it at lunchtime when it costs less or better yet, stay at a Japanese inn, *ryokan*, where dinner is included in the room rate. The best *ryokan* stand as excellent restaurants in their own right.

There is no standard *kaiseki* menu. The set meals are named individually by restaurants, but you choose by price. A typical meal consists of a starter, *sashimi*, a dish of grilled food, *nimono* (steamed vegetables), a vinegared dish, clear soup (to cleanse the palate), fried food such as *tempura*, rice and pickles.

IZAKAYA - DRINKING PLACES

Izakaya are casual pubs popular for after-work get-togethers. They serve beer, *sake* and usually whiskey and *shochu*, a strong liquor usually made from sweet potatoes, as well as a variety of foods to accompany the beverages. Not potato chips, but substantial food to make a dinner of it. Usually you order a number of dishes and share with your group. *Izakaya* tend to be fairly inexpensive.

Many are chains with branches all over the country, such as Tengu (logo is red mask with long nose), Tsubohachi and Murasaki. While *izakaya* menus are almost always written in Japanese, the chains have menus with a lot of pictures. If they don't, use our food guide.

Remember, if your neighbor is eating something interesting, point discreetly to his food and tell the waiter *"Onaji no onegai shimasu."*

Important note: If you see a sign for a place that says pub but looks unwelcoming, don't go in. Many small, exclusive Mama-san bars call themselves pubs.

Yakitori	grilled chicken on skewers
Tsukune	chicken meat balls on skewers
Niku jaga	potatoes stewed with bits of meat and onions
Hiya yakko	cold tofu
Age dashi tofu	fried tofu in a sauce
Tofu suteiki	grilled block of tofu
Guriin sarada	green salad
Tsuna sarada	tuna salad
Wakame su	vinegared seaweed
Harumaki	spring rolls
Eda mame	young boiled soy beans, don't eat the pod; especially good with beer
Kara age	deep fried morsels of chicken
Yaki nasu	grilled eggplant
Yose nabe	one pot stew: fish, seafood, chicken, vegetables (winter only)
Ika somen	thin strips of raw squid
Sashimi moriawase	assorted *sashimi* (slices of raw fish)
Miso shiru	*miso* (fermented bean paste) soup
Onigiri	rice balls filled with pickled plum *(ume)*, salmon *(shake)* or cod roe *(tarako)*
Yaki onigiri	grilled rice balls, outside is crunchy like rice crispies
Ochazuke	rice with tea poured over it and flavored with plum *(ume)*, salmon *(shake)*, seaweed *(nori)*, or cod roe *(tarako)*
Zosui	thick rice soup flavored with egg *(tamago)* or chicken *(tori)*

FAMILY RESTAURANTS

Names like Denny's and Royal Host may sound familiar, but did you think you could ever order *miso* soup or *tonkatsu* in one? The family restaurants are all over Japan and while the atmosphere is similar to their American cousins, both Japanese and Western food are served.

The food is predictable and uninspired but will do in a pinch. These casual eateries are good for kids because they offer a wide variety of food and have high chairs and a large dessert menu with a lot of dressed-up ice cream. No one minds if your kids are a little noisy; Japanese kids are noisy too.

Western food in family restaurants leans towards spaghetti, hamburger steak, pilaf and salads. Japanese food is heavy on the cutlets and noodles. Prices are reasonable; coffee has unlimited refills; and there are usually smoking and nonsmoking sections. The menu may be written in Japanese only, but pictures of everything make ordering a cinch.

WESTERN & ETHNIC RESTAURANTS

In addition to the many types of Japanese food, cities have many foreign restaurants serving French, Italian, German, American, Mexican, Chinese, Thai, South Asian and other types of food. Some of the top French and Italian restaurants can hold their own against any in the world. The recent popularity of Italian food has put a trattoria on almost every city street corner.

Over the last few years, there has been a boom of restaurants serving ethnic food sometimes devoted to one cuisine, but more often having a cross section of South and Southeast Asian food. The spiciness of these other cuisines is often toned down for the Japanese palate.

JAPANESE SWEETS

In urban areas you'll see patisseries selling beautiful cakes and pastries. Then you'll pass a Japanese sweet shop and everything looks so unusual. Since the procedure for making sweets is so complicated, Japanese do not make them at home. Instead Japanese buy them in shops, preferably in a nice old shop that has been producing sweets for generations.

Japanese sweets don't use butter or flour; most use sweetened beans and rice pounded into a dough. Yes, they are virtually fat free, but not low calorie.

Sweets are eaten in the afternoon with green tea. Japanese do not eat sweets for dessert; if they have anything at all, it will be a small piece of fruit. Don't be disappointed when you are served three strawberries or a thin slice of melon on a lacquer dish. Chocolate cake after a Japanese dinner is unheard of.

We like to pick up some sweets and have a snack when we get back to our hotel room. Although you may think it's strange to eat beans as a sweet, give it a try. They grow on you.

Yokan	a gelatin made from beans and served in slices
Mitsumame	cubes made from agar-agar, and mixed with fruit and beans
Anmitsu	agar-agar cubes, sweet bean paste, fruit and beans

Gyuhi	sweetened *omochi*, pounded rice cakes
Zenzai	warm sweetened beans with pounded rice cakes
Warabimochi	jellied cube made from *kuzu* root and coated with bean flour
Higashi	a dried sweet made of sugar taken with bitter green tea
Namagashi	bean paste sweets shaped into flowers in season, often eaten as a second "course" at tea ceremony

TEA

Foreigners may think that all Japanese tea is the same, but there are many different varieties. Restaurants usually serve complimentary *o-cha*. In Japanese restaurants, you'll have to ask for water: "*Mizu o kudasai.*"

O-cha	Generic name for Japanese tea
Hoji cha	Roasted tea, brown color, no caffeine
Mugi cha	Barley tea, served chilled in summer
Matcha	Powdered green tea, used in tea ceremony
Genmai cha	Tea made from tea leaves and roasted brown rice

BARS

Most Japanese eateries have a limited drink menu (but not a limited supply!). Beer, *sake*, whiskey and sometimes *shochu* are standard. If you would like something more exotic, you'll have to go to a bar.

There shouldn't be any trouble finding one in entertainment districts and hotels in large cities. In rural areas, you're out of luck.

Japanese love the bottle-keep system. In Japanese society, everyone (well, almost everyone) wants to belong to a group and what better way than having your own bottle at a bar. In most bars you'll see bottles lined up on shelves on the walls. If you'd like to do the same, here's how the system works. You purchase a bottle the first time and, at the larger bars, receive a membership card. At the small places, they just know you. Then, when you come back, you pay a small set-up charge for ice and soda water.

In bars, they will have the mixed drinks you're familiar with at home. You can order in English but put a Japanese spin to it so the bartender will understand. For instance, gin and tonic becomes "jin tonikku."

One word of warning: drinking can be expensive in Japan. Even in average bars, mixed drinks run ¥1000 and up and more in hotel bars.

BENTO SHOPS

Bento, literally meaning lunch box, is the Japanese answer to sandwiches. They are the ultimate fast food and are popular at lunchtime as well as for an inexpensive dinner. Usually included are rice, meat or fish, vegetables, salad and pickles. At *bento* shops you can often buy instant soup as well as small portions of salad. They're also available at many chain stores such as Hoka Hoka, but usually mom and pop operations — often part of a meat store — have better food. It isn't gourmet cuisine, but it's good and the price is right.

Bento are popular to eat when traveling, and stations on long-distance train lines will have at least one stand selling *bento* with regional specialties. The prepackaged boxes are even stamped with their assembly time. It's unlikely they are more than a few hours old. For health reasons, *sushi* with raw fish is not sold.

Some popular *bento* are:

Katsu	bento with *tonkatsu*, breaded and fried pork cutlet
Shogayaki	sautéed slices of pork, ginger and onion
Kara-age	morsels of chicken dipped in batter and deep fried
Hanbaagaa	hamburger
Chikin teriyaki	chicken sautéed in a sweet soy sauce

FAST FOOD

Western fast food is everywhere. McDonalds, Burger King, Wendy's and Arby's are around as are homegrown versions like Lotteria and First Kitchen. But none is a carbon copy of their American cousins. You can find familiar Big Macs, but they have also tailored their offerings to suit the Japanese palate. When was the last time you ordered a *matcha* (green tea) shake or a *teriyaki* burger at a McDonalds? How about a soy burger at Mos Burgers or a grilled rice ball at KFC (Kentucky Fried Chicken)? Where else could you buy a squid and corn pizza at Dominos?

Fast-food outlets run pretty much the same way they do in America. You order at the counter, pay, and take your food either to a table or outside. When you belly up to the counter, the staff person mumbles something quickly to you in Japanese. They are most likely asking *"Kochira de meshi agarimasu ka?"* meaning "Are you going to eat here?" Say *"Hai"* for yes or, if you want to take out, say *"Motte kaerimasu."*

The menu posted over the counter will most likely be in Japanese, but don't let it intimidate you. On the counter itself are menus with pictures. Fast-food joints like to package sets: you get a hamburger or some other item with french fries and a drink for a slightly cheaper price than buying them separately. Morning set is about ¥390 and includes burger, fries and drink.

If all else fails, remember fast food has English names, so just say hamburger, fries and coke with a Japanese accent, and you'll be understood.

DEPARTMENT STORES

In your quest for good food, don't overlook the department stores. Almost all have a variety of restaurants selling reasonably priced food on the top floor. These restaurants are nothing like the greasy spoons some department stores have back home. Many are branches of well-known restaurants. Department store eateries tend to have generous plastic food displays, making ordering a cinch. Be forewarned that they tend to be crowded at lunch time, so lines are not uncommon. Most restaurants in department stores stay open past the store's closing hour, so you don't have to eat an early supper. If you are unsure of where to eat, you can always find a good place in a department store.

You must go down to the food floors in the basements of department stores. You'll find counters selling baked goods, bread, meat, fish, *bento*, Chinese, Japanese, Western and South Asian prepared food, *yakitori*, *tempura, sushi, tonkatsu, oden* stew, fruit, Japanese and Western sweets, tea and pickles. It's a feast for the eye and great entertainment. You can buy prepared food and take it back to your hotel or eat it outside. Many stalls also give samples. Unless you're shameless, you probably can't make a meal of the samples, but it will take the edge off your hunger.

One warning: while the *tempura* and fried cutlets look great, if they aren't eaten piping hot, they tend to be greasy.

BAKERIES

Many bakeries produce high-quality bread far superior to anything you find in an American supermarket. In addition to plain bread, they make bread filled with cheese, bacon and other fillings suitable for lunch. Every department store has a bakery on its food floor. In rural areas, the offerings may be limited to prepackaged items.

Bakeries are always self-service. As you enter, take a tray and tongs, make your selections, and carry them to the cash register. You will probably find bread stuffed with potato, cheese, or bacon. Many bakeries sell sandwiches, usually on soft, crust-free white bread, but occasionally on rolls or brown bread. Japanese love mayo-laden sandwiches with unlikely ingredients such as potato salad, macaroni salad or strawberries. The possibilities are endless.

Bakeries also sell donuts, but beware, many an unsuspecting foreigner has bought a jelly donut only to bite in and find curried tuna or bean paste. If an object appearing to be a jelly donut has fried crumbs on the surface, it's probably a curry donut. If not, it's probably filled with bean paste.

You'll find drinks and individually portioned salads in a refrigerator case, so it's easy to find an entire and inexpensive meal in a bakery.

If you have a yearning for a jelly donut, Mr. Donut seems to have branches near the train station of every sizable city.

MISO PASTE OR PEANUT BUTTER?

A recently arrived American friend prepared her husband's lunch as she'd always done in the US. He hungrily opened his bag and was thrilled to see what he assumed was his favorite – a peanut butter and jelly sandwich. From his first big bite, he knew something was really wrong and spit it out immediately. It looked like peanut butter, but what had happened to its taste? He carefully wrapped his sandwich and took it home for further investigation.

When he presented it to his wife, she was rather surprised to see it again and to hear his tale of woe. Trying to figure out what was wrong, together they carefully examined the peanut butter in a plastic container that she bought at a local grocery. The following day, a Japanese friend solved the mystery – what they both thought was peanut butter was, in fact, light miso paste!

CONVENIENCE STORES

Seven-Eleven, Lawsons, AM-PM and other convenience stores are nearly everywhere except in remote villages. You can get an inexpensive meal here. Amongst the wide array of products are *bento* meals, sandwiches, hard-boiled eggs and instant noodles. Most have Chinese buns called *man* warming on the counter. Meat-filled dumplings are called *niku-man;* sweet bean-paste filled are *an-man*. In winter they may have a pot of *oden*: fish cakes and vegetables simmering in broth. All you need to do is point to what you want and the clerk will pack up everything to go.

When you buy a *bento* at a convenience store, the cashier will ask you *"Atatame masu ka?,"* "Do you want it heated?" Say *"Hai"* for yes, *"Ii desu"* for no. Somewhere on the counter, there's usually a thermos of hot water for making instant noodles. If you don't see it, ask *"Oyu?"*

Convenience stores sell instant coffee; one kind is packaged with a cup, creamer, sugar and a stirrer. Great coffee it isn't, but if you're desperate for coffee after a night in a Japanese inn, it will do the trick.

In addition to food, convenience stores are mini community centers. They have copy machines, fax machines (usually you can send only

MAKE SURE THOSE EGGS ARE SOFT-BOILED!

Another newly arrived friend was making pastry early on a Thanks-giving morning. How early was it? Too early to disturb a neighbor to borrow a couple of eggs to finish her pies. Undaunted, our heroine jumped on her Japanese housewife's bicycle and raced to a nearby convenience store where she bought two neatly-wrapped plastic containers holding two eggs each. "Only in Japan," she thought.

Back again in her kitchen and ready for anything, she gently tapped the first egg on the edge of the counter; nothing happened. She tapped a little harder; again nothing happened. Finally she banged the egg as hard as she could only to discover she'd bought hard-boiled eggs. "Only in Japan," ran through her mind again and again as she giggled about the experience while finishing her early morning project about noon.

domestically), delivery service pick-up, and sell telephone cards and stamps. They're open until late in the evening or 24 hours.

VENDING MACHINES

It seems there are more vending machines than people in Japan. They are everywhere, often two or three side by side, across the street from another half-dozen. The good news is there's no reason to go thirsty. The bad news is they add nothing to the decor.

The majority of vending machines sell soft drinks, but you can also find ones purveying cigarettes, batteries, fast food (complete with micro-wave), rice, snacks, film, disposable cameras, condoms, movies tickets, beer, whiskey and *sake*. Drink machines sell hot and cold canned juice, soda, coffee, tea, Japanese tea, and sometimes soup. The standard price is ¥120, but it is higher in hotels and resort areas. Sometimes "hot" and "cold" are written in English on the vending machine. When the signs are in Japanese only, heated drinks will have a red stripe under them and chilled drinks will have a blue one. With typical Japanese efficiency, in winter half a vending machine sells heated drinks while in summer the machines are adjusted so nearly all drinks are chilled.

Japanese are addicted to canned coffee and a single vending machine may stock as many as 10 different varieties from black to cafe-au-lait. You'll also find cocoa and a number of teas, including English tea, green tea, barley tea and oolong tea. Sports drinks, with names like Pokari Sweat and Aquarius vie with soda, juice, yogurt drinks (our favorite brand name is Calpis) and other concoctions. On most cans, there's something in English to identify its contents but, if you can't find anything, chances are the drink is either Japanese or Chinese tea.

PLASTIC FOOD

Japan has so many different kinds of restaurants and many have menus written only in Japanese. This could mean that you'd either have to do a lot of pointing at other diner's meals (hoping that they are eating something appealing) or you'd be stuck eating at hotels or tourist restaurants. But fortunately, Japanese invented plastic food. Lots of restaurants have colorful displays in their windows. Just a glance will tell you what type of food the restaurant serves and usually the price. Gesture for the waiter or waitress to come to the display to order your meal.

Several words of warning:

• Displays of stew-pot type meals such as shabu-shabu and nabe will often show the quantity of food served to two people, but the price listed is per person.

• Avoid eating in restaurants where the plastic food is dirty and faded. If the restaurant doesn't care how it looks to the public, chances are the kitchen doesn't care either.

Making plastic food is an art perfected in the postwar era. At first the models were made of wax, but they melted in the hot sun. Now made of molded plastic, they are remarkably realistic representations. You can buy some to take home, but they are not cheap. Pieces of sushi cost about ¥500 each; a bowl of noodles is ¥4000; and a complicated food display can run in the tens of thousands. Several shops in the Kappabashi district in Tokyo sell them. We have a friend who puts a sunny-side-up egg on her living room carpet to see guest's reactions. Actually, not all the food on display is plastic. A friend, telling his visiting girlfriend about plastic food, touched the daily special on display outside a restaurant to illustrate his point. Turns out it was real food. What a surprise! And he was trying to impress his girlfriend with his knowledge of the local culture.

10. TAKING THE KIDS

Traveling with kids can be a lot of fun in Japan. Even hard-to-please teenagers love castles and ninja stories. These combined with the Japanese natural affinity for children make for a great family trip.

Naturally, you have to plan and pace your trip specially. Most of our friends who have toured as families have balanced their sightseeing; they don't rush from temple to temple because, basically, the kids won't stand for it. For most families, one major activity a day is enough. Some of the major activities can be aquariums, zoos, science museums and other sights, the same places Japanese families go.

Kids are a great icebreaker. Japanese love children and will go out of their way for them and for you. Since they don't often see very many foreign kids, especially outside the big cities, they quickly drop their normal reserve to make a big fuss of them. Over and over again, Japanese will say of your children *Kawaii, kawaii! (cute)*. Patrice's daughters began to think *kawaii* was their name.

We've divided our suggestions by age to give you some ideas how to make the best of a family trip.

A few advance preparations will get your trip off to a good start:
• Children need passports (and if adults need visas, children do also).
• Shoes that slip on and off greatly simplify touring with children (and adults!).
• To give a sense of adventure, have the children practice using chopsticks at home.
• Teach the children a few simple words of Japanese: *domo* (thank you), *hai* (yes) and *sayonara* (good-bye).
• Get an English translation of Japanese fairy tales.

BABIES

Traveling with babies takes surprisingly little adjustment. With a baby backpack or stroller, you can go about your day. Most train and subway stations don't have elevators so be prepared to lug a stroller up and down the stairs.

No need to carry all your supplies from home. Disposable diapers are available everywhere. You'll find the familiar Pampers name as well as an assortment of Japanese diapers equally as good. Drug stores and department stores carry powdered baby formula. SMA by Wyeth is one common brand name but there are several others. Soy-based formula is also easy to find. Buy diaper wipes and jars of baby food as well as freeze-dried baby food in drugstores, supermarkets and department stores.

Department stores provide special rooms with cribs and nursing areas near the children's department. Many rest rooms have changing tables.

Health concerns shouldn't be a major worry. You can drink the water anywhere in the country. High standards of hygiene mean there's little fear of catching exotic diseases.

Make sure you have children's medicine such as pain relievers and cold and cough medications because the Japanese brands will be unfamiliar. Japan has good medical care and in an emergency ask your hotel to call a doctor. (See the Medical Emergency section of Basic Information.) If the child has special medication, make sure you bring it with you. Americans should have a thermometer with them because Japanese ones register in Celsius.

Babysitting

Large hotels can arrange baby-sitting for you, but it may be a problem at smaller inns. The Japanese generally do not use baby-sitters and rely on family members.

TODDLERS & YOUNG CHILDREN

Parents must be creative in planning interesting schedules for young children. Sandwich your sightseeing with stops in parks, playgrounds and other kid-friendly places. Every sizable city sports a zoo and natural history and science museums. Aquariums are commonplace as are theme and amusement parks. Department store toy sections usually have some samples on display to amuse children and most department store rooftops have play equipment to keep the kids occupied. And if all else fails, there's Tokyo Disneyland.

If your child will only eat hamburgers, you are in luck. The ubiquitous fast food restaurants provide inexpensive meals. But you should be able to find food for finicky eaters in other restaurants also. Most children will eat fried chicken chunks (*kara-age*), noodles, and deep fried shrimp *tempura*. So try to branch out. And plain white rice is available everywhere.

SURVIVING THE FLIGHT WITH KIDS

No matter what you do, the international flight is going to be long. And traveling with children you probably won't have the luxury of immersing yourself in a good book to help the time pass quickly. But with some preparation, the flight doesn't have to be an ordeal.

While many people hesitate to travel with infants, we find that traveling long distances with babies under the age of one is easier than with slightly older children. Children between one and three are mobile and difficult to keep occupied on a long flight. Steel yourselves for countless trips up and down the aisles. By age three, most children are able to sit still, look at books and entertain themselves, at least for part of the trip.

On international flights, children under two can travel free but are not entitled to a seat. This isn't a problem with an infant, but a long trip in economy class with a nearly two-year-old on a lap is our idea of hell on earth. Ask the airline how full the plane is and consider springing for a ticket if you have little hope of getting an extra seat. Airlines generally charge two-thirds of an adult fare for children age two through eleven.

Get your seat assignments when you make your reservations; you don't want to get to the airport and discover you can't sit together (or do you?). For babies, you want to be in the bulkhead seats where bassinets fasten, but with older children the bulkhead seats are a hindrance. They're right under the movie screen, a distraction for children trying to sleep. The armrests of bulkhead seats don't raise, so a child can't stretch out on your lap. And since you cannot put your carry-on luggage under the seats in front of you, it's a nuisance to get toys and snacks.

With smaller children, make sure you pack in your carry-on baggage at least two changes of clothes (and one for yourself). Dress your children in layers so you can adjust for temperature changes on and off the aircraft. Bring a variety of toys and games to keep them entertained. We buy something new and surprise the children with it on the airplane; the novelty keeps them occupied for a while.

Make sure you have enough diapers to see you through the flight and to your destination. Airplanes usually supply diapers, but you don't want to count on it and sometimes they have only one size. Bring a cup with a cap for small children to prevent spills.

Take along healthy snacks for the flight. Look into children's meals, which must be ordered in advance. On some airlines this means hamburgers, which may not be appealing to your child. The regular meal or another type of special meal may be a better choice. But we find it's best not to rely on the airline for meals. Taking some of your children's favorite foods can make the dining experience more pleasant. Make sure the children drink plenty of liquids to avoid dehydration.

For older children, a selection of books and a gameboy helps the time pass faster.

Traveling with younger children means paying closer attention to your travel schedule. You want to avoid being on subway and commuter trains at rush hour, usually 8 to 9:30am. Be careful boarding the train; sometimes there's a large gap between the train and the platform. You may want to consider using a stroller for a child as old as age four or five because chances are you'll do a lot of walking. You can rent strollers at zoos and amusement parks or take your own.

You'll need to carry baby wipes *(wetto tissue)* for hands and faces, if not bottoms, and a package of tissues for bathrooms. Japanese drugstores sell *benza kurina* to sanitize toilet seats.

OLDER CHILDREN & TEENAGERS

Older children and teenagers have a higher tolerance for sightseeing, but you still need to customize the schedule. Make sure you visit at least one castle. Break up sightseeing days with amusement parks, theme parks, zoos, aquariums, and science and natural history museums. Don't overlook the video arcades and the growing number of virtual reality arcades.

TRAVEL COSTS

Traveling by train, subway and buses, children under six years old ride free and six through eleven pay half fare. On a long distance train, a child under six is not entitled to a seat, so if it's crowded, the child will have to sit on your lap. If this would be a problem, buy a child's ticket. The Japan Rail Pass is available for children six through eleven at one-half the adult cost.

On domestic airplane flights, children under three fly free but do not get their own seat. Children three through eleven are half price.

At hotels and Japanese inns, the tariff for children gets tricky. Many Western hotels don't have rooms with two double beds because the rooms are small. Many charge per person, even if the person is a child. The large American chains like Hyatt, Hilton and Holiday Inn are a plus here because they generally have a policy of no extra charge for children in the room with their parents.

At Japanese inns, if the child is under three or four, you can request a *futon* only (no meals for the child) and usually will be charged a few thousand yen. (Don't worry about not having a meal for a small child, there will be more than enough food on your plate to share.) For an older child, the tariff is usually half the adult price. But there is no standard policy and it has to be negotiated with the inn.

Most temples, amusement parks and other attractions have reduced prices for children, often one price for elementary school children, another for junior and senior high school and a third for college students. Usually children under six are admitted free to museums and temples, but amusement parks and zoos generally charge admission for children three and older.

GREAT PLACES TO TAKE THE KIDS

National Children's Land (Kodomo no Kuni) is a large hilly park popular with families. It used to be an ammunition depot so there still are cement bunkers in the hills; hopefully, they're empty but we didn't get close enough to check. The verdant park geared to children is refreshingly noncommercial. Activities include a cycling course, boating, pony rides, swimming pools in summer, ice skating in winter, a dairy farm complete with homemade ice cream, a small zoo, a nature study center, a plum garden, a swan pond, and a playground with unusual climbing structures and sculptures. The food sold on the grounds leaves a lot to be desired, so it's best to take a picnic lunch. *Tel. (045-961-2111. Open 9:30am to 4:30pm; 5pm July and August. Closed Monday and December 31 and January 1. ¥600. From Shibuya take the Shintamagawa line to Nagatsuda and change for the shuttle train to Kodomo no Kuni, about 45 minutes from Shibuya.*

Tokyo Sesame Place. Unlike most amusement parks, this one doesn't have rides; children have to participate actively. The climbing apparatus is first rate, and all the favorite Sesame Street characters perform live in a studio. The whole place is in a green area on top of a mountain. Small children love it. *403 Ajiro, Itsukaichi-machi, Nishitama-gun, Tokyo. Tel. (0425)96-5811. Open 9am to 5pm. Closed Thursday. Children ages 3 to 12 ¥1000, adults ¥2000. From Shinjuku Station take the JR Chuo line to Hachioji Station and then 30 minutes by bus.*

Sanrio Puroland. If you have a small child who loves Hello Kitty, put Puroland on your itinerary. It's an indoor amusement park where the terminally cute cat holds court. There are rides and shows. After 4pm, ticket prices drop; we find three hours is enough, so this is a cheaper alternative. *Tel. (0423)72-6500. Open 10am to 7pm. Closed Tuesday. ¥4400 adults, ¥4000 children. Take the Odakyu or Keio line from Shinjuku Station to Tama Center Station, about 45 minutes.*

Tama Zoo (Tama Dobutsu Koen). The zoo is in the hills of suburban Tokyo, and it's worth the trip to enjoy the park-like atmosphere. You can ride a special bus through a large lion pen. The insectarium has a fantastic conservatory filled with lush plants, butterflies and other insects. *7-1-1 Hodokubo, Hino-shi, Tokyo. Tel. (0425)91-1611. Open 9:30am to 5pm (enter by 4pm). Closed Monday and December 29 through January 3. ¥500. Keio*

Line express train to Takahata-Fudo Station, change for shuttle train to Keio Dobutsu Koen Station. Entrance is across the street from the station.
Tokyo Disneyland. You didn't travel all the way to Japan to see Mickey and his friends. But, if you have kids, Disneyland is sure to keep them amused for a day. It's also an interesting sociological study to see Japanese and other Asian people enjoying themselves in such an overwhelmingly American experience. Tokyo Disneyland has been a big hit since it opened in 1983 and boasts that it has had more than 190 million visitors. Unless you're a masochist, avoid going on weekends or during Japanese school holidays; it may seem that all 190 million are there at one time. *1-1 Maihama, Urayasu. Tel. (0473)54-0001. Tickets with admission to unlimited attractions are ¥5200 for 18 and over, ¥4590 children 12 through 17 and ¥3570 children 4 through 11. Opening hours vary with the season and day, but at a minimum: 9am until 7:30pm. The easiest way to get there is to take the JR Keiyo line from Tokyo Station to Maihama Station.*

Shinagawa Aquarium. This aquarium is one of the best in Tokyo. Our kids can't get enough of the dolphin and sea lion shows and the underwater tunnel with fish swimming all around you. *Tel. (03)3762-3431. Open 10am to 5pm. Closed Tuesday (open daily July 23 through September 2) and December 29 through January 1. ¥900. 5-minute walk from Omori Kaigan Station on the Keihin Kyuko line – board train at Shinagawa Station.*

11. TOKYO'S BEST PLACES TO STAY

Tokyo's wide range of hotels, inns and lodges adds to the allure of any trip. As in most countries, you'll find the full spectrum of accommodations, from deluxe international hotels to youth hostels. But in Japan, traditional inns provide another layer. They range from ¥100,000 per person a night for luxury accommodations with personal service to small family-run inns at about ¥4500 per person where you put out your own bedding. To enjoy your stay at a Japanese inn, you will need to shift from Western cultural expectations of hospitality, fine dining and accommodations to those of the Japanese. Staying at a traditional inn adds a uniquely Japanese dimension to your trip, and so we've included two inns in this chapter for those of you interested in getting away from the city.

Of all the different places we stayed, we'll always cherish the memory of our unique experiences at this handful of hotels and inns.

PARK HYATT HOTEL, *3-7-1-2 Nishi Shinjuku, Shinjuku-ku, Tokyo, 163. Tel. (03)5322-1234, Fax (03)5322-1288. US and Canada toll free: 800-233-1234. Singles from ¥41,000. Doubles from ¥46,000. Credit cards.*

Perched high atop the 52-storied Shinjuku Park Building, high tech meets high hospitality. The architecturally stunning hotel floats above Tokyo, setting a new standard for luxury hotels.

The Park Hyatt creates a warm, small-hotel atmosphere in a postmodern skyscraper by successfully dividing the grand public spaces and restaurants from the guest rooms. Guests use a private internal elevator to reach their floors and check in and out in a small, living room-like area. The 178 guest rooms, the largest in Tokyo, sport contemporary furniture and large windows to maximize the stunning views. The oversized, opulent bathrooms feature both a tub and a shower. Equipped with two telephone lines, a fax machine, dataport and voice mail, the guest rooms readily double as offices.

The public areas are equally grand. Three glass pyramids top the skyscraper. The elevator whisking you to the 41st floor opens onto the four-storied glass pyramid of the Peak Lounge and Bar; the view is incredible. During the day, enjoy tea and light meals overlooking the sprawling city. When the sun goes down, the lounge transforms itself into a glittering candle-lit space with the lights of Tokyo forming a nightscape.

The second glass pyramid provides one of the most magnificent settings for a health club anywhere. Swim in the 20-meter pool and work out on the exercise equipment under the glass dome with Tokyo spread out in front of you.

The third and largest pyramid houses the chic New York Bar and Grill, one of Tokyo's most popular restaurants. In the evening, enjoy live jazz in the bar. The restaurant, serving continental fare, pulsates with the excitement of the Big Apple.

The two-storied Kozue Restaurant serves refined Japanese cuisine in a contemporary setting. The wooden decor provides a warm ambiance, and all tables have a view of Mt. Fuji – at least on the days when Mt. Fuji allows itself to be seen.

The Park Hyatt provides an oasis high above the hustle and bustle of Tokyo.

FOUR SEASONS HOTEL, *2-10-8 Sekiguchi, Bunkyo-ku, Tokyo, 112-0014. Tel. (03)3943-2222, Fax (03)3943-2300. Toll Free in the US: 800/332-3442. Singles from ¥31,000. Doubles from ¥35,000. Credit cards. Mejiro Station.*

Tokyo is filled with top-of-the-line hotels offering deluxe rooms and superior service, but the Four Seasons offers one luxury in this crowded city that no one else can match: space. The low-rise hotel is built on the grounds of the century-old Chinsan-so Garden, a rambling 17-acre expanse of greenery. And the hotel itself exudes spaciousness: grand foyers, wide hallways, airy restaurants and, foot for foot, some of the largest rooms and suites in Tokyo.

With only 283 rooms, the Four Seasons is an oasis of serenity in a chaotic city. No detail is too small. Hot spring water is trucked in from the famous springs of Izu to fill the traditional hot spring onsen bath. The health club and spa includes an indoor heated pool, a sauna, a steamroom, a gym and services more befitting a resort than an urban hotel.

The elegant restaurant Bice ranks among Tokyo's top Italian restaurants, but you can also dine on Japanese, Chinese and continental cuisine.

The Four Seasons runs a shuttle bus to the nearest train and subway stations. The biggest drawback is the hotel is located outside the city center. If every minute is programmed during your trip to Tokyo, stay at a more centrally located hotel. But if you will have some extra time, take advantage of the Four Season's luxuries.

PALACE HOTEL, *1-1-1 Marunouchi, Chiyoda-ku, Tokyo, 100-0005. Tel. (03)3211-5211, Fax (03)3211-6987. 393 rooms. Singles from ¥24,000. Doubles and twins from ¥32,000. Credit cards. Otemachi Station.*

Location. Location. Location. It doesn't get better than this, no matter if your travel is for business or pleasure. The Palace Hotel is in the Otemachi/Marunouchi business district, but just across from the Imperial Palace grounds. Look out one direction to the high-rise buildings of the financial district, the other direction to the sturdy stone walls of the moat and lush greenery of the Imperial Palace. (Make sure you request a room facing the palace). A transportation nexus, Otemachi features a half-dozen subway lines at Otemachi Station and myriad JR trains at Tokyo Station, just a few blocks away.

The Palace Hotel is relatively small — and uncrowded — for a deluxe hotel and is only ten stories tall. Non-smokers can revel that two floors are reserved exclusively for their use. An extensive renovation a few years ago has updated all the rooms. The well-staffed business center provides the services travelers need, including free computer use.

Guests seeking exercise can walk or jog around the Imperial Palace, but can also avail themselves of the facilities of the private fitness club "Sky Across" located on the 25th floor of the nearby Nomura Building. A 25-meter pool, gym, squash courts, aerobics and sauna beckon even the most adamant couch potato.

The Crown Restaurant, on the 10th floor, offers some of Tokyo's best French cuisine with stunning views and equally stunning prices, while the more down to earth Exchange features New York deli-style sandwiches. Buy a sandwich and then cross the street and enter the Imperial Palace's East Garden for a quiet lunch in a most memorable setting.

FAIRMONT HOTEL, *2-1-17 Kudan Minami, Chiyoda-ku, Tokyo, 102-0074. Tel. (03)3262-1151, Fax (03)3264-2476. Singles from ¥11,000. Doubles from ¥20,000. Credit cards. Kudanshita Station.*

We love this hotel for its quiet location, intimate setting and its excellent value. Located on a quiet street on the north side of the Imperial Palace, the Fairmont Hotel is reasonably central yet offers tranquillity and tree-top views. Facing the Imperial Palace's Chidorigafuchi Moat, rooms look out on cherry blossoms during their short spring season and lush greenery at other times. And the stone castle walls rising from the water of the moat are an awesome sight which will transport you back to the time of the shoguns.

The Fairmont's friendly staff go out of their way to make you feel welcome and the small size of the hotel — 207 rooms — provides an intimacy not found at larger places. The expertly arranged fresh flowers which always adorn the lobby add to the Fairmont's graceful charm. Make sure you request a room with a moat view.

The famed Yasukuni Shrine and war museum, the Imperial Palace's East Garden and the National Science, Modern Art and Craft museums in Kitanomaru Park are all within a short walk. The nearby Kudanshita station provides fast transportation across the city on the Hanzomon and Shinjuku subway lines.

PRESIDENT HOTEL, *2-2-3 Minami Aoyama, Minato-ku, Tokyo, 107-0062. Tel. (03)3497-0111, Fax (03)3401-4816. Doubles ¥17,000. Twins from ¥17,000. Credit cards. Aoyama Itchome Station.*

The President combines very reasonable rates with an excellent location and is a good value for the money. The Aoyama Itchome subway station is just across the street, providing excellent access on the Ginza and Hanzomon lines. The Aoyama area is a mecca for shoppers and the nearby Akasaka Detatched Palace is not open to the public, but its greenery is an oasis of open space in the congested central city.

The hotel's lobby has a European air to it and even has a reading corner well-stocked with magazines and newspapers. Many of the guests are foreigners, and to cater to them the hotel offers CNN on television. The staff provides excellent service. The hotel has two good restaurants, Japanese and French and even provides room service. For a greater variety of food, go across the street to the basement of the Aoyama Twin Tower.

The rooms are on the small side, but are comfortable. Request a room on the upper floors for a view of the Akasaka Detached Palace. The President Hotel is a perfect place for travelers who want a central location, good value and who are too busy to spend a lot of time sitting in their hotel room.

CHUJIKAN, *2036 Fuegashima, Miyagi-mura, Seta-gun, Gunma, 371-1100. Tel. (0272)83-3015, Fax (0272)83-7522. From ¥10,000 per person with two meals. Credit cards.*

For a great getaway from Tokyo, Chujikan can't be beat. The small rural inn features outdoor hot spring baths overlooking a deep ravine and waterfall and serves delicious country fare. Chujikan takes its name from an Edo period Robin Hood who hailed from this area. Kunisada Chuji robbed the rich and shared his booty with the poor. Each of the inn's 13 guest rooms bears the name of one of Chuji's followers.

Chujikan was recently rebuilt in a traditional rural style. The result is the best of both worlds, an authentic building containing amenities you would expect to forego: central heating and air conditioning plus private toilets. Attention was paid to the authenticity of every detail of this farmhouse-style building including the long sloping roof, which resembles its thatched relatives. Beams crisscross the high ceiling of the corridor leading to the guest rooms. Dark wood is used throughout, giving a much more rustic feel than the blonde wood usually favored in Japanese buildings. The hallway's dark wooden floors glisten. Throughout the stucco walls are a light cream color, and farm implements decorate the entryway.

Unlike most Japanese inns, you do not wear slippers in Chujikan. Instead guests are provided with soft white *tabi* socks to wear with a cotton *yukata* robe.

Meals are served in a Japanese-style central dining room where guests sit at low tables. Before dinner, the cheerful cook explains what she has prepared. Her love of food is obvious and shows in her eyes when she appears to serve her finished products. Dinner is good mountain fare including *sashimi* of river fish, mountain vegetables, *tempura* and locally raised steak you grill at your table. The day we were there, the cook served special fern fritters which she made from perfect tender ferns she found in her garden.

Another highlight at Chujikan is the outdoor hot spring baths, one for men and one for women, side by side but separated by a bamboo fence. The stone baths have stunning views of the deeply wooded ravine and waterfall. At night basket torches light the baths and powerful lamps illuminate the waterfall. But this being Japan, the men's bath affords a better view of the waterfall.

HORAI, *750 Izusan, Atami, Shizuoka, 413. Tel. (0557)80-5151, Fax (0557)80-0205. From ¥41,000 per person with two meals. Credit cards.*

Mt. Horai is the Buddhist depiction of heaven. Its namesake's inn re-creates an idyllic paradise on earth. Situated high on a hill above Sagami Bay in Atami on the Izu Peninsula, Horai's superb location sets it apart from other deluxe Japanese inns. Each of the 16 rooms of this elegant Japanese inn features an entire wall of *shoji* screens that open to offer stunning views of the bay.

Stay at Horai for a delightful retreat. Take time to appreciate the simplicity, beauty and attention to detail found not only in the physical surroundings, but also in the meals served in your room, your personal attendant's thoughtful service and the pervasive presence of mother nature.

The experience of staying at Horai is heightened by journeying down the many steps and corridors to the open air hot spring bath located much closer to the water. With so few guest rooms, you can find a time to relax in total privacy surrounded by views of nature.

Horai awaits you less than an hour from Tokyo on the *shinkansen* train. While it is pricey, splurge for an experience you will remember for a long time.

12. WHERE TO STAY

Tokyo is chock full of hotels: deluxe hotels, moderately priced hotels, business hotels and budget Japanese inns. No matter what kind you choose, look for a hotel convenient to train or subway lines; otherwise you can spend a lot of time stuck in traffic.

Tokyo's top-of-the-line **deluxe hotels** are on a par with the best worldwide. The international groups — Hilton, Intercontinental, Hyatt, Four Seasons, Westin — are joined by top Japanese names — Okura, Imperial, New Otani— to provide a standard of service for which Japan is famous. Notoriously expensive Tokyo real estate means rooms are often smaller than at similar hotels overseas. This trend is changing because the newer deluxe hotels like the Park Hyatt and Westin Tokyo have larger rooms.

Deluxe hotels offer all the services business travelers expect — translators, secretarial assistance, meeting rooms, shopping arcades and travel agencies. You'll also find standard cable television with CNN and BBC, concierges to assist you, a plethora of restaurants and bars, 24-hour room service, and a pool and sports facilities. One quibble is many of these hotels charge an additional fee for the sports club and pool.

If you are searching for a deluxe hotel, our advice is to choose one based on location. Frankly, the decor may vary, but they all offer top service and amenities. A deluxe hotel will cost ¥25,000 and up plus a 10% or higher service charge and 8% tax. In this bracket, there's only a minor differential between a single and double room.

Moderately priced hotels are a good option for those who don't need all the amenities of a deluxe hotel. They have at least one or two restaurants on the premises and room service although it probably won't be 24-hour. The room will be equipped with a hair dryer, cotton *yukata* robe, shampoo and toothbrush. Since these hotels tend to be smaller, the atmosphere is more personal. Often in moderately priced hotels, double or twin rooms cost nearly twice as much as a single.

Plan to spend ¥12,000 to ¥25,000 for a twin room in a moderately priced hotel. Expect a 10% service charge and 5% tax, 8% if the room rate is over ¥15,000.

Business hotels cater to Japanese road warriors. Japanese corporations are notoriously cheap so the staff travels on limited budgets. Business hotels offer no-frills accommodations. The rooms are minuscule — we have been in some singles where we could spread our arms and touch both walls — but the rooms are clean and they have private baths though you may have to use a shoehorn to get in. Service is minimal; most serve a breakfast for ¥1000 or under, but there may not be a regular restaurant. Forget about room service; the best you can do is a vending machine for drinks and snacks. Business hotels tend to be in central locations close to train stations. If you view a hotel only as a place to spend the night, staying at business hotels stretches your travel dollar.

Business hotels run between ¥7000 and ¥12,000, and do not add a service charge.

Japanese Budget inns are another alternative. They are simple places providing basic Japanese-style accommodation. The inns are usually small and run by friendly people. Often you won't have a private bath. You tend to find Japanese budget inns in interesting old neighborhoods like Asakusa and Ueno. They are a little far from central Tokyo, but people who choose to stay at them usually find that the atmosphere makes up for the inconvenience. Budget inns cost between ¥4500 and ¥7000 per person, less for two in a room, and do not add a service charge. The doors are usually locked at 11pm or 12 midnight.

No matter what sort of accommodation you wish to stay in, do yourself a favor and make reservations before you arrive Tokyo. You don't want to have the task of finding a place after a long trans-Pacific flight. Tokyo hotels do fill up at times you would never anticipate such as when a large convention is in town. In February, students and their mothers come from all over Japan for university entrance exams, and hotel rooms can be almost impossible to find even in the top price range.

Tokyo unfortunately is not the place to try out a traditional Japanese inn. The few Japanese inns in Tokyo are budget accommodations and although acceptable as such, do not have the service, standards and charm of traditional Japanese *ryokan* inns. Save the *ryokan* experience for an out of town trip.

Also missing from the Tokyo scene are intimate, reasonably priced small hotels. Perhaps because the cost of land is so high, most hotels are large and impersonal or small and impersonal with cookie-cutter rooms. Although service may be excellent, Tokyo doesn't have the quirky, eccentric inns found in many other large cities. It doesn't have the grand

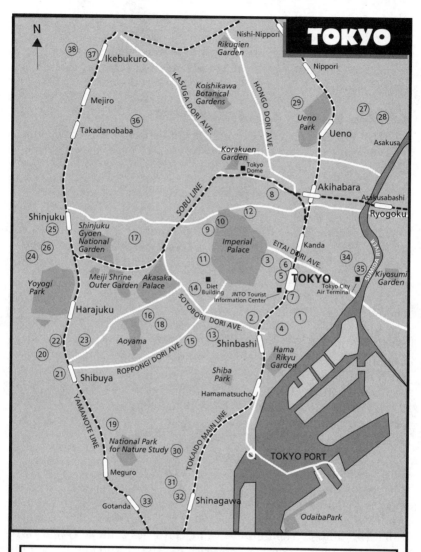

Tokyo Hotels

1. Hotel Seiyo Ginza
2. Imperial Hotel
3. Palace Hotel
4. Ginza Tobu Hotel
5. Tokyo Station Hotel
6. Tokyo Marunouchi Hotel
7. Yaesu Fujiya Hotel
8. Yamanoue Hotel (Hilltop Hotel)
9. Hotel Kayu Kaikan
10. Fairmont Hotel
11. Tokyo Diamond Hotel
12. Kudan Kaikan
13. Hotel Okura

14. Capitol Tokyu Hotel
15. Roppongi Prince Hotel
16. President Hotel
17. Hotel JAL City
18. Asia Center of Japan
19. The Westin Tokyo
20. Creston Hotel
21. Hillport Hotel
22. Shibuya Tobu Hotel
23. Kodomo no Shiro Hotel
24. Park Hyatt Hotel
25. Keio Plaza Hotel
26. Shinjuku Washington Hotel

27. Asakusa View Hotel
28. Ryokan Shigetsu
29. Sawanoya Ryokan
30. Miyako Hotel
31. Tobu Takanawa Hotel
32. Shinagawa Prince Hotel
33. Ryokan Sansuiso
34. Royal Park Hotel
35. Hakozaki Terminal Hotel
36. Four Seasons Hotel
37. Hotel Metropolitan
38. Kimi Ryokan

old hotels either. They were bulldozed long ago in Tokyo's quest for newer, bigger and better.

To help you orient yourself, we list the convenient sightseeing areas to each hotel district, which you'll find later in this chapter in the *Seeing the Sights* section.

GINZA, HIBIYA & MARUNOUCHI

The centrally located area east of the Imperial Palace is convenient to shopping and business centers. Transportation is excellent with a slew of subway lines serving the area. This district is convenient to our Seeing the Sights area 1, *Around the Imperial Palace*; and area 2, *From Ginza to Nihonbashi*.

1. HOTEL SEIYO GINZA, *1-11-2 Ginza, Chuo-ku, Tokyo, 104-0061. Tel. (03)3535-1111, Fax (03)3535-1110. US toll free: 800/44-SEIYO. Doubles from ¥48,000. Credit cards. Home page: http://www.travelweb.com/thisco/rosewood/seiyo/seiyo. Ginza Itchome Station.*

If money is no object and privacy and service are your priorities, choose the Hotel Seiyo. This small, luxurious hotel offers a nearly unparalleled level of service including being assigned a personal secretary. The hotel has only 200 rooms and, in place of a lobby, there is a small, tastefully decorated reception room. Hotel Seiyo takes great pride in its opulent and spacious bathrooms that have separate tubs and showers.

2. IMPERIAL HOTEL, *1-1-1 Uchisaiwai-cho, Chiyoda-ku, Tokyo, 100-0011. Tel. (03)3504-1111, Fax (03)3581-9146. Toll free in USA and Canada: 800/223-6800. Singles from ¥30,000. Twins from ¥35,000. Credit cards. Hibiya Station or JR Yurakucho Station.*

Legendary service and a great central location make the Imperial a top choice for businessmen or tourists willing to pay the price. Some of the rooms overlook Hibiya Park and the Imperial Palace. Their concierges go to extraordinary lengths to assist you, be it to send flowers to Aunt Mabel in Kansas or track down that Hiroshige woodblock print you can't live without. The business center provides computers and secretarial service; every room has a fax machine. The large lounge in the lobby is filled with businessmen from around the world making deals. One piece of advice: taxi drivers do not know the name Imperial Hotel; you have to tell them *Teikoku Hotel*, its name in Japanese.

The present hotel, which opened in the late 1960s, is on the site of the Frank Lloyd Wright-designed Imperial Hotel. Step into the Old Imperial Bar on the mezzanine floor of the main building for a glimpse of the old masterpiece; the interior was moved from the old hotel. The original lobby has been preserved at Meiji Mura, an open air museum near Nagoya.

3. PALACE HOTEL, *1-1-1 Marunouchi, Chiyoda-ku, Tokyo, 100-0005. Tel. (03)3211-5211, Fax (03)3211-6987. 393 rooms. Singles from ¥24,000. Doubles and twins from ¥32,000. Credit cards. Otemachi Station.*

The Palace Hotel is a good deluxe hotel in the Marunouchi business district. Relatively small for a luxury hotel, and only ten stories tall, it's an oasis in a district of high-rise office buildings. Located across the street from the Imperial Palace moats, the Palace Hotel has great views of the verdant grounds. Ask for a room facing the palace. Their 10th floor French restaurant, Crown, is one of the best in the city and has panoramic views, but isn't for those on limited budgets.

Selected as one of our Best Places to Stay; see Chapter 11 for more details.

4. GINZA TOBU HOTEL, *6-14-10 Ginza, Chuo-ku, Tokyo, 104-0061. Tel. (03)3546-0111, Fax (03)3546-8990. 206 rooms. Singles from ¥17,000. Doubles from ¥23,000. Credit cards. Ginza or Higashi Ginza Station.*

We recommend this hotel not only for its great location but also for its personalized service. The room size is larger than most in this class. The restaurants are good but with so many eateries within walking distance, there's no need to eat in. The hotel offers good value.

5. TOKYO STATION HOTEL, *1-9-1 Marunouchi, Chiyoda-ku, Tokyo, 100-0005. Tel. (03)3231-2511, Fax (03)3231-3513. Singles from ¥13,000. Doubles from ¥19,000. Credit cards. Tokyo Station.*

This old-fashioned Western hotel in the station in the heart of Tokyo is often overlooked; we think it's one of Tokyo's best-kept secrets. The hotel opened in 1914, the same year as Tokyo Station. The rooms have high ceilings and the tile bathrooms are charming. The long narrow Georgian windows are double sealed so the rooms are quiet. The main dining room's French food is good and offers great station views. And just think, you can leave the hotel just a few minutes before your train's departure.

6. TOKYO MARUNOUCHI HOTEL, *1-6-3 Marunouchi, Chiyoda-ku, Tokyo, 100-0005. Tel. (03)3215-2151, Fax (03)3215-8036. Singles from ¥13,000. Twins from ¥21,000. Credit cards. Tokyo Station, Yaesu exit.*

Marunouchi Hotel is one of the oldest hotels in Tokyo. It has an excellent location in the heart of the Marunouchi business district and is only minutes away from Tokyo Station and a number of subway stations. The old-fashioned hotel is fairly intimate yet offers a variety of restaurants: a French restaurant called The Bamboo, a *sushi* bar, a Kyoto-style Japanese restaurant and a Chinese restaurant. The lobby is on the small side but has a comfortable café called Samurai.

7. YAESU FUJIYA HOTEL, *2-9-1 Yaesu, Chuo-ku, Tokyo, 104-0028. Tel. (03)3273-2111, Fax (03)3273-2180. Singles from ¥14,850. Doubles from ¥18,700. Twins from ¥24,200. Credit cards. Tokyo Station, Yaesu exit.*

Yaesu Fujiya Hotel is just a few minutes walk away from Tokyo Station and a number of subway stations, so it's conveniently located for business and sightseeing. The rooms are on the small side and the decor is nothing to write home about, but it has all the basics.

NORTH OF THE IMPERIAL PALACE

The hotels located close to the Imperial Palace offer pleasant walks around the moat, which doubles as Tokyo's most popular jogging route. The area is convenient to Seeing the Sights areas 1, *Around the Imperial Palace*; area 2, *From Ginza to Nihonbashi*; and area 15, *North of the Palace*.

8. YAMANO-UE HOTEL (HILLTOP HOTEL), *1-1 Kanda Surugadai, Chiyoda-ku, Tokyo, 101-0062. Tel. (03)3293-2311, Fax (03)3233-4567. Singles from ¥17,000. Doubles from ¥24,000. Twins from ¥26,000. Credit cards. Jimbocho Station.*

Built in 1937, Yamano-ue Hotel is one of Tokyo's older hotels and still has a very old-fashioned air. The hotel is on a hill in a district filled with universities, so the atmosphere is very different from the chic veneer of Ginza or Shinjuku. Yamano-ue was a favorite haunt of novelists including Mishima Yukio, who wanted to finish work undisturbed. Rooms with old style wooden furniture are like stepping back into your grandmother's house. On clear winter days, you may be able to see Mt. Fuji and the surrounding mountains. Transportation is convenient: Tokyo Station, Ginza, Ikebukuro, Shinjuku, and Akasaka are within a 10-minute train ride away.

9. HOTEL KAYU KAIKAN, *8-1 Sanban-cho, Chiyoda-ku, Tokyo, 102-0075. Tel. (03)3230-1111, Fax (03)3230-2529. US toll free: 800/421-0000. Doubles from ¥21,000. Twins ¥25,000. Credit cards. Hanzomon Station.*

Managed by the Hotel Okura, Kayu Kaikan is a quiet hotel offering good service and food. Known for catered affairs given by government ministries, not many Japanese realize it is actually a hotel. Located only a few minutes walk from Marunouchi, a major business area, we find it convenient for business as well as touring around the city.

10. FAIRMONT HOTEL, *2-1-17 Kudan Minami, Chiyoda-ku, Tokyo, 102-0074. Tel. (03)3262-1151, Fax (03)3264-2476. Singles from ¥11,000. Doubles from ¥20,000. Credit cards. Kudanshita Station.*

This smallish hotel is one of our favorites. It's location, on the north side of the Imperial Palace, is reasonably central yet offers tranquillity and tree-top views. Facing the Imperial Palace's Chidorigafuchi Moat, the rooms look out on cherry blossoms during their short spring season and offer lush greenery at other times. Rumor has it if you want to stay here during the cherry blossom season, you need to make reservations one year in advance! With or without the cherry blossoms, the hotel is cozy yet elegant. Beautiful fresh flower arrangements always adorn the lobby. Selected as one of our Best Places to Stay; see Chapter 11 for more details.

11. TOKYO DIAMOND HOTEL, *25 Ichiban-cho, Chiyoda-ku, Tokyo, 102-0082. Tel. (03)3263-2211, Fax (03)3263-2222. Singles from ¥12,000. Doubles from ¥20,000. Twins from ¥24,000. Credit cards. Hanzomon Station.*

Located just one minute from Hanzomon subway station, the hotel is a stone's throw from the Chidorigafuchi Moat, one of the all-too-few open green areas in Tokyo. Their twin rooms are reasonably spacious for the price. Restaurants include Chinese, Japanese, *sushi* bar, coffee bar and a Western main dining room.

12. KUDAN KAIKAN, *1-6-5 Kudan Minami, Chiyoda-ku, Tokyo, 102-0074. Tel. (03)3261-5521, Fax (03)3221-7238. Singles from ¥8500. Twins from ¥15,000. Doubles from ¥16,000. Credit cards. Kudanshita Station.*

One of the few Meiji era hotels remaining in Tokyo, Kudan Kaikan overlooks the Imperial Palace moat. It is a tranquil and cozy medium-sized hotel with basic comforts. Although nothing fancy, the rooms are well kept and the staff is very friendly and helpful. It's close to Kudanshita Station on the Tozai, Shinjuku and Hanzomon subway lines and only a 10-minute taxi ride from Tokyo City Air Terminal.

AKASAKA & ROPPONGI

The districts of Akasaka and Roppongi are centrally located and are filled with restaurants, bars and clubs. This district is convenient to Seeing the Sights areas 3, *Tsukiji to Roppongi*; and 13, *Aoyama and Akasaka*.

13. HOTEL OKURA, *2-10-4 Toranomon, Minato-ku, Tokyo, 105-0001. Tel. (03)3582-0111, Fax (03)3582-3707. Singles from ¥32,000. Twins from ¥35,000. Doubles from ¥36,000. Credit cards. Kamiyacho Station.*

The Okura is one of Tokyo's best hotels. American presidents and other dignitaries use it as their Tokyo base. The hotel opened in the early 1960s and the lobby has a sort of 1950's Eisenhower charm, low ceilings, retro chairs and soft light filtering in through *shoji* screens. The rooms are fairly standard and are on the small side, given the price. The hotel is enlarging some of its rooms to stay competitive with the newer luxury hotels. Service is extraordinary; the staff jumps through hoops to accommodate the guests. Slightly away from central Tokyo, the closest subway stop, Kamiyacho Station, is about a five-minute walk down the hill.

14. CAPITOL TOKYU HOTEL, *2-10-3 Nagata-cho, Chiyoda-ku, Tokyo, 100-0014. Tel. (03)3581-4511, Fax (03)3581-5822. Singles from ¥32,500. Doubles from ¥37,500. Credit cards. Akasaka Mitsuke Station or Kokkaigijido-mae Station.*

The Capitol Tokyu, one of our favorite hotels, has all the services of a big hotel, but is intimate enough that the doormen know your name by your second day. The hotel used to be a Hilton, but in the 1980s, Hilton moved to a new site in Shinjuku and Tokyu management took over. The understated lobby is always decorated with a huge seasonal floral arrangement; in spring, you find fully opened cherry branches arranged in an enormous bamboo basket; and in autumn, red maple branches mixed with green pines are on display. The lobby looks out on a small, peaceful garden. Located at the top of a hill adjacent to Tokyo's popular Hie Jinja Shrine, it is a superb place to stay for business as well as sightseeing. The good-sized rooms have some Japanese touches such as *shoji* paper screens that give a special softness to the atmosphere.

15. ROPPONGI PRINCE HOTEL, *3-2-7 Roppongi, Minato-ku, Tokyo, 106-0032. Tel. (03)3587-1111, Fax (03)3587-0770. US Toll free: 800/542-8686. Singles from ¥19,500. Doubles and twins from ¥23,000. Credit cards. Roppongi Station.*

Designed by Kurokawa Kisho, an internationally known architect, the Roppongi Prince Hotel is built around an inner court with an open air sky-blue swimming pool in the center. The sides of the pool are transparent so coffee shop patrons have the weird experience of having a fish-eye view of the swimmers — reason enough to make sure we're in shape before swimming here. The hotel has a very postmodern feel with its bright colors and contemporary furniture. It has only 216 rooms. Located just off noisy Roppongi Dori, the hotel is a quiet oasis. It's an especially good choice for someone interested in Roppongi's nightlife since it's an easy walk downhill from the entertainment district.

16. PRESIDENT HOTEL, *2-2-3 Minami Aoyama, Minato-ku, Tokyo, 107-0062. Tel. (03)3497-0111, Fax (03)3401-4816. Doubles ¥17,000. Twins from ¥17,000. Credit cards. Aoyama Itchome Station.*

The President offers some of the best, moderately priced accommodations in Tokyo. The hotel has a comfortable, casual feel. All our friends who have stayed liked it and many are repeat customers. The rooms are on the small side; but its good location, around the corner from the Aoyama Itchome subway stop, more than compensates.

Selected as one of our Best Places to Stay; see Chapter 11 for more details.

17. HOTEL JAL CITY, *3-14-1 Yotsuya, Shinjuku-ku, Tokyo, 160-0004. Tel. (03)5360-2580, Fax (03)5360-2582. Singles from ¥11,000. Doubles from ¥17,000. Twins from ¥18,000. Credit cards. Yotsuya san-chome Station.*

JAL City is a new, moderately priced hotel, a step up from a business hotel. The attractive rooms are larger than in a business hotel and are equipped with trouser presses and hair dryers. Yotsuya san-chome, a stop on the Marunouchi subway line, is only one minute away.

18. ASIA CENTER OF JAPAN, *8-10-32 Akasaka, Minato-ku, Tokyo, 107-0052. Tel. (03)3402-6111, Fax (03)3402-0738. Singles with bath from ¥6500. Twins with bath from ¥10,500. Member of Welcome Inn Reservation Center. Aoyama Itchome Station.*

Asia Center is one of Tokyo's best inexpensive hostels. Located in a quiet area near Akasaka and Roppongi, the Asia Center is convenient to transportation and for sightseeing and shopping. The simple rooms are almost like college dorms, but clean. The atmosphere is very international, and the staff is friendly and helpful. Make sure you book here far in advance because it fills up.

AOYAMA, SHIBUYA & EBISU

The Shibuya-Ebisu-Aoyama area didn't have many hotels, but this situation has changed with the opening of the Westin Tokyo and a number of smaller hotels. This area is convenient for sightseeing, shopping, eating and entertainment. Seeing the Sights areas 10, *Ebisu*; 11, *Shibuya*; 12, *Harajuku and Omotesando*; and 13, *Aoyama and Akasaka* are close by.

19. THE WESTIN TOKYO, *1-4-1 Mita, Meguro-ku, Tokyo, 153-0062. Tel. (03)5423-7000, Fax (03)5423-7600. Singles from ¥30,000. Twins and doubles from ¥36,000. Credit cards. Ebisu Station.*

Opened in 1994 in the new Yebisu Garden Place, Westin Tokyo offers generous-sized rooms with opulent European-style decor. All the rooms have large desks, and fax machines are available upon request. The hotel exudes a feeling of spaciousness; even the restaurants have lots of elbow room. The many shops and restaurants of Ebisu Garden Place are outside the front door, and Ebisu Station is a five-minute, moving-sidewalk ride away.

20. CRESTON HOTEL, *10-8 Kamiyama-cho, Shibuya-ku, Tokyo, 150-0047. Tel. (03)3481-5800, Fax (03)3481-5515. Singles from ¥13,000. Doubles from ¥19,000. Twins from ¥20,000. Credit cards. Shibuya Station.*

Creston Hotel is a pleasant, tranquil place to stay in the Shibuya area. Although located just a few blocks from the energetic shopping and nightlife center, the streets around the hotel are quiet. The interior is done in soothing, subdued colors. The rooms and bathrooms are relatively spacious for the price. Each room is equipped with an outlet for a fax machine, which you can rent at the front desk. The basement houses a delicious, popular and reasonably priced *shabu-shabu* restaurant called Shabuzen.

21. HILLPORT HOTEL, *23-19 Sakuragaoka, Shibuya-ku, Tokyo, 150-0033. Tel. (03)3462-5171, Fax (03)3496-2066. Singles from ¥11,000. Twins from ¥17,000. Credit cards. Member of Welcome Inn Reservation Center. Shibuya Station.*

Located just a few minutes walk from the south exit of JR Shibuya Station, Hillport Hotel is a reasonably priced family hotel one step up from a business hotel. The work of architect Hara Hiroshi, the stylish marble lobby is especially attractive, and the hotel is artfully designed. The rooms are on the small side, but adequate. The hotel has several "function rooms" with beds that fold into the wall so you can hold meetings during the day.

22. SHIBUYA TOBU HOTEL, *3-1 Udagawa-cho, Shibuya-ku, Tokyo, 150-0042. Tel. (03)3476-0111, Fax (03)3476-0903. Singles from ¥11,800. Doubles from ¥16,400. Twins from ¥20,000. Credit cards. Shibuya Station.*

The Tobu Hotel is in the middle of Shibuya's shopping and entertainment district; by walking outside, you have instant entertainment. The rooms are small but cheerfully decorated in pastel colors. Twin rooms are much larger than doubles. It's a good choice for a moderate hotel in an excellent location.

23. KODOMO NO SHIRO HOTEL (CHILDREN'S CASTLE), *5-53-1 Jingumae, Shibuya-ku, Tokyo, 150-0001. Tel. (03)3797-5677, Fax (03)3406-7805. Singles ¥6120. Twins ¥12,630. Credit cards. Member of Welcome Inn Reservation Center. Shibuya or Omotesando Station.*

Children's Castle, an activity center for children from toddlers to high school age, houses a hotel. It's an ideal place to stay with the kids; most guests also have the kids with them. Reservations can be made six months in advance, and it fills up. The hotel is conveniently located close to Shibuya and Omotesando. Stay away from the single rooms because they don't have windows. They also have a few Japanese-style rooms, which kids usually enjoy.

SHINJUKU

Shinjuku is home to at least a half-dozen high-rise deluxe hotels that all provide first-rate service and accommodations. Shinjuku is a busy commercial and business center with lots of department stores, restaurants and bars. A dozen train lines go through Shinjuku so transportation is excellent. For sightseeing, refer to Seeing the Sights areas 14, *Shinjuku* and 16, *Ikebukuro*.

24. PARK HYATT HOTEL, *3-7-1-2 Nishi Shinjuku, Shinjuku-ku, Tokyo, 163-1055. Tel. (03)5322-1234, Fax (03)5322-1288. US and Canada toll free: 800/233-1234. Singles from ¥41,000. Doubles from ¥46,000. Credit cards. Hatsudai or Shinjuku Station, south exit.*

Perched on floors 39 to 52 of the Shinjuku Park Tower Building, the Park Hyatt is an architecturally stunning hotel that seems to float above the city. The three towers of the building have glass atriums and provide incredible panoramic views from the hotel's lounge, swimming pool and New York Grill restaurant. Despite its location, the hotel has only 178 rooms and provides personalized service. The rooms are the largest in Tokyo and come equipped with fax, video and laser disc machines. The large, opulent bathrooms have separate baths and showers.

Selected as one of our Best Places to Stay; see Chapter 11 for more details.

25. KEIO PLAZA HOTEL, *2-2-1 Nishi Shinjuku, Shinjuku-ku, Tokyo, 160-8330. Tel. (03)3344-0111, Fax (03)3344-0247. US toll free: 800/222-KEIO. Singles from ¥20,000. Doubles and twins from ¥24,000. Credit cards. Shinjuku Station, west exit.*

The Keio Plaza was the first high-rise hotel in west Shinjuku. From the upper floors, you're ensured spectacular views through the hotel's large windows. Only a few minutes from Shinjuku Station, it's the closest of the area's hotels. The Lo Spazio restaurant has a stunning, high-Milan interior and serves delicious Italian food. Be sure you have a drink in the Polestar bar on the top floor bar where you'll enjoy a memorable panoramic view.

26. SHINJUKU WASHINGTON HOTEL, *3-2-9 Nishi Shinjuku, Shinjuku-ku, Tokyo, 160-8336. Tel. (03)3343-3111, Fax (03)3342-2575. Singles from ¥11,300. Doubles from ¥17,000. Twins from ¥17,500. Credit cards. Shinjuku Station, west exit.*

This large (1600 rooms) hotel has ship-like portholes for windows. Check-in is completely computerized although there are real people to assist you. Rooms are small, but adequate. Service is minimal: no bellboys and no room service. There are, however, more than a dozen restaurants in the complex. Choose the Washington Hotel for a no-frills stay in Shinjuku.

ASAKUSA & UENO

Stay in Asakusa if you want a nostalgic journey to old Tokyo. It's not that the district is perfectly preserved, but the atmosphere takes you back to bygone days even though very few wooden buildings remain. The downside is Asakusa is fairly inconvenient to western Tokyo; just keep in mind that it's a 35-minute subway ride to Shibuya.

Seeing the Sights areas 4, *Asakusa*; 5, *Ueno*; 6, *Yanaka*; 7, *Akihabara*; and 8, *Asakusabashi, Ryogoku, Fukagawa and Kiba* are close by.

27. ASAKUSA VIEW HOTEL, *3-17-1 Nishi Asakusa, Taito-ku, 111-0035. Tel. (03)3847-1111, Fax (03)3842-2117. Singles from ¥15,000. Doubles from ¥21,000. Twins from ¥28,000. Credit cards. Asakusa Station.*

We find it jarring to see the Asakusa View Hotel, a 28-storied, modern concrete complex that towers over Asakusa, Tokyo's center of traditional culture where most buildings don't top three stories. Yet, it is an option if you want to be in Asakusa but don't want to stay at small, Japanese budget inn. The marble lobby as well as the rooms are faux art-deco style. Inside the hotel, you feel a million miles away from the commotion of Tokyo. On the 6th floor, the Japanese rooms face a Japanese garden; they start at ¥40,000 for two people. The swimming pool is covered by a roof that is open in good weather.

28. RYOKAN SHIGETSU, *1-31-11 Asakusa, Taito-ku, Tokyo, 111-0032. Tel. (03)3843-2345, Fax (03)3843-2348. Singles from ¥7000. Twins from ¥14,000. Japanese or Western Breakfast, ¥900; Japanese dinner ¥2500. Credit cards. Part of the Japanese Inn Group and Welcome Inn Reservation Center. Asakusa Station.*

This inn is our budget choice in Asakusa. The small inn, recently reconstructed, has 10 Japanese rooms and 14 Western rooms, all with private baths. Located only a stone's throw from Asakusa Kannon Temple, traditional downtown Tokyo is all around you. On the top floor, there's a spacious Japanese-style bath with a grand view. The clientele is overwhelmingly foreign.

29. SAWANOYA RYOKAN, *2-3-11 Yanaka, Taito-ku, Tokyo, 110-0001. Tel. (03)3822-2251, Fax (03)3822-2252. ¥4500 for one person without meals. ¥8800 without bath, ¥9200 with bath for two persons without meals. Credit cards. Member of the Japanese Inn Group and Welcome Inn Reservation Center. Nezu Station.*

This small economical inn is located in Yanaka, an old downtown area that has retained its old-Tokyo feeling. It's a good budget choice if you're looking for Japanese accommodations in a traditional district. The building itself is nondescript, but the rooms are all Japanese style and comfortable. The inn is convenient to Ueno and is just a few minutes by taxi from the Keisei Ueno Station for Narita Airport trains. The friendly owner is one of the organizers behind the Japan Inn Group.

SHINAGAWA AREA

The large concentration of hotels in this area goes back to feudal times when Shinagawa was the first stop on the road from Edo to Kyoto. Today Shinagawa is nine minutes from central Tokyo. Shinagawa doesn't have major sightseeing spots but is on the Yamanote line, which means you can easily reach any part of Tokyo. Seeing the Sights area 9 is really convenient from hotels in this district.

30. **MIYAKO HOTEL**, *1-1-50 Shiroganedai, Minato-ku, Tokyo, 108-0071. Tel. (03)3447-3111, Fax (03)3447-3133. Singles from ¥18,000. Doubles from ¥30,000. Twins from ¥22,000. Credit cards. Meguro Station.*
Built on the estate of a prominent businessman and politician, the Miyako Hotel has a quiet atmosphere surrounded by lush greenery. The Japanese garden, seen through the huge glass windows of the cafe, gives the impression of looking at an eight-panel screen. The rooms are a good size and have large windows. They have a swimming pool and sports club for guests for a ¥2000 fee. The hotel is fairly far from train stations but runs a shuttle bus to Meguro Station. This situation will improve drastically once the new subway line opens sometime around the year 2000.

31. **TOBU TAKANAWA HOTEL**, *4-7-6 Takanawa, Minato-ku, Tokyo, 108-0074. Tel. (03)3447-0111, Fax (03)3447-0117. Singles from ¥13,000. Twins ¥20,000. Doubles from ¥25,000. All include Western or Japanese breakfast. Credit cards. JR Shinagawa Station.*
Tobu Takanawa is a lovely small hotel in a very convenient location and offers personalized service. Three minutes walk from Shinagawa Station, the neighborhood is surprisingly quiet. The lobby faces a small inner court, so the atmosphere is especially tranquil. The business corner offers translation and other services.

32. **SHINAGAWA PRINCE HOTEL**, *4-10-30 Takanawa, Minato-ku, Tokyo, 108-0074. Tel. (03)3440-1111, Fax (03)3441-7092. Singles from ¥8000 (main building), ¥14,000 (annex) and ¥18,000 (new wing). Twins from ¥14,000. Credit cards. JR Shinagawa Station.*
The Shinagawa Prince Hotel consists of three different buildings, each with varying room sizes, and is a good choice for a moderately priced hotel. To us, the singles in the main building are absolutely claustrophobic. Instead, we prefer the new wing because the high rise puts you above everything making the rooms appear light and airy. The hotel's many restaurants include a food court, Aji Kaido Gojusantsugi, on the 38th floor: the *sushi, tempura, yakitori, kushiage* and *teppanyaki* areas all have a grand view.

33. **RYOKAN SANSUISO**, *2-9-5 Higashi Gotanda, Shinagawa-ku, Tokyo, 141-0022. Tel. (03)3441-7475, Fax (03)3449-1944. Singles without bath ¥5000. Twins with bath ¥9000. Credit cards. Part of the Japanese Inn Group and Welcome Inn Reservation Center. Gotanda Station.*
For the budget traveler who wants Japanese-style accommodations in a central location, Sansuiso may be for you. Still, we have to be honest about the accommodations. The location is convenient, the price is reasonable, and the atmosphere is Japanese. But the slightly run-down inn is on small street, surrounded by office buildings — most of the rooms don't get sunshine. But it is quiet. The owner is hospitable, friendly and caters to foreigners. The inn doesn't serve meals, but there are tons of

restaurants in the neighborhood. Try Tokyu Supermarket next to Gotanda Station for a wide variety of take-out foods on the first floor — *sushi* to sandwiches.

TOKYO CITY AIR TERMINAL (TCAT) HAKOZAKI AREA

If you are staying in Tokyo for a very short time, you might want to consider the TCAT area. You won't waste time getting from airport to the hotel, and it's built above a subway station. Seeing the Sights area 2, *From Ginza to Nihonbashi* is most convenient.

34. ROYAL PARK HOTEL, *2-1-1 Nihonbashi Kakigara-cho, Chuo-ku, Tokyo, 103-0014. Tel. (03)3667-1111, Fax (03)3665-7212. US and Canada toll free: 800/223-0888. Singles from ¥21,000. Doubles from ¥28,000. Twins from ¥30,000. Credit cards. Suitengu-mae Station.*

If you take a limousine bus from Narita Airport to TCAT, you'll be relaxing in your room before your fellow passengers reach their hotels. Located literally next to TCAT, the hotel is popular with airline crews. Although it's a little far from the center of things, being right above Suitengu-mae subway station means you can get anywhere in Tokyo easily. The hotel is equipped with a good business center and a fitness club as well as a variety of restaurants including 20th-floor eateries with good views. You can even watch CNN. When it's time to leave Tokyo, you won't even have to drag your suitcase next door to TCAT to catch the airport bus — the bellman will roll it over for you.

35. HAKOZAKI TERMINAL HOTEL, *4-7 Nihonbashi Nakasu, Chuo-ku, Tokyo, 103-0008. Tel. (03)3808-2222, Fax (03)3808-2221. Singles from ¥7000. Twins ¥10,000. Credit cards. Suitengu-mae Station.*

This small business hotel is close to the Royal Park. Like most business hotels, the rooms are minuscule and service minimal. But if you are looking for basic accommodations, it's right by the Suitengu-mae subway station, so you can get around Tokyo easily.

MEJIRO & IKEBUKURO

Mejiro is a fairly quiet residential area. Ikebukuro, a busy commercial center in the northwest corner of Tokyo, is loaded with stores, restaurants and bars. It's far from the downtown business centers, but being on the JR Yamanote loop line as well as several subway lines, it offers good transportation.

Seeing the Sights areas 14, *Shinjuku*; 15, *North of the Palace*; and 16, *Ikebukuro* are the most convenient.

36. FOUR SEASONS HOTEL, *2-10-8 Sekiguchi, Bunkyo-ku, Tokyo, 112-0014. Tel. (03)3943-2222, Fax (03)3943-2300. Toll Free in the US: 800/*

332-3442. Singles from ¥31,000. Doubles from ¥35,000. Credit cards. Mejiro Station.

Located on the grounds of a large Japanese garden, the Four Seasons has one of the best settings in Tokyo. Lush greenery surrounds you and since the hotel is not high rise, you feel part of the garden. The spacious feeling carries over into the large lobby that's attractively decorated with Asian objects. Also on the grounds is one of Tokyo's most well-known wedding reception halls, Chinzanso; you may see many beaming couples gathered with their families. The guest rooms are large by Tokyo standards and well appointed. Bice, the elegant main restaurant, serves delicious Italian food — it's the first major hotel in Tokyo not to have French cuisine in the main dining room. Four Seasons' only drawback is its poor location relative to a train station; the hotel runs a shuttle to Mejiro Station.

Selected as one of our Best Places to Stay; see Chapter 11 for more details.

37. HOTEL METROPOLITAN, *1-6-1 Nishi Ikebukuro, Toshima-ku, Tokyo, 171-0021. Tel. (03)3980-1111, Fax (03)3980-5600. Toll free from US and Canada: 800/465-4329. Singles from ¥18,000. Doubles and twins from ¥22,000. Credit cards. Ikebukuro Station, west exit.*

The hotel is also called Crowne Plaza Metropolitan, part of the Holiday Inn group. It's an 814-room new hotel that has a half-dozen restaurants, an outdoor swimming pool (open July to September) and business amenities. Located a few minutes walk from Ikebukuro Station and next to the Tokyo Metropolitan Art Space, you have easy access to transportation and the shopping and restaurants of Ikebukuro. Removed from the commotion of Ikebukuro's streets, the hotel is quiet and less expensive than the top deluxe hotels. The Metropolitan is good value for a full-service hotel.

38. KIMI RYOKAN, *2-36-8 Ikebukuro, Toshima-ku, Tokyo, 171-0014. Tel. (03)3971-3766. No fax. Single ¥4,500. Twin from ¥6,500. No credit cards. Ikebukuro Station, west exit.*

This inn is legendary among budget travelers, and the guests are almost exclusively foreigners. The 37 Japanese-style rooms are very clean; none has a private bath. The singles and regular twins are very small; we suggest you spring for the larger twin that costs ¥7500. The brothers who own the inn backpacked extensively in Europe in the 1970s and realized Japan lacked inexpensive pension-style accommodations, so they decided to open the inn. The place is very popular, especially on weekends, so book in advance. The police box at the west exit of Ikebukuro Station has maps to Kimi Ryokan.

13. WHERE TO EAT

No doubt about it, Tokyoites are obsessed with eating. The city has over 150,000 restaurants and bars. It's a shame we can only eat three meals a day. At that rate, it would take us about 137 years to try them all.

If you think restaurants are nearly always found at street level, you're in for a surprise in Tokyo. Six- and eight-storied buildings sometimes house dozens of restaurants. You find them in basements, on penthouse floors, and scattered throughout department stores. And as if there weren't enough, when darkness falls, wooden carts drop down their sides and become portable restaurants.

Japanese cuisine is varied and restaurants tend to specialize. You won't be able to get *tempura* in a *sushi* bar, nor *sushi* in a *tempura* restaurant. But sometimes, especially in areas frequented by tourists, you'll find restaurants serving a wide variety of Japanese food. But why limit yourself to Japanese food? Tokyo has excellent French, Italian, Indian, Thai and other cuisines. So when you tire of soy sauce, branch out.

Tokyo has restaurants to suit all budgets. Inexpensive noodles, the original Japanese fast food, compete with Western fast food and revolving *sushi* bars to fill the bellies of budget travelers. At the other end of the spectrum, posh restaurants serve top-of-the-line fare to the well heeled and those on expense accounts. Fortunately, most restaurants fall between the two, providing tasty food and reasonable value.

Tokyo goes through food fads. When a particular cuisine becomes the rage, restaurants multiply with alarming speed until a new trend replaces it. Generic ethnic and Thai have peaked, but Italian trattorias, Parisian cafes and California Asian eateries are still on the rise. Restaurants appear and disappear almost overnight and then, they sometimes reappear. More than once we've gone and have found a construction site where there once was a restaurant; in six months, the same restaurant is ensconced in shiny new digs. But to be on the safe side, call before you go far out of your way.

Successful restaurants often open branches. Although the name is the same, sometimes the menu is different. For instance, many famous

RESTAURANT PRICE CATEGORIES

A word on how we have categorized the restaurants:
* *inexpensive is under ¥3000 per person*
* *moderate is ¥3000 to ¥6000*
* *expensive is between ¥6000 and ¥12,000*
* *very expensive is over ¥12,000*

restaurants have branches in department stores, but the menu in the department store is usually less expensive than at the main shop.

Japanese restaurants tend to serve fixed meals called sets, courses or *teishoku*. In some places you cannot order a la carte, while others will offer both. A typical Japanese course includes a starter, main dish, rice, pickles and soup. But with *kaiseki*, Japanese haute cuisine, the entire meal seems in search of a main dish; you are served small dish after small dish.

Restaurants have wide variations in price. A restaurant expensive in the evening can easily have a ¥1500 lunch special. Or a restaurant may have a ¥7000 set dinner, but if you only want one or two courses, your bill can be less. It's a sweeping generalization, but we'll say it anyway: in Western restaurants, the set meals can be boring, and you may have a better meal by ordering a la carte. Alcoholic beverages, especially wine, can add substantially to the cost of a meal — even beer or *sake* (rice wine) adds up.

Lunch is Tokyo's big bargain. Even very expensive restaurants have a more reasonably priced menu at noontime. If you want to try a specific restaurant but don't want to pay the high price, look into eating your mid-day meal there. For office workers, 12 noon is the universal lunch hour, so expect restaurants in business areas to be packed at this time. Eat before noon or after 1pm to avoid the crowds. But don't wait too late because most restaurants stop serving lunch by 2pm. Tokyoites also eat dinner on the early side, around 6:30 to 7pm. Many restaurants stop serving by 8:30pm or 9pm.

Restaurants have a last-order time, but you usually have about an hour after that time to eat. The closing time we list is actually the last-order time. If you arrive later, you will almost always be refused; restaurants take their hours seriously.

There's a 5% tax added. Sometimes it's included in the menu price, but usually it is additional, and if your meal is over ¥7500, another 3% tax is charged. Hotel and high-end restaurants usually add a 10% service charge. Do not tip, ever, even if there is no service charge. Usually you settle the bill at the counter near the exit, not at the table.

If you can't figure out where to eat, head to the closest department store or to the basement of a large office building. Both will have a number of reasonably priced restaurants usually with lots of plastic food samples outside their doors. And department store restaurant floors stay open later than the store itself.

Do yourself a favor, and slip out of your hotel to try some of Tokyo's many restaurants. If the menu posted is only in Japanese, look at it as an adventure. Use the extensive menu listings in Chapter 10, *Food & Drink*, to order any type of Japanese food. Eating in Tokyo is a great cultural and culinary experience. *Bon Appetit*, or, as the Japanese say, *Itadakimasu.*

We have divided Tokyo restaurants into the following dining areas:

1. Akasaka, *pages 184-186*
2. Asakusa, *pages 186-189*
3. Ebisu, *page 189*
4. Ginza, Hibiya, Marunouchi and Tsukiji, *pages 189-192*
5. Harajuku and Aoyama, *pages 192-195*
6. Kanda, *page 195*
7. Odaiba (Tokyo waterfront), *pages 195-196*
8. Roppongi, Hiroo and Nishi Azabu, *pages 196-199*
9. Ryogoku, *pages 199-200*
10. Shibuya and Daikanyama, *pages 200-202*
11. Shinagawa and Takanawa, *page 203*
12. Shinjuku, *pages 203-205*
13. Shirogane and Meguro, *pages 205-207*
14. Ueno, *page 207*
15. Tokyo outskirts, *page 208*

AKASAKA

MIMIU *(Udon-suki, moderate). 3-12-13 Akasaka, Minato-ku. Tel. (03)3505-3366. Open 11:30am to 8:30pm. Closed Sunday. Akasaka Mitsuke Station.*

A branch of the well-known Osaka restaurant, Mimiu serves *udon-suki*, a one-pot dish with *udon* noodles, chicken, fish and vegetables cooked in broth. Special noodles that stay firm when cooked and the nearly clear, tasty broth are the secrets to success. We really feel warmed up eating here on cold wintry days. *Udon-suki* costs ¥3500.

ROSSO E NERO *(Italian, moderate). 2-A Kioi-cho Building, Chiyoda-ku. Tel. (03)3237-5888. Open daily 11:30am to 2pm; 5:30pm to 10pm. Akasaka Mitsuke Station.*

True to its name, the interior decor is red and black with lots of plants creating a cozy atmosphere. Although the selection of Italian wine is fine, Noriko adores their orange juice. Its color is almost as red as tomato juice and the taste is superb. Some of our favorites are *bruschetta del conte* (garlic toast topped with perfectly ripened diced fresh tomatoes, basil and olive oil); *vitello tonnato* (thin slices of veal in tuna and anchovy sauce); and *gnocchi* in pesto sauce. The homemade pastas are served perfectly al dente.

GRANATA *(Italian, inexpensive to moderate). B1, TBS Kaikan, 5-3-3 Akasaka, Minato-ku. Tel. (03)3582-3241. Open daily 11am to 10:30pm. Akasaka Station.*

Granata is a Tokyo institution. Located in the basement of a local landmark, the TBS building, it's easy to find. We suspect it's popular with Tokyoites because it is authentic Roman style rather than adjusted to local taste. Platters of antipasto sit on a table in the center of the room so you have a sense of what's to come. The restaurant is divided into several semiprivate corners, giving an intimate feeling. Pastas are delicious and fish and meat are cooked well: the chicken a la Roma is our favorite. They offer lunchtime service ranging from ¥950 to ¥3000. Dinner courses are ¥5000 and ¥7000 and include two starters, fish, meat, dessert and coffee. A la carte is also available.

HINAZUSHI *(Sushi, inexpensive to moderate). B1, Nambu Building, 3-3 Kioi-cho. Chiyoda-ku. Tel. (03)3230-1884. Open weekdays 11:30am to 2:30pm; 5pm to 11pm. Saturday, 12 noon to 10:30pm, Sunday and national holidays, 12 noon to 10pm. Akasaka Mitsuke Station.*

From the exterior, Hinazushi looks rather exclusive so you may wonder if this is the right place. But as you enter, a friendly, kimono-clad hostess greets you. The interior is contemporary Japanese — long paper lanterns and fresh flower arrangements placed on a beautiful stone floor. The lunchtime set consist of nine kinds of *sushi* and one *temaki* roll for ¥980. If you want to choose your *sushi*, ask for the *okonomi nigiri:* you select 12 pieces for ¥2300. At dinner an all-you-can-eat course costs ¥4300. Hinazushi has an English menu; you merely write down your order. It's a perfect place to eat *sushi* to your heart's content. Juni-an, the adjacent restaurant sharing the same entrance, is a *kaiseki* restaurant managed by the same company. If you'd prefer, *kaiseki* meals cost ¥4300 (lunchtime only), ¥5300, and two different courses for ¥7300.

TAJ *(Indian, inexpensive to moderate). 3-2-7 Akasaka, Minato-ku. Tel. (03)3586-6606. Open 11:30am to 2pm; 5:30pm to 10pm; 11:30am to 10pm on national holidays. Closed Sunday. Akasaka Mitsuke Station.*

Conveniently located near the Akasaka Mitsuke subway station, Taj has been serving authentic Indian food in Tokyo for quite sometime. It's a popular restaurant with Indian expatriates. Lunchtime specials start from ¥830 and lunchtime *tabe hodai* (all you can eat) costs only ¥1200. Noriko loves their Masala Dosa, a South Indian dish, which costs ¥1300.

SUSHI SEI *(Sushi, inexpensive to moderate). 3-7-12 Akasaka, Minato-ku. Tel. (03)3584-2552. Open weekdays 11:30am to 2pm, 5pm to 10:30pm;*

Saturday 11:30am to 2pm, 4:30pm to 10pm. Closed Sunday and national holidays. Akasaka Mitsuke Station.

One of the many branches of the reasonably priced Sushi Sei, we love this shop with its immaculate *sushi* bar and friendly staff. Lunch *nigiri sushi* set costs ¥900; dinner will cost under ¥5000 per person.

TORAYA *(Japanese sweets, tea room). 4-9-22 Akasaka, Minato-ku. Tel. (03)3408-4121. Open 8:30am to 8pm, until 6pm Sunday; tea room in the basement open 11am to 6:30pm; to 5pm weekends. Akasaka Mitsuke Station.*

When the emperor moved from Kyoto to Tokyo in 1868, Toraya moved with him. The Kurokawa family has been making Japanese sweets since the 10th century and enjoys the connoisseurship of the Imperial family. The shop faces busy Aoyama Dori; its traditional Japanese gray and white stucco walls make it easy to find. Toraya sells freshly made bean paste sweets in seasonal flowers shapes for ¥370. It's rather expensive for a small sweet, but it's a piece of art. In the basement is a contemporary tea room where you can enjoy tea and sweets in a relaxed atmosphere. Toraya even has a branch in New York City.

ASAKUSA

BON *(Japanese temple vegetarian, expensive). 1-2-11 Ryusen, Taito-ku. Tel. (03)3872-0234. Weekdays lunch at 12 noon, dinner at 5pm; weekends: 12 noon, 3pm and 5pm. Closed Tuesday. Iriya Station.*

Fucha-ryori is a special Zen Buddhist vegetarian cuisine introduced by a Chinese monk who founded Mampuku-ji Temple at Uji, near Kyoto, in the 17th century. Tucked away among the low houses in a quiet residential area of old downtown Tokyo, Bon is an oasis of serenity. The moment you see the entrance, you know that even the smallest details have not been neglected – the paving stones have been sprinkled with water as a symbol of purification. Note the flower arrangement at the front desk, the dynamic calligraphy of the character for Bon (meaning Buddhist devotee), and the well-polished cobblestone entrance where you remove your shoes. Bon has eight private *tatami* mat rooms with under-the-table pits so you can stretch your legs. Your meal consists of dish after dish of delectable tidbits served on beautiful plates. The set meals, consisting of 12 courses, cost ¥7000 and ¥8000 at lunchtime on weekdays, and ¥10,000 on weekends and evenings. Reservations necessary.

KUREMUTSU *(Japanese, expensive). 2-2-13 Asakusa, Taito-ku. Tel. (03)3842-0906. Open 4pm to 10pm. Closed Thursday. Asakusa Station.*

Set in a small traditional house, Kuremutsu's interior is filled with farmhouse furniture and implements. The food is cooked Kaga style from Kanazawa; there's lots of fresh fish. Their specialty is steamed red snapper stuffed with *okara* (the chaff left from making tofu); it can serve three people. Courses cost ¥8000 and ¥10,000.

ICHIMON *(Japanese, moderate). 3-12-6 Asakusa, Taito-ku. Tel. (03)3875-6800. Open 5pm to 11pm. Closed Sunday and holidays. Iriya or Asakusa Station.*

When you are in Asakusa at the end of the day, stop here for dinner. Ichimon is a drinking establishment so the beer and *sake* rice wine flows freely, and the atmosphere is lively. When you enter, purchase ¥5000 worth of *mon*, a now extinct small coin, which you use to pay for drinks and food. When you leave, return any remaining coins. Ichimon is old farmhouse style with tables as well as *tatami* mats. There are lots of different types of *sake*. The food is simple fare that goes with drinking: *nabe* stews in winter and *takebue tofu* in summer are two favorites.

ASAKUSA IMAHAN *(Sukiyaki, inexpensive to expensive). 3-1-12 Nishi Asakusa, Taito-ku. Tel. (03)3841-1114. Open daily 11:30am to 9:45pm. Asakusa Station.*

Imahan is justifiably the most well-known *sukiyaki* restaurant in Tokyo. The secrets are using marbled beef from Omi province (present Shiga prefecture) and a sugarfree sauce. At lunch Imahan serves *sukiyaki* sets for ¥1800 and ¥3500. Dinner *sukiyaki* courses cost ¥6000, ¥8000 and ¥10,000. The difference in the price depends on the cut of meat. Try it for a change from fish and vegetables.

SANSADA *(Tempura, inexpensive to expensive). 2-2-1 Asakusa, Taito-ku. Tel. (03)3841-3400. Open 11am to 9pm. Closed the last Monday of the month. Asakusa Station.*

"First Asakusa, second Kannon (Buddha of Mercy) and third Sansada's *tempura*," is an old expression. Known for its crispy, honey-colored Edo-style *tempura* (versus Kansai style that is a lighter color), the Sansada family has been frying *tempura* for seven generations – 160 years at the same site. It is located by Kaminarimon Gate that leads to the temple. At lunch they serve a *tendon* set for ¥1250 and a variety of set menus including *tempura*, soup, rice and pickles starting at ¥2000. The annex has *tatami* mat rooms with views of the garden and has sets consisting of *sashimi*, vinegared vegetables, soup, rice, pickles and their special *tempura* ranging from ¥4300 to ¥8000. The shop is large enough that you don't need to make reservations unless it's imperative you eat at a certain time. They charge an additional 10% if you make a reservation.

KAWAMATSU *(Japanese, moderate). 1-4-1 Asakusa, Taito-ku. Tel. (03)3841-1234. Open 11:30am to 9pm. Closed Thursday. Asakusa Station.*

A Japanese restaurant with efficient service and good food on a busy street just a stone's throw from the Kaminarimon Gate, Kawamatsu offers Edo-style Japanese meals at comparatively reasonable prices. The friendly kimono-clad owner of the shop speaks English and is always happy to explain the shop's history to customers. She will probably recommend you try *Kawamatsu-zen*, a lunch box filled with lots of different food

---

TEMPURA

Do you wonder why we've listed so many tempura shops in Asakusa? Asakusa Kannon Temple was a major pilgrimage site – a beacon for people all over Japan. Once they arrived, they looked for more than religious salvation; they wanted to have a good time and eat good food. Japan adopted tempura from the Portuguese who arrived in the 16th century, so it was exotic and trendy.

Asakusa is on the Sumida River, so the shops were always able to get fresh tempura ingredients including fish and shrimp. The tradition has survived although, fortunately, today the fish and shrimp don't come directly from Tokyo Bay.

---

cooked in a variety of ways, ¥3200; *tempura teishoku* (starter, *tempura*, rice, soup, pickles and ice cream) for ¥2600, *sashimi teishoku* for ¥2800, or *unagi teishoku* at ¥2900. They also offer *kaiseki* meals for ¥7000.

AOIMARUSHIN *(Tempura, inexpensive to moderate). 1-4-4 Asakusa, Taito-ku. Tel. (03)3841-0110. Open daily 11am to 9pm. Closed first and third Mondays. Asakusa Station.*

Aoimarushin is famous for crispy Edo-style *tempura* served with a sweet and sour sauce. You'll love it. The house specialty is *kakiage tempura*, mixed vegetables and seafood all mixed together. The *kakiage* course costs ¥2300. *Tendon* is also good at ¥1400. We love their *yasai tendon* (vegetable *tempura* on rice with sauce), ¥1600.

OWARIYA *(Soba, inexpensive). 1-1-3 Asakusa, Taito-ku. Tel. (03)3841-8780. Open daily 11:30am to 8:30pm. Asakusa Station.*

This *sóba* noodle shop has been around more than 100 years. The specialty, *tempura soba* at ¥1200, is famous for its monster shrimp that are larger than the bowl. Frying in sesame oil makes the *tempura* very light.

LA FLAMME D'OR *(Beer hall, inexpensive). 1-23-1 Azumabashi, Sumida-ku. Tel. (03)5608-5381. Open daily 11:30am to 11pm (April through September), 11:30am to 10pm (October through March). Asakusa Station.*

Everyone who goes to Asakusa looks across the Sumida River and says "What's that strange building with a gold curlicue on top?" The answer is the Asahi Beer Company's headquarters. According to designer Philippe Starck, the golden object symbolizes beer froth — use your imagination. The contemporary interior decor gives a sense of spaciousness. You definitely feel you're going through a time warp as you cross the bridge from the traditional atmosphere of Asakusa to the 21st century. Along with cold, frothy beer, the hall serves inexpensive food such as sausages and noodles. Budget ¥1500 for lunch and ¥3500 for dinner.

TOWADA *(Soba, inexpensive). 1-33-5 Asakusa, Taito-ku. Tel. (03)3841-8270. Open 11:30am to 8pm. Closed Monday. Asakusa Station.*

Towada is known for its special *soba* noodles made of 100% buckwheat flour. Standard *soba* is made with a combination of buckwheat and wheat flour; the latter is needed to make a smooth dough. Towada prides itself on a secret recipe that eliminates the need for wheat flour. This is the place to try genuine *soba*. *Zaru* (plain *soba* with dipping sauce) costs ¥750 and *tempura soba* ranges from ¥1100 to ¥1650.

EBISU

CHATEAU RESTAURANT TAILLEVENT ROBUCHON *(French, very expensive). 1-13-1 Mita, Meguro-ku. Tel. (03)5424-1338. Main restaurant open daily 12 noon to 1:30pm; 6pm to 8:30pm. Cafe open daily 11:30am to 1:30pm; 5:30pm to 9pm. Ebisu Station.*

Taillevent Robuchon is a collaborative effort of two Parisian rivals. The original plans called for moving a French chateau to Tokyo stone by stone, but building codes became too cumbersome — instead they built a new one. The chef, Bernard Clays, is Belgium born and trained with one of France's top chefs. When the restaurant opened, it was booked solid for months, but reservations are much easier to come by today. The set dinners cost ¥22,000 and ¥27,000. If the main restaurant is too pricey, try the more casual Cafe Français that serves lunch sets for ¥3500 and ¥4800 and dinner sets for ¥4800, ¥6000 and ¥8000.

IL BOCCALONE *(Italian, moderate). 1F, Silk Ebisu Building, 1-15-9 Ebisu, Shibuya-ku. Tel. (03)3449-1430. Open 6pm to 11pm. Closed Sunday. Ebisu Station.*

For a change from Japanese food, Il Boccalone is an ideal place. One of the most popular Italian restaurants in Tokyo, Il Boccalone is always crowded with people of all ages who enjoy eating and love a festive atmosphere. The staff is Italian. The open kitchen area gives a very up-to-date touch to the place, and the large fresco paintings make you think you might be in Rome. The pastas are delicious, but their real specialty is charcoal grilled fish and meat. We recommend you make reservations as far in advance as possible because the restaurant fills up.

GINZA, HIBIYA, MARUNOUCHI & TSUKIJI

KAMOGAWA *(Japanese, moderate to expensive). B1F, Okura Bekkan Building, 3-4-1 Ginza, Chuo-ku. Tel. (03)3561-0550. Open 11:30am to 3pm; 5:30pm to 10pm. Closed Sunday and national holidays. Ginza Station.*

Special gardeners and carpenters came from Kyoto to build this elegant traditional restaurant in the midst of bustling Ginza. Indeed, as you go down the stairs, you enter a serene and peaceful world. Attention has been paid to the most minute details: stepping stones, dimly lit lanterns and bamboo hedges that separate the private rooms. The fresh fish comes directly from Kamogawa in Chiba Prefecture where the owner has a hotel. The vegetables are always the freshest of the season. What amazes us most is how the food is presented. Kamogawa has such a variety of plates and lacquer bowls and dishes that it is a delight to see the innovative serving. If you don't have time to go to Kyoto, Kamogawa is a good place to experience *kaiseki* in a traditional Japanese atmosphere. We recommend you go at lunchtime for *shokado bento* (lunch packed in a lacquered box) for ¥3000 and ¥4000; *kaiseki* courses run from ¥5000 to ¥30,000. At dinner *kaiseki* courses begin at ¥13,000.

ZAKURO (*Japanese, inexpensive to expensive*). *B1, Sanwa Building, 4-6-1 Ginza, Chuo-ku. Tel. (03)3535-4421. Open daily 11am to 9pm. Ginza Station.*

This Ginza shop is a branch of a famous Japanese restaurant. We like it because of the high quality of the food and the reasonable price. (The main shop, located in Akasaka across from the American Embassy, is rather expensive — the *shabu-shabu* set meals run ¥11,000, ¥13,000 and ¥16,000.) The staff, dressed in kimono, are friendly and efficient, bringing hot towels and tea as soon as you sit down. At lunchtime there's a special set menu called *wa-teishoku A* for ¥2500; it consists of small starters, *sashimi* and a main course (meat or fish), rice, *miso* soup, pickles and dessert. *Tempura teishoku* costs ¥2800. The lunchtime *tempura* course is an excellent value at ¥5000. Fresh hot tea is served frequently, usually just when our current cup cools down enough to drink.

At dinnertime the menu moves to the higher side, but their seasonal *wa-teishoku*, a type of *kaiseki* course, is worth the ¥6800. For an appetizer, enjoy seasonal vegetables that are followed by *sashimi*, grilled fish, vinegared vegetables, steamed vegetables and mixed rice. Noriko loves a refreshing special dessert, cooked plums in syrup. It's best to make reservations for dinner.

KOOMIYA (*Taiwan-style shabu-shabu, inexpensive to moderate*). *B1, Nakaya Ginza Building, 5-8-16 Ginza, Chuo-ku. Tel. (03)3573-3540. Open daily 11:30am to 2pm; 5pm to 10:30pm. Ginza Station.*

This small restaurant serves *shabu-shabu* Taiwan style. Just like Japanese *shabu-shabu*, thin strips of beef and vegetables are cooked in broth at the table, but the dipping sauce is richer. Lunch courses for ¥1000 and ¥1200 do not include *shabu-shabu*, but you can have it if you order in advance. *Shabu-shabu* course, ¥3800, includes dessert. Koomiya is next to Matsuzakaya Department Store.

SUSHI SEI (*Sushi, inexpensive to moderate*). *Dai Nana Kanai Building B1, 8-2-13 Ginza, Chuo-ku. Tel. (03)3571-2772. Open weekdays 11:45am to 2pm, 4:45pm to 10:40pm. Saturday 11:45am to 2pm, 4:30pm to 10pm. Closed Sunday and holidays. Ginza Station.*

There are more than one hundred *sushi* shops in the area, including six Sushi Sei branches. No doubt this is really the land of *sushi* and with good reason — Tsukiji fish market, the source for all, is close by. We like this shop for its beautifully presented fresh fish, contemporary Japanese decor, quiet ambiance, friendly staff and high-tech toilet. The lunchtime *sushi* set includes a tiny starter, *sushi* for the main course, and soup; it costs only ¥1000. You can also order *omakase* (the customers let the chef choose the best of the day), which costs ¥2400. Or you can sit at the counter and point to whatever you fancy. Remember the price of fish varies according to the season and the weather (if the seas are rough or calm). An average bill is ¥2500 per person.

BUONO BUONO *(Italian, inexpensive to moderate). 2F, Nishi Ginza Department Store, 4-2-15 Ginza, Chuo-ku. Tel. (03)3566-4031. Open daily 11:30am to 11pm. Yurakucho Station.*

Located just two minutes from Yurakucho Station on the Yamanote line, Buono Buono is a favorite for Milan-style Italian cuisine. Choose from three set lunch menus ranging from ¥1600 to ¥3000. The ¥1600 offers great value: antipasto, pasta, dessert and coffee. The atmosphere is bright and cheerful; watch the passersby through the large glass windows. One warning: at lunchtime, plan to arrive before 12 noon or after 1pm because Buono Buono is popular with area office workers. Set dinners cost ¥6000 and ¥8000; you can also order a la carte.

EDOGIN *(Sushi, inexpensive to expensive). 4-5-1 Tsukiji, Chuo-ku. Tel. (03)3543-4401. Open 11am to 9:30pm. Closed Sunday. Tsukiji Station.*

Edogin serves some of the best *sushi* in Tsukiji, which is why there will often be a line of people waiting. *Nigiri sushi* sets start at ¥1000 and include soup. Have lunch here after tramping around the fish market.

SUSHI KO *(Sushi, inexpensive to moderate). 6-5-8 Ginza, Chuo-ku. Tel. (03)5568-0505. Open daily 11:30am to 2pm; 5pm to 4am. Ginza Station.*

The chef of this reasonably priced *sushi* shop spent 10 years in California and will happily tell you everything about his fish in fluent English. *Nigiri sushi* sets run ¥700 to ¥3000; you can also order a la carte.

TOUTOUKYO *(Chinese dim sum, inexpensive to moderate). B1, Ginza World Town, 5-8-17 Ginza, Chuo-ku. Tel. (3)3572-5666. Open 11:30am to 9pm. Ginza Station.*

This restaurant makes 84 different kinds of *dim sum* by hand. We love to come here with a large group and choose food from wagons wheeled around the restaurant. The lunch sets start at ¥750 — choice of noodles, Chinese dumpling, vegetable and dessert. The ¥2500 weekday special course is discounted to ¥2000 on weekends.

FARM GRILL *(American, inexpensive). 2F, Ginza Nine Sango-kan, 8-5 Ginza, Chuo-ku. Tel. (03)5568-6156. Open 11am to 9:45pm. Shimbashi Station.*

Farm Grill serves all-American fare like chicken, steak and ribs at very reasonable prices. Their Sunday all-you-can-eat-and-drink buffet from 3pm to 9:45pm for ¥3470 is one of the best deals in town, but it gets crowded.

YAKITORI UNDER THE TRACKS One of our favorite inexpensive places to eat dinner is at one of the many *yakitori* pubs under the tracks south of Yurakucho Station. Eating here is definitely no frills. Protected from the elements by hanging plastic sheets, most shops are half-indoors and half-outdoors. Weekday evenings the places are crowded with office workers from the nearby areas. Beer, *sake* and whiskey flow freely, so the atmosphere is lively and noisy. The food is basic *yakitori* and other Japanese pub fare. From Ginza 4-chome crossing, walk in the direction of the Imperial Palace. Just after you walk under the expressway, turn left after the New Tokyo building; you can't miss the dozen or so eateries.

HARAJUKU & AOYAMA

ASADA *(Japanese, moderate to expensive). B1, 2-7-13 Kita Aoyama, Minato-ku. Tel. (03)5411-0171. Open daily 11:30am to 2:30pm; 5:30pm to 9:30pm. Gaien-mae Station.*

This restaurant is a branch of the famous Asadaya in Kanazawa on the Japan Sea. During the 17th-19th centuries, under the connoisseurship of the Maeda feudal lords, a special cuisine called *Kaga ryori* developed. Asada uses fresh ingredients sent directly from Kanazawa and the food reflects the seasons. At lunch the *Godan Bento* (a five-layer lunch box) costs ¥4000 and *kaiseki* course is ¥7000. At dinner the *Kaga kaiseki* course is served at tables (¥12,000) and *Tateyama* course (¥16,000) is served in private Japanese-style rooms. The special seasonal weekend *kaiseki* course costs ¥10,000. The serene atmosphere of this restaurant is a treat at any time.

KIHACHI *(Nouvelle French, moderate to expensive). 4-18-10 Minami Aoyama, Shibuya-ku. Tel. (03)3403-7477. Open 11:30am to 2:30pm; 5:30pm to 9:30pm. Sunday 11:30am to 8pm. Omotesando Station.*

Kihachi is the perfect place to have lunch after browsing around the designer boutiques of Aoyama; it is a continuation of contemporary Japan. Fashionable Japanese women fill the restaurant at lunchtime. At dinner time, the mood changes and the clientele includes more couples. Kihachi serves French cuisine using Japanese ingredients — especially lots of fresh fish. The chef's salad, which is to die for, includes fresh raw fish and lots of herbs; it's topped with roasted almond slivers. The lunch sets include appetizer, fish or meat, authentic French dessert and coffee and cost ¥2500 to ¥5000. Set dinners cost ¥8000 and ¥10,000, but the chef encourages customers to order a la carte at dinner for maximum appreciation of his inventive culinary talent. The decor is bright and open, and the staff is friendly.

YUZEN *(Japanese, moderate to expensive). B1, Sumitomo Minami Aoyama Building, 5-11-5 Minami Aoyama, Minato-ku. Tel. (03)3486-0206. Open 11:30am to 2pm; 6pm to 9pm. Closed Sunday and national holidays. Omotesando Station.*

Once seated at this charming restaurant, you wonder if you are getting French or Japanese cuisine because the pastel interior and pink tablecloths have a very French feel. The answer is both. The chef worked at Maxim de Paris in Ginza for 13 years and now works his magic in his own kitchen. The menu is a wonderful combination of French and Japanese, and food is served on carefully selected Japanese plates and garnished with seasonal flowers and herbs. The set lunches cost ¥3500 and ¥5000: two starters, pasta, main dish, special rice, dessert and coffee. Set dinners are ¥7500, ¥10,000 and ¥12,000.

KIKU *(Japanese, inexpensive to expensive). 4-16-27 Jingu-mae, Shibuya-ku. Tel. (03)3408-4919. Open 11am to 2pm; 5pm to 9:30pm. Closed Sunday. Harajuku or Meiji Jingu-mae Station.*

Tucked away on a small alley off Omotesando, this restaurant is a real find. Kiku is in a private, renovated house with a very contemporary feeling. Entering the foyer, you step on small paving stones that in the old days must have been part of the narrow garden. Bamboo trees provide serenity and a nice contrast from the commotion of Harajuku. Beautiful indigo banners hang in an atrium. The waiters wear indigo colored *samui*, originally working outfits for Buddhist monks. It's one of our favorite places for a light lunch but, alas, we are not alone. If you go to Kiku after 12 noon you may have to wait for 30 minutes; try to arrive before 11:45am or after 1:15pm.

The food is home-style Japanese; perhaps that's why it's so popular — many Tokyoites don't take the time to prepare it at home. Kiku's lunch set for ¥800 includes a small vegetable starter, main dish (usually fish), rice, *miso* soup and pickles. They also serve more elaborate lunchtime courses costing up to ¥2000. For dinner, the *gyofuzen* set costs ¥2600, *Kiku bento* ¥3600 and *yosenabe* and *kamo* (duck) *nabe* stews (winter only) cost ¥4500. Dinnertime *kaiseki* courses run ¥5500 to ¥12,000. You'll need to make a reservation if you're going to splurge on the ¥12,000 course.

LUNCHAN *(American, moderate). 1-2-5 Shibuya, Shibuya-ku. Tel. (03)5466-1398. Open daily 11am to 11pm. Omotesando Station.*

Bright and airy, Lunchan serves upscale American home cooking. Meat loaf is on the menu, but so are pastas and duck. The decor is open and bright, and you can see the chefs at work in the open kitchen. Sunday brunch is a treat. So are the desserts —they're American sized. Entrees run from ¥1500 to ¥2600.

BARBACOA GRILL AOYAMA *(Brazilian, inexpensive to moderate). B1, Evergreen Building, 4-3-24 Jingumae, Shibuya-ku. Tel. (03)3796-0571. Open 11:30am to 4pm; 5:30pm to 10pm. Omotesando Station.*

This basement restaurant serves an enormous lunch for ¥970 and a lunch buffet for ¥1500. At dinner they have Brazilian all-you-can-eat for ¥3300; it's heavy on barbecued beef. The dinner salad bar course is ¥2500. Come here if you need a meat fix at a reasonable price.

IL FORNO *(Italian cafe and pizzeria, inexpensive to moderate). 2F, La Mia Building, 5-1-3 Minami Aoyama. Tel. (03)3400-0517. Open daily 11:30am to 3pm; 5:30pm to 10:30pm. Omotesando Station.*

For a real cross-cultural experience, try Il Forno for California-Italian food in the heart of Tokyo. A branch of the Santa Monica eatery, the atmosphere is more California than Japan. The menu includes pasta, pizza, meat and fish, and there's a spa section for calorie counters — we said it was California, didn't we? The pizza has a delicious thin crust; you can choose from 15 different toppings. Tea and coffee refills are free, a rarity in Japan. The young waiters and waitresses, sporting T-shirts and black pants, are friendly. Lunchtime specials cost ¥1200.

LAS CHICAS *(Eclectic, inexpensive to moderate). 5-47-6 Jingumae, Shibuya-ku. Tel. (03)3407-6865. Open daily 11am to 10pm. Omotesando Station.*

Tucked away on a back street off Aoyama Dori — turn at Citibank — funky Las Chicas is popular with Tokyo's young expats. The restaurant has a front garden terrace and several rooms inside. The food is eclectic combining American, Continental and Asian. Service is irregular, but everyone is having too good a time to notice. You can even play on the internet. Entrees average ¥1400.

MAISEN *(Japanese tonkatsu, inexpensive). 4-8-5 Jingumae, Shibuya-ku. Tel. (03)3470-0071. Open daily 11am to 10pm. Omotesando Station.*

There are thousands of *tonkatsu* shops in Tokyo, but Maisen stands out. The deep-fried pork cutlet is so tender you can cut it with your chopsticks (if you can manipulate them, that is). Maisen serves *tempura* and *sashimi* in addition to *tonkatsu*, but we recommend you stick with what they do best — *tonkatsu*. Maisen serves an inexpensive lunch until 5pm. The *katsu* set (*tonkatsu*, rice, soup and pickles) costs ¥850; *hitokuchi-katsu teishoku* (bite-sized pieces of *tonkatsu* with rice, soup and pickles) costs ¥800. No item on the menu costs more than ¥2800. Considering Maisen's location in pricey Omotesando, it is a bargain.

BINDI *(Indian, inexpensive to moderate). 7-10-10 Minami Aoyama, Minato-ku. Tel. (03)3409-8755. Open daily 11:30am to 2pm; 6pm to 9:30pm. Omotesando Station or Hiroo Station.*

Tokyo has many Indian restaurants, but tiny Bindi offers one of the most versatile menus. The Mehtas serve delicious home cooking at incredible prices. *Sag* chicken (chicken and spinach) costs ¥1000; *boti kabab* (three pieces of grilled lamb) ¥1000; fish *tikka* (four pieces of swordfish) ¥1300. If you are craving a certain Indian dish, call Mr. Mehta and he'll do his best to accommodate your request.

KANDA

YABU SOBA *(Soba, inexpensive). 2-10 Awaji-cho Kanda, Chuo-ku. Tel. (03)3251-0287. Open 11:30am to 7pm. Closed Monday. Ogawamachi Station.*

Yabu Soba is a classic noodle shop known all over Japan; for more than 100 years, it's served *soba* noodles in the same place. It's worth a detour to visit. The setting is like a movie: a traditional wooden two-storied building with a garden and a small pond in front. Patrons sit at tables as well as on *tatami* mats. The waiters announce your order to the kitchen in voices so resonant, some claim to come only to hear them. But it would be a shame not to order the wonderful noodles with their out-of-this-world broth. *Zaru soba* costs ¥600; *tempura soba* is ¥1500. Best picks include *kamo-nanban (soba* with duck), ¥1500, and *anago-nanban (soba* with freshly cooked sea eel), ¥1700.

ODAIBA

ODAIBA CAFE *(Continental, moderate). 1-3-5 Daiba, Minato-ku. Tel. (03)5531-2771. Open daily 11:30am to 11pm Monday through Thursday; 11:30am to 5am Friday through Sunday. Odaiba Kaihin Koen Station.*

Odaiba, part of the new waterfront development, is the hottest area in Tokyo. Odaiba Cafe is on Sunset Restaurant Row, a string of a half-dozen restaurants that all have terraces to see the beach across the street. We like Odaiba Cafe's food and atmosphere, which is both casual and romantic. The succulent grilled salmon for ¥2600 is a favorite; the portions are large by Japanese standards. Every evening they have live jazz. And if you want to stay up late, they don't close until 5am on weekends. Figure on ¥5000 per person. Make reservations to avoid disappointment.

SAM CHOY *(Hawaiian, moderate). 1-3-5 Daiba, Minato-ku. Tel. (03)5531-5036. Open 11:30am to 2:30pm; 5pm to 11pm weekdays; 11:30am to 5am weekends. Odaiba Kaihin Koen Station.*

This sister restaurant of Sam Choy at Hawaii's Diamond Head is one of Tokyo's new hot spots. Sam Choy, the celebrity-chef, is a Chinese-American born to a family that loves good food. Choy excels at combining the best ingredients of the East and the West. Mahi mahi, steamed white fish wrapped in leaves, is a signature dish. Costing ¥2800, it's large enough to share. He also has a slew of mouth-watering appetizers. Reservations are a must.

ROPPONGI, HIROO & NISHI AZABU

TAKAMURA *(Japanese kaiseki, very expensive). 3-4-27 Roppongi, Minato-ku. Tel. (03)3585-6600. Open 12 noon to 3:30pm; 5pm to 10:30pm. Closed Sunday and national holidays. Roppongi Station.*

Surrounding this quaint and tranquil restaurant in a private house, a bamboo grove insulates you from the commotion of Roppongi. The restaurant has eight private *tatami* mat rooms, all different but charming. One has a pit under the table, so specify it if you'd like to stretch your legs. The *robata* room has a rustic open hearth. *Sake* rice wine is served in freshly cut bamboo containers. Using the freshest seasonal ingredients course after course, the *kaiseki* is a visual treat. Lunchtime set meals cost ¥13,000 and ¥15,000 including a flask of *sake* and service charge. Dinner sets cost ¥17,000, ¥20,000 and ¥25,000 plus a ¥1000 room charge, 15% service charge and 8% tax. So unless someone else is picking up the tab, lunch is the time to enjoy one of Tokyo's most exquisite dining experiences.

INAKAYA *(Robata-yaki, expensive). East branch: 1F, Reine Building, 5-3-4 Roppongi, Minato-ku. Tel. (03)3408-5040. West branch: 7-8-4 Roppongi, Minato-ku. Tel. (03)3405-9866. Open daily 5pm to 5am. Roppongi Station.*

Inakaya is a boisterous restaurant popular with tourists. It's a country-style *robata-yaki* restaurant with a folk art ambiance. All the patrons sit at a large u-shaped counter. Chefs dressed in traditional garb sit behind charcoal grills surrounded by baskets filled with ingredients waiting to be cooked. You merely point at what you want to eat, and it will be cooked for you. The staff shouts out your order, so it's a noisy, festive place. Our biggest complaint is the restaurant is too expensive. By the time you have a beer or two, *sake* and a few dishes, your bill is over ¥10,000.

KISSO *(Japanese kaiseki, inexpensive to moderate). 1B, Axis Building, 5-17-1 Roppongi, Minato-ku. Tel. (03)3582-4191. Open 11:30am to 2pm; 5:30pm to 9pm. Closed Sunday and national holidays. Roppongi Station.*

Located in the basement of the Axis Building, a center of contemporary design, Kisso fits right in. The ambiance is modern Japanese, accented with paper lanterns and artfully arranged fresh flowers. The food is presented on a black lacquered tray and contemporary Japanese dishes. The food emphasizes what's in season, and the fresh citrus-fruit sherbet is to die for. Lunch set costs ¥1200; it changes every day depending what the chef finds at the morning market. *Donburi* is available at ¥1200. *Kaiseki* courses start at ¥3500. Dinner sets begin at ¥8000. After your meal, browse in a corner section where they sell dishes like the ones used to serve you.

ERAWAN *(Thai food, inexpensive to moderate). 13F, Roi Building, 5-5-1 Roppongi, Minato-ku. Tel. (03)3404-5741. Open daily 5pm to 11:30pm. Roppongi Station.*

Erawan, a Thai restaurant with a view, ranks among our favorite Tokyo eateries. On the 13th floor of the Roi Building, it offers fantastic views of Tokyo. The teak wood decor makes you think you're in Bangkok. The food is authentic and the price reasonable. Unlike many Thai restaurants, they don't tone down the spices for the Japanese palate. Each dish costs between ¥1200 and ¥2000; we always order several dishes and share. Some of our favorites are spicy fish cake (¥1200); *mee krob*, crispy vermicelli (¥1200); spicy eggplant salad (¥1200); fried rice served in a fresh pineapple half (¥1500); and *pad thai* noodles (¥1200). The menu indicates how spicy the food is.

NANBAN-TEI *(Japanese yakitori, inexpensive to moderate). 4-5-6-Roppongi, Minato-ku. Tel. (03)3402-0606. Open 5:30pm to 2am. Roppongi Station.*

Nanban-tei serves inventive *yakitori*. In addition to the usual array of chicken and vegetables, you can have pork with asparagus, beef with Japanese basil leaves, and other tantalizing combinations. Course A, ¥3500, comes with 14 different sticks including raw vegetables you dip in a thick *miso* sauce; Course B, ¥3000, has 10 different sticks. You can also order a la carte. The friendly staff speak English, and there is an English menu. Nanban-tei is popular with locals as well as with foreign residents, so it is best to make reservations. There are several branches around central Tokyo.

MIKASA *(Continental, inexpensive to moderate). Arisugawa West, 1F, 5-14 Minami Azabu, Minato-ku. Tel. (03)3448-8924. Open 11:30am to 10:30pm weekdays; 11am to 10:30pm weekends and national holidays. Hiroo Station.*

Mikasa is a light and airy place for a casual lunch in the Hiroo area. In fair weather, you can eat on the patio under large cloth umbrellas. The menu is heavy on Italian, but they also serve fish cooked in nouvelle French style. Mikasa emphasizes using fresh, local seasonal ingredients. Also, unlike many Tokyo restaurants that serve an assortment of bite-size portions for dessert, Mikasa lets you choose from among its tantalizing desserts. The lunch menu starts at ¥1800 for a beef set (starter or soup, mini-steak, raspberry sorbet and coffee), but we prefer the pasta menu for ¥2000 (starter, pasta of the day, dessert and coffee).

NEW HOKKAIEN *(Chinese, inexpensive to moderate). 2F, No. 23 Togensha Building, 3-16-15 Roppongi, Minato-ku. Tel.(03)3505-7881. Open daily 11:30am to 10:30pm. Roppongi Station.*

As a long-standing Beijing-style Chinese restaurant, New Hokkaien is always crowded with young and old, Japanese and foreigners. It's one of Tokyo's few Chinese restaurants that hasn't adjusted its recipes to suit the

Japanese palate. In addition to standard and authentic Chinese dishes, you can choose delicate and tasty dim sum.

KITCHEN 5 *(Southern European and Middle Eastern, moderate). 4-2-15 Nishi Azabu, Minato-ku. Tel. (03)3409-8835. Open from 6pm to 9:45pm. Closed Sunday, Monday and holidays. Also closed for five weeks late July to early September, four weeks around New Year's and three weeks around Golden Week. Hiroo Station.*

Kobayashi-san, the female chef, closes the restaurant for extended periods several times a year when she travels to Europe and the Middle East to try out new cuisines. She returns and incorporates what she has learned to make delicious, eclectic fare. There is no menu; Kobayashi-san goes to the market every morning, chooses the freshest food and cooks it. The offerings are placed on the counter and you tell her your choices. While you never know what you'll find, we adore her spicy chicken, ratatouille, and pasta in fresh tomato and basil sauce. The restaurant is tiny—there's only a small counter and one table. Come before 7pm or you may have to wait. Dishes cost about ¥1800 each; ¥5000 should buy enough for an average appetite.

LA TERRE *(French, inexpensive to moderate). 1-9-20 Azabudai, Minato-ku. Tel. (03)3583-9682. Open 11:30am to 2pm; 6pm to 8:30pm. Closed Sunday and national holidays. Kamiyacho Station.*

Tucked away on a little alley across from the Russian Embassy, La Terre is a cozy and romantic French bistro. When the weather is good, there are a few tables outside. La Terre is especially popular in the spring when cherry trees blossom and new leaves sprout; reservations are a must. The cherry trees are right outside the restaurant; even if you are facing the back, you can see them reflected in the mirror. The food is French but on the light side. The lunchtime sets cost ¥2000, ¥2500 and ¥4000. Dinner courses are ¥6000, ¥8000 and ¥10,000. You can also order a la carte.

LE FRICOTEUR *(French bistro, inexpensive to moderate). 4-11-28 Nishi Azabu, Minato-ku. Tel. (03)3498-4508. Open 11:30am to 2:30pm; 6pm to 9:30pm. Closed Sunday. Hiroo Station.*

This intimate French bistro has a friendly chef and staff and serves good, honest fare. The specialty is red wine beef stew, which melts in your mouth (¥2700). The lunchtime ¥1050 set menu is a bargain: appetizer, main dish and coffee. For the lunchtime D course, the chef chooses the best available (¥3400). Evening set meals cost ¥6000.

KUSHIHACHI *(Yakitori, expensive). 3F, Seshido Building, 3-10-9 Roppongi, Minato-ku. Tel. (03)3403-3060. Open 5:30pm to 10:30pm. Closed Sunday and national holidays. Roppongi Station.*

It's pricey but a lively traditional Japanese dining experience. The ¥7000 basic set includes 10 kinds of *yakitori* and other delicacies on skewers plus four side dishes.

HONMURA-AN *(Soba, inexpensive). 7-14-18 Roppongi, Minato-ku. Tel. (03)3401-0844. Open 11:30am to 9pm. Closed Tuesday. Roppongi Station.* Located behind Hotel Ibis, Honmura-an dishes up some of Tokyo's best *soba* noodles. Walk up the few steps to reach this lively shop always crowded with aficionados. *Soba* can cost more here than at average shops, but it's worth every yen. The house specialties are *tempura seiro,* cold *soba* with *tempura* on the side (¥1700) and *kamo seiro,* cold *soba* you dip in duck broth (¥1300). *Tempura soba,* (the *tempura* shrimp floats in the hot broth on top of noodles) is ¥2100. *Sansai* (mountain vegetable) *soba* costs ¥900. After you finish eating cold *soba,* the staff brings hot water in a square lacquer container. Mix this water with your remaining dipping sauce and drink as a soup.

JOHNNY ROCKETS *(American, inexpensive). 2F, Coco Roppongi Building, 3-11-10 Roppongi, Minato-ku. Tel. (03)3423-1955. Open 11am to 11pm Sunday to Thursday; 11am to 6am Friday and Saturday. Roppongi Station.*

For that hamburger craving, bypass McDonalds. Johnny Rockets is a retro American diner serving burgers, fries and shakes. Most of the fun-loving staff are foreigners. The shop's most popular "original hamburger" costs ¥900, soft drinks are ¥450. Yes, it's more expensive than fast food, but worth it. Weekend evenings Johnny stays open all night so you can fill up after dancing nearby.

KAOTAN RAMEN *(Ramen, inexpensive). 2-34-30 Minami Aoyama, Minato-ku. Tel. (03)3475-6337. Open 11:30am to 5am; holidays until 4:30am. Roppongi Station.*

Located at the foot of Aoyama Cemetery, it is hard to miss this shack that serves legendary *ramen.* Their Benzes parked nearby, people queue up to eat the ¥600 bowl of noodles.

RYOGOKU

CHANKO DOJI *(Chanko nabe, inexpensive to moderate). 1-28-4 Midori-cho, Sumida-ku. Tel. (03) 3635-5347. Open daily 11:30am to 1:30pm; 5pm to 9:30pm. Ryogoku Station.*

Chanko Doji serves *chanko nabe,* the stew that sumo wrestlers eat: vegetables, tofu, *udon* noodles, chicken and fish are cooked together in a broth. Don't worry, it's not fattening, sumo wrestlers just eat a lot of it. At lunchtime, the *nabe* is ¥1800 and ¥2000 and *kamo chanko* (duck chanko) is ¥2200. Dinnertime, *tori chanko* (chicken chanko) is ¥4000, *yokozuna chanko* (champion chanko) is ¥5000.

MOMOJIYA *(Japanese, inexpensive to moderate). 1-10-2 Ryogoku, Sumida-ku. Tel. (03)3631-5596. Open 5pm to 9pm. Closed Sunday. Ryogoku Station.*

Momojiya serves venison and boar dishes and badger soup. The *inoshishi* (boar meat) set is ¥4000. *Inoshishi teishoku* (¥4500) includes boar meat, rice, pickles and mushroom soup. Ask them to substitute badger soup if you prefer.

SHIBUYA & DAIKANYAMA

HASSAN (*Shabu-shabu, moderate*). *B1F, Junikagetsu Building, 1-18-7 Jinnan, Shibuya-ku. Tel. (03)3464-8883. Open daily 11:30am to 11pm. Shibuya Station.*

The restaurant is known for its special ceramic plates, *Takatori-yaki* ware, introduced to Japan by a Korean potter named Hassan during the 17th century. Located in the basement of the Junikagetsu Building, Hassan has a quiet, traditional air; the windows look out on bamboo trees. Lunchtime menus consist of two *shabu-shabu* sets: ¥1500 for imported beef and ¥2500 for Japanese beef. All you can eat *shabu-shabu* (*tabehodai*) costs ¥3900 and ¥4500 at lunchtime, and ¥4500 and ¥5900 at night. After 4:30pm they add a 10% service charge.

SHABU ZEN (*Shabu-shabu, sukiyaki, and kaiseki, moderate*). *B1, Shibuya Creston Hotel, 10-20 Kamiyama-cho, Shibuya-ku. Tel. (03)3485-0800. Open 11:30am to 3pm; 5pm to 11:30pm weekdays; 5pm to 11:30pm weekends. Shibuya Station.*

Shabu Zen serves *shabu-shabu* at a very reasonable price. You can order a set for ¥3000 but for just ¥800 more you can have *tabehodai*, all you can eat. The least expensive set uses US beef, the next up (¥4000) uses Japanese beef and the highest (¥5000) uses Kobe beef, raised where the animals are drinking beer and listening to Mozart and Bach. They also serve *sukiyaki* and *kaiseki*. The basement has high ceilings and a contemporary Japanese ambiance. Most of the customers sit at tables but there are *tatami* mat rooms along one side.

TABLEAUX (*Continental/American, moderate*). *B1, Sunrise Daikanyama Building, 11-6 Sarugaku-cho, Shibuya-ku. Tel. (03)5489-2201. Open daily 11:30am to 2pm; 5:30pm to 10:30pm. Tea lounge open weekdays 2pm to 5:30pm. Daikanyama Station.*

Popular with models and expats, this restaurant has a richly textured decor of deep red brocades and velvets; in other words, early bordello. The food is eclectic and good — surprisingly inexpensive given the surroundings and clientele. Their pasta is delicious as is the seafood. Tableaux is in Daikanyama, an area known for fashionable boutiques and eateries. The American manager is very friendly and will be more than happy to assist you with choosing your food and wine.

KAIKA-YA (*Japanese home-style cooking, moderate*). *23-7 Maruyama-cho, Shibuya-ku. Tel. (03)3770-0878. Open 11:30am to 2pm Monday, Wednesday and Friday; 6pm to 10pm daily except Sunday and holidays. Shibuya Station.*

This tiny Japanese bistro ranks among our favorite places for original and inventive Japanese home-style cooking. There is only one offering at lunch (¥1000), decided by the chef after he goes to the morning market. For dinner, the menu is written only in Japanese. We recommend that you tell the chef "*omakase* course," ¥3000, and the chef will give you a sampling of the best dishes of the day. One specialty is tuna ribs, tuna cooked on the bone in a thick soy sauce. The sign for the restaurant is in Japanese, but you'll see "By the Sea" in English.

RAJ MAHAL *(Indian, inexpensive to moderate). 5F, JOW Building, 30-5 Udagawa-cho, Shibuya-ku. Tel. (03)3770-7680. Open daily 11:30am to 10pm. Shibuya Station.*

Raj Mahal is an excellent Indian restaurant. The decor is suitably Indian without being over the top and the *tandoori* oven, visible through the kitchen's glass window, lends an air of authenticity. The *tandoori* meats, fish and *nan* bread are wonderful as are the curries. Fortunately, the flavors haven't been toned down for the Japanese palate. Raj Mahal's manager, Mr. Panda, is always very helpful with dining suggestions. The menu is both in English and Japanese. Lunchtime specials range from ¥950 to ¥1800 and most entrees are in the ¥1500 range.

SAMRAT *(Indian, inexpensive to moderate). Koyas One Building, 6F, 13-7 Udagawa-cho, Shibuya-ku. Tel. (03)3496-9410. Open daily 11am to 10pm. Shibuya Station.*

One of several Indian chain restaurants in Shibuya, Samrat serves good food at reasonable prices. The chef and most of the staff are Indian so communication in English is no problem. The curries are good and so is the *nan* bread. The lunchtime menu is served until 4pm, a real plus. For ¥890 you can have two kinds of curry, a drink, and all the rice and *nan* you can eat. Samrat has other shops in Roppongi *(Shojikiya Building 2F, 4-10-10 Roppongi, Minato-ku. Tel.(03)3478-5877)*; in Ueno *(OAK Building 2F, 4-8-9 Ueno, Taito-ku. Tel.(03)5688-3226)*; and in Shinjuku *(Seno Building 7F, 3-18-4 Shinjuku, Shinjuku-ku. Tel.(03)3355-1771)*.

ANATOLIA *(Turkish, moderate). B1, Miyamasuzaka Building, 2-19-20 Shibuya, Shibuya-ku. Tel. (03)3486-7449. Open daily 11am to 11pm; 3pm to 11am Sunday. Shibuya Station.*

Anatolia is a small basement restaurant serving hearty Turkish food. The picture menu is in English as well as in Japanese. They have three set courses costing ¥3300 to ¥4400, but we prefer to order a la carte. Our favorite is the *iskender* kebobs.

SUSHI SEI *(Sushi, inexpensive). B2, Shibuto Cine Building, 2-6-17 Dogenzaka, Shibuya-ku. Open 11:30 to 2pm, 5pm to 10pm weekdays, 11:30am to 9:30pm weekends and national holidays. Closed the 3rd Monday of the month. Shibuya Station.*

This *sushi* bar in the basement of the Shibuto Cine Building, right across the street from the Shibuya 109 Building, is popular for its fresh and reasonably priced *sushi*. It gets crowded, so come for dinner before

7pm or else you'll have to wait. We usually go with the chef's course, an assortment of *nigiri sushi*, for ¥2500. You can also order a la carte.

KABALA *(Thai, moderate). B1F, Pink Dragon Building, 1-23-23 Shibuya, Shibuya-ku. Tel. (03)3498-0699. Open 6pm to 11pm. Closed Sunday. Shibuya Station.*

As you go down the stairs, you'll notice that the owner's taste is most peculiar. Kabala has more to offer than the delicious Thai food it serves. The interior decor is closer to continental Europe, and the cutlery is decorated with unusual heavy patterns without a Thai connection. The Thai food is out of this world; two of our favorites are *pad thai*, a translucent noodle dish, and minced pork with basil leaves. Entrees run about ¥1600.

CHOTOKU *(Udon noodles, inexpensive). 1-10-5 Shibuya, Shibuya-ku. Tel. (03)3407-8891. Open 11:30am to 9pm. Closed Monday. Shibuya Station.*

Most noodle shops serve both *soba* and *udon* but Chotoku is one of the most authentic *udon* shops in Tokyo. The handmade *udon*, its serving bowls, the waitresses in working kimono, the furniture, the folk art interior decor and the soothing classical music remind customers of the good old days. Carefully chosen seaweed and mushrooms go into the broth that's made fresh daily. We love the al dente texture of the *udon*. Try the *tempura udon* (¥2000) that is served in a rustic brown bowls. The menu has pictures of each item. Noodles cost ¥1400 and up; it's pricey for *udon* but worth every yen.

IROHANIHOHETO *(Japanese/Western, inexpensive). 1-19-3 Jinnan, Shibuya-ku. Tel. (03)3476-1682. Open daily 5pm to 4am. Shibuya Station.*

This large and noisy drinking establishment is popular with young people on limited budgets. The decor is country, with farm implements and other stuff decorating the interior. The food is inexpensive and the menu extensive; ordering is easy because the menu has pictures. The food is a combination of Japanese and Western. It's not haute cuisine, but then again, neither are the prices. Try the *ika somen* (thin strips of raw squid on ice), fried noodles and Hokkaido potatoes.

MELA *(Indian, inexpensive). 3F, Kasumi Building, 2-25-17 Dogenzaka, Shibuya-ku. Tel. (03) 3770-0120. Open daily 11:30am to 2pm. Shibuya Station.*

There are a zillion Indian restaurants in Shibuya, but this ranks among the best. Tucked away in a small alley, it's popular with shoppers and people working in the area. The decor tries to copy a village hut. The lunch special is three different curries and a drink for ¥850. The waitresses speak a bit of English.

SHINAGAWA & TAKANAWA

AJIKAIDO GOJUSANTSUGI *(Japanese, inexpensive to moderate). 38F, Shinagawa Prince Hotel. 4-10-30 Takanawa, Minato-ku. Tel. (03)3440-1111. Open 11am to 2pm. Shinagawa Station.*

The top floor of the newest wing of the Shinagawa Prince Hotel offers a slew of casual Japanese eateries gathered together. Shinagawa was the second of 53 stations on the Tokaido Road between old Tokyo and Kyoto. This floor features the foods that feudal era travelers enjoyed on their way. You can choose from *yakitori, sushi, oden, teppanyaki, tempura* and *shabu-shabu.* The views are spectacular.

CACCIANI *(Italian, inexpensive to moderate). 1F, 3-11-3 Takanawa, Minato-ku. Tel. (03)3473-3939. Open daily 11am to 2:30pm; 5pm to 10pm. Takanawadai Station.*

If you are staying at one of the Shinagawa/Takanawa hotels, try this lovely neighborhood Italian restaurant for a good change. Cacciani offers light and tasty Italian cuisine. Pizza is thin and crusty — the house special is Pizza Bianca with mozzarella cheese and homemade ham for ¥1900. The *antipasti misti* always includes a variety of local mushrooms and eggplant marinated in a herb vinaigrette. We have friends who come all the way across town to eat chicken *diavola*— a small tasty chicken slowly grilled until it's golden (¥2200). It is big enough for two people. Lunch set starts from ¥850.

SHER, *In the tennis court building behind the Shinagawa Prince Hotel. Open daily 11am to 9:30pm. Shinagawa Station.*

This unlikely site houses a surprisingly good, Japanese-style curry shop. Chicken curry costs ¥850; mushroom curry, ¥850, dry chicken curry with five small pieces of chicken on top of curried rice, ¥1000. You can specify if you want your curry medium, hot or very hot.

SHINJUKU

NEW YORK GRILL *(American Continental, moderate to expensive). Park Hyatt Tokyo, 3-7-1-2 Nishi Shinjuku, Shinjuku-ku. Tel. (03)5323-3458. Open daily 11:30am to 2:30pm; 5:30am to 10:30pm. Shinjuku or Hatsudai Station.*

One of Tokyo's hottest restaurants sits on the 52nd floor of the Park Hyatt Hotel. The New York Grill's views are spectacular. The weekday lunchtime buffet offers an appetizer, salad and dessert buffet, and you order the main course from the menu (¥4200). On weekends, the system is the same but includes champagne, and the cost is ¥5800. Dinner set menus cost ¥10,000 and ¥15,000. We prefer lunch because the daytime views of Tokyo are more interesting than nighttime. Four large murals are reminiscent of New York, but if you look closely, a little of Japan slips in.

The adjacent bar has live jazz music in the evenings. Try to avoid coming on a cloudy day. Be sure you make reservations.

KOZUE (*Japanese, moderate to expensive*). *Park Hyatt Tokyo, 3-7-1-2 Nishi Shinjuku, Shinjuku-ku. Tel. (03)5323-3460. Open daily 11:30am to 2:30pm; 5:30pm to 10pm. Shinjuku or Hatsudai Station.*

We love the open, spacious feeling Kozue exudes: the large glass windows, high ceiling and wide tables. High up in the Park Tower Building, the huge glass windows afford a bird's-eye view of western Tokyo and on a clear day, a glimpse of Mt. Fuji. The lunch box set menus are ¥3900 and ¥4800, and *tendon* set costs ¥2800. *Tendon* set includes beautifully presented *sashimi* as a starter, *tendon*, clear soup and pickles. On weekdays they have a special course that ends with dessert and coffee served in the adjacent lounge (¥5000). Dinner *kaiseki* courses start at ¥12,000, *shabu-shabu* at ¥15,000. Kozue is a lovely place for a special Japanese meal.

CARMINE EDOCHIANO (*Italian, moderate*). *9-13 Arakicho, Shinjuku-ku. Tel. (03)3225-6767. Open 12 noon to 2pm; 6pm to 10pm. Closed Sunday. Yotsuya Station.*

This is a sister restaurant to Carmine and it's in an out-of-the-way place. But we think it is worth a visit to enjoy authentic Italian food in a very Japanese atmosphere, a fascinating combination. Located in a Taisho-era wooden house, the small reception hall is like entering a friend's home. But you are requested not to take your shoes off. Most of the tables are upstairs although the Japanese room downstairs also beckons invitingly. The waiters wear navy blue monk's working outfits.

Each room is small because they have converted a small private house into a restaurant. And yet the kitchen in this very Japanese environment produces delicious Italian food. The ¥2500 lunch sets includes antipasto, pasta, dessert and coffee; the ¥3500 set adds a fish or meat dish. The set dinner is ¥6000. Pasta a la carte runs ¥1600 to ¥2000.

TSUNAHACHI-KADOHAZU-AN (*Tempura, inexpensive to expensive*). *3-28-4 Shinjuku, Shinjuku-ku. Tel. (03)3358-2788. Open daily 11am to 10:30pm. Shinjuku Station.*

Tsunahachi-Kadohazu-an ranks among Tokyo's top *tempura* shops. Located a few minutes east of Shinjuku Station, the entire six-storied building is dedicated to serving *tempura*. The automatic glass door leads you to a reception desk where you are directed to a floor. The elevator's door is lacquered. Each floor is decorated differently: one floor is modern Japanese with black, gray and white colors and another has an ancient Heian soft pastel color scheme. You can either sit at a table or on *tatami* mats. The business lunch consists of *tempura*, appetizer, cooked vegetable, rice, soup and pickles and costs ¥1200. The lunch set is ¥2500.

We like the special salad; the marinated tuna makes an unusual combination with tomato and minced leek in a soy-based dressing. The *tempura* is fried crispy and the vegetables and fish are tender. At dinner you can sit at the counter and enjoy *tempura* cooked right in front of you, these sets start at ¥5000. You can also order a la carte.

CARMINE *(Italian, moderate). 21 Naka-machi, Shinjuku-ku. Tel. (03)3260-5066. Open 12 noon to 2pm; 5:30pm to 10pm. Closed Sunday. Ichigaya Station.*

Though located in an inconvenient place, a 15-minute walk from Ichigaya Station, Carmine serves delicious and authentic Italian food. The small restaurant has a casual atmosphere. The *penne al gorgonzola* alone is worth the trek. Lunch sets start at ¥1800. The special course A at dinner is a great deal for ¥3500; it includes antipasto, pasta, main dish, dessert and coffee. Don't go without a reservation.

AGIO *(Italian, inexpensive). 7F, Isetan Department Store, 3-14-1 Shinjuku, Shinjuku-ku. Tel. (03)3354-6720. Open 11am to 9pm. Closed Wednesday. Shinjuku Station.*

Agio, a cozy Italian restaurant, serves delicious pasta and pizza. It almost always has people waiting outside, but they provide chairs so the usually brief wait is comfortable. From the entrance you see fresh tomatoes, colorful peppers, garlic, zucchini and a chef kneading pizza dough. The atmosphere is casual and the staff attentive.

SHIROGANE & MEGURO

KASHO *(Teppanyaki, moderate to expensive). Gajo-en Hotel, 1-1-8 Shimo Meguro, Meguro-ku. Open 11:30am to 2:30pm; 5:30pm to 9:30pm weekdays. 11:30am to 9:30pm weekends. Meguro Station.*

Kasho is one of the many restaurants at Meguro Gajo-en Hotel, which we think is an incredible example of Japanese aesthetics with a twist of Chinese style. The hotel personifies the Japan-Fujiyama-Geisha style: gaudy, kitschy, inscrutable, static and strange. Don't miss the lacquered bathroom that you reach by crossing a small red-lacquered drum-shaped bridge. Now, about the food — Kasho serves delicious *teppanyaki* in this fascinating environment. Food is served on plates too tasteful for the rest of the hotel.

Once seated, you receive a napkin-apron lest you get splattered by the food that's grilled in front of you. Lunch courses start at ¥3000; they include a starter, vegetables, small salad, fish or meat. Watching the chef at work with his knife cutting meat and vegetables is a treat, but don't expect Benihana theatrics. A small Japanese sweet and coffee are served at lounge tables away from the grill. At dinner time courses range from ¥6000 to ¥15,000.

TSUKASA *(Japanese, moderate to expensive). Happoen, 1-1-1 Shiroganedai, Minato-ku, Tokyo. Tel. (03)3443-3111. Open daily 11:30am to 2pm; 5pm to 7:30pm. Meguro Station.*

Happoen is a wedding palace but has several restaurants not geared to wedding parties. One is Tsukasa, a lovely place to enjoy Japanese delicacies sitting at a Western-style table. From its huge glass window you see the large and lush Japanese garden. Go for a stroll around the pond after you eat. *Tempura* and *soba* sets cost ¥2500, *sashimi* or *sukiyaki* course are ¥3000. If you feel like splurging the *mini-kaiseki* courses are ¥5000 and ¥6000. At dinner, *kaiseki* courses costing ¥7000 to ¥11,000 are served.

SHIROGANE *(Japanese, moderate). 3F, Ritz Shirogane, 6-16-28 Shirogane, Minato-ku. Tel. (03)3449-0033. Open daily 11:30am to 2:30pm; 5:30pm to 9pm. Meguro Station.*

A very contemporary Japanese restaurant, Shirogane is located in a chic contemporary concrete building. Its interior combines the modern with traditional touches like bamboo branches covering the ceiling. The thick wooden tables are comfortable for a long, leisurely meal. The lunchtime *shokado bento* (¥3000) is an elegant lunch. It includes an appetizer, a variety of vegetables, fish and meat tidbits served in a lacquered box and either *tempura* or steak with a Japanese sauce, rice, soup, and dessert. When we want a quiet lunch and a place where we can talk, we go here. Set dinners are ¥5000, ¥7000 and ¥10,000. Unlike most Japanese restaurants, Shirogane ends its meals with dessert and coffee.

DAIGO *(Japanese tonkatsu, inexpensive). 1-25-21 Shirogane, Minato-ku. Tel. (03)3444-2941. Open 12 noon to 2pm; 6pm to 9pm. Closed Monday and 3rd Tuesday. Meguro or Ebisu Station.*

Daigo is located in the middle of nowhere from the tourist's point of view, but we love this tiny *tonkatsu* shop so we often go out of our way to have lunch here. The delicious and tender *tonkatsu* is accompanied by lots of shredded fresh cabbage and a tasty thick sauce. The special tofu salad is sublime (¥600). *Hire katsu* set costs ¥1800 and *rosu katsu* set ¥1500. They even have an English menu.

TONKI *(Japanese tonkatsu, inexpensive). 1-1-2 Shimo Meguro, Meguro-ku. Tel. (03)3491-9928. Open 4pm to 10:45pm. Closed Tuesday and 3rd Monday. Meguro Station.*

Tonki raises cooking *tonkatsu* to an art form. A special formula dips the pork cutlets in batter three times for a thick crust and tender meat. Tonki is popular and you may have to wait; opt for a seat at the counter instead of upstairs. When you enter you'll be asked to choose either *hire* (fillet) or *rosu* (chop). While you are waiting for a seat, your dinner is being prepared, so by the time you sit down, your food is almost ready. *Hire teishoku* and *rosu teishoku* each cost ¥1550.

TOSHI-AN *(Soba, inexpensive)*. *5-17-2 Shiroganedai, Minato-ku. Tel. (03)3444-1741. Open 11:30am to 7pm. Closed Monday and Tuesday. Meguro Station.*

It's not unusual to see people standing in line waiting, not so patiently, to get into Toshi-an. Homemade *soba* is the specialty here. The dipping sauce and broth is real Edo-style dark brown. The decor includes beautiful *tansu* chests and broad wooden tables with matching chairs. Plates are selected to match the rustic folk art decor.

UENO

HANTEI *(Japanese kushi-age, moderate to expensive)*. *2-12-15 Nezu, Bunkyo-ku. Tel. (03)3828-1440. Open 5pm to 10:30pm. Closed Sunday. Nezu Station.*

We love to take visitors to this restaurant in a charming old wooden building. Our favorite is to eat in the cozy, thick-walled storehouse, but there's also a room with tables and *tatami* mat rooms are upstairs. Ask for the *kura* (storehouse) when making a reservation. *Kushi-age* are deep fried morsels on sticks. You don't order, they just start bringing you sticks. After twelve, they'll ask if you want to continue. Just tell them when you don't want any more. Twelve sticks cost ¥4000.

SASA-NO-YUKI *(Tofu, inexpensive to moderate)*. *2-22-15 Negishi, Taito-ku. Tel. (03)3873-1145. Open 11am to 9pm. Closed Monday. Uguisudani Station.*

As vegetarian food becomes more popular, Sasa-no-yuki's popularity grows. Make a reservation to eat here the day you decide to wander around the old traditional downtown areas. Sasa-no-yuki, which literally means "snow on the bamboo leaves," has been producing tofu for nearly 300 years. Only Japanese soy beans and fresh well water are used, so the tofu is sublime. An American friend who tasted its tofu for the first time described it as "cool, clean, slightly sweet, with an almost buttery texture." The restaurant knows how to cook tofu 300 different ways, but don't worry about having to slog through a fat menu. There are several courses: from three different dishes of tofu for ¥1500 to eight dishes for ¥4200. There's even an English menu. The seating is all on *tatami* mats looking out over a lovely garden — come dressed to sit on the floor.

HONTE PONTA. *3-32-2 Ueno, Taito-ku. Tel. (03)3831-2351. Open 11:30am to 2pm; 4:30pm to 8pm. Closed Monday. Ueno or Okachimachi Station.*

This old-fashioned shop serves *yoshoku*, Japanized Western food. The ¥2500 *rosu tonkatsu teishoku* is popular; it includes pork cutlet, rice and *miso* soup.

OUTSKIRTS OF TOKYO

UKAI TORIYAMA *(Japanese, moderate to expensive). Minami Asakawa-machi, Hachioji-shi. Tel. (0426)61-0739. Open 11am to 8pm weekdays, 11am to 7pm Sunday and national holidays. Takao-san guchi Station.*
Mt. Takao is a popular destination for Tokyoites fleeing urban congestion. Only 55 minutes from Shinjuku, suddenly you are in a heavily wooded cedar forest. Ukai Toriyama is the perfect escape for lunch or dinner. The restaurant, on a river ravine, is a collection of farm and teahouses moved from all over Japan. Dine in a thatched roof farmhouse or in a teahouse that once belonged to the powerful Maeda feudal lord. The setting personifies the Japanese ideal many Western tourists seek.

You'll have the choice of several different set meals; all include charcoal grilled *ayu* river fish, our favorite. The chicken course includes an appetizer, *sashimi,* soup, grilled *ayu,* chicken you grill over charcoal, special rice and pickles for ¥4500. The beef course, which uses Hida beef from the Takayama area in central Japan, costs ¥7500. *Sake* rice wine is served from fresh bamboo containers.

It is hard to believe that Ukai Toriyama is so close to Tokyo. From Shinjuku Station take the Keio express train to Takao-san-guchi Station, the end of the line (55 minutes). The restaurant runs a complimentary shuttle bus from the station. If it doesn't come within a few minutes, call to request one.

14. SEEING THE SIGHTS

Each of Tokyo's many districts has its own special character. The best way to get a feel for Tokyo is to explore it on foot: wander along busy shopping streets, down little alleys and meander through temple compounds. Tokyo still has small neighborhoods with tiny specialized shops where local residents buy tofu, fish, vegetables and other daily necessities. Merchants are friendly and life is at a pace more akin to small villages. There are also business districts like Marunouchi and Shinjuku where Japan's office workers spend most of their waking hours. Finally, there are the glittering shopping and entertainment areas like Ginza, Shinjuku, Shibuya and Harajuku where Japanese relax and play.

We divide Tokyo into 18 areas and give directions for informal walking tours. Be aware of two different Tokyo's existing side by side — the contemporary and the traditional. Some remnants of old Japan still exist in Asakusa and Ueno, but the up-to-the-moment places are Shibuya, Harajuku and Shinjuku.

And take your time to sit in a cafe and watch the world go by. Spend a few hours in a museum savoring its art. Participate in a tea ceremony or take a flower arranging class. Have a traditional *shiatsu* massage. Explore a flea market.

AREA 1: AROUND THE IMPERIAL PALACE

Time for the walk: about 1/2 day and longer if you visit all the museums. The closest subway station is Nijubashi-mae on the Chiyoda line.

We'll start at the **Imperial Palace**. Although it sounds like it is an important sight, in reality, there's no Buckingham Palace-type mansion to gaze upon and no stately imperial guard standing watch. The emperor lives in a low residence not visible from the street, but the formidable castle walls and moats are beautiful.

The palace grounds are an oasis of green in the center of the city. The five-kilometer sidewalk around the perimeter of the palace is a popular place to jog although we find the car exhaust makes it less than perfect. On Sundays from 10am to 4pm, the roads on the eastern and northern sides are closed to cars; bicycles are available free of charge from the Babasakimon Police Station.

On the east side of the palace along Hibiya Dori, there's a wide open area called Kokyo-mae Hiroba, graced by many pruned pine trees. **Nijubashi Bridge**, a double-arched iron bridge designed by a German architect in the 19th century, is now the main entrance to the palace. It's

HOPELESSLY LOST?

Tokyo began as a castle town, and castle towns are notoriously difficult to navigate. Designed to confuse the enemy, roads that start out parallel to each other suddenly end up perpendicular. And you can go into a maze of tiny alleys and find that the only way out may be the way you came in. Tokyo not only confounded invading armies, it still confounds residents and visitors alike. But don't let that get in your way. Wander around. What's the worst that could happen?

*If you become hopelessly lost, here's our foolproof method for getting yourself where you want to be: Hail a taxi and tell the driver: "**Ichi ban chikai eki ma-de**," and he'll take you to the closest subway station or JR train station. From there you can get anywhere in the city. Another way, but not as foolproof, is to jump on the nearest city bus. Buses usually begin and end their routes at train or subway stations. Although this approach is a little more risky, you'll eventually end up at a train station having seen another part of Tokyo.*

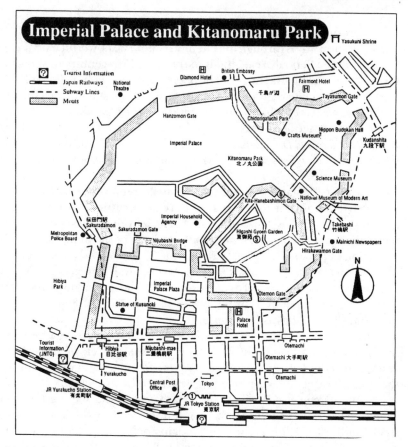

Imperial Palace and Kitanomaru Park

Courtesy of Japan National Tourist Organization

nearly mandatory for Japanese tourists to be photographed in front of this bridge. Walk north parallel to **Uchibori Dori** (literally Inner Moat Avenue) until you reach the **Otemon Gate** (literally Principal Gate) across from the Palace Hotel.

If you are dying to go into the inner grounds of the palace other than on January 2 and December 23 when the emperor gives audiences, take a tour in Japanese given by the Imperial Household Agency. Apart from the idea that you have entered the palace's inner sanctum, we don't think it's worth the trouble, but here's the information: *90-minute tour leaves from the Kikyo-mon gate, across from the Palace Hotel, at 10am and 1:30pm weekdays. You must call the Imperial Household Agency, Tel. (03)3213-1111, ext. 485, to make an appointment and then go to the Sankan-gakari Visitor's Office to pick up your permit card at least one day in advance of the tour. The office is open 9am to 4:30pm weekdays, closed for lunch from noon to 1pm. It's best to have a Japanese speaker make the phone call.*

There are three ways to enter the **East Garden** (Higashi Gyoen); the most common way is through the Otemon Gate. The powerful feudal lord Date, from the Sendai area, built it in the early 17th century to show his loyalty to the Tokugawa shogun. The present gate is a replica built in 1967; the tall wooden gate is imposing with its heavy doors and fine metalwork.

The garden is open from 9am to 4:30pm (until 4pm November through February), but you must enter at least one-half hour before closing. Closed Monday, Friday and December 25 through January 3. Admission is free. Pick up a plastic tag at the office just past the gate and surrender it when leaving. You do not have to leave by the same gate.

The peaceful garden is psychologically far removed from the bustle of Tokyo that's outside the gates. Inside are more castle walls, lots of trees and bushes and a few buildings. The **Imperial Court Museum** (Sanno-maru Shozokan), a tiny museum, displays pieces of the imperial family's collection of Japanese art. *Tel. (03)3213-1177. Open 9:15am to 4pm. Closed Monday and Friday. No admission fee.* The **Fujimi Turret** and **Fujimi Armory** are the only two Tokugawa-era buildings remaining. As their names suggest, they were prime places for viewing Mt. Fuji as well as important places for castle defense.

Inside the East Garden lies a small but exquisite Japanese garden that has beautiful iris flowers in June. This was the garden of the private residence of the Tokugawa shoguns. A stone foundation marks the site of the Tokugawa's castle keep that was destroyed by fire in 1657.

From a steep slope called Shiomizaka, you could see the tides on Tokyo bay 130 years ago, but today it only offers views of the concrete and steel buildings of Hibiya. The weird looking octagonal building, with its mosaic walls, is the **Togaku-do**, a concert hall built for the (then) empress in 1969.

Exit the East Garden on the north side to enter **Kitanomaru Park** that was once the home of the imperial guard and is now the abode of a number of cultural institutions. The heavily wooded park even has nature trails.

Just across from the gate is the **National Museum of Modern Art** (Tokyo Kokuritsu Kindai Bijutsukan). This museum houses a large collection of modern Japanese art — from the Meiji Period onward. If you've seen traditional Japanese art, a stop here will fill you in on what happened after the floodgates to the West opened in the late 19th century. *3-1 Kitano-maru Koen. Tel. (03)3214-2561. Open 10am to 5pm. Closed Monday. ¥410, additional fee for special exhibitions.*

A few minutes walk from the museum takes you to **The Crafts Gallery** (Kogeikan). The museum, exhibiting contemporary renderings of traditional crafts such as pottery, lacquer and weaving, is housed in a 1910 red brick building, the former headquarters of the old Imperial Palace Guard.

CASTLES & PALACES

When Tokyo became the capital of Japan in 1868, stripping Kyoto of this status, the emperor made the bold decision to move to Tokyo. He needed somewhere to live and what better place than the castle grounds that the Tokugawa shoguns vacated – they were sent packing to the Shizuoka area. In its heyday, the castle's area was 608 acres, and the outer walls formed a 16-kilometer circle. Today the inner area is a mere 28 acres, but the names of some of Tokyo's streets show how large the castle grounds were: half of central Tokyo is inside Sotobori Dori, which means Outer Moat Avenue.

The Tokugawa built a large castle keep and a splendid residence, but fire destroyed the keep in 1657. Their power was so secure they didn't bother to rebuild it. When the Meiji Emperor moved to Tokyo, he built a Western-style palace in 1889; it was destroyed in an air raid during World War II. The current palace is a low structure built for Emperor Akihito after his father's death. If you want to take a peek, the upper floors of office buildings along Hibiya Dori look down on the palace grounds; we find the most convenient place is from the Idemitsu Museum. The place's green copper roof is in the middle of so many trees. Don't bother to go too far out of your way; there's not much to see.

The outer precincts of the palace – the East Garden, Kitanomaru Park and Chidorigafuchi Park – are accessible to the public. The inner part, containing the emperor's residence, is open to the public only two days a year when the emperor greets his people: January 2 to celebrate New Year's and December 23, the emperor's birthday. It's a pretty subdued affair, but go if you happen to be in Japan. Most likely, it will be your only chance to see the emperor.

As you wait to enter the inner precincts, you are given a Japanese paper flag. Then you walk over Nijubashi Bridge with about 2000 other people and end up in a plaza in front of one of the palace buildings. With his family members beside him, the emperor stands on a glass-enclosed balcony. He says a few words of welcome and people wave their flags. Some people seem to get carried away by the mere sight of the emperor, but to most it's just another event. The newspapers report how many people went to visit the emperor. Now it's usually between 30,000 and 50,000; when the emperor's father, the Showa Emperor, was alive, many more people attended.

We like to visit to get a sense of what's happening in the contemporary craft scene. *Tel. (03)3211-7781. Open 10am to 5pm. ¥420.*

Turn left as you leave the Crafts Gallery and the **Japan Science Museum** (Kagaku Gijutsukan) will be on your right. Despite its austere, institutional facade, the museum is a great place to take the kids — lots of hands-on exhibits related to robots, electronics, technology and space exploration. *Tel. (03)3212-8471. Open daily 9:30am to 4:50pm, enter by 4pm. Closed Monday. ¥600.*

At the northern tip of Kitanomaru Park is the **Budokan**, a hall built for martial arts for the 1964 Olympics. Until Tokyo Dome was built in the late 1980s, the Budokan was a favored venue for rock concerts – the Beatles played there in 1966. From the Budokan, exit over the moat. The area along the moat is **Chidorigafuchi Park**; its hundreds of cherry trees ensure a spectacular sight in the spring, but it's pretty any time of year. You can rent boats and row along the moat. The main street is Yasukuni Dori.

Walk up Yasukuni Dori for about five minutes or until you see the bronze *torii* gate on the right, which is the entrance to **Yasukuni Shrine**. Yasukuni, founded in 1869, is a controversial Shinto shrine because it enshrines soldiers killed in war. Every year some Cabinet members participate in a special ceremony on August 15 to mark the end of World War II. The cabinet members are asked if they visit Yasukuni as public figures or as private individuals. It's not a moot question. Leftists accuse the ministers of violating the Constitution that separates state and religion by honoring convicted war criminals. Right wingers denounce the ministers as unpatriotic if they don't show up. The only way to avoid the entire controversy is not to be a cabinet minister.

Politics aside, the buildings themselves are very low key; hundreds of cherry trees on the premises make it one of Tokyo's prettiest places to see cherry blossoms. Actually, the Meteorological Agency uses two trees at Yasukuni as the standard to predict Tokyo's blossom season. When those trees bloom, the cherry blossom season begins officially.

While you are there, stop at the **Yushukan**, the yellow building to the right of the shrine, Japan's war museum. Inside you will find war memorabilia from samurai costumes to a *kamikaze* torpedo and glider planes. Unfortunately there isn't much description written in English, but the graphic exhibits need little explanation. *3-1-1 Kudankita, Chiyoda-ku. Tel. (03)3261-8326. Open daily 9am to 5pm. ¥300.*

AREA 2: FROM GINZA TO NIHONBASHI

This walk takes the better part of a day, less if you don't do too much window shopping or don't stop in museums. The streets in this area are laid out in a grid, so it's easy to find your way.

This area, east of the Imperial Palace, contains some of Tokyo's most famous shopping districts and office centers, art galleries and a handful of excellent museums. You can combine this area with the Imperial Palace (see above).

GINZA

*The mention of **Ginza** to Japanese conjures up visions of high society and shopping. This idea goes back a hundred years to a time when Ginza came to stand for all that was fashionable. Ginza was the site of the Tokugawa government's silver mint, established in 1612, and many silversmiths had their workshops here. They gave the area its name: Ginza means "silver guild."*

Fire destroyed Ginza in 1872 so the Meiji government, in the early days of its rapid Westernization program, had British architect Josiah Conder design a Western-style center. Hundreds of brick buildings were built and sidewalks were planted with willow trees and lit by gas lights. People turned out to see the development and soon a thriving commercial center was born. They flocked to see Western products like men's suits and women's dresses. Department stores opened branches here. Woodblock prints depict large-nosed foreigners wearing frock coats accompanied by women wearing hoop skirts. They strolled in Ginza under cherry trees and gas lights, and horse-drawn carriages were in the street.

World War II air raids flattened Ginza; the Wako Department Store building is one of the few structures that survived. Ginza recovered quickly and resumed its position as the country's foremost retail area.

Today, Ginza attracts a sophisticated, middle-aged crowd to its expensive shops and art galleries. The name Ginza has become synonymous with the best, and we find it used everywhere we travel in Japan: Ginza bar in Kumamoto, Ginza Dining Hall in Hokkaido, Ginza shopping mall in Hiroshima and Ginza Dori in small towns in the middle of nowhere.

This walk can start with an early morning visit to the Tsukiji Fish Market (see its description under Tsukiji). From the fish market, walk north along Shin Ohashi Dori and turn left on Harumi Dori. The Kabuki-za will be several blocks down on the right. If you sleep late and skip the fish market, take the Hibiya subway line to Higashi Ginza Station and get off at the central exit. The Kabuki-za will be in front of you.

You can't miss the **Kabuki-za**. Built in 1924, the gaudy building exudes the brashness of *kabuki* theater itself. You can buy a one-act ticket to get a glimpse of this vibrant art form that combines music, dance and singing (see Performing Arts later in this chapter for ticket information).

Return to Harumi Dori and continue walking down toward the center of Ginza. Across the first large intersection after the Kabuki-za, there's a small wooden building at an angle on the far side. This tiny shop sells *tabi* (Japanese socks), small towels and other cotton goods. We often pick up some inexpensive gifts there. Continue walking on the left side of Harumi Dori. If you feel like resting your feet or having breakfast, turn left after Togeki, a movie theater, and you'll find the Ginza Tokyu Hotel. The cafe is a pleasant place to have a cup of tea or a bite to eat.

Return to Harumi Dori. Just before you reach Chuo Dori, the **Nihonshu Center**, the Japanese Sake Center, is on the left. It offers tastes of four different types of Japanese rice wine for ¥300 — one of the best deals in town. They have *sake* from all over Japan so it's a good place to figure out which type you like best.

Continue walking down Harumi Dori to the heart of Ginza, the 4-chome intersection where Harumi Dori and Chuo Dori meet. At night, the neon lights on this corner are so bright you can easily read a newspaper. On the corner are two of Japan's most exclusive department stores: **Mitsukoshi** where the prices are merely high and **Wako**, where they are astronomical. Make sure you go inside Wako; the ground floor has some of the most expensive watches on this planet. The basement has a corner featuring Japanese goods where you can find some reasonably priced items. Wako's clientele tends toward old-fashioned women from good families. This Mitsukoshi is a branch of the Nihonbashi store; the ground floor Tiffany Boutique is popular with the twenty-something set. With a 300-year history, Mitsukoshi knows how to make money on some of the most expensive real estate on this globe.

From Harumi Dori, turn left onto Chuo Dori. On the corner is the **Ginza Core Building**; its basement restaurant, **Shabuzen**, has some of the least expensive *shabu-shabu* in town. We don't know how it survives because during the peak of the economic bubble in the late 1980s, this property was so expensive that a two *tatami* mat (6 feet by 6 feet) piece of land cost more than one million U.S. dollars. One block further along, you'll come to **Matsuzakaya**, another of Ginza's large department stores; this one is especially famous for its kimono, and **Familiar**, exclusive children's fashions. Walking along the same street you reach the **Lion Sapporo Beer Hall** with good beer and neat mosaic walls. Soon after is **Ginza Pocket Park**, which, despite its name, is a building, an amazingly small one that houses an architectural studio run by Tokyo Gas. Next to it is **Yamaha Hall**, a music store selling Japanese as well as Western sheet music, hot-off-the-design-table electones and Yamaha's latest models.

On the other side of Chuo Dori, just before the expressway, is **Hakuhinkan Toy Park**, one of Tokyo's largest toy stores. Walking back toward the Ginza 4-chome intersection, you'll come to **Shiseido**, where the cosmetics' manufacturer started in 1872. The cafe is a pleasant place to stop for a cup of coffee. At Shiseido, turn left and walk down five short blocks to Sotobori Dori, turn left and you'll find **Takumi**, a great folk craft shop. The area between Sotobori Dori and Chuo Dori is filled with art galleries, boutiques and bars with Ginza in their names.

Retrace your steps to Chuo Dori and be sure you stop at **Kyukyodo** where incense, paper, tea ceremony utensils, fancy greeting cards, brushes and other calligraphy equipment have been sold for 300 years. Kyukyodo is next to the bright San-ai Building at the Ginza 4-chome crossing. Crossing Harumi Dori, you'll see **Mikimoto Pearls** on the left. Mikimoto invented the culturing process and is the name-brand place to buy pearls. The quality is excellent and some goods are priced low enough so you may not have to mortgage your house. On the right is **Matsuya** Department Store and **Itoya**, a great shop for stationery and paper goods, where half the goods are imported and half are Japanese.

Return to the Ginza 4-chome crossing and turn right on Harumi Dori, heading in the direction of the Imperial Palace. **Jena Books** on the left has a cramped but good selection of English-language books. Farther down on the left is the **Sony Building**, with electronic showrooms and the exclusive Maxim's and Sabatini's restaurants. On the other side of the street, after you walk under the expressway, are the twin department stores, **Hankyu** and **Seibu**. In a novel design, they connect on each floor. The clock in the plaza comes alive with a miniconcert every hour; it is one of the area's most popular meeting places.

When Harumi Dori meets Hibiya Dori — the green trees and open spaces of Hibiya Park and the Imperial Palace are on the far side — turn left and walk a few short blocks to the **Imperial Hotel**, one of Tokyo's most famous. This was the site of the Frank Lloyd Wright-designed hotel that opened in 1923 but succumbed to the wrecking ball in 1968. Actually, the Wright low-style lobby has been reassembled in Meiji Mura, an open air park outside of Nagoya. The current Imperial Hotel's bar, on the second floor, has some of the fittings of Wright's original bar.

Across the street on the northern side of the hotel is the **Tokyo Takarazuka Theater** where the all-female revue performs. The performances are really kitschy, but great fun — a cross between Las Vegas and *kabuki*.

Keep walking down this road; under the railroad tracks, you'll find the **International Arcade**, a slightly run-down shopping arcade catering to foreign tourists. You can get export model electronics, old kimono, jewelry and souvenirs. Despite the surroundings, it's not a bad place to shop for souvenirs. **Hayashi Kimono** has an especially good selection of old kimono.

In this same area, under the railroad tracks, there are some good hole-in-the-wall *yakitori* restaurants. Most are closed during the day but come alive in the evening when office workers are looking for cheap beer and eats.

The front of the Imperial Hotel faces **Hibiya Park**, the first Western-style park in Tokyo; while it's filled with office workers searching for some greenery and fresh air at lunchtime, it has little to recommend it to a visitor. Behind Hibiya Park is **Kasumigaseki**, a ghetto of government ministry buildings. Unless you want to see institutional architecture, there's no reason to spend any time there.

From the front of the Imperial Hotel, walk north on Hibiya Dori, in the direction of the Imperial Palace. Soon after crossing Harumi Dori, the **Daiichi Mutual Life Insurance Building** is on your right. Built in 1938, it was one of the few buildings that survived the bombing of World War II. General Douglas MacArthur used it to as headquarters for the Occupation forces; his office is preserved today.

One block further takes you to the **Idemitsu Museum of Arts**, one of our favorite museums in Tokyo. It's funded by the Idemitsu Oil Company so clearly it has the resources to continue adding to its superb collection of Oriental art. Located on the 9th floor of an uninspired office building, the display space is divided into three main rooms. It's not too large so we find we can look at the objects with appreciation. This museum is where you can admire monk Sesshu's 15th-century monochrome paintings, Momoyama and early Edo lively, gold-leafed genre paintings and the exquisite colors of Ninsei's world famous vase. The temporary exhibitions are top notch. After viewing a show, sit and enjoy a complimentary cup of tea overlooking the verdant Imperial Palace grounds. *Imperial Theater Building, 9F, 3-1-1 Marunouchi, Chiyoda-ku. Tel. (03)3272-8600. Open 10am to 5pm. Closed Monday. ¥500.*

From the Idemitsu Museum you can cross Hibiya Dori and enter the palace grounds and pick up our tour under Imperial Palace. But we are going to walk east, away from the palace. You'll run into the massive **Tokyo International Forum** complex. One of the most recent offerings on the cultural scene, this building finally gives Tokyo the grand architectural statement it has long wanted. Designed by New York-based architect Rafael Vinoly, the glass, steel and stone structure houses performance halls for concerts, dance and theater as well as a conference center, restaurants and the **Tourist Information Office**, an excellent source of information. The soaring 60-meter-high, all glass atrium is a sight to behold. Even if you are not going to a concert here, stop by to see what ¥1.65 billion, not including the price of the land, will buy.

After leaving the Forum, follow the train tracks north a few blocks to **Tokyo Station**. Designed by Tatsuno Kingo, a leading turn-of-the-century Japanese architect, the western facade of the station was built in 1914. Tatsuno built the station in Queen Anne style with red brick. Today Japanese traveling to Amsterdam always say, "There's Tokyo Station" when they see Central Station. The entrance facing west was used exclusively by the imperial family, but is now used by mere mortals, and plenty of them. Over 2500 trains pass through the station every day. The Tokyo Station Hotel, part of the station, is a convenient and pleasant place to stay.

TOKYO'S RAIL STATIONS

Tokyo Station was not Tokyo's first train station; that honor falls to **Shimbashi Station**. *Built with the technical assistance of British engineers – employed by the Meiji government at an outrageous cost – the first railway opened between Shimbashi and Yokohama in 1872. At that time Shimbashi was on the waterfront. The train took 53 minutes and stopped at four stations en route. The excitement of this engineering feat came just four short years after the overthrow of the feudal Tokugawa government and can be seen in ukiyo-e woodblock prints. In 1879, a railway between* **Ueno Station** *and Aomori, in northern Japan, commenced operations; and in 1889, service began on the Tokaido railway between Shimbashi and Kobe. Ueno wasn't connected to Shimbashi until Tokyo Station opened in 1914.*

Shimbashi remained Tokyo's major railway station until the government commissioned Tatsuno Kingo to design a new station to commemorate Japan's victory in the Russo-Japanese War. Tatsuno studied in Europe and designed a red-brick, three-storied building. The roof and interior were heavily damaged by bombing during World War II and after the war, the station was rebuilt as a two-storied building. With the construction of the shinkansen line in the 1960s, the eastern side of the station now shows no traces of the original building, but the western side still maintains its graceful facade.

The skyrocketing cost of land in the 1980s tempted JR to raze the building, but the outcry was so strong that the building was spared.

The district around Tokyo Station is **Marunouchi**, literally "within the citadel." During the Edo period, feudal lords had their official residences in this area. But at the end of the era, in the mid-19th century, they packed up and went back home. By the late 19th century, the district was so deserted that foxes and badgers lived side by side. The savvy Mitsubishi family bought the land for next to nothing and constructed Western-style buildings designed by Josiah Conder. Now, in the mid-1990s, Mitsubishi has decided to move south of Shinagawa Station to develop a new business center, but Marunouchi remains one of the most prestigious office districts.

North of the station is Eitai Dori; turn right to head east on this major thoroughfare. This area is called Otemachi and is a banking and business center. Soon you will reach the intersection of Eitai Dori and Chuo Dori. This area is Nihonbashi. A turn to the right will take you to the famous and now, unfortunately, totally unremarkable **Nihonbashi Bridge**, literally the Bridge of Japan, that's half swallowed by an overhead expressway. The bridge is considered the center of Japan and distances are measured from here. During the Edo period, Nihonbashi was the intersection for the five roads that connected Edo to the provinces. Once the bridge was a beautiful, curved wooden structure (see a reconstruction in the Edo Tokyo Museum), but today it's cement.

Cross the Nihonbashi Bridge and continue on Chuo Dori. You'll come to **Mitsukoshi**, the prestigious department store's main store. Some purists insist on buying their goods at Mitsukoshi's main store, not at the newer Ginza or Shinjuku or other branches. Mitsukoshi developed into a department store from a kimono shop in the Edo period and was the first shop to display its goods in glass cases at the turn of the century. Before that, goods were brought from the storage areas at the customer's request.

From Chuo Dori, turn left right after Mitsukoshi. Incidentally, Kiya, Tokyo's most famous knife store, is on the right of this intersection. The **Bank of Japan Building**, built in 1898, was Japan's first major Western-style building designed by a Japanese — in this case by Tatsuno Kingo who also designed Tokyo Station.

NIHONBASHI

*Located along the canals, **Nihonbashi** was the heart of the downtown area in the Edo Period. Boats carrying goods from all over Japan flocked to the docks. Apparently, Nihonbashi was cursed because five, large, ruinous fires started there.*

*During the Meiji period, Nihonbashi was a district that exemplified the drive to Westernize. At the turn of the century, **Maruzen Book Store**, a center for the intelligentsia, became the first in Japan to sell foreign books and luxury goods. **Takashimaya** was one of the first Japanese department stores. Across the Renaissance-style Nihonbashi Bridge stands the **Bank of Japan**, the centerpiece of the modern banking system. Nihonbashi was one of the trendy places of that time as Omotesando is now.*

After a long period of neglect and construction of an overhead expressway that bisects the district, Nihonbashi is being resurrected as an area that, ironically, has retained its Japaneseness.

Retrace your steps and cross back over the Nihonbashi Bridge and walk to the Tokyu Department Store. Behind Tokyu is a tiny **Kite Museum** that's jam packed with Japanese and foreign kites. These aren't your run-of-the-mill diamond-shaped kites; some resemble birds, warriors and squid. The collection belongs to the owner of the first floor restaurant, Taimei Ken. *Tel. (03)3275-2704. ¥200. Open 11am to 5pm. Closed Sunday and holidays.*

Walk back to Chuo Dori. Two blocks past the Eitai Dori intersection is **Takashimaya**, an old-time department store. Across the street is **Maruzen** that has been selling foreign language books and goods since the turn of the century. The selection of Japanese novels translated into English is especially good. Maruzen also has an area with an excellent selection of Japanese crafts.

Walk south about four blocks on Chuo Dori to Yaesu Dori. On the far corner is the Bridgestone Building, which houses the **Bridgestone Museum of Art** (Bridgestone Bijutsukan). This museum has one of Japan's best collections of modern European art and focuses especially on the Impressionists and Western-style works by Japanese artists. The Japanese works incorporate some elements of Japanese aesthetics into their works. *2F, Bridgestone Building, 1-10-1 Kyobashi, Chuo-ku. Tokyo. Tel. (03)3563-0241. Open 10am to 6pm. Closed Monday. ¥500.*

Retrace your steps along Chuo Dori and turn right on Eitai Dori. On the right is a well-known paper goods shop called **Haibara** that sells Japanese *washi* paper, stationery and other goods made from the paper. We like to buy lightweight gifts here.

Continue down Eitai Dori and cross under the expressway. The **Yamatane Museum** is on the left corner of the next major intersection near the Kayabacho subway station. The museum has a strong collection of modern Japanese art. Surrounded by securities dealers, this site is an unlikely spot for an art museum, but the collection belonged to the head of Yamatane Securities. *7-12, Nihonbashi-Kabutocho, Chuo-ku, Tokyo. Tel. (03)3669-4056. Open 10am to 6pm. Closed Monday and New Year's. ¥700.*

Walk along the small street where Yamatane Museum is located. Several blocks down on the left, you'll find the **Tokyo Securities Exchange**, the stock market. The exchange's glassed-in area provides an excellent view of the trading floor. To teach you about the market, the extensive Exhibition Plaza features many interactive displays in English as well as Japanese.

Visitors are welcome Monday through Friday, 9am to 4pm and an English tour is given at 1:30pm. It's best to telephone to reserve a spot on the hour-long tour. 2-1 Nihonbashi-Kabutocho, Chuo-ku. Tel. (03)3666-0141. Free admission.

SENIOR PRIVILEGE

Senior Citizens 65 and over are admitted free to the following museums. You'll need to present your passport for admission.

- *National Science Museum, Ueno*
- *National Museum of Modern Art, Kitanomaru Park*
- *Crafts Gallery, Kitanomaru Park*
- *Tokyo Metropolitan Teien Museum, Meguro*
- *Tokyo Metroplitan Art Museum, Ueno*
- *Tokyo National Museum, Ueno*
- *Edo Tokyo Museum, Ryogoku*
- *Tokyo Metropolitan Museum of Photography, Ebisu*
- *Silk Museum, Yokohama*
- *Kanagawa Museum of Modern Art, Kamakura*
- *Japan Open Air Folk House Museum, Kawasaki*

AREA 3: FROM TSUKIJI TO ROPPONGI

A walk from Tsukiji to Roppongi takes the better part of a day.

When Japan opened to the West in the middle of the 19th century, the government assigned Tsukiji as a foreign settlement. When restrictions were lifted around the turn of the century, most foreigners didn't stick around; many moved to Yokohama. Today, Roppongi is an international district filled with restaurants, discos, bars, clubs and shops.

Tokyo Central Wholesale Market/Tsukiji Market (Tsukiji Shijo). *5-2-1 Tsukiji, Chuo-ku. Tel. (03)3542-1111. 10-minute walk from Tsukiji Station of Hibiya Subway Line; use exit 1, walk down Shin Ohashi Dori, cross Harumi Dori and turn left at the next corner. Turn right at the small shrine and go over the bridge. The fish market is in front of you. Alternatively take bus #1 from Shimbashi Station's east exit to Tsukiji Chuo Shijo stop (5 minutes). Open 5am to 3pm. Fish auction is 5:10am to 5:50am. The fruit and vegetable auction is at 6:30am to 7:30am. Closed Sunday, holidays and some Wednesdays. Have your hotel call the market or check with the Tourist Information Office before setting out on Wednesday morning.*

Fishermen all over the world are early risers, and Japan's are no exception. When you wake up jet lagged at 4am, jump out of bed and head for Tsukiji market, Japan's largest fish market. See the huge frozen hulks lined up on the floor for the 5am tuna auction's high-speed drama — it's great fun to watch. If you prefer to sleep later than 4am, there's still lots of activity afterwards.

The fish market moved from Nihonbashi after the 1923 earthquake. Today there are over a thousand wholesalers, and no one minds if you wander up and down the aisles as long as you stay out of the way of the carts that whiz by – they stop for no one. Make sure your shoes can survive a good soaking as the floor is wet and slippery. If you feel like having an escorted tour in Japanese, phone for reservations for a 9:30am tour. There's really no need to bother – it's more fun to wander around on your own.

The back streets around the intersection of Harumi Dori and Shin Ohashi Dori are filled with retail shops catering to the chefs. You'll find the most amazing kinds of kitchenware, knives and dry goods at reasonable prices.

Finish off your morning with a breakfast or lunch of *sushi*. **Tsukiji Sushi Sei**, founded in the Edo period, is really popular; people line up even before it opens at 8am. *4-13-9 Tsukiji, Chuo-ku. Tel. (03)3541-7720.* Sushi Sei even has a branch in New York. If you don't feel like eating raw fish, we suggest you go to Uogashi Ramen that faces Shin-Ohashi Dori. Once again you'll find many people waiting in line to be served delicious Chinese noodles in broth with sliced roasted pork for only ¥500.

Across Harumi Dori is **Tsukiji Hongan-ji Temple** originally built in Nihonbashi in 1617. The current building, constructed in 1934, is based on an Indian temple design and is one of the most unusual temple buildings in Japan.

From the fish market, it's a short walk to Hama Rikyu Garden. From the market, continue walking south on Shin Ohashi Dori, staying on the left side of the road. After the road curves right, the entrance to the garden is on the left.

Hama Rikyu Garden. *1-1 Hamarikyu Tei-en, Chuo-ku. Tel. (03)3541-0200. Open 9am to 4:30pm. ¥300. Free to seniors over 65 and juniors under 12. Closed Monday and at New Year's.* This large, Japanese-style strolling garden was once the private duck-hunting preserve of the Matsudaira, a branch of the Tokugawa family. The Imperial Household took it over in the late 19th century and entertained foreign dignitaries on the grounds. U.S. President Ulysses S. Grant was feted at one of the teahouses. The salt water pond rises and falls with the tides of the Sumida River inlet and is the home of many ducks; none is hunted today. The low, zigzagged

EARLY MORNING ACTIVITIES IN TOKYO

•*Jog around the Imperial Palace: traffic is light, so car exhaust isn't bad*

• *Tsukiji Fish Market*
• *Asakusa Kannon Temple*
• *Shrine flea markets on Sunday mornings*

wooden bridge over the pond offers changing views of the garden around you. Since the garden is on the water, it gives you a feeling of space as it is much more open than the usual, meticulously calculated Japanese garden.

From the Hama Rikyu Garden's pier, one alternative is to take the ferry up the Sumida River to Asakusa — see the Asakusa write-up. Boats leave every 40 minutes.

If you prefer to stay on land, walk south alongside the expressway for about 10 minutes to reach **Kyu-Shiba Rikyu Garden**. Although fairly small and now surrounded by tall buildings, it's one of our favorite gardens in Tokyo. This strolling garden was once at the water's edge; the sand at the pond's edge maintains a little of the waterfront feeling. The pond's water level, connected with the sea, rises and falls with the tide. In mid-May, the wisteria and azaleas are in full bloom. *1-4-1 Kaigan, Minato-ku. Tel. (03)3434-4029. Open 9am to 4:30pm. Closed Monday and December 29 through January 3. ¥100. 1-minute walk east of JR Hamamatsucho Station.*

The area east of the garden, **Takebashi**, has recently undergone redevelopment and offers a pleasant stroll along the waterfront. The new Intercontinental Hotel's Asian Tables restaurant has good Asian food and a spectacular view of the Rainbow Bridge. Walk to Hamamatsucho Station, just west of the Shiba Rikyu Garden. The street just north of the station leads west to **Zojo-ji**, a temple in Shiba Park. Several blocks before the park you'll see a wooden gate in the middle of the road. **Daimon** (literally big gate) is the outer gate for Zojo-ji; all the land inside the gate used to belong to the temple.

Near the gate, turn left onto a tiny road sandwiched between Sanwa Bank and Yoshinoya fast food. On the left, in a beautifully restored former *geisha* house, is the **Tolman Collection**. Run by Americans Norman and Mary Tolman, long-term residents, the gallery sells contemporary Japanese prints. *2-2-18 Shiba Daimon, Minato-ku. Tel. (03)3434-1300. Open 11am to 7pm. Closed Tuesday.*

Tokyo doesn't have grand temples like Kyoto — most have only pocket-sized lots. **Zojo-ji**, established by the Tokugawa shogunate is the exception. This temple, along with Kan'ei-ji in the northern part of the city, was one of the Tokugawa's family temples and could have been used as a fortress to protect the castle against an invasion from the south. The buildings, rebuilt in the 1970s, are unremarkable, but the impressive main gate has stood since 1605.

From Zojo-ji, fans of Asian art can take a detour to the **Matsuoka Museum of Art** — walk north on Hibiya Dori until the 7th block on the right. In an old building, this small museum houses a superb collection of Chinese ceramics and other Oriental art. *5-22-10 Shimbashi, Minato-ku. Tel. (03)3431-8284. Open 10am to 5pm. Closed Monday and at New Year's.*

¥550. 3-minute walk from the A4 exit of Onarimon Station on the Toei Mita subway line.

Behind Zojo-ji, you can't help but notice a transplanted Eiffel Tower — **Tokyo Tower**. Built in 1958, the 333-meter structure is the tallest stand-alone steel structure in the world. Unlike Paris' Eiffel Tower that sits gracefully in a large park, Tokyo's is plopped on top of a concrete building in the middle of an urban neighborhood. Some 3.7 million people visit the tower each year; it's a sightseeing destination second only to Disneyland. But we don't recommend that you join the long queue. Tokyo Tower is tacky, rundown, and overpriced; you can get as good a view from the Tokyo Metropolitan Government Building in Shinjuku without paying an admission charge. We really hate how the down elevator deposits you on the fourth floor of the building and forces you to walk down the stairs past an aquarium, a wax museum, a chamber of horrors, a trick art gallery and whatever else the owners think will get you to part with your yen. *Open daily 9am to 8pm mid-March to mid-November; until 6pm mid-November through mid-March. ¥270 to the main observatory; an additional ¥520 to the higher special observatory.*

The road that goes past the main entrance to Tokyo Tower leads you to a large intersection on Sakurada Dori. On the far right side, behind some buildings, is a huge Darth Vadar-like building that is the temple of the **Reiyukai**, one of the new Buddhist sects. Go inside for a closer look at the neo-Buddhist architecture.

Return to the intersection and walk up the hill on Gaien Higashi Dori, past the Russian Embassy and the Azabu Post Office and walk under the expressway. Continue on the same road; you are deep in the heart of **Roppongi**, a nightlife area filled with restaurants, discos and bars. The area is fairly quiet in the daytime, but when the sun goes down, it's all-night party time.

Roppongi has a few daytime attractions. One of our favorite places is the **Axis Building** on the left side of Gaien Higashi Dori about two blocks past the expressway as you walk away from Tokyo Tower. The building is devoted to modern design. The street floor has a **Living Motif** store, which reminds us of Pottery Barn in the U.S. Downstairs, **Nuno** is a fabulous textile store that supplies Issey Miyake with his raw material. There's also a selection of clothes of their own design. **Kisso**, on the same floor, sells pottery and is a *kaiseki* restaurant that serves its food on its own plates. **Bushy** has beautiful contemporary lacquer ware from small bowls to furniture and matching lamps.

Continue walking in the same direction and in a few blocks, you'll reach another large intersection under the expressway. This is **Roppongi Crossing** and is known to nearly every taxi driver in town. The **Almond coffee shop**, on the corner, is THE place to meet. Virtually every set of directions for anything in Roppongi starts at Almond. Incidentally, Almond is famous as a landmark, but not for its coffee.

Walk under the expressway, and continue north on Gaien Higashi Dori. Take the 3rd right to reach the **Azabu Museum of Arts** (Azabu Bijutsu Kogeikan), a contemporary concrete structure, where you may find an excellent exhibition of Japanese crafts. *4-6-9 Roppongi, Minato-ku. Tel. (03)5474-1371. Open 10am to 6pm. Closed Monday. ¥800. 3-minute walk from Roppongi Station of Hibiya subway line.*

The Hibiya subway line's Roppongi Station is near Roppongi Crossing or if it's close to dinner time, why not try one of Roppongi's many restaurants.

EDOKKO

*Old time Tokyoites love to use the term **Edokko**. In the strictest sense Edokko (literally a child of Edo) is a person who is at least the third generation born in Edo (or Tokyo). In other words, if your grandparents were born in Tokyo, you are full-fledged Edokko. But in feudal times, Edokko meant more than just genealogy. An Edokko had to live in **shitamachi**, the crowded area the Tokugawa shogunate designated for merchants, entertainers, apprentices and traders. In the Edo period, 70% of the population lived in shitamachi whereas 70% of land in Edo was occupied by the warrior class.*

Edokko were fun-loving people, who could cry easily over sentimental stories; were contemptuous of the snobbish high-class warriors whom they felt didn't know how to enjoy life; and were very proud of being Edokko. Their distinctive language can be compared to Cockney in London – it's hard to imitate unless you are born to it.

Edokko took great joy in the pleasures of everyday life. The Tokugawa shogunate restricted every aspect of their lives from the types and colors of their clothes to the materials they could use to build their houses. Although people quickly learned to circumvent these rules, conspicuous consumption was out. As a result, people spent their money on enjoying life; an old expression says that if they had extra, they would spend it in a night. Pleasure quarters flourished throughout shitamachi and samurai, barred from mingling, would often disguise themselves so they could get in. To capture the fleeting moment, people took great delight in fireworks and cherry blossoms.

AREAS 4, 5, 6, 7, 8: SHITAMACHI - TOKYO'S OLD DOWNTOWN

The walking tours listed below —Akihabara, Asakusa, Asakusabashi, Fukagawa, Kanda, Kiba, Ryogoku, Yanaka, and Ueno — are all part of old *shitamachi*, commoners' districts in the feudal days. To this day there are vestiges of old Edo.

Shitamachi (low city) was Edo's eastern edge along the Sumida River where merchants and artisans resided. Even today, people are more friendly to each other than in other areas. It was the tradition that the *shitamachi* people supported each other in every aspect of life — from sharing food they cooked in their small kitchens to sharing money. Inevitably such close contact has diminished and relationships have become more impersonal. Today Japanese talk nostalgically about the good old days. Keep this in mind as you explore Tokyo's *shitamachi*.

AREA 4: ASAKUSA

You can reach Asakusa by boat from Hama Rikyu Garden or Hinode Pier at Hamamatsucho. Boats depart every 40 minutes to cruise up the Sumida River. ¥660 to Hinode, ¥620 to Hama Rikyu. To reach by subway, take the Ginza subway line to Asakusa Station; use the stairway in the middle of the train platform and go out exit 1.

Asakusa is one of the few areas in Tokyo that retains the earthy *shitamachi* atmosphere of old Edo. Although most buildings are postwar constructions, the low-rise buildings, shops selling crafts and kimono, and traditional restaurants evoke the memory of an age that has all but disappeared from most Tokyo neighborhoods. Asakusa is definitely not glitzy and the contrast with contemporary Tokyo makes a visit a must. Plan to spend at least a half-day; longer if you want to explore lots of shops.

While the Sumida is a rather plebeian river with undistinguished low bridges, the boat ride is fun and a change from the usual subways and trains. At the Asakusa boat pier, cross Edo Dori and walk on the wide street, Kaminarimon Dori, until the gate with the large red lantern is on your right.

If you've come by subway, you will be on Kaminarimon Dori. Walk west, away from the river, for one block to reach **Kaminarimon Gate**, the large red gate with a huge red paper lantern. Every group of Japanese tourists must have its picture taken under the lantern. Across the street is a **Tourist Information Office**, which has maps and information in English. Ask for the map of Kappabashi, the restaurant supply district. This map lists every store and the goods it sells. *Open daily 10am to 5pm.*

The Kaminarimon Gate has large statues of the guardian gods of thunder and wind, Raijin and Fujin. Pass through the gate and you enter the lively world of the **Nakamise** (literally inner shops) with its bazaar atmosphere and crowded with people and tiny shops selling everything from cheap trinkets to expensive kimono, wigs and hair ornaments, traditional toys, Japanese paper umbrellas, exquisite origami paper, swords, sweets and freshly grilled rice crackers. You'll see shops grilling rice crackers over charcoal and others making bean-filled cakes so you know they are fresh. You may think it's a special festival, but it's like this every day.

Although the buildings are postwar, this area has been a thriving souvenir center for hundreds of years catering to the pilgrims who came to the temple area in search of salvation and entertainment. Many of the stores have been run by the same family for generations.

We especially like **Bairindo**, the first store on the left selling sugar-covered beans; **Okadaya**, in the last block on the left, sells traditional Japanese umbrellas; and in the last block on the right before reaching the inner gate, you find **Tsuruya** selling tortoise shell crafts; **Sukeroku** selling miniature wooden toys complete in every detail; and **Kimuraya** selling *ningyo-yaki*, molded cakes filled with sweet bean paste.

At the end of the long promenade is a second gate, the Hozomon Gate, that leads to the precincts of **Senso-ji Temple**, also called Asakusa Kannon Temple. The Main Hall, Kannondo, is straight ahead. *Open daily 6am to 5pm, April through September and 6:30am to 5pm, October through March.* The temple's history dates to the 7th century when fishermen found a tiny golden statue of Kannon, the Bodhisattva of Mercy, in their nets. In the 16th century, the Tokugawa shogun donated the land on which the temple now stands. Senso-ji was one of the most important temples in the Edo period. World War II air raids destroyed the temple buildings; the present concrete main hall was constructed in 1958. People don't visit Senso-ji to admire architectural relics; they go for the overall atmosphere and, to be fair, some people pray for salvation.

There's a bronze incense stand in front of the main hall; you'll notice people directing the smoke to parts of their bodies. Believers feel the smoke will cure ailments and protect from illness. To the left of the main hall is **Asakusa Jinja**, a Shinto shrine that honors the three fishermen who found the Kannon image. This building is one of the few in the area that dates from the 17th century as does the Nitenmon Gate, which is to the right as you face the shrine. The fishermen who found the golden Kannon statue in the 7th century are not honored in the Buddhist temple; instead, they have their own Shinto shrine. This is a good example of the long and (generally) harmonious relationship between Shintoism and Buddhism.

On the third Sunday of May, the shrine runs the **Sanja Festival**, one of Tokyo's largest festivals. Large *mikoshi* (portable shrines) are carried through the neighborhood to commemorate the fishermen finding the golden Kannon statue. Lots of *sake* and beer ensure that everyone has a good time and that the bearers feel no pain.

The **pagoda** to the left of the main hall was originally built at the command of the third Tokugawa shogun. The present structure was built

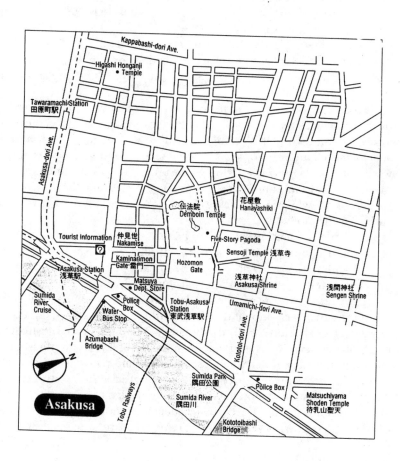

Asakusa

in 1973. Behind the pagoda is the **Hanayashiki Amusement Park**, Tokyo's oldest. Unless you have kids with you, it's definitely skippable. South of the pagoda is **Dempoin Garden**, Senso-ji's chief abbot's residence. The beautiful, peaceful strolling garden is attributed to the 17th century master Kobori Enshu. You can enter the garden if the temple doesn't have any religious events planned. It's best to make a reservation — have a Japanese speaker call *(03) 3842-0181;* if you don't have a reservation, go to the temple's administrative office at the left side of the pagoda. Go into the *Shomuka* office (third door on the left), sign a book and receive a ticket. The garden closes at 3pm and is closed on Sunday and holidays.

To enter the garden, you must return to Nakamise and turn right at the first street, Dempoin Dori. The entrance to the garden is on the right. There are some wonderful shops along the way: **Yonoya**, a comb shop; an abacus shop; kimono shops; and **Daikokuya**, a good *tempura* restaurant with *tendon* as its specialty. If you go past the garden's entrance gate, on the left is **Nakasei**, another good *tempura* restaurant that has a nice garden, and **Yoshikami** that serves Japanized Western fare such as steaks and fried shrimp.

Entering the garden, you leave behind all the bustle of the streets outside and take a step back in time. The strolling garden has a large pond, Japan's oldest temple bell, cast in 1387, and a teahouse. There are wonderful views of the pagoda from around the pond.

Turn left as you leave the garden; cross over the busy Nakamise arcade and turn left — not at the back of the Nakamise stores, but on the next street. On the left is **Fujiya**, a shop selling *tenugui*, small cotton towels printed with beautiful traditional Japanese designs — dragonflies, plum blossoms, thunder, water wheels, snow and cloud patterns to name just a few. These reasonably priced items make great gifts. A little further down is **Hyakusuke**, a shop that sells traditional Japanese cosmetics such as safflower lipstick and **Kuremutsu**, a delicious country-style restaurant. On the right is a bell tower that used to ring on the hour to tell time in old Edo.

Then turn around and retrace you steps on the same street. After Fujiya, on the left is a noodle shop easily recognized by the counter for rolling noodles that's behind a glass window. The tasty noodles make it a good place for lunch. In an old wooden building next door is **Tatsumiya** Restaurant, chocked full of antiques. Its food is reasonably priced. And on the right side, in the last block before the main street, is a wonderful little paper crafts shop called **Kurodaya**. This area has an extensive maze of covered streets with stores selling inexpensive clothing and traditional crafts. It's a fun place to wander, especially on a rainy day.

Return to the main road, Kaminarimon Dori. If you want to call it quits, turn left. You'll go past **Kamiya**, Japan's oldest bar, established in the 1880s and known for its *denki* brandy (electric brandy) drink. The Ginza subway station is there or you can cross Edo Dori. To the left of the Azumabashi Bridge is the pier where you board the **Sumida River Cruise** boats that can take you down the river to Hama Rikyu Garden and Hinode Pier at Hamamatsucho. One more travel alternative is to catch the **double-decker bus** to Ueno from in front of Kaminarimon Gate. It leaves a few times an hour and costs ¥200.

Across the Sumida River is an unusual contemporary building: a black box topped with a golden curlicue. This building is Asahi Beer headquarters and has a beer hall inside.

Unless you are ready for a drink, turn right on Kaminarimon Dori, and go away from the river. Several blocks down on the right is a wonderful shop, **Tachikichi**, selling a wide range of Japanese ceramics.

Continue walking on the same road until it ends at Kokusai Dori. Across the street to the right is the **Drum Museum** (Taikokan). The shop downstairs sells drums and festival instruments, but upstairs is where the real fun begins. The museum has drums from all over the world, and you can play them — except for a few of the rarest ones. There's even a large Japanese *taiko* that's 3 feet in diameter. Our kids love this place. *Miyamoto Unosuke Store, 4F, Kokusai Dori, 2-1-1 Nishi Asakusa, Taito-ku. Tel. (03)3842-5622. Closed Monday and Tuesday. Open 10am to 5pm. ¥300.*

Turn right as you exit the Drum Museum and walk a few short blocks to a main street, Asakusa Dori. Turn right on Asakusa Dori. The south side of the street is lined with shops selling Buddhist altars and other religious goods.

Several blocks further along, you'll easily see a building on the far right corner with a giant chef's head on the roof. This landmark announces your arrival at **Kappabashi**, the restaurant supply district. Turn right; shops on both sides of the street sell dishes, pots and pans, knives, signs, uniforms for chefs, waiters and waitresses and anything else the restaurant trade could possibly use. We love **Biken** and **Maizuru**, both in the first block on the right, selling brightly colored plastic display food that looks good enough to eat. Bring home some *sushi* that will never spoil. About two blocks down on the left, there's a shop selling *noren*, the curtains that hang in a doorway to identify a shop, at a fraction of department store prices. Don't worry if you don't want to buy things by the case; small quantities are okay. Ironically, there are few restaurants in the area.

From Kappabashi, return to Asakusa Dori; turn left, the Ginza subway station is a few blocks down. Ueno is just two stops away.

IF YOU'RE ON A BUDGET...

Maybe not all the best things in life are free, but these are:
- *East Garden of Imperial Palace*
- *Meiji Shrine*
- *Asakusa Kannon Temple*
- *Kappabashi*
- *Tokyo Metropolitan Building Observatory in Shinjuku*
- *Flea markets at shrines on Sunday mornings*
- *Department Stores: the merchandise may be expensive, but there is*
enough to entertain you for hours – from craft galleries on the top floors to
food samples in the basement – without ever dipping into your pockets.

AREA 5: UENO

To reach Ueno, take the JR Yamanote line to Ueno Station. Use the park exit on the west side.

Ueno is a mixture of people and cultures: well-dressed women who go to museums and concert halls mix with wide-eyed tourists from the Japanese provinces; children of all ages on school excursions; shoppers

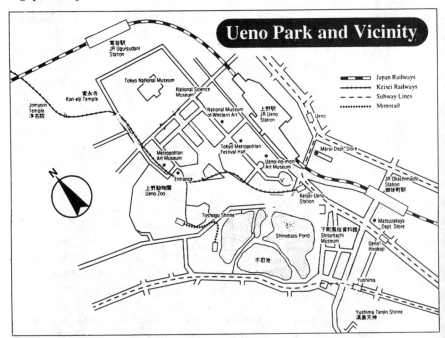

Courtesy of Japan National Tourist Organization

seeking the bargains of Ameyoko; illegal aliens, many of whom work in areas served by trains from Ueno Station; and the homeless.

Back in the days of Edo, Ueno was a major commercial center for the merchant and artisan classes. The large Ueno Park, now the home of a half-dozen cultural institutions and countless cherry trees and pigeons, is on the grounds of the once powerful **Kan'ei-ji Temple**, the Tokugawa's family temple. This temple, along with Zojo-ji in the south, was designed to act as a first fortress against attacks on the castle as well as offer protection from the evil spirits who dwelled in the northeast.

After the surrender of the Edo Castle in 1868, some of the Tokugawa's warriors retreated to Kan'ei-ji Temple. Their fighting with supporters of the emperor destroyed the temple's main buildings. The temple never recovered. Eager to cut the influence of the temple, in 1878 the new Meiji government converted the area into a park that contained Japan's first zoo and museums. Inside Ueno Zoo, a **five-storied pagoda** built in 1631, is all that remains of Kan'ei-ji within the park's boundaries.

When you arrive by subway and depart Ueno Station, the building in front of you is **Tokyo Metropolitan Festival Hall** (Tokyo Bunka Kaikan). Built in 1961, the hall was one of Japan's first postwar structures to receive international acclaim. For two decades it remained Tokyo's main concert hall; now there are over twenty.

Follow the wide path to the right of the hall; the **National Museum of Western Art** (Kokuritsu Seiyo Bijutsukan) is on the right. Le Corbusier designed this three-storied building that houses the Matsukata collection of Western art. It won't give New York's Museum of Modern Art a run for its money, but the museum has an extensive Rodin sculpture collection and often offers outstanding traveling exhibitions. The museum re-opened in Spring 1998 after a long renovation. *Tel. (03)3828-5131.*

Continuing along the same path, you'll reach a large plaza filled with pigeons. Straight ahead is the **Ueno Zoo**; on the right is the **Science Museum**, and the **Tokyo National Museum** is at the end of the plaza on the right.

Ueno Zoo (Ueno Dobutsu Koen), Japan's first zoo (1882), is a pleasant urban zoo and the only place where pandas live in Japan. If all you want to do is see pandas and leave, enter by the main gate near Ueno Park's central plaza; the panda house is just a few minutes walk to the right. You can then duck back out. Pandas sleep in the afternoon, but you can still see them in their air-conditioned comfort. A monorail connects the two parts of the zoo. The western part is around Shinobazu pond and has a nice petting zoo for children. Shinobazu Pond is the home to many ducks and other water birds. *9-83 Ueno Koen, Taito-ku. Tel. (03)3828-5171. Open daily 9:30am to 4:30pm. Closed Monday and December 29 through January 3. ¥500.*

National Science Museum (Kokuritsu Kagaku Hakubutsukan). This museum is a favorite of our kids. There are exhibitions on physics, chemistry, zoology and botany, astronomy and oceanography. The dinosaur exhibition is a big hit. *Tel. (03)3822-0111. Open 9am to 4:30pm. Closed Monday and December 26 through January 3. ¥400.*

Tokyo National Museum (Tokyo Kokuritsu Hakubutsukan). The National Museum holds Japan's largest collection of art — over 88,000 objects. Only a fraction is on display at any time, but a stroll through the galleries will give you an excellent overview of Japanese and Asian art. The National Museum is not an exhaustive (or exhausting) museum like the Louvre or British Museum. You don't have to devote a lifetime to see it; a few hours is enough. The temporary exhibitions are often very crowded, but the regular galleries rarely are. And if you don't want to see the temporary exhibition, purchase a ticket for the permanent collection only *(josetsu-ken)*.

The museum is a complex of four buildings. The large main building, straight ahead as you enter, houses Japanese art. Completed in 1937, the building has concrete walls and Japanese-style roofs, representing a synthesis of East and West. This hall houses Japanese art and temporary exhibitions. On the first floor are sculpture, arms and armor, textiles and ceramics while paintings, lacquer ware and calligraphy are on the second. A few of our favorites from the permanent collection are Hasegawa Tohaku's superb early 17th century brush painting of a pine forest — we can almost hear the wind rustling through the pines; the lively and humorous masks used for the court dances in the Nara period; and a Muromachi period six-panel screen, *Pine Trees on the Beach,* painted on gold leaf.

The building to the left of the main gallery, a faithful imitation of Western architecture constructed at the turn of the century, houses Japanese archaeological materials and Ainu artifacts. The Asian art collection is in the gallery to the right of the main building; it contains Chinese, Korean, South Asian and Middle Eastern art. The final gallery houses treasures from Horyu-ji temple in Nara but is under reconstruction and is scheduled to reopen in autumn 1999 along with a new temporary exhibition hall. *13-9 Ueno Koen, Taito-ku. Tel. (03)3822-1111. Open 9am to 5pm. Closed Monday and December 26 through January 3. ¥400, additional for special exhibitions.*

Tokyo Metropolitan Art Museum (Tokyo-to Bijutsukan) exhibits mainly modern Japanese art. There's no standing exhibition so check to see what is on display. *8-36 Ueno Koen, Taito-ku. Tel. (03)3823-6921. Open 9am to 5pm. Closed Monday and New Year's. Admission fee varies.*

Just south of Ueno Zoo is **Toshogu Shrine** that was built in 1651 to honor the first Tokugawa shogun. Like the Toshogu Shrine in Nikko, the

TOKYO UNIVERSITY

*Nicknamed **Todai**, Tokyo University is at the pinnacle of Japan's higher education system – the dream of tens of thousands of ambitious students. Founded in 1877, Todai was the first imperial university and was built on the estate of the Maeda family. The Maeda feudal lords' domain was second only to the shogun's. When the Tokugawa shogunate collapsed in 1868, the Maeda packed up and returned home to Kanazawa.*

The main gate, Akamon (literally the red gate), was built to commemorate the wedding between a Maeda and the daughter of Shogun Ienari. She was above him in the social hierarchy and apparently she never let her hapless husband forget it. Tales abound about how she always seated herself in a higher position and how her husband talked to her in public using honorific language suited to a daughter of the shogun rather than the way a normal husband would speak to his wife.

The university's campus spans 124 acres and includes a garden belonging to the Maeda estate. To visit, take the Marunouchi subway line to Hongo-san-chome Station.

style is very ornate; if you don't have a chance to get to Nikko, you can get some idea from this shrine. The stone and bronze lanterns that line the approach were donated by the feudal lords. The descending dragons of the Karamon (Chinese Gate) were carved by Hidari Jingoro, the same sculptor who worked on Nikko's famous, ornate Yomeimon Gate. The dragons are so vividly portrayed it was believed they would drink water from Shinobazu Pond at night. The shrine is designated a National Treasure. *Open 9am to 4:30pm or 6pm, depending on the season. ¥200.*

Benzaiten Shrine is on an island in the middle of the Shinobazu Pond, the southwest part of Ueno Park, and is dedicated to the only female among the seven deities of good fortune. Benten is a patron of music, beauty and the arts and is often depicted playing a lute near the water, which explains why Benzaiten shrines are often found on islands.

At the southern tip of Ueno Park, east of Shinobazu Pond, is the **Shitamachi Museum**. This small museum displays a reproduction of a downtown merchant's area in old Edo. The district was a center for commoner's culture. The second floor houses exhibits of goods and toys used in everyday life. It's quite a charming museum and is a nice break from the high culture of Ueno's other museums. *2-1 Ueno Koen, Taito-ku. Tel. (03)3823-7451. Open 9:30am to 4:30pm. Closed Monday. December 29 through January 3. ¥200.*

From the Shitamachi Museum, walk south until you reach Kasuga Dori. Turn right. About two blocks after the Yushima subway station, **Yushima Tenjin Shrine** is on the left. This small shrine is dedicated to Sugawara Michizane, a 9th century scholar who has been deified as the god of scholarly achievement. In February, when the universities have entrance exams, it is crowded with students praying to pass their entrance exams. On the grounds there's a small grove of plum trees, Michizane's favorite blossom.

Walk back east along Kasuga Dori until you reach Okachimachi Station of the elevated JR Yamanote line. The area north from Okachimachi to Ueno Station is **Ameyoko Market**, a free-wheeling, boisterous place where bargains abound. Ameyoko started as a black market after World War II. Ame is short for America; originally goods pilfered from the Occupation army were the main commodities.

The outdoor market that runs alongside the train line has fishmongers, green grocers and dry goods sales people all barking out their specials to passersby. What a small world we live in: fresh Maine lobsters, Norwegian salmon, smoked salmon, Southeast Asian spices, imported coffee and tea are just a few of the items available in a few short blocks.

The shops, in a warren under and east of the tracks, sell mostly imported clothing, cosmetics, suitcases, shoes and whatever else is popular at the moment. Recently some fairly glitzy buildings have gone up in the Ameyoko area.

From Ueno, the Yanaka and Akihabara/Kanda areas are convenient.

AREA 6: YANAKA

To reach Yanaka, take the JR Yamanote line to Nippori.

Yanaka is a quiet backwater with lots of narrow roads with old temples, residences and shops recalling the Tokyo of 100 years ago. Yanaka has alleys where small houses, with lots of potted plants placed outside, stand so close to one another that they practically touch. We enjoy the quiet atmosphere of the district conveniently located north of Ueno Park. You can easily spend two or three hours wandering around.

The Tokugawa shogunate ordered temples to move to Yanaka as a first wall of defense against invasion. The area was spared major fires and bombing so many of these temples still remain although on much smaller plots of land than in the Edo period.

Don't think of Yanaka as a perfectly preserved district of wooden houses. Most people prefer modern houses over drafty and damp wooden ones, which means that if they have enough money, they usually rebuild. Since most of Yanaka's residents are of modest means, they haven't rebuilt to the same extent as in other areas.

When you arrive at Nippori station, walk to the north exit at the very end of the platform, go up the stairs and take the west exit. Stairs to the left lead to Yanaka Cemetery; this detour is lovely during cherry blossom season. Instead, take the road heading away from the station and turn left at the third street where there's a bright orange post box on the corner. The **Asakura Sculpture Gallery** (Asakura Chosokan) is on the left. This museum was the studio-residence of Asakura Fumio (1883-1964) who's considered to be the father of modern Japanese sculpture. You'll recognize it by the ragged cement pillars making a wall around the residence. Asakura designed his house without any angular forms, even to the point of using round cypress poles. His lovely, albeit small, water garden has a pond that occupies most of the space and an assortment of plants that bloom in white all year round — only one has red flowers. Asakura's teahouse is elegant and rustic. *7-18-10 Yanaka, Taito-ku. Tel. (03)3821-4549. Open 10am to 4:30pm. Closed Monday and Friday and New Year's. ¥300.*

Turn left as you exit the sculpture gallery. This road runs into another road where Sun Royal Star store is on your left. Turn right onto this road; it leads to Sendagi subway station. On the right in the block before the station, you'll find **Kikumi Sembei**, a charming rice cracker shop. Turn around, retrace your steps, and a block or so down on the right is **Isetatsu**. Located in a traditional wooden house with a large picture of a *kabuki* actor above the door, this shop has an excellent assortment of Japanese handprinted paper and crafts. You'll find paper with unusual patterns like *kabuki* actors' make-up styles and feudal lords' family crests. Isetatsu also has beautifully printed cotton cloth with traditional patterns. *2-18-9 Yanaka, Taito-ku. Tel. (03)3823-1453. Open daily 10am to 6pm.*

As you exit Isetatsu, turn right on the little street to the right of the store. **Chika**, a small folk craft shop, is on the left. Turn left at the first street and turn right when the street ends — about a five minute walk. On the right is the **Daimyo Clock Museum** (Daimyo Dokei Hakubutsukan). This museum displays Japanese clocks made during the Edo period. These clocks are unique: time was geared to sunrise and sunset, and the length of the hours varied depending on the season. In summer, one daylight hour could last almost twice as long as a nighttime hour. This extremely complicated system meant clocks had to be reset twice a day. Only *daimyo* (feudal lords) could afford such an luxury; hence, the name, *daimyo* clocks. Two of our favorites are the pillow clock used in the bedroom and a tiny clock made into an *inro*, a tiny decorative medicine bottle. *2-1-27 Yanaka, Taito-ku. Tel. (03)3821-6913. Open 10am to 5pm. Closed Monday, July through September and December 25 through January 15. ¥300.*

Turn right as you leave the museum and then take your first left. This road takes you to Kototoi Dori. Turn right and Nezu Station of the

Chiyoda subway line is a few blocks down at the intersection of Shinobazu Dori. If you turn left onto Shinobazu Dori, the road will lead you to Ueno Park.

AREA 7: AKIHABARA/KANDA

To reach Akihabara, take the JR Yamanote line to Akihabara Station, one stop from Okachimachi Station or two stops from Ueno Station. Or you can walk south from Ueno, parallel to the Yamanote train tracks, for about 15 minutes.

Akihabara is a high-tech shopper's paradise. Dubbed "Electric Town" by JR's sign makers, the area is enveloped in a neon glow. Shop after shop has its goods spilling onto the street. Figure on spending a half-day in this area.

Akihabara began its electronic reputation after World War II by selling black market goods. Later it began to stock household appliances and became the place Tokyoites went to buy their televisions, washing machines and transistor radios. Now, while you can still buy household appliances, computers and software overwhelm the visitor. The area's many alleyways have booths selling semiconductors and all sorts of parts that require a Ph.D. to identify.

One of the largest shops is **Laox**, pronounced "Raokkusu," which has eight shops within a two or three block area. They and other large shops have duty free departments that specialize in export goods in 120 and 240 volts and have an English-speaking staff. Take your passport to be exempt from paying the 5% consumption tax.

Unlike most shops in Japan, you can usually bargain for a slightly cheaper price at Akihabara's shops as well as at discount electronic shops in other areas. Or in lieu of a cheaper price, you can negotiate some freebies such as extra batteries. So don't be shy about asking for a discount.

You may find that goods are cheaper in New York than they are in Akihabara, but you're sure to find the latest or fully loaded models that have not yet left Japan's shores. We don't know a capacitor from a widget, but we love to browse around Akihabara. There's still a free-wheeling, black market atmosphere even though highly sophisticated goods are now for sale.

Electronic junkie friends have told us that recently Akihabara has lost some of its competitive edge to other big discount shops like Bic Camera, Sakuraya and Yodobashi Camera in Shibuya and Shinjuku. For the foreign visitor, these shops are fine for cameras and video cameras, but they don't have the selection of overseas models for electronic appliances

If you want to have a peek in a traditional Chinese (Oriental) herb medicine shop on Chuo Dori, the main road of Akihabara, turn right at Ishimaru Denki, just before the bridge over the Kanda River. On the right is **Kinokuniya Kan Yakkyoku**, *1-2-14 Soto Kanda, Chiyoda-ku*. This old shop is still flourishing and sells authentic Chinese medicines at reasonable prices, reasonable, that is, as long as you aren't looking for rare items like powdered antlers of a young deer, ¥100,000 for a one month supply.

If you're interested in seeing a few temples, continue along this road for several blocks until **Yushima Confucian Shrine** (Yushima Seido) is on your right. This shrine was affiliated with the Tokugawa shogunate's top samurai school. The Chinese-style building was rebuilt in 1934 after the 1923 earthquake. The main temple building houses a statue of Confucius and is open on Saturday, Sunday and holidays — the grounds are a good escape from the city.

Across Hongo Dori, the street at the back of the shrine, is the entrance to **Kanda Myojin Shrine**, a Shinto shrine with history that goes back to the 8th century. The Tokugawa Shogunate designated it Edo's guardian shrine. While the building was reconstructed in the 1930s, it's faithful to earlier architectural styles. Kanda Myojin holds one of Tokyo's largest and noisiest festivals every other year on May 15. On the shrine's grounds, the Mikoshi-den houses the ornate *mikoshi* (portable shrines) that men, decked out in festival gear, carry through the streets. Fortified with plenty of *sake* and beer, they feel very little pain.

Walk back along the Kanda River to the Akihabara area. Turn right on Chuo Dori and cross over the Mansei Bridge. The **Transportation Museum** (Kotsu Hakubutsukan) is on the right at a fork in the road just past the bridge. The building is old and has a run down feeling, but its heart is in the right place. What a great place to take kids! You can't miss it because a *shinkansen* train is on display at the side of the building. The first floor has trains; cars and ships are on the second; and aviation is on the third. The first steam locomotive used in Japan, which began service between Shimbashi in Tokyo and Yokohama in 1872, is on display. You can sit in the driver's seat of a Yamanote car while a film takes you on the loop all around Tokyo. The model train panorama has about 20 trains, and there's a demonstration of them a few times each hour. We loved the 1938 Datsun car and the primitive stop lights, but our kids loved driving the trains. *25 Kanda Sudacho, 1-chome, Chiyoda-ku. Tel. (03)3251-8481. Akihabara Station on JR Yamanote line. Open 9:30am to 5pm. Closed Monday and December 29 through January 3. ¥300.*

The small road forking off from Chuo Dori at the Transportation Museum leads to Yasukuni Dori, a major thoroughfare. Walk along Yasukuni Dori to reach the heart of Kanda Jimbocho — about 20 minutes. First you'll walk through a **sporting goods** district with nearly 100 shops that sell discounted skiing equipment and ski ware as well as paraphernalia for other sports. The biggest shops are Victoria Sports and Minami Sports. Discounts can reach 80% for last year's goods. *If you want to bypass* *sporting goods, hop on the Toei Shinjuku subway line at Ogawamachi Station on Yasukuni Dori; and take it one stop to Jimbocho. Use the A-6 exit and you'll come out on the corner of Yasukuni Dori and Hakusan Dori.*

Jimbocho is Tokyo's book store center with lots of shops selling new, used and rare books in Japanese and English and sometimes other languages, and maps and woodblock prints. The concentration of universities in this area during the Meiji era made it a natural. Rumor has it that the area wasn't bombed during World War II because of the precious antique books in the old shops, but we're skeptical that anyone's aim could be so accurate.

Many of the shops are on Yasukuni Dori on one side of the street. A few of our favorites are **Ohya Shobo** *(1-1 Kanda Jimbocho, Chiyoda-ku, Tel. (03) 3291-0062)* for a good collection of woodblock prints, illustrated books and maps; **Hara Shobo** for woodblock prints *(2-3 Kanda Jimbocho, Chiyoda-ku, Tel. (03) 3261-7444);* and **Kitazawa Books** for an excellent selection of used and rare books in English *(2-5 Kanda Jimbocho, Chiyoda-ku, Tel. (03) 3263-0011).*

WHERE CAN YOU GO ON MONDAYS WHEN ALMOST EVERY MUSEUM IS CLOSED?

• *MOA Museum in Atami*
• *Kamakura*
• *Meiji Shrine, Omotesando and Harajuku*
• *Asakusa Kannon Temple*
• *Japan Traditional Craft Center in Aoyama*

Area 8: Asakusabashi/Ryogoku/Fukagawa/Kiba

Allow the better part of a day for this tour. To reach Asakusabashi, take the JR Sobu line to Asakusabashi Station.

Asakusabashi is a bustling wholesale and retail shopping district. Across the Sumida River, Ryogoku is the center of sumo wrestling, Japan's national sport, and is known for a large fireworks display every summer. The sumo stadium is there as well as most of the sumo stables where wrestlers live and train. The large wrestlers, dressed in cotton *yukata* robes, are often on the streets. But sumo isn't the only act in town. Near the stadium are the Edo Tokyo Museum, a small strolling garden and an earthquake memorial; all are worth seeing.

The Asakusabashi Station exit lets you out on Edo Dori, a main road lined with doll and paper goods shops. For paper products, we love to browse in **Shimojima**, there are a half-dozen stores in the area, each selling different products. **Sakura Horikiri**, located on the road along the south side of the train tracks east of the station, sells craft kits using Japanese paper. You have the option of assembling your kit under expert instruction. Shimojima has so many kinds of reasonably priced wrapping paper, both Japanese and Western, that we find it difficult to choose and always come home with more than we need. Also on Edo Dori are several large stores selling elegant dolls in glass cases. Year round you can find dolls for Girls' Day, March 3, and Boys' Day, May 5.

Walk north on Edo Dori and turn right on Kuramae Dori, crossing over the Sumida River. On the right one block after the bridge is the Earthquake Memorial Park. The architecturally eclectic **Centotaph Hall** memorializes the victims of World War II bombing raids as well as the 40,000 people who perished on this site in the fire storm after the 1923 earthquake.

Exit the park from the rear of the hall; across the street is the **Kyu Yasuda Garden**. The quiet park preserves the spirit of Edo gardens. This strolling garden was constructed about 300 years ago; the pond's water level used to rise and fall with the tide of the nearby Sumida River, but today it's controlled artificially. Like the residences of so many other feudal lords, the garden was purchased by a wealthy businessman – in this case the founder of Yasuda Bank, today's Fuji Bank – in the late 19th century. *1-12 Yokoami, Sumida-ku. Open 9am to 4:30pm. Closed at New Year's. Free admission.*

Just south of the park is the **Sumo Stadium** (Kokugikan), home of three sumo tournaments each year. In the building is the small **Sumo Museum** (Sumo Hakubutsukan). The museum is not worth a trek across town, but if you are at the Edo Tokyo Museum, stop in. It has sumo paraphernalia. The trophies aren't very interesting, but some of the old photos are fun. During sumo tournaments, the museum is open only to ticket holders. For information on sumo tickets, see "Sports" later in this chapter. *To go directly to the Sumo Stadium, use the Ryogoku Station of the JR Sobu line. 1-3-28 Yokoami, Sumida-ku, Tokyo. Tel. (03)3622-0366. Free admission to museum.*

Next to the stadium is the **Edo Tokyo Museum** (Edo Tokyo Hakubutsukan). *1-4-1 Yokoami, Sumida-ku, Tokyo. Tel. (03)3626-9974. Ryogoku Station on the JR Sobu line. Open 10am to 6pm; until 8pm Thursday and Friday. Closed Monday and December 28 through January 4. ¥400, additional admission fee for special exhibitions.*

Flush with cash in the middle of the bubble economy of the 1980s, Tokyo decided to build a museum to immortalize its past. It's a Darth Vadar-like building – a silvery steel raised platform with a long escalator taking you from street level into the guts of the building. Designers say the building imitates a rice storehouse that sits on stilts to prevent rodents from eating the grain; the only similarity we see is tall pillars. Instead of the earthy organic feeling of a wooden rice storehouse, the building reminds us of an overgrown robot.

Half the museum is dedicated to Edo, as Tokyo was known during the Tokugawa shogunate (1603-1868), and begins with a reconstruction of the gracefully arched wooden Nihonbashi Bridge, the place from which all distances were measured and where all roads began. Crossing the bridge, imagine how an Edo-period traveler in straw sandals and straw hat must have felt beginning his journey. The museum depends heavily on reconstructions but succeeds in vividly displaying Edo. The other half of the museum displays Tokyo from 1868 onward, through the Meiji craze for all things Western, the 1923 earthquake, the destruction of World War II and the reconstruction in the postwar period. A gallery in the basement has special exhibitions.

Earphones with an English tape are available free of charge at the ticket booths at street level; you pay a refundable deposit. We think they're unnecessary because the text is the same as the English panels in the museum. The museum shop in the basement has an excellent selection of traditional crafts, some of which you find only in the Shitamachi area.

Kiyosumi Dori is the main road running along the eastern side of the Edo Tokyo Museum. Walk south on Kiyosumi Dori one block to the intersection of Keiyo Dori. Here is **Lion-do**, a clothing store that caters to sumo sizes. Stock up on your sumo sized T-shirts here. *Tel. (03)631-0650.* Also near this intersection is **Chanko Doji**, which serves *chanko nabe* sumo fare: raw vegetables, tofu, *udon,* chicken and fish cooked together in a broth. *Tel. (03) 3635-5347.*

Two short blocks south of Keiyo Dori on the left side of Kiyosumi Dori is **Kikuya**, a shop specializing in *tabi,* one-toed socks. *1-9-3 Midori, Sumida-ku. Tel. (03)3631-0092. Closed Sunday and holidays.*

Another good place to eat in the Ryogoku area is **Momojiya** (see *Where to Eat*), which serves venison, boar dishes and badger soup. *1-10-2 Ryogoku, Sumida-ku. Tel. (03)3631-5596.*

Fukagawa is fairly close to Ryogoku. Continue walking along Kiyosumi Dori for about 20 minutes until the Kiyosumi Garden is on your right or hop in a taxi since it's not a particularly pleasant walk. **Kiyosumi Garden** (Kiyosumi Tei-en). This beautiful and peaceful garden was the site of the villa of feudal lord Kuze Yamato-no-kami. Iwasaki Yataro, founder of the Mitsubishi empire, purchased the estate in the late 19th century and seriously upgraded the garden by adding lots of rare rocks from all over Japan. Its large pond is home to thousands of carp. *3-3-9 Kiyosumi, Koto-ku. Tel. (03)3641-5892. Open daily 9am to 4:30pm. Closed December 28 through January 4. ¥150.*

SEEING THE SIGHTS 243

Return to Kiyosumi Dori and turn on to Moto Kuyakusho Dori, across the street from the park. Down several blocks on the left is the **Fukagawa Edo Museum** (Fukagawa Edo Shiryokan). This small museum has 11 buildings all moved from the Fukagawa area. They've been reconstructed to show a working class neighborhood during feudal times and include stores, warehouses, merchants' houses and tenements. It's smaller and less pretentious than the Edo Tokyo Museum. When we were here, some older Japanese touring the museum kept saying, *"Natsukashii,"* – "I'm nostalgic for the good old days." *1-3-28 Shirakawa, Koto-ku. Tel. (03)3630-8625. Open daily 9:30am to 5pm; closed December 28 through January 5. ¥300.*

From the museum, turn left on Kiyosumi Dori and walk about 15 minutes to the Monzen Nakacho Station on the Tozai subway line. You can also take #33 bus to the station. To visit one of the premier alternative art spaces in Tokyo, turn right onto Eitai Dori , the main road where the subway station is, and make the first right after the canal. Turn right at the first corner to reach the **Sagacho Exhibit Space**. This gallery, housed in a refurbished art deco building, formerly the laboratory of the All-Japan Rice Market, is one of the best venues in Tokyo to see the work of up-and-coming artists. The gallery reminds us of New York's Soho galleries. *3F, Shokuryo Building, 1-8-3 Saga, Koto-ku. Tel. (03)3630-3243. Open 11am to 6pm. Closed Sunday and holidays.*

At Monzen Nakacho Station, take the subway one stop to **Kiba**, which literally means timber place. In the Edo period, logs were carried by boats to the canals of the district. To get from the Fukagawa Edo Museum or Sagacho Exhibit Space to the Museum of Contemporary Art (next stop below), it's actually much more efficient to take a taxi.

The only reason to go to Kiba is the **Museum of Contemporary Art, Tokyo** (Tokyo-to Gendai Bijutsukan), with the self-proclaimed nickname "MOT." This museum opened in 1995, and is another large public project planned during the heyday of the bubble economy. The large postmodern stone and glass complex has a zillion little nooks and pathways. It seems as though more thought was put into creating a signature piece of architecture than a working museum. However, the museum holds excellent exhibitions of contemporary art by both Japanese and international artists and, if there's a good exhibition, it's worth the trek even though it's located in the middle of nowhere. We find the practice of charging separate admission fees for each exhibition annoying. Usually several exhibitions run simultaneously and charge anywhere from ¥500 to ¥1000 each. *4-1-1 Miyoshi, Koto-ku. Tel. (03)5245-4111. Open 10am to 6pm, until 9pm Friday. Closed Monday and December 28 through January 4.*

AREA 9: SHINAGAWA & MEGURO

On the southern part of the Yamanote loop, the sights in the Shinagawa and Meguro areas are spread out. Rather than walking long distances, we recommend that you take a taxi from one to another. **Sengaku-ji**. From Shinagawa Station, walk about 10 minutes north on Hibiya Dori. An otherwise ordinary temple, Sengaku-ji is famous because the 47 *ronin* (masterless samurai) are buried here. This story is one of Japan's favorites about samurai loyalty — the revenge by the retainers of a feudal lord who was forced to commit suicide. People come and pray for the *ronin*, putting one stick of incense on each grave. By the 47th, we were pretty dizzy from breathing the incense.

A five-minute walk will take you to **Tozen-ji** Temple. From Sengaku-ji, walk back towards Shinagawa Station and turn to the right after you pass the pedestrian overpass. Tucked away on a quiet, small alley lined with willow trees, Tozen-ji's simple and austere Zen atmosphere is impressive. The temple was used as the British Legation between 1859 and 1873. It's a shame that the part the British used is not accessible to the public. Still it's a lovely small temple, so drop in when you are in the neighborhood.

From Sengaku-ji, it's a 25-minute walk or 5-minute taxi ride to the **Hara Museum of Contemporary Art** (Hara Bijutsukan). *4-7-25 Kita Shinagawa, Shinagawa-ku. Tel. (03)3445-0651. Open 11am to 8pm weekdays, 11am to 5pm weekends and holidays. Closed Monday. ¥700. 15-minute walk from JR Shinagawa Station or from Shinagawa Station Takanawa exit, take bus #90 to Gotenyama stop. Web site: http://www.haramuseum.or.jp.*

The Hara Museum is one of the best places to see the cutting edge of contemporary art in Tokyo. Housed in a 1930s Bauhaus-style residence, the museum features Japanese and international artists. The prominent Hara family produced a free-thinking mayor of Tokyo in the early part of this century. His grandson is one of Japan's biggest collectors of contemporary art. The museum has a cafe serving good food, a rarity among Tokyo's museums. In summer you can dine in the garden, a truly delightful experience.

Turn right as you leave the grounds of the Hara Museum and at the large intersection with Yatsuyama Dori, cross the street and continue walking on the narrow road. On the right is **Kaitokaku**, the estate of Baron Iwasaki, the founder of the Mitsubishi empire. The grounds are not open to the public, but today Mitsubishi uses the turn-of-the-century robber baron's mansion for entertaining. Kaitokaku is one of the few large estates left intact in Tokyo.

After about a seven-minute walk, the street merges into a larger road and the Takanawa Prince Hotel is on the right. Continue walking straight; just past the end of the hotel's property is a street light. There's always a

THE TALE OF THE 47 RONIN

This tale of samurai loyalty has captured the imagination of the Japanese even 400 years after it occurred. The story begins when Asano Takuminokami, a young feudal lord head of a small domain west of Himeji, arrives in Edo. A country bumpkin, he didn't follow common practice and go to see Kira Kozuke-no-suke, the shogun's head of protocol, to present a gift and ask for his guidance. Asano expected to be informed of the protocol of an engagement at the shogun's castle. But the head of protocol, miffed over the breach of etiquette, refused to coach Asano, so he wound up wearing the wrong clothes to the castle.

Humiliated, Asano angrily drew his sword against Kira, but others stopped Asano from killing him. As a result, Asano committed ritual suicide since samurai were prohibited from drawing their swords within the castle grounds. After Asano's death the shogun confiscated his domain and divided it among other feudal lords. Asano's retainers became **ronin** *(masterless samurai). The ronin were so incensed they vowed to do what their lord could not – kill Kira – even though they knew that they themselves would have to commit suicide for this action.*

The ronin planned meticulously – the leader left his wife to live a dissolute life in brothels to make sure no one was suspicious of the plan. Forty-seven of Asano's retainers broke into Kira's residence on a snowy evening, December 14, 1702, and killed him. They then killed themselves.

The pathos of this feat has been immortalized in kabuki, bunraku, movies, TV dramas and even in contemporary opera. Naturally, some take artistic license with the facts. While only about a year elapsed between Asano's suicide and Kira's death, in many plays it stretches out to a decade. Something in the Japanese psyche has great empathy towards tragedy and glorifies the losers; the tale of the 47 ronin pulls all the right strings to make it a classic.

police guard at this intersection. Turn left. In one block, you'll come to a large intersection. Cross Sakurada Dori and on the other side the road forks into two small streets. Take the one on the right. Several blocks down, past a playground, is a big red sign that says **Han-nya-en**. Turn left and follow the road as it curves around to the right. Turn left at another red sign; the Hatakeyama Collection and Han-nya-en are just past the parking lot. The walk takes about 20 minutes; if you want to save your time and energy, take a cab.

The **Hatakeyama Collection** has one of the best museum settings in Tokyo and is a must-see for anyone with a serious interest in the tea ceremony and its arts. The museum is tucked away on a quiet side street in a verdant compound of gardens, teahouses and an elegant residence. Hatakeyama Issei, a successful machine industry businessman and a tea ceremony connoisseur, collected tea utensils, hanging scrolls and ceramics. Hatakeyama himself designed the gallery that includes three tea ceremony rooms. The famous collection includes a beautiful handscroll that is the result of the collaboration between two of the most versatile artists in the Edo period: Hon'ami Koetsu and Tawaraya Sotatsu. There are also dynamic tea bowls and square plates by Ogata Kenzan. The museum exhibits about 50 objects at a time, changing shows with the seasons. *2-20-12 Shiroganedai, Minato-ku. Tel. (03)3447-5787. Open 10am to 5pm. ¥500.*

The museum shares a garden with Han-nya-en, an elegant, traditional building, the former Hatakeyama residence. Today it is an extremely pricey restaurant, dinner runs about ¥50,000 per person. Mishima Yukio used Han-nya-en as the setting for his novel *After the Banquet.*

From the museum, walk back to Sakurada Dori, turn right and walk about five minutes down the hill to Gotanda Station. Take the JR Yamanote line one stop to **Meguro Station**. Come out the east exit of the station and walk east along Meguro Dori for five minutes. Just after you pass under the expressway, you'll come to the **Tei-en Museum** (Tokyo-to Tei-en Bijutsukan) on the left. The only remaining Art Deco building in Tokyo, the Tei-en Museum is the former residence of Prince Asaka. Built in 1933, Henri Rapin designed the building, and much of the glasswork is by Rene Lalique. The museum does not have a permanent collection but often has exhibits relating to Art Deco. We love to bring a picnic lunch and eat in the museum's French and Japanese gardens — admission to the garden only is ¥200. *5-21-9 Shiroganedai, Minato-ku. Tel. (03)3443-8500. Open 10am to 5pm. Closed 2nd and 4th Wednesday. Admission varies with the exhibition.*

Just beyond the Tei-en Museum is the **Nature Study Park** (Shizen Kyoiku-en), a heavily wooded area with educational programs to teach Tokyoites about nature because they see little of it in their real lives. It's a good place to surround yourself with some trees. This park is one of the few original forests of the Musashino plain and is left in an authentic state. Don't get disgusted by the crows that have decided to move in; the Tokyo government would like to move them out, but hasn't discovered how.

Continue walking down Meguro Dori for another five minutes. Just after the pedestrian overpass, on the right corner is **Happo-en**, a catering hall that is popular for weddings. The complex has a lovely strolling garden that once belonged to the Okubo family, chief retainers to the Tokugawa shoguns. You can have a nice meal here or just enjoy the garden.

Walk back to the west side of Meguro Station. On the southeast side is a small road coming off to the left of Sakura Bank at an angle. Walk down this road about five minutes until you come to Meguro Gajoen.

Meguro Gajoen is a wedding palace and hotel, and even though you have no intention of getting married, you must stop in. The place was an early 20th century building that was completely rebuilt a few years ago, and some of the art has been incorporated into the new structure. An outrageous project undertaken at the height of the economic bubble, it's as "bubbly" as you can get — a real tribute to the crazy 1980s when cost was no object for anything. It is so way out, we love to show it off to visitors.

The hotel really functions as a wedding palace with rooms on the side. The large contemporary structure has a tall atrium overlooking a Japanese garden. There are several restaurants, including a good *teppanyaki* restaurant, Kasho, where lunch courses begin at ¥3000.

The long hallway has huge paintings of Japanese women; be sure to look up at the ceiling where fan-shaped paintings look down on you. Sneak a peek into the *tatami* mat lobby of the Japanese-style banquet room. It's Japanese rococo with paintings moved from the original building. And don't forget to go into the rest rooms in the lobby; they, too, are works of art.

You can walk back up the hill to Meguro Station for the JR Yamanote line.

AREA 10: EBISU

On the western side of Tokyo, one stop south of Shibuya on the JR Yamanote line.

Ebisu was a quiet and nearly forgotten neighborhood until **Yebisu Garden Place** opened. It's one of Tokyo's few urban complexes incorporating offices, commercial and residential space, a luxury hotel, and numerous restaurants. Until the late 1980s, the site was Yebisu's beer brewery. The moving sidewalk at the south exit of Ebisu Station delivers you to the complex. The plaza has lots of open space, but unfortunately most is bricked over — more grass would have been nice. The area is packed with young people, especially dating couples, on evenings and weekends.

The Westin Tokyo Hotel is there as is a small branch of Mitsukoshi Department Store. The site used to house the Yebisu beer factory, so naturally there is a beer hall and a beer museum. The upscale French restaurant, Taillevent Robuchon, is in a faux chateau; plans to move a real one from France were nixed because of building codes. Dinner is pricey; lunch is less so or why not try the basement cafe. A host of other restaurants serve everything from *sushi* and *tonkatsu* to spaghetti.

The **Tokyo Metropolitan Museum of Photography** (Tokyo-to Shashin Bijutsukan) alone is worth the trip to Yebisu Garden Place. The museum is the premier place to view photography and video art in Tokyo. *Yebisu Garden Place, 1-13-3 Mita, Meguro-ku. Tel. (03)3280-0031. Open 10am to 6pm, Thursday and Friday until 8pm. Closed Monday. ¥1000. http://www.tokyo-photo-museum.or.jp.*

The commercial area around the northern exit of Ebisu Station has lots of shops catering to area residents and makes for some interesting strolling.

AREA 11: SHIBUYA

Shibuya is three stops on the Yamanote line from Shinjuku.

Shibuya has an entirely different feel than most other districts of Tokyo. The Shibuya area is one of Tokyo's trendiest areas; it's always crowded with people and exudes energy and excitement. Filled with shops and restaurants, it caters to a young crowd dressed from head to toe in the latest fashions. It's much smaller and doesn't have the same massive office buildings and hotels. People come to Shibuya to play, not work. Even if you are over 25, don't stay away from Shibuya. There are enough "establishment" places so you won't feel out of place.

The area was once the boondocks, far removed from the population center around and east of the castle. After the 1923 earthquake, people started moving west, searching for open space, and Shibuya's prosperity began. For the last two decades, two parvenu department store companies, Tokyu and Seibu, have been competing to build the best department stores and fashion buildings; in the process, they've put Shibuya on the map.

This walk through Shibuya can take one hour if you don't stop or all day for shopaholics. Begin at Shibuya Station, a fairly small place when compared to Shinjuku or Ikebukuro but served by six train and subway lines. There's a small plaza at the northwest quadrant of the station, with a statue called **Hachiko**, named after a famous dog, where friends wait to meet each other (see above sidebar). On evenings and weekends the area is so crowded it's almost impossible to find someone unless he or she has pink hair. Actually, being blonde is a plus. There's a small police box in **Hachiko Plaza**.

The buildings around Hachiko Plaza have bright neon lights, billboards and video screens that light up the evening sky. The noise level can be unbearable when people concerned about the future —politicians, right wingers, left wingers, you name it — park their sound trucks next to the plaza and blast out speeches no one wants to hear.

The large intersection has to be one of Tokyo's most crowded; literally a thousand or more people cross at the same time and, naturally,

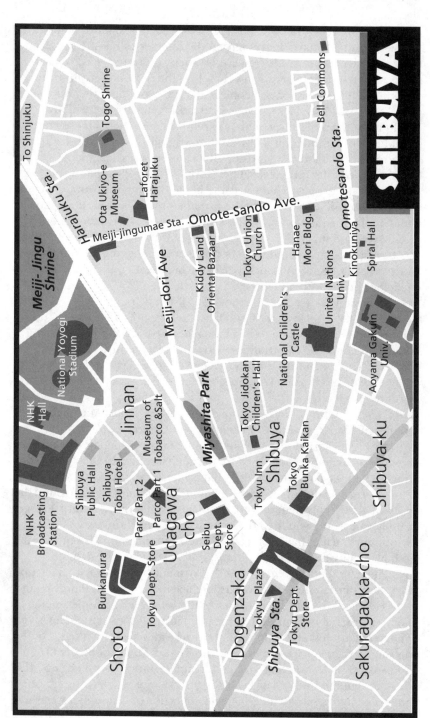

SHIBUYA

all go in different directions. Sometimes it feels like all of Tokyo's 12 million residents have converged on the intersection at the same time. The experience can be disconcerting when you're not used to crowds; instead of letting it overwhelm you, follow the person in front of you by looking at his or her shoes. People will try to avoid bumping into you.

From Hachiko Plaza, locate and walk towards the **Shibuya 109** building; it has a big silver silo; be careful because there are several 109 Buildings. In the time you walk the block, you will probably receive at least three packets of tissues advertising all sorts of services imaginable. On the left you'll see a discount electronics store with its goods spilling out onto the sidewalk and hear its advertising jingle blasting over loudspeakers. Welcome to **Bic Camera**. Despite its name, Bic sells computers, household appliances, stereos and nearly anything else electronic. Where else would you find small foot warmers in winter and ice sherbet makers in the shape of a penguin in summer? The prices are comparable to Akihabara's, but export models aren't stocked. Next to Bic is **Kobe-ya**, a bakery that has delicious bread and sandwiches.

Shibuya 109 was one of the first "fashion buildings" — basically vertical malls chocked with small stores and restaurants. At the Y intersection in front of the 109 building, bear to the right. Along the right side of the building is a traditional-looking restaurant with plastic food displays. This restaurant is **Kujira**, one of the few places in Japan serving whale meat. Leave your Greenpeace membership card at home if you want to give it a try.

As you continue along the road, a *pachinko* parlor, **Maruhan**, is on your right. Japan's largest, this parlor was one of the first of the new upscale breed. To get first shot at the best machines, people line up long before the 10am opening. Next to Maruhan is a money exchange office run by Bank of Tokyo-Mitsubishi that is open from 12 noon to 6pm.

The road leads to Tokyu Department Store's main store. Around the back of the department store is **Bunkamura**, literally Culture Village. Under one roof, you'll find Orchard Hall, the home of the Tokyo Symphony; smaller halls; art movie theaters; Bunkamura Museum, home to high-quality traveling exhibitions; gallery space and restaurants.

The main entrance of Tokyu Department store is a Y intersection; walk along the left side of the Y. Turn right at the next traffic light; Shibuya City Hotel will be on the left. Follow this road along the perimeter of Tokyu Department Store and up the hill. The road ends at the **Kanze Noh Theater**. Turn left and follow the red brick sidewalk for a block. On the right, in a yellow brick building, is the **Toguri Museum of Art** (Toguri Bijutsukan). The building is architecturally undistinguished, but this small museum is one of our favorites and is a must for anyone seriously interested in ceramics. The 2000-piece collection of Chinese, Korean and

HACHIKO, MAN'S BEST FRIEND

Shibuya would not be complete without an explanation of **Hachiko,** *the famous dog statue that has to be Tokyo's most famous meeting place. Who is this dog? Hachiko, an Akita (a Japanese species which is almost extinct today), was born in Akita Prefecture in 1923. His master was a professor at Tokyo Imperial University. Hachiko always accompanied his master to the train station and would return to the station in the afternoon to meet him coming home.*

In 1925, when Hachiko was only two years old, his master died while teaching a class. Even though the gardener, who lived in Asakusa, adopted Hachiko, the faithful dog walked across Tokyo everyday to wait at Shibuya Station for his master to return. Commuters came to know Hachiko. In 1932 he was featured in the Asahi Shimbun newspaper and became an instant celebrity. The dog died at the age of 13. Every year on April 8, a special commemorative festival is held in front of the bronze statue at Shibuya Station. Such dogged loyalty has won the hearts of the Japanese.

Japanese ceramics belonged to a businessman; only a small portion is on display at a time. The Imari and Nabeshima pieces are outstanding. The museum organizes four exhibitions a year. *Tel. (03)3465-0070. Open 10am to 5:30pm. Closed Monday. ¥1030.*

Continue along the red sidewalk. Shoto Park will be on your left. Just past the park, at the intersection with the traffic light, in a contemporary concrete building is **Gallery TOM**, a unique gallery where you can touch the art as well as see it. Bronze, stone and wooden sculptures are on display including works by Rodin. *Tel. (03)3467-8102. Open 10:30am to 5:30pm. Closed on Sunday, Monday and national holidays. ¥600 (¥300 for visually handicapped).*

Retrace your steps; pass the Toguri Museum and turn right when the Kanze Noh Theater is on your left. Go down the hill. At the traffic light where Shibuya City Hotel is on your right, continue up a narrow road. This is Rambling Road, which will take you up the hill to the heart of **Maruyama-cho**. Once the exclusive preserve of love hotels and sleazy bars, these have now been joined by legitimate establishments, making it one of Shibuya's main entertainment areas. There must be more love hotels per square meter here than anywhere else in Japan. Their rates are listed outside; "rest" is for two or three hours, and "stay" is for overnight. On the legitimate side, **On Air East** and **On Air West** have live music performances; **Club Asia** is a restaurant and disco; and **Dr. Jeekans** is a virtual reality amusement parlor. Its first floor bar, **Wood and Stone**, features inexpensive food and drinks.

Continue rambling along Rambling Road until it descends slightly. At this intersection is a traffic light. Turn left on to Dogenzaka, another of Shibuya's main roads. A few blocks on the left is the **Prime Building**; on the second floor there's a food court serving all sorts of cuisines at reasonable prices. Dogenzaka leads you back to Shibuya Station. Just before the station, turn left, 109 Part 2 building will be on the far corner. **Seibu Department Store**, one of Tokyo's most trendy, is on the left and offers an especially good selection of Japanese designer wear. Seibu's Loft Building is a rival to Tokyu Hands (see below) and its SEED building has avant-garde clothing, gallery space and a performance hall. A little further down the road is **Tower Records**, the world's largest CD and tape store. The book store has an excellent selection of English-language books, magazines and newspapers from all over the world and some of the lowest prices in Japan.

Walk back to Seibu; turn onto the street between the two Seibu buildings and follow it for several blocks. Stay on the road while it curves to the right. Just past McDonalds is the back entrance to **Tokyu Hands**. Tokyu Hands invented the "Do-it-yourself" genre of stores. It has everything you could ever think you need or want for your hobby or leisure time. We recommend you take the elevator to the top floor and walk down. You go past sections for bicycles, automotive supplies, hardware, cooking, sewing, art supplies, party supplies, outdoor equipment, paper goods, lumber, posters, frames and more. Even if you aren't interested in buying anything, it's a major cultural experience just to see what the store offers. One of our favorite, truly original souvenirs is a clock made with plastic *sushi*. One warning: avoid this cultural experience on Sunday afternoons. There may be as many people as there are items in the shop.

Exit Tokyu Hands from the main exit on the first floor; turn right as you leave the store and walk about two short blocks to a traffic light. This street is Koen Dori. At the intersection are several buildings called **Parco**, one of the best "fashion buildings." There's an especially good selection of Japanese and Japan-inspired designers such as Issey Miyake, Yohji Yamamoto and Jurgen Lehl.

Turn left onto Koen Dori. The **Tobacco and Salt Museum** is in a red brick building one block up on the right. Tobacco may not be politically correct, but no one has told this museum. Tobacco and salt were government monopolies, which is why this unlikely combination exists. The museum displays pipes, Edo period woodblock prints depicting smoking and antique cigarette manufacturing equipment. Salt production equipment is also on display. The museum puts on temporary exhibitions on a wide range of themes. *1-16-8 Jinnan, Shibuya-ku. Tel. (03)3476-2041. Open 10am to 6pm. Closed Monday. ¥100.*

SHIBUYA WITH CHILDREN

Shibuya has lots of great places for children:

• **TEPCO Electric Energy Museum**. *Run by the Tokyo Electric Power Company, this eight-storied building is filled with hands-on displays – everything you always wanted to know about electricity. Kids love it. Tel. (03)3477-1191. Open 10:30am to 6:30pm. Closed Wednesday. Admission free. From Hachiko Plaza, take the road to the left of the 109 Part 2 building running parallel to the tracks. When the road curves to the right, the glass and steel museum building with a domed roof is on the right.*

• **Tokyo Metropolitan Children's Hall** *(Tokyo-to Jido Kaikan). This hall entertains children from toddlers through junior high students. It has climbing equipment, computers, crafts, music room and a lot more to keep children and their parents occupied for the better part of the day. 1-18-24 Shibuya, Shibuya-ku. Tel. (03)3409-6361. Open 9am to 5pm. Closed usually the 2nd and 4th Mondays and around New Year's. No admission fee. From Hachiko Plaza at Shibuya Station, walk under the train tracks and turn left at the major road, Meiji Dori. At the first traffic light, turn right and the hall is on the left, one block in.*

• **Children's Castle** *(Kodomo no Shiro). Kids are definitely kings and queens in this castle. There is everything to entertain them on a rainy day and on sunny days too. Younger children love the climbing equipment, crafts and story book areas. View videos in the audio-visual room – they have a fair number in English. Older children enjoy the more extensive craft program, music room, performances and more. Don't overlook the roof garden with bicycles and a jumping-on-balls area. Children's Castle even has a hotel on the premises – an ideal place to stay with children. 5-53-1 Jingumae, Shibuya-ku. Tel. (03)3797-5666. Open 12:30pm to 5:30pm, weekdays; 10am to 5:30pm weekends, holidays and school holidays. Closed Monday. ¥500. From Hachiko Plaza at Shibuya Station, walk under the train tracks and continue on that street up the hill. You'll pass the large post office. When the road ends, bear left onto wide Aoyama Dori. Children's Castle is two blocks on the left. You can't miss the unusual sculpture out front.*

Continue along the same road until it opens into a large intersection. Yoyogi Park is straight ahead; NHK, the public television station, is to the right. **NHK Studio Park** is on the 3rd and 4th floors of the NHK Broadcasting Center. You can see the stage sets of popular TV dramas. *Open 10am to 6pm. Closed 2nd Monday. ¥200.*

Across a wide brick walkway from NHK is the **National Gymnasium**, two distinctive buildings designed by Tange Kenzo for the 1964 Olympic

Games. The smaller one, with a seashell spiral roof, is for basketball, and the larger one is for swimming and diving, but other events are also held. These buildings look so contemporary that they belie their age.

Yoyogi Park is an oasis of green in the city. The wide open area is great for running around, playing frisbee or having a picnic lunch. The park has a bicycle course; children under 15 can borrow bicycles at no charge between 9am and 4pm, except Monday.

Adjacent to Yoyogi Park is **Meiji Shrine**, which is the first stop in our Harajuku tour (see next sights section, area 12, below). Harajuku Station is one minute away from the entrance to the shrine.

Side trip from Shibuya: Japan Folk Craft Museum (Nihon Mingei-kan). The museum is a little out of the way, but worth the effort. Housed in a folk-style building, itself a piece of art, the museum has a collection of folk art gathered together by Yanagi Soetsu, a pioneer in the *mingei* (folk art) movement of the 1930s. On top of Yanagi's collections, the museum has an extensive assortment of earthy Japanese ceramics, dynamic woodblock prints by Munakata Shiko and country-style furniture.

We enjoy seeing the sunlight streaming through the paper windows of the *shoji* screens. Temporary exhibitions change with the seasons. The museum's charming and tiny shop is well stocked with folk craft items. *From Shibuya Station, take the Inokashira line train two stops to Komaba Todai-mae. At the station, cross the tracks and take the road parallel to the tracks up the hill. 4-3-33 Komaba, Meguro-ku. Tel. (03)3467-4527. Open 10am to 5pm. Closed Monday and at New Year's. ¥1000.*

AREA 12: HARAJUKU & OMOTESANDO

To reach Harajuku, take the JR Yamanote line to Harajuku Station or the Chiyoda subway line to Meiji Jingumae Station.

Harajuku offers a contrast between the traditional and the contemporary. The staid and solemn Meiji Shrine, hidden deep inside a forest, is only a few hundred meters away from the trendy shops of Takeshita Dori and Omotesando. This sums up the dichotomy of modern Japan.

Harajuku is an area for the young and the young at heart. Students throng the streets to see the latest teen fashions and to be seen. Some come to this mecca from as far away as Osaka and Sendai. The age of Harajuku's customers has been getting younger and younger. Once the haunt of high school students, the streets are now crowded with junior high students.

Omotesando (literally pilgrim's main path) is the fashionable area along the approach road to Meiji Shrine. This wide avenue is often called Tokyo's Champs Elysees. Both are lined with tall trees and have some cafes and McDonalds on them, but the similarity doesn't go much beyond that.

Built in 1924, Harajuku Station is one of the few in Tokyo that has retained its original architecture, a European half-timbered look. Head for the green trees across the bridge spanning the Yamanote line's tracks. The plaza gives way to a dense forest beyond a wooden *torii* gate. It's about a 10-minute walk through the woods to **Meiji Shrine** (Meiji Jingu). The woods were designed as part of the shrine and contain trees and plants gathered from every Japanese prefecture. It's almost impossible to believe you're in the center of Tokyo.

Meiji Shrine was built to deify the Meiji Emperor who died in 1912. He was restored to power at the end of the Tokugawa era (1868) and helped Japan usher in the modern era. With the exception of the Treasure House, the original buildings were destroyed in World War II. The present shrine was built in 1958.

The understated plain buildings made of cypress wood have long, sloping copper roofs. Maiden priestesses wearing white kimono over orange *hakama* pants sell amulets and other good luck items at the stalls on the side. On weekends, Shinto priests formally dressed in pale blue costumes perform weddings, bless newborn babies and conduct other ceremonies. We love to see couples dressed in wedding kimono or a baby, dressed in a formal kimono, held by a mother in traditional dress — fathers almost always dress in Western attire; all look delighted to be there.

Meiji Shrine is one of the most popular places to visit at New Year's to welcome the gods and pray for good luck; several million people crowd the shrine during the first days of the year. Look closely at the pillars of the main hall — the exterior sides have lots of dents from being hit by flying coins.

Behind the shrine is the **Treasure House** that displays artifacts belonging to the Meiji Emperor and Empress. The 1921 building is a good example of the religious revival architecture of the time. *Treasure House is open 9am to 4pm, November through February, and 9am to 4:30pm, March through October. Closed 3rd Friday. ¥400.*

Also on the grounds of the shrine is the peaceful **Inner Garden**, built by the Meiji Emperor for his wife whose favorite flower was the iris. The iris garden is beautiful in June; we are always amazed by the many hues of the purple iris. The garden also has a lovely teahouse overlooking a water lily pond; we find it more dramatic to see the water lily pond before approaching the irises. *¥300.*

Meiji Shrine is open from dawn until sunset, making it a good place to go for an early morning stroll; guards do not permit jogging.

Return to Harajuku Station; walk along the station's side, parallel to the train tracks. There's a traffic light at the back exit; turn right at this light and you are on **Takeshita Dori**. You'll immediately notice that the average age of the people around you is about 15. Takeshita Dori used to be a hangout for high school students, but now junior high students have taken over. The stores sell inexpensive clothes and jewelry. You'll also find a number of stores selling crepes, a popular snack with this age group.

Walk down Takeshita Dori until you reach Meiji Dori. If you turn left, you'll come to **Togo Shrine**; its lively antique and junk market will captivate you the first and fourth Sundays of the month.

Rather than going to Togo Shrine, on Meiji Dori turn right and walk to the next major intersection, where Meiji Dori meets Omotesando. Turn right and then right again at the first little street. You'll come to the **Ota Memorial Ukiyo-e Museum** (Ukiyo-e Ota Kinen Bijutsukan). Exchange your shoes for slippers before entering this tiny museum. The museum has an exhaustive *ukiyo-e* collection put together by a businessman in the insurance field; it includes woodblock prints by Hokusai, Utamaro, Hiroshige and other famous artists of the Edo period. Only a small portion is shown at a time. Exhibitions change every month. You need to step onto *tatami* mats to see some of the works. Exhibitions change every month. *Tel. (03)3403-0880. Open 10:30am to 5:30pm. Closed Monday and the last few days of every month to change the installation. ¥500.*

Near the Ota Museum is the unusually named **Do! Family Museum of Art** that features exhibitions for the whole family. *1-12-4 Jingumae, Shibuya-ku. Tel. (03)3470-4540. Open 11am to 6pm. Closed Monday. ¥300.*

Return to Omotesando. On the far side of the road is a shop called **Chicago**. Most of the store sells recycled clothing from America, but there's also a good used kimono section.

As you exit Chicago, turn right. Just before you cross Meiji Dori, a small shop called **Condomania** is on the right. It caused a small stir when it opened several years ago.

The boulevard of Omotesando is lined with shops, boutiques and restaurants. The many cafes and bakeries will surely tempt you. **Peltier** and **Cafe de Rope**, both on the right, have tasty pastries. Make a detour

OUR FAVORITE TOKYO MUSEUMS

- *Idemitsu Art Museum, Hibiya*
- *Nezu Institute of Art, Omotesando*
- *Toguri Art Museum, Shibuya*
- *Japan Folk Craft Museum, Komaba, near Shibuya*
- *Sagacho Exhibit Space, Fukagawa*
- *Taiko Drum Museum, Asakusa*
- *Suntory Museum of Art, Akasaka*
- *Ota Memorial Museum of Art, Harajuku*

for an excellent restaurant: across from the Vivre 21 building is a police box. Go down the steps to the left of the box and walk along the little alley; just before the barrier, in a traditional building on your left, you'll find the restaurant **Kiku**, featuring homestyle Japanese cooking. The interior decor is Japanese modern.

Return to Omotesando. On the far side of Omotesando is **Kiddyland**, a large toy store popular with children of all ages. Next door is **Fuji Tori**, which has both new and antique ceramics, screens and other traditional goods. In the next block is **Oriental Bazaar**, stocking new and antique items and catering to foreigners.

Across the street, you'll notice some old brown buildings. The Dojunkai Apartments were built in 1925 after the big earthquake and look slightly out of place. These were among the first apartments built in Japan. Today, many of the ones that line Omotesando have been turned into charming shops and galleries taking advantage of the old-time atmosphere.

Under the coffee shop named **Chat Noir**, is one of Tokyo's best known revolving *sushi* restaurants. This restaurant is very popular and its high turnover ensures that the *sushi* hasn't spent the afternoon going around and around on the conveyor belt. You'll also pass **Cafe de Flore**, a cousin to the shop in Paris, a trendy French-style cafe serving espresso for ¥600 and hot chocolate for ¥900. Further along is the boutique of **Hanae Mori**, the first Japanese fashion designer to make it big on the international scene. The basement has small shops selling Japanese and Western antiques, and on the fifth floor, **L'Orangerie** serves a delicious Sunday brunch. Across the street is **Asahi Gallery**, an antique shop with absolutely beautiful works. The collection of screens on the second floor is excellent.

As you continue along Omotesando, you'll come to McDonalds; turn left at the small road before it. The road ends in one block; turn left and then immediately right. On the right is **Gallery Kawano** that sells vintage textiles. Continue down the road and the large building on the left is **Maisen**, a popular *tonkatsu* restaurant — lunch specials are a bargain.

Retrace your steps to Omotesando and go to the large intersection where Aoyama Dori and Omotesando meet. Cross Aoyama Dori and continue straight ahead. The road narrows substantially. On the left corner is an old shop that sells flower arrangement supplies. You are sure to find vases unlike anything in the West. You'll also find *kenzan* (iron flower holders) and special scissors. Make a slight detour onto Aoyama Dori for a good bakery, **Andersen's**. They have deli-style sandwiches in the basement and slightly more upscale restaurant on the second floor.

The narrow road, the continuation of Omotesando, has boutiques of many of Japan's best-known contemporary fashion designers as well as

TWO DIFFERENT MUSEUMS

Burned out on museums? Does the idea of visiting just one more make you catatonic? Here are a few that are sure to whet your appetite.

Meguro Parasitological Museum *(Meguro Kiseichukan). 4-1-1 Shimo Meguro, Meguro-ku. Tel. (03)3716-1264. Open 10am to 5pm. Closed Monday and holidays. Free admission. This museum is the only one in the world devoted to parasites. Is it a coincidence that a country that has raised eating raw fish to an art form should have this museum? Parasites of all shapes and forms are cheerfully presented in glass jars. The museum's prized possession is a tapeworm 9 meters long – they even have a tape measure that you can pull out to get an idea how long 9 meters really is. Their T-shirts with the museum's theme, "the wonderful world of worms," make great presents. And, unlike most museums, you can photograph to your heart's content. Just make sure you go after lunch or you may never eat again.*

Bicycle Culture Center *(Jitensha Culture Center). 1-9-3 Akasaka, Minato-ku. Tel. (03)3584-4530. Open 10am to 4pm. Closed weekends. Free admission. Located across the street from the American Embassy, you have to go through the building's parking garage to reach the center. It's a well-done display on biking and includes some of the earliest bikes produced.*

international designers —Issey Miyake, Yohji Yamamoto, Kawakubo Rei's Comme des Garçons and Jurgen Lehl. A ten-minute walk will show you the latest in men's and women's fashion design. Even if you are not interested in buying clothes, we are sure you'll enjoy seeing the conspicuously creative contemporary designs as well as the simple and subdued interior decorations. Make sure you stop in the From First and Collezione buildings, on the right just before the Nezu Museum.

Before you reach these two buildings, on the right will be the **Tessenkai Noh Institute**, a most unlikely contemporary concrete building with a steel door. Inside is an authentic *noh* stage where *noh* is performed several times a month.

The road leads to a large intersection. Cross the main road, and you'll be standing in front of a stucco wall on the far right side. This wall surrounds the grounds of the **Nezu Institute of Fine Arts** (Nezu Bijutsukan); the entrance is about a half-block down the road. This small gem of a museum is tucked away behind high walls, possibly to keep trendy Aoyama at arms length. The museum houses the collection of Nezu Kaichiro, founder of the Tobu Railway Company. During the early part of this century, he assembled a first-rate art collection, especially strong in tea ceremony utensils. The museum has Ogata Korin's *Irises*, a masterpiece screen painting, and the *Nanchi Waterfall* scroll painting from the Kamakura era. The Nezu Institute has two galleries: one displays temporary exhibitions — not always from the museum's collections — and the second has a permanent display of the museum's holdings. The museum's collection is so extensive that only a small portion is on view at any one time. The Iris screen, for instance, is shown every spring in late April and early May.

The Institute has a large strolling garden open to the public at no charge. It's a serene place that we love to visit to escape from the overload of all the shops in Aoyama. *6-5-1 Minami Aoyama, Minato-ku. Tel. (03)3400-2536. Open 9:30am to 4:30pm. ¥1000.*

Across the street from the museum is a small art gallery, **Honjo**, which carries new and antique items. As you exit Honjo, turn right. On the right you'll come to **Zero First Design**, a store selling contemporary Japanese furniture and crafts. Across from Zero First is a small alley. At the end of the alley is the **Ishii Collection**, a tiny antique shop. Return to the main road.

When the road ends at Kotto Dori, literally Antique Street, turn right (many of the antique shops have been forced out by high rents). The ones remaining make for fun browsing. This road ends at Aoyama Dori. Turn right and a few blocks down is the Omotesando subway station served by the Ginza, Hanzomon and Chiyoda lines. If you continue walking down Aoyama Dori , you'll tour Aoyama and Akasaka Mitsuke.

AREA 13: AOYAMA & AKASAKA

From the Omotesando Station on the Ginza, Hanzomon and Chiyoda subway lines, exit onto Aoyama Dori. If you come out at Fuji Bank, cross Omotesando, the road with stone lanterns at the entrance, going in the direction of the police box.

These two districts are fashionable areas lined with elegant boutiques and restaurants.

As you walk along Aoyama Dori, you'll pass premier retailers. Brooks Brothers looks so authentic you may think you are on Madison Avenue. Several blocks down, on the right is the **Japan Traditional Craft Center** (Zenkoku Dentoteki Kogeihin Senta). It's on the second floor and can be difficult to locate: look for Haagen Dazs ice cream parlor. This gallery has an excellent selection of crafts from all over Japan. Although you can purchase anything in the shop, it feels like a museum. The center also has video tapes showing different Japanese crafts; many are in English. There is no charge to view the videos. *2F, Plaza 246 Building, 3-1-1-Minami Aoyama, Minato-ku. Tel. (03)3403-2460. Open 10am to 6pm. Closed Thursday and December 29 through January 4.*

The Traditional Craft Center is at the intersection of Killer Dori, a street known for its fashion and other boutiques, and Aoyama Dori. Heading south, the road leads to Aoyama Cemetery. North leads to the National Stadium. On the corner diagonally across from the Craft Center is **Bell Commons**, a "fashion building" with stores and restaurants. It has a branch of the good and reasonably priced *sushi* shop, **Sushi Sei**. The north side is more interesting for it has **Watari-um**, an art space showing avant-garde international and Japanese artists *(3-7-6 Jingumae, Shibuya-ku. Tel. (03)3402-3001)*. **On Sundays**, a great art book shop, in the same building and run by the same people, has one of the world's most extensive selection of postcards.

Return to Aoyama Dori and continue walking in the same direction. On the left is Meiji Outer Garden that has several stadiums, the **Meiji Memorial Picture Gallery** (Kaigakan) and **Meiji Jingu Outer Garden Children's Park** (Meiji Jingu Gaien Jido Koen). The Picture Gallery is housed in a large, turn-of-the-century Western building. Inside it has an 80-panel mural illustrating Japan's history which is of interest only to Japanese history buffs.

This Children's Park, in the Meiji Outer Garden, is to the right as you face the Picture Gallery. Young children cannot get enough of this place; it's one of the nicest playgrounds in Tokyo. The extensive climbing structures keep the kids amused for hours. In the summer months, a beer garden which also serves noodles and barbecue is set up next to the park. *9 Kasumigaoka, Shinjuku-ku. Tel. (03)3478-0550. Open daily 9:30am to 4pm. ¥150 adults, ¥50 children.*

Continuing on Aoyama Dori, on the left is a long wall with lots of trees behind it. Behind the wall is the **Akasaka Detached Palace**, which holds the residences of the imperial princes and princesses.

Across the street is the **Canadian Embassy**; its gallery often has excellent exhibitions. A block further along is the **Sogetsu Kaikan**; designed by Tange Kenzo, it is the contemporary hall of the Sogetsu flower arranging school. Stunning displays decorate the lobby; the stones there were sculpted by Isamu Noguchi and symbolize flowers, stone and water. Flower arranging classes in English are held regularly (see Flower Arranging under *Sports & Recreation* later in this chapter).

Two blocks along on the right is a modern building; the ground floor has an old Japanese motif of blocks placed at an angle. This building houses **Toraya**, one of Japan's most famous confectioners. The main shop used to be based in Kyoto where it served the imperial family, but it moved to Tokyo with the emperor. The treats are a feast for the eyes. The shop has a tea room as well as a small exhibition space.

For a short detour to see Japan's imitation of European court architecture, turn left at the edge of the Akasaka Detached Palace grounds

FLOWERS, FLOWERS EVERYWHERE

Japanese adore cherry blossoms and also enjoy other flowers. Flower viewing seems to be a major preoccupation for large segments of the population. Here are a couple of favorite places to view flowers in season. But beware, you will not be viewing them in solitary splendor.

Plum *(mid-February to mid-March)*
Yushima Tenjin Shrine. Yushima Station on Chiyoda subway line.
Shinjuku Gyoen Garden. Shinjuku san-chome on Marunouchi subway line.

Peonies *(May)*
Nishi Arai Taishi. Nishi Arai Station on the Hibiya line – transfer to a special train that takes a few minutes to the temple.

Wisteria *(May)*
Kameido Tenjin Shrine. Kameido Station on the JR Sobu line. Follow the crowds for the 10-minute walk. The garden was destroyed in the World War II firebombing, but the roots survived and the plants grew again.

Azaleas *(May)*
Nezu Shrine. Nezu Station on Chiyoda Subway line.

Iris *(mid-June)*
Meiji Shrine Garden. Harajuku Station on the JR Yamanote line.
Koishikawa Korakuen Garden. Iidabashi Station on JR Sobu line.
Yasukuni Shrine. Kudanshita Station on Tozai, Hanzomon and Shinjuku subway lines.
East Garden of the Imperial Palace. Otemachi Station for five subway lines.

Hydrangeas *(early June to early July)*
Hakusan Shrine. Hakusan Station on Toei Mita subway line.
Meigetsuin. Kita Kamakura Station on JR Yokosuka line.

and follow the road that runs next to the palace walls. You'll be parallel to the expressway for a short time. On the left is the **Akasaka Detached Palace** (Geihinkan), which was built in 1909. Designed by architect Katayama Tokuma as the residence of the Taisho Emperor when he was crown prince, the prince found it too luxurious to live in. Today it is the official guest house for heads of state. The palace is probably the greatest Western-style architectural work of the Meiji period.

Retrace your steps to Aoyama Dori. On the left, just before the expressway, is the Suntory Building, home of the **Suntory Museum of Art**. The museum has a strong collection of traditional Japanese art including paintings, ceramics, lacquer ware and textiles. The permanent collection is supplemented with borrowed art works to organize excellent exhibitions. *Suntory Building, 11th floor, 1-2-3 Moto Akasaka, Minato-ku. Open 10am to 5pm. Until 7pm on Friday. Closed Monday. ¥700.*

The large intersection with the overhead highway is Akasaka Mitsuke, a business and entertainment center. During the day, restaurants are filled with businessman enjoying inexpensive lunch specials. At night it's still a businessmen's haunt, but the atmosphere changes and they crowd into dimly lit, sophisticated restaurants and private clubs. This area has several large hotels that are popular with foreign business executives (See *Where To Stay*).

As you reach the intersection just beyond the Suntory Museum, you'll see the **New Otani**, a large hotel on the left across the moat. Open to the public, it has a beautiful Japanese garden that you enter by going through a building that adjoins the hotel's main building and tower. Across the street, the **Akasaka Prince Hotel**, is a stark, modern hotel designed by Tange Kenzo. You can't help noticing the **Akasaka Tokyu Hotel**, nicknamed the pajama hotel because of its stripes.

Walk on Sotobori Dori, in front of the Akasaka Tokyu Hotel. This is the heart of **Akasaka Mitsuke**, a commercial area filled with restaurants and bars. Most of the establishments are on the roads running parallel to Sotobori Dori. Several blocks down Sotobori Dori on the left is a large *torii* gate. Pass through the gate and follow the road around to enter the quiet compound of **Hie Jinja Shrine**. The shrine was founded by the first feudal lord of Edo, Ota Dokan, and became Edo's most popular shrine during the Tokugawa era. Held every other year in June, the shrine's Sanno Festival is one of Tokyo's largest.

Walk back down the hill and continue on Sotobori Dori. At the overhead expressway, turn left. This road will take you to the **Japanese Diet Building** (Kokkai Gijido) where parliament meets. The building took 18 years to build and was completed in 1936. The Kokkai Gijido-mae Station of the Chiyoda line is located at the Diet Building.

AREA 14: SHINJUKU

The JR Yamanote, Chuo, Sobu, and Saikyo lines; the Marunouchi and Toei Shinjuku subway lines; and the private Odakyu and Keio train lines all serve Shinjuku Station.

Shinjuku is really two cities, one east and one west of the station. Nishi (West) Shinjuku is a forest of high-rise buildings. When seen from a distance, it looks like the city of Oz rising from the plains. East of the station, there's a jumble of stores, restaurants, bars and raucous nightlife spots. You can party there all night long. Dividing the two is **Shinjuku Station**, Japan's and maybe the world's busiest — over two million people pass through each weekday.

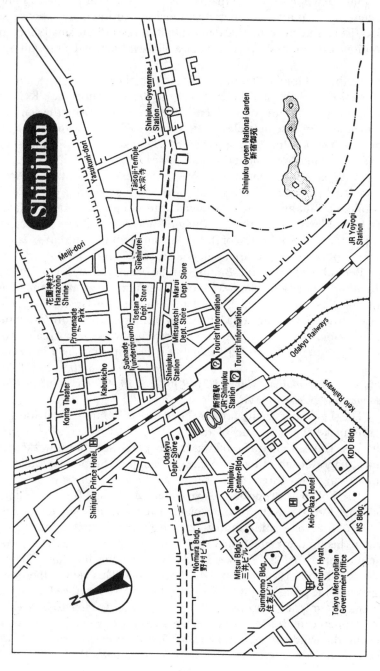

Shinjuku

Courtesy of Japan National Tourist Organization

Shinjuku epitomizes all that is Tokyo — masses of people, a railway system that runs with amazing precision, bombardment by street noises, high-rise architecture, myriad department stores, infinite small shops and boutiques, discount shops, and a maze of alleys filled with entertainment of all sorts.

Begin at Shinjuku Station, but not during the morning rush hour. At the west exit of the station are two large department stores, Keio and Odakyu. West of these department stores, one block from the station, is a small area of discount electronic stores, *pachinko* parlors and cheap eateries. **Yodobashi Camera** has an excellent selection of cameras and other electronic gear, all at discount prices.

Walk back to the main plaza of the west exit of the station. Across from **Odakyu Halc**, a store selling furniture and interior goods, is the Shinjuku L Building. **Toto** and **Inax**, bathroom equipment manufacturers, have showrooms on the 26-27th floors and 20-21st floors respectively. Stop in for an amazing view of the bathroom of tomorrow that's available today. Both showrooms are open daily from 10am to 6pm.

Behind the Shinjuku L Building is the Yasuda Kasai Kaijo Building. The 42nd floor **Seiji Togo Memorial Yasuda Kasai Museum of Art** (Yasuda Kasai Togo Seiji Bijutsukan) displays van Gogh's *Sunflowers,* bought a dozen years ago by a Japanese for a mere ¥5.3 billion. Other than the van Gogh, a few Cezannes and Renoirs and works by surrealist Togo Seiji, the museum is unremarkable, but it has a spectacular view. *Yasuda Kasai Kaijo (Yasuda Fire and Marine) Head Office Building, 1-26-1 Nishi Shinjuku, Shinjuku-ku. Tel. (03)3349-3081. Open 9:30am to 5pm. Closed Monday and New Year's. ¥800.*

The skyscrapers in this area are lined up like dominoes — atriums and plazas make the area one of the most open of Tokyo's commercial districts. The Keio Plaza Hotel was the first high rise, but now there are more than a dozen others. We like the Shinjuku Sumitomo Building's inner triangular courtyard that's open all the way to the sky.

The **Tokyo Metropolitan Government Building** (Tocho), designed by Tange Kenzo, has such an interplay between the different textures and colors of the stones and windows that we get vertigo looking at it. Tange said his inspiration came from Paris' Notre Dame Cathedral. The government complex has three towers and a low assembly building. The twin towers have observatories on their 45th floors. This view is the best in town, and the price is right — free. On a clear day you can see Mt. Fuji and all Tokyo's grayness sprawled out in front of you. We like to have coffee in the open cafe, but don't bother on a cloudy day — you may not see beyond the windows. *Open 9:30am to 5:30pm weekdays; 9:30am to 7:30pm weekends and holidays. Closed Monday. Free admission.*

West of the municipal building is **Shinjuku Central Park**. While its name may conjure up images of skating rinks and hansom carriages, the reality is far different. This park has more cement than trees, but is a respite from the city.

South of the park, on Koshu Kaido, is the **Shinjuku Park Tower**. Run by Tokyo Gas, architect Tange Kenzo designed the 52-storied postmodern structure. A number of floors are devoted to architectural and interior design. **Conrans**, the British store, has a shop there. The top floors house the **Park Hyatt Hotel**, which has some of the best views in the city; its restaurant, the **New York Grill**, is one of Tokyo's most popular. Stop and have a drink in the 52nd-floor lounge.

Just beyond Park Tower is another high-rise complex, **Tokyo Opera City**. It's at Hatsudai Station on the Keio train line or about a 20-minute walk from Shinjuku Station; use the south exit and walk left along Koshu Kaido. One of Tokyo's newest office and cultural complexes, the center has a wide array of cultural offerings. The 4th to 6th floor **NTT InterCommunication Center** (ICC) has state-of-the-art multimedia technology and puts on exhibitions, film and video showings, workshops and provides electronic information. The **New National Theater** has an opera house plus a medium and a small theater. The 200-meter long glass-roofed Galleria runs the length of the complex. And there are enough stores and restaurants in the complex to keep you busy for a long time.

From Opera City, walk east along Koshu Kaido, and cross over the train tracks at Shinjuku Station. The east side of the station has an entirely different feel. In contrast to the high rises with large plazas, east Shinjuku is a warren of tiny streets and a million little shops, restaurants and bars.

After you cross the train tracks, turn right at the Shin Minami-guchi building of Shinjuku Station. Alongside this building is a path leading to **Shinjuku Times Square**, the new building that houses a branch of Takashimaya Department Store; Kinokuniya, Tokyo's best selection of English books; Sega Joyopolis, a virtual reality arcade; lots of other shops; restaurants and movie theaters.

Return to Koshu Kaido; across the street is the south annex of **Mitsukoshi Department Store**; sometimes its 7th floor museum has excellent exhibitions. *Tel. (03)3342-1111. Open 10am to 7:30pm. Closed Monday.*

Beyond Mitsukoshi's south annex, Koshu Kaido meets Meiji Dori in a large, triangular intersection. Bear to the left and in one block you'll be at the large Shinjuku san (3)-chome intersection where Meiji Dori and Shinjuku Dori meet. **Isetan**, one of Japan's premier department stores is on the far left corner and is the only major prewar building left in Shinjuku. The large store has an especially good selection of clothes by young Japanese designers. The store also has a foreign customer service desk where a bilingual staff can assist you with your shopping.

Across the street from Isetan is **Marui Fashion Kan**, a store popular with young women. Behind it is **Tsunahachi**, an excellent *tempura* restaurant serving reasonably priced set meals.

Next to Marui is **Mitsukoshi Department Store**. Continue along Shinjuku Dori past Mitsukoshi and the many discount electronic shops that blare theme songs to sidewalk strollers. You'll come to the **Studio Alta** building with its large video screen; it's one of the most popular meeting places in Shinjuku because it is close to the east exit of Shinjuku Station. Walk down one of the narrow roads on either side of Studio Alta, and you'll come to Yasukuni Dori, a wide street.

The small streets on the other side of Yasukuni Dori put you in the heart of **Kabuki-cho**, one of Tokyo's entertainment districts where legitimate and raunchy establishments exist side by side. During the day, it's a pretty tame place. Kabuki-cho has legitimate inexpensive restaurants, bars, taverns, movie theaters, *pachinko* parlors, and video arcades as well as peep shows, strip shows, massage parlors, soaplands (full service baths), porno shops and girlie shows of every kind. Kabuki-cho parties till dawn. Unlike the sleazy entertainment districts in most cities around the world, women are rarely threatened physically even at night; but drunken men may make rude comments. It's best for women to stick to the main alleys. A word of warning: don't go by the prices posted outside establishments; they may be only the admission charge. Make sure you know the real costs up front, and don't be shy about asking.

To continue our exploration of Shinjuku, return to Yasukuni Dori and turn left, walking east. After Isetan Department Store, turn left onto Meiji Dori, a large thoroughfare. Two blocks down is a small shrine called **Hanazono** where there's a good flea market on the 2nd and 3rd Sunday of each month. This shrine has existed for a long time and is a popular place to pray for commercial success.

Retrace your steps along Meiji Dori and turn left on Yasukuni Dori. At the next large intersection, turn right onto Gyoen Dori. The area on the left between Yasukuni Dori and Shinjuku Dori is **Shinjuku ni (2)-chome** and has Tokyo's largest concentration of gay bars.

Gyoen Dori leads you to **Shinjuku Gyoen Park**. The garden was once the site of the feudal lord Naito's mansion and became an imperial garden after the emperor moved to Tokyo in 1868. It has Japanese and Western-style gardens, including a formal French garden and English landscape gardens and is a popular place to view cherry blossoms in the spring. *Open 9am to 4:30pm. Closed Monday. ¥200.*

CHERRY BLOSSOMS IN TOKYO

The whole city goes cherry crazy at the end of March and in early April. One of the first official duties of new corporate recruits is to spend the day sitting on blue tarps to safeguard prized prime space under the cherry trees. The rest of the office troops down after work for an evening of booze, food and song under the cherry blossoms. As a foreigner, groups will ask you to join them for a drink.

Some of the favored viewing spots follow:

Ueno Park *has over one thousand trees. Unfortunately, Ueno is one of the most popular party places and gets pretty messy by the end of the evening.*

Chidorigafuchi Park*, along the northern perimeter of the Imperial Palace, is a beautiful place; some of the trees lean into the castle moat.*

Yasukuni Shrine*, just up the street from Chidorigafuchi Park, has about a thousand trees, two of which the Meteorological Agency uses as the measure to determine Tokyo's official cherry blossom season.*

Yoyogi Park *is technically only open from 5am to 5pm so you don't get the drunken rowdiness that mars other sites.*

Aoyama Cemetery *is one of our favorite viewing sites. The trees form a archway over the road.*

Shinjuku Gyoen Garden *has 1500 trees.*

Koishikawa Korakuen*, a lovely Japanese garden, is a good place to see cherries in a serene and traditional setting.*

Sumida River *near Asakusa Station has 1100 trees lining the river.*

AREA 15: NORTH OF THE IMPERIAL PALACE

These places are most easily reached by subway or JR train. Take the JR Yamanote line to Mejiro Station; board the #60 bus in front of Sakura Bank and get off at Chinzan-so stop. Alternatively, take the Yurakucho subway line to Edogawabashi Station.

Here are a handful of our favorite places fairly close together and north of the Imperial Palace:

Formerly the estate of Yamagata Aritomo, a Meiji Restoration leader and founder of the Japanese army, **Chizanso** is a wedding palace with one of Tokyo's prettiest gardens. The Four Seasons Hotel is on the grounds. Chizanso's garden restaurant serves Genghis Khan barbecue.

Across the street from Chizanso is **St. Mary's Cathedral**. A study in steel and concrete, this contemporary church was designed by Tange Kenzo and built in 1966 to commemorate the 100th year anniversary of Japan lifting its ban on Christianity.

Take the Yurakucho subway line two stops to Ichigaya Station to reach the **Takagi Bonsai Museum**. It's just a one-minute walk from exit #3. The JR Sobu line's Ichigaya station is also close. Walk along Nittere Dori, away from the moat, and turn left at the Bank of Yokohama. The museum is just past the bank. You'll know the building by the statues of two guard dogs.

Bonsai are trees that may be hundreds of years old, but because of special pruning, they are only one or two feet tall. This little gem of a museum exhibits *bonsai* trees and changes the display weekly to show trees at the peak of their seasons. An elevator whisks you to the 9th floor roof where trees are displayed around a spring-fed pond. The white clay walls provide a lovely backdrop to view the dwarfed plants. The museum has an audio tape in English. On the 8th floor, *ukiyo-e* woodblock prints show that *bonsai* have been part of Japanese life for a long time. Also, seasonal *bonsai* and antique pots are on display.

If you notify the museum one week in advance, an English-speaking person will be available to guide you. Included with the price of admission is coffee or tea so you can sit and contemplate *bonsai*. *1-1 Goban-cho, Chiyoda-ku. Tel. (03)3221-0006. Open daily 10am to 5pm. ¥800. On the 8th and 9th floors of the Meiko Shokai Building.*

From Ichigaya Station, take JR Sobu line two stops to Suidobashi where **Koishikawa Korakuen Garden**, a traditional Japanese garden, is located behind Tokyo Dome. It's also convenient to Korakuen Station on the Marunouchi and Nanboku subway lines. Koishikawa Korakuen is a lovely place that was the strolling garden of the Mito branch of the Tokugawa family. First constructed in 1629, Chinese influence is evident in the bridges and design. The Naitei area, near the east gate, has changed little from the Edo times. The contrast between this quiet, peaceful garden and the hustle-bustle of the Tokyo Dome area couldn't be greater. *1-6-6 Koraku, Bunkyo-ku. Tel. (03)3811-3015. Open daily 9am to 5pm. Closed Monday and December 29 through January 3. ¥300.*

Tokyo Dome, the Big Egg, is at Korakuen and Suidobashi stations. It's Japan's first huge, domed stadium and hosts everything from baseball and rock concerts to flower shows. The Yomiuri Giants and Nippon Ham Fighters baseball teams play there. The Baseball Hall of Fame Museum is located just outside the dome.

Hop on the Nanboku subway line at the Tokyo Dome and go four stops north to Komagome Station. **Rikugi-en Garden** is a seven-minute walk away. The JR Yamanote line also goes to Komagome Station. Anyone seriously interested in Japanese gardens can't miss this garden that dates from 1695 when it was built by Yanagisawa Yoshiyasu, an aid to the fifth Tokugawa shogun. The garden, deserted after Yoshiyasu's death in 1714, saw new life in 1879 when Iwasaki Yataro, the founder of the Mitsubishi industrial empire, bought it and restored it. The park is filled with scenes alluding to masterpieces of literature and was designed so strollers walk clockwise around the large pond; be sure you go in the right direction.

There are several teahouses in the park, including Takimi-no-Chaya and Tsutsuji Chaya. Fujishiro-toge, an artificial hill constructed to view Mt. Fuji, provides the best vantage point. *6-16-3 Hon-Komagome, Bunkyo-ku. Tel. (03)3941-2222. Open daily 9am to 5pm. Closed Monday and December 29 through January 3. ¥300.*

AREA 16: IKEBUKURO

The JR Yamanote and Saikyo lines; the Marunouchi and Yurakucho subway lines; and the private Seibu and Tobu train lines all serve Ikebukuro Station.

Ikebukuro has metamorphosed over the last decade or so from a nondescript suburban neighborhood to a major transportation, commercial and cultural nexus. Everything in Ikebukuro seems to take on gigantic proportions: some of Japan's largest department stores — Sunshine 60 was Japan's tallest building for a while — and a zillion clothing, record and electronic stores. Nothing is in moderation.

Ikebukuro Station itself is a study in chaos. There are two huge department stores in the station, **Seibu** on the eastern side and **Tobu** on the western. Between the two, you'll find everything you could ever want. Tobu's restaurant "floor" spans six stories — from the 11th to 17th. The central building's 9th floor has an extensive variety of Japanese goods. The **Tobu Museum** has first-rate exhibitions. On the other side of the station, equally gigantic Seibu is home to lots of restaurants. The basement, filled with edibles from all over Japan and the world, is a sight to behold. The amount and variety is incredible; if it's not in Seibu's basement, it may not exist. Seibu's **Sezon Museum of Art** has excellent traveling exhibitions.

Two blocks west of Ikebukuro Station is **Tokyo Metropolitan Art Space**. The 28-meter atrium houses a three-storied waterfall and lush green trees that certainly create a different atmosphere from what is outside. The complex has theaters, concert halls and exhibition space. Long escalators lead to a huge concert hall; its acoustics are excellent for a full scale orchestra, but the hall is too big for a chamber orchestra. The Tokyo Metropolitan government spent lavishly by inviting first-rate orchestras from all over the world. We have to admit that we find it quite jarring to leave the serenity of the hall to go out into the noise, chaos and crowds of Ikebukuro.

Sunshine City is Ikebukuro's other famous complex. Use the east exit of Ikebukuro Station, walk along Green Dori, which is perpendicular to the station, and turn left onto Sunshine 60 Dori. After crossing the expressway, the **Amlux building** is on your right. Run by Toyota, the large, neon-lit building is a motor enthusiast's dream and includes a massive display of cars, a simulated factory, a 3-D theater and a computer-equipped studio where you design your own car. If you get lost at night, the brightly lit building will help you get your bearings.

Just beyond Amlux is Sunshine City. Sunshine 60, as its name implies, is a 60-storied tower. The **World Import Mart** has merchandise from all over the globe and its 10th floor houses the **Sunshine International Aquarium**. Our recommendation — save the ¥1600 cost of admission and visit Shinagawa Aquarium or Tokyo Water Life Park. *Tel. (03)3989-3467.*

Sunshine City's Bunka Kaikan has the **Ancient Orient Museum** on its 7th floor. It displays pottery and other antiquities from the Middle East to Japan. *Tel. (03)3989-3491. Open 10am to 4:30pm. Closed Monday. ¥400.*

AREA 17: TOKYO WATERFRONT (ARIAKE/RINKAI FUKUTOSHIN)

A new monorail, Yurikamome, named after a type of seagull alluded to in historic poetry, connects Shimbashi Station with Ariake. You can also get there by ferry from Hamamatsucho – 20 minutes, ¥350. One word of warning: the Yurikamome monorail can be incredibly crowded over the weekend. The whole area is new and Tokyoites find it fashionable to visit. There are sometimes long lines to board the monorail even though it departs every ten minutes. We've heard horror stories of people waiting more than two hours when there's been a big convention. The alternative is to take the Yurakucho subway line or JR Keiyo line to Shin Kiba Station and change for the Rinkai Fukutoshin line. Take it three stops to Tokyo Teleport Station.

When a city like Tokyo runs out of space, it turns to the water. Landfill has been going on at least 400 years — the Ginza was once a marsh. The latest development is the Tokyo Waterfront Project, a landfill island called **Rinkai Fukutoshin**. It's the brainchild of a long-term governor of Tokyo who lost his fifth-term reelection bid in the early 1990s mainly because taxpayers became disgusted at the outrageous price tag.

The waterfront has a lot of empty lots, but it also has some postmodern buildings that look like the opening scenes of the futuristic film, *Bladerunner.* The entire scene is surreal with futuristic buildings like Tokyo Big Site (Convention Center), the Hotel Nikko, Fuji Television Headquarters and Ariake Frontier Building just a few minutes walk from the water's edge — sand, shells and all.

Rainbow Bridge is a graceful 800-meter suspension bridge. You can cross on foot between *9am and 9pm April through October and 9am to 6pm November through March.* To reach the bridge on the Shibaura side, it's a ten-minute bus ride or 25-minute walk from JR Tamachi Station, or a five-minute walk from the Shibaura Futo Station on the Yurikamome Mono-rail. *The pedestrian walkway is closed every 3rd Monday and December 29-31. ¥300.*

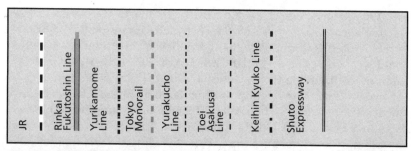

JR

Rinkai Fukutoshin Line

Yurikamome Line

Tokyo Monorail

Yurakucho Line

Toei Asakusa Line

Keihin Kyuko Line

Shuto Expressway

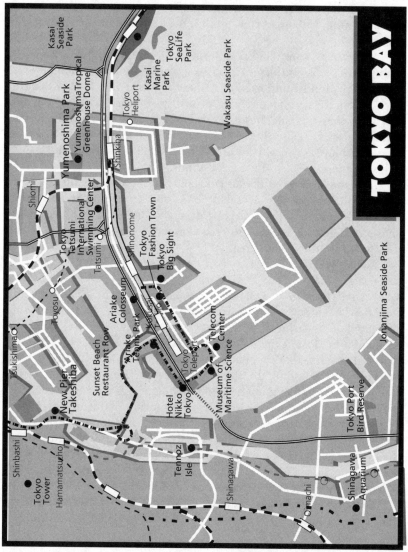

TOKYO BAY

Shinbashi

Tokyo Tower

Hamamatsucho

Tsukishima

New Pier Takeshiba

Sunset Beach Restaurant Row

Toyosu

Shiomi

Yumenoshima Park

Yumenoshima Tropical Greenhouse Dome

Kasai Seaside Park

Tatsumi

Tokyo Tatsumi International Swimming Center

Shinonome

Tokyo Fashion Town

Tokyo Big Sight

Ariake Colosseum

Ariake Tennis Park

Kokusai-Tenjijo

Tokyo Teleport

Telecom Center

Museum of Maritime Science

Hotel Nikko Tokyo

Shiokaze Park

Shinkiba

Tokyo Heliport

Kasai Marine Park

Tokyo SeaLife Park

Wakasu Seaside Park

Tennoz Isle

Shinagawa

Omachi

Shinagawa Aquarium

Tokyo Port Bird Reserve

Jonanjima Seaside Park

On the other side of Rainbow Bridge is **Odaiba Marine Park**, which is complete with a sandy beach. **Sunset Beach Restaurant Row**, across the street from the Marine Park, has a half-dozen restaurants each with an outdoor patio. The large **DECKS Tokyo Beach** is a shopping and amusement building that includes a virtual reality game arcade called Joyopolis. If you don't walk across the Rainbow Bridge, the most convenient mode of transportation is the Yurikamome Monorail from Shimbashi Station. Get off at the Odaiba Kaihin Koen Station. You can also take a water bus from Hamamatsucho's Hinode Pier to Odaiba Keihin Koen.

The **Telecom Center**, at the monorail's Telecom Center Station, has an observatory with great views of the entire waterfront area. *Open 11am to 8pm. ¥600.*

At the next monorail stop, Kokusai Tenjijo Seimon, **Tokyo Big Sight**, is a huge new convention center. The signature building resembles four upended pyramids supported by a tinker-toy structure. It's worth a stop to check out the architecture of this futuristic building; the large atriums that let the sun shine in. The Observation Bar Lounge on the 8th floor has great sea views. *Tel. (03)5530-1115.* On the other side of the station is Tokyo Fashion Town, which would like to become center of the fashion industry; there are also some retail shops.

The Hotel Intercontinental Tokyo Bay is on the mainland side of the waterfront development at Takeshiba at the Takeshiba Station of the Yurikamome monorail or JR Hamamatsucho station. A free observatory on the 24th floor of South Tower has wonderful views of Rainbow Bridge and the entire waterfront area.

Tokyo Sea Life Park is only a subway ride away. *6-2-3 Rinkai-cho, Edogawa-ku. Tel. (03)3869-5152. Open 9:30am to 5pm (enter by 4pm). Closed Monday and December 29 through January 3. ¥800. Kasai Rinkan Koen Station on JR Keiyo line or ferry from Hinode Pier at Hamamatsucho (55 minutes, ¥800).* This fabulous aquarium is on the waterfront in the newly developed Kasai Rinkan Park. Most of the structure is below ground. You enter through a large glass dome that's similar to an upside-down goldfish bowl, and you descend into the body of the building — goldfish never had it so good. The aquarium has a huge donut-shaped tank filled with tuna and other fish. Walking through the center, you have a great view of the tuna that are so silvery they look like they've been spray painted. The aquarium opens out onto the sea, and has an artificial beach where children can pick up shellfish and other shore creatures. The penguin area is out on the patio overlooking the sea. The way the pen is constructed, we can look longingly at the open seas, but the penguins can't.

Tokyo Sea Life Park is located inside Kasai Seaside Park, a large park that is reclaiming Tokyo's beachfront. Crystal View, a wonderful postmodern, glass observation building near the aquarium, is a popular place for couples to enjoy the sunset.

Nearby Tokyo Sea Life Park is a botanical garden called **Yumenoshima Tropical Plant Dome**. *3-2 Yumenoshima, Koto-ku. Tel. (03)3522-0281. Open 9:30am to 4:30pm. Closed Monday and December 29 through January 3. ¥300. 15-minute walk from Shinkiba Station on the Yurakucho subway line and JR Keiyo line.* This botanical garden is constructed in an attractive greenhouse dome.

The **Tokyo Port Wild Bird Park** (Tokyo-ko Yacho Koen) is in the waterfront area, but you approach it using the Tokyo Monorail from Hamamatsucho Station, heading toward Haneda Airport. Get off at the second stop, Ryutsu Senta Station. You'll be sure we sent you to the wrong place because all you'll see are large, ugly warehouses. But walk east toward the water, and you'll reach a large water bird reserve, divided into sea and freshwater bird reserves. The reserve has an observatory with telescopes. *Open 9am to 5pm, until 4:30pm November through January. Closed Monday. ¥200.*

AREA 18: OUTSKIRTS

Tokyo has lots of great spots to visit outside the city center. When you factor in transportation time, each place listed takes the better part of the day to visit.

Gotoh Museum (Gotoh Bijutsukan) and **Seikado Bunko Library** (Seikado Bunko) are both located in suburban Tokyo. Both museums are surrounded by greenery and are fairly close together; a visit makes a good outing to see art and culture and gives you a break from downtown Tokyo.

Seikado Bunko Library. Seikado Bunko's collection once belonged to the famous businessman Iwasaki Yataro who started the Mitsubishi empire at the end of 19th century. The outstanding collection includes Japanese, Korean and Chinese art. The display of about 40-50 items changes quarterly. Some of the masterpieces include the illustrated diary of Lady Murasaki, the author of the *Tale of Genji;* Edo-period artist Sotatsu's famous screen painting of the *Tale of Genji*; and a world famous black *temmoku* (oil spot) tea bowl. *2-23-1 Okamoto, Setagaya-ku. Tel. (03)3700-2250. Open 10am to 4pm. Closed Monday. ¥800. Take the Shin Tamagawa line from Shibuya Station. Get off at Futako Tamagawa Station. Take bus # 4 and get off at Seikado Bunko-mae.*

To go to the Gotoh Museum, return to Futako Tamagawa Station, and take the Tokyu Oimachi line one stop to Kaminoge.

The **Gotoh Museum** houses the collection of Gotoh Keita, the founder of the Tokyu rail, real estate and retail empire. The museum has masterpiece scroll paintings of the *Tale of Genji* from the 12th century; because of their fragility, they are only shown during a brief period each

ENJOY THE NEW YEAR JAPANESE STYLE!

The biggest holiday is New Year's – a special festive season and a highlight of the year. Japanese start preparations several weeks in advance just as Westerners start enjoying Christmas weeks in advance. The end of the year is regarded as the time to settle all financial transactions and unfinished business. Museums close from about December 27 through January 3. Department stores stay open through December 31; usually they're packed the morning of the 31st as people buy last minute items, but all close January 1, and many stay closed on January 2.

So what's there to do at year's end?

• Go to Tsukiji Outer Market. You don't have to go early in the morning. December 28-31 it's thronged with people buying food and decorations for New Year's.

• Eat soba noodles the night of December 31st; they symbolize longevity.

• Go to a Buddhist temple at midnight December 31st to ring the bells to repent and get rid of the sins of the past year. Buddhist temples ring their bells 108 times, once for each type of sin according to Buddhist belief. At Kan'ei-ji in Ueno, pay ¥3000 to ring the bell; at Enkaku-ji 100 pairs of people can ring the large bell, a National Treasure, for free. At Tokei-ji in Kamakura, you can ring the bell for ¥100; you must be in line by 11:40pm, and the bell is rung 108 times.

• Watch TV. Kohaku Uta Gassen is a New Year's Eve program as classic as Guy Lombardo and the Times Square ball. More than half the population has the TV tuned to NHK, the national television station. Japanese popular singers divide into two teams, red (women) and white (men) who compete by singing songs.

• Go to a concert. Many orchestras have programs beginning at 10pm so you can welcome in the New Year with music.

• Trains run all night long on December 31.

• During New Year's, go to a Shinto shrine with millions of Japanese to welcome in the gods. If you really want to get fancy, do a pilgrimage circuit of seven shrines representing the seven lucky gods.

• Go to the Imperial Palace on January 2 to see and hear the emperor give his New Year's greetings.

• Chinese restaurants open on January 2; go to Yokohama's Chinatown.

• Go for a hike. Mt. Takao is close, and you're rewarded with a temple at the top.

• Kabuki begins the year on January 3. All month, some people attend wearing formal kimono and the atmosphere is festive.

Tokyo is lovely during the New Year's holidays. Best of all, the streets are empty. Almost all restaurants, except in hotels, are closed January 1; but shopping areas like Shibuya and Shinjuku are bustling on January 2. Convenience stores stay open throughout the holiday so you can always get basic commodities.

spring. Gotoh's fine collection also includes Chinese and Japanese paintings, calligraphy and ceramics — there's always something to see. Behind the museum is a peaceful hillside garden with two tea huts. *9-25-3 Kaminoge, Setagaya-ku. Tel. (03)3703-0662. Open 9:30am to 4:30pm. Closed Monday. ¥700. To return to Shibuya Station, take the Tokyu Oimachi line one stop to Futago Tamagawa Station and change to the Shin Tamagawa line to Shibuya Station.*

Jindai-ji Temple and **Jindai-ji Botanical Park** (Jindai-ji Shokubutsukan). If the city is closing in on you but you don't want to go too far, take this day trip. Less than an hour from Shinjuku Station, the area is an oasis of calm. *From Shinjuku Station, take the JR Chuo line to Mitaka and board the #56 bus heading to Chofu.*

Jindai-ji Temple goes back a thousand years. The thatched-roof entrance gate and meditation center, located in a large building to the right of the entrance, are two of the few thatched-roof structures left in Tokyo. Most temple buildings were rebuilt in the Edo era after a disastrous fire. The temple has lots of statues, but the most famous is the Hakuhobutsu, which was carved around 700 and discovered under a temple building in 1909. The statue is displayed under glass in the Shaka-do, a modern building.

Take the cobblestone path at the left of the temple. You climb up a wooded hill to reach a tall spire with a building encircling it. This pet cemetery makes sure that Fido also attains everlasting peace. When you get hungry, head for one of the many *soba* stands all over the temple precincts. The local specialty is Jindai-ji *soba,* eaten by the Tokugawa shogun. Supposedly, the fresh spring water makes the *soba* noodles special; whatever the reason, they sure are tasty.

Behind Jindai-ji is the **Jindai-ji Botanical Park**, Tokyo's largest botanical garden that was once part of the temple complex. The garden has many different trees and plants including dogwoods given to the Japanese government by the US government in exchange for the cherry trees that grace Washington, D.C. Ask at the entrance gate for a strolling map in English. *Jindai-ji Botanical Garden. Tel. (0424)83-2300. Open 9:30am to 4pm. Closed Mondays. ¥400.*

Japan Open Air Folk House Museum (Nihon Minka-en).This place is one of our favorites to take guests to soak up some greenery and history. It's an easy trip out of central Tokyo and gives you a glimpse of how people lived in the countryside. Until about 100 years ago, Japan was primarily an agricultural country — yes, it's difficult to believe when you see metropolitan Tokyo. From all different areas of Japan, 20 old farmhouses were reassembled in this hilly and heavily wooded park. The buildings have been meticulously restored and furnished. Wooden chests, storage bins for rice, *sake* and soy sauce, clay cooking stoves and cooking utensils and other objects give some sense of how people lived.

We find the variety of buildings amazing — some have thatched roofs, others tile or shingle. Some from very snowy areas needed steep roofs so the snow wouldn't accumulate while others have flat ones. One farmhouse has a noodle shop or you can pick up something to eat near the station and have a picnic in the large park. *7-1-1 Masugata, Tama-ku, Kawasaki. Tel. (044)922-2181. Open 9:30am to 4pm. Closed Monday and December 27 through January 4. ¥300. From Shinjuku Station take the Odakyu train (local or express) to Mukogaoka-yuen. It's about a 15-minute walk alongside the monorail until the monorail veers to the left at a small river, you continue straight ahead on a fairly narrow street until you reach the parking lot. If you don't want to walk, it's less than 5 minutes by taxi.*

Mt. Takao (Takao-san). When Tokyo starts closing in around us, we head for our favorite, easy getaway. Mt. Takao is a mere 55 minutes from Shinjuku Station, but it could be another planet. After traveling through a seemingly endless urban mass, the green hills suddenly open up and the air becomes fresher.

Take the Keio line from Shinjuku Station to Takao-san guchi. Make sure you take an express and that your car says Takao-san guchi. Some trains split at Hachioji Station. If in doubt, ask. And the stop before Takao-san guchi is Takao, so don't get off too early. At Takao-san guchi Station, turn right as you exit and walk along the path to the cable car station. Along this path are some *soba* noodle shops. The local specialty is *tororo soba*, buckwheat noodles with grated mountain potatoes, but you'll find other varieties of noodles also.

From the cable car station, you can board a cable car or ski lift chair to the top of Mt. Takao. The fare for either is ¥470 one way; ¥900 round trip. The cable car is faster but if you factor in waiting time, you arrive at the top at about the same time. Service begins as early as 8am during the summer. There are also several hiking trails up, and since we've seen women hike in high heels, you know the mountain isn't too challenging. We usually take a lift up and walk down. The walk up takes about 90 minutes; the mountain is about 600 meters high.

At the top of the lift, you walk another 10 minutes or so to **Yakuo-in Temple**, which has a history spanning 1200 years. Belonging to the esoteric Shingon sect, Yakuo-in has statues and masks of long-nosed spirits called Tengu. These are beings who live deep in the mountains and help fulfill the wishes of believers.

Continue up the mountain to the peak. On clear days you have a nice view of Mt. Fuji. There's also a small nature museum at the top. Go down the mountain by cable car, chair lift or on your own two feet.

TAKAO'S HIWATARI FESTIVAL

*Mt. Takao is one of the mountains where **yamabushi** (ascetic priests) go for rigorous training to attain salvation and enlightenment. Two of the other mountains are Dewa Sanzan in Yamagata Prefecture and Mt. Yoshino in Nara Prefecture.*

*On the second Sunday in March, priests dressed in brilliant orange and yellow robes participate in **Hiwatari**, a walking-on-fire ritual, to complete their annual training. A monstrous bonfire, as big as the buildings around, is built in front of the Museum of Natural History, not far from the train station. After the flames are extinguished and the coals are still smoldering, the chief priest chants sutras and walks barefooted on the ashes as if he were walking on velvet lawn. Other priests follow him across the coals.*

Spectators are invited to join and many, including children, follow. No one seems to get burned. We were really tempted to join in the fun, but foolishly wore panty hose. The moral: wear socks if you feel like experiencing foot toasting.

The area has a charming restaurant that we highly recommend: **Ukai Toriyama**. It's a short ride from the Takao-san guchi Station. A complimentary shuttle bus operates between the restaurant and the station, but if it's an off-hour, you might have to call and ask for a pick-up.

Ukai Toriyama is nestled deep in the mountains along a small river gorge. The restaurant consists of about a dozen teahouses; some are several hundred years old and others are more recent constructions. There is also a large farmhouse for big groups. If you are a group of four or more, you will be seated in your own teahouse. Several different set menus are offered; you'll grill the main course on a charcoal hibachi. The food is good and the mood is peaceful. When we eat there, we feel we're a million miles away from Tokyo.

Reservations are recommended, especially on weekends. The staff speaks some English, and there is an English menu. *Set menus begin at ¥4500. Tel. (0426)61-0739.*

Ski Dome (SSAWS Gelande). On the trip in from Narita Airport, you may have noticed a huge, sloping building with steel girders for legs. This is the Ski Dome, Japan's first and largest indoor ski slope. Want to go skiing on a sweltering August day? No problem. The dome is open all year round and, ironically, is most crowded in winter. Here, high-tech meets snow. When you enter, you receive a computer card that keeps track of your expenses including food, ski and clothes rental and how much time on the snow. The snow making itself is computer controlled. In only two minutes, two high-speed ski lifts whisk you to the top of the 500-meter slope. And there's a tow rope for beginners. It's one of those experiences that only the Japanese could have invented.

After skiing, dip in the heated pool for ¥500. Or shop in the many stores selling pricey ski gear. *2-3-1 Hamacho, Funabashi, Chiba. Tel. (0474)32-7000. Admission: all day pass (ichi-nichi ken) ¥5400 or by the hour (jikan ken) ¥2200 plus ¥1000 per hour; ski equipment: ¥1800, ski wear: ¥1800. Generally open from 10am to 10pm but varies with the day and season. Take the JR Keiyo line to Minami Funabashi Station.*

IF YOU ONLY HAVE ONE OR TWO DAYS...

If you only have one day in Tokyo, it's really a shame, but here's how we would spend one very full day.

If you are jet lagged and wake up early, go to the Fish Market in Tsukiji where the tuna auction begins around 5am. Explore the retail shops outside the market itself. Have sushi for breakfast at one of the many shops in the area or hop a taxi to a Ginza hotel – the Ginza Tokyu has a nice café for a Western breakfast if raw fish doesn't do it for you in the morning. Walk through the Ginza district, but not too early because most of the shops don't open until 10am. Make sure you go into one of the big department stores such as Mitsukoshi or Matsuya.

Take a taxi to Hama Rikyu Garden (except on Monday when it's closed) for a stroll in one of Tokyo's best gardens and jump on the ferry up the Sumida River to Asakusa. Have a late lunch in the Asakusa area; see the Asakusa Kannon Temple and buy your souvenirs from the shops along the Nakamise arcade. Eat dinner at Nanbantei or Honmura-an in Roppongi. If you can still keep your eyes open, go to Roppongi, Shibuya or Shinjuku to see the lights and the nightlife.

If You Have Two Days

***Day 1:** Go to Asakusa to see the Kannon Temple and the shops in the area. Take the ferry to Hama Rikyu Garden. Then walk over to Ginza, taking in one act at the Kabuki-za. Explore Ginza and walk west to the Imperial Palace and go into the East Garden.*

***Day 2:** Start your day at Meiji Shrine; then walk around Harajuku stopping at the tiny Ota Museum to view its woodblock print collection. Walk along Omotesando and stop at the nearby Nezu Museum and garden. If you still have energy, walk to Shibuya.*

15. NIGHTLIFE & ENTERTAINMENT

In the evening, Tokyo transforms itself from a monotonous city into a glittering entertainment center. *Salariman* (Japanese-English for male, white-collar workers) and office ladies (Japanese-English for female clerical workers) escape from their concrete office buildings and head to bars, restaurants and clubs to eat and drink with their friends and colleagues or to continue business discussions with their customers. It's an essential part of the bonding process.

Friday night is date night and the party goes on late into the evening. In Roppongi, Shibuya and Shinjuku, the sidewalks are as crowded at midnight as they are at 7pm.

Each entertainment district has it's own feel. **Ginza** is very establishment, popular with middle-aged businessmen and up. **Akasaka** is a real hodgepodge: *geisha* houses catering to titans of industry and politics are side by side with inexpensive bars. **Roppongi** is popular with foreigners and Japanese who want a slightly more international atmosphere. **Shibuya** attracts a young crowd. Shinjuku's **Kabuki-cho** is a raucous, anything-goes area.

Tokyo's music scene is lively. International names come through, playing at the Tokyo Dome, clubs called "live houses" or intimate jazz joints. Discos rock until the wee hours of the morning. Cover charges usually run between ¥1500 and ¥5000. Sometimes drinks are included; sometimes they are extra.

Bars and clubs come and go with alarming speed. Here are a few that have some staying power, but to be on the safe side, check before you trek across town. The *Tokyo Journal* has the most complete listings in English.

LIVE HOUSES & DISCOS

Roppongi

BIRDLAND (jazz), *Basement of the Square Building. 3-10-3 Roppongi, Minato-ku. Tel. (03)3478-3456.*

There are a bunch of discos in the building, but you would never know it in Birdland. The intimate jazz club is far removed from all the craziness outside.

DESPERADO TOKYO, *B1F, Elsa Building, 3-13-12 Roppongi, Minato-ku. Tel. (03)3475-6969.*

Live 70s and 80s rock. ¥1500 cover; none if you sit in the bar.

ROPPONGI PIT INN (jazz and soul), *3-17-7 Roppongi, Minato-ku. Tel. (03)3585-1063.*

A Roppongi institution that features acts by top-notch Japanese and international musicians.

BODY AND SOUL (jazz), *7-14-12 Roppongi, Minato-ku. Tel. (03)5466-3348.*

This really relaxed club features jazz usually played by Japanese musicians.

VOLGA, *3-5-14 Shiba Koen, Minato-ku. Tel. (03)3433-1766.*

You can't miss the Russian onion dome facade. The extremely ornate restaurant has blues shows at 9 and 11pm. It's located in the outskirts of Roppongi near Tokyo Tower.

CAVERN CLUB, *5-3-2 Roppongi, Minato-ku. Tel. (03)3405-5207.*

Live Beatles music by sound-alike bands. You don't have to close your eyes to think the Fab Four have returned; even though the musicians are Japanese, they look like the Beatles. Alas, dancing is not allowed. Cover ¥1400.

KENTOS, *5-3-1 Roppongi, Minato-ku. Tel. (03)3401-5755.*

Next to and under the same management as the Cavern Club. Kentos has live 1950s and 1960s music and the tiny dance floor is packed. Cover ¥1400.

LEXINGTON QUEEN, *3-13-14 Roppongi, Minato-ku. Tel. (03)3401-1661.*

Granddaddy of Tokyo's discos, it's still going strong. It's a favorite drop-in place for movie stars when they're in town. Cover: ¥4000 men, ¥3000 women.

VALFARRE, *7-14-22 Roppongi, Minato-ku. Tel. (03)3746-0055.*

Tokyo's largest disco — the entrance is a spectacular staircase. Open only until midnight. Men ¥5000. Women ¥4000. Sundays women are free before 9pm; Wednesdays ¥2000.

Aoyama

BLUE NOTE TOKYO (jazz), *FIK Minami Aoyama Building, B1, 5-13-3 Minami Aoyama, Minato-ku. Tel. (03)3407-5781.*
A sister of New York's legendary Blue Note; top international musicians perform at top prices.

Shinjuku

SHINJUKU PIT INN, *3-16-4 Shinjuku. Tel. (03)3354-2024.*
Jazz and rock.
LIQUID ROOM, *Shinjuku Humax Pavilion, 7th floor, 1-20-1 Kabuki-cho, Shinjuku-ku. Tel. (03)3200-6831.*
Usually has live music, but sometimes djs.
INDIGO BLUES, *7F, Lumine 2 Building at Shinjuku Station. Tel. (03)3344-0471.*

Shinjuku-ni (2) chome is Tokyo's gay district and home to several hundred bars. A few that are welcoming to non-gays are: **Fuji** *(2-12-16 Shinjuku, Tel. (03)3354-2707);* **Kinsmen** *(2-18-5 Shinjuku, Tel. (03)3354-4949);* **Kinswomyn** for women only *(Tel. (03)3354-8720);* **Delight** for dancing *(Dai-ni Hayakawaya Building, B1, 2-14-6 Shinjuku, Tel. (03)3352-6297).*

Shibuya

ON AIR WEST, *2-3 Maruyama-cho, Shibuya-ku. Tel. (03)5458-4646.*
"Live house" with mostly rock performers. Cover varies with the musicians.
CLUB QUATTRO, *5F, Quattro Building, 32-13 Udagawa-cho, Shibuya-ku. Tel. (03)3477-8750.*
A popular live house with a rock focus. Cover varies with musicians.
CLUB ASIA, *1-8 Maruyama-cho, Shibuya-ku. Tel. (03)5458-5962.*
Asian pop music.

Meguro

BLUES ALLEY JAPAN, *Meguro Station Hotel, B1, 1-3-14 Meguro, Meguro-ku. Tel. (03)5496-4381.*
A branch of the Washington, D.C. blues club, Blues Alley serves French and Italian food and has live music on Fridays.

KARAOKE

Karaoke, a peculiarly Japanese invention now spread worldwide, has people crooning out songs in bad voices in bars and pubs. A recent addition is karaoke boxes, private rooms that mercifully save the ears of strangers. Most karaoke bars have only a small selection of songs in English — *My Way* and *Diana* are the favorites. An exception is **Keets** in Roppongi; they have over 3000 English songs, so you are sure to find your favorites. And it won't blow the bank: ¥2000 cover charge includes two drinks. *Dai-ju Togensha Building, 4F, 2-4-9 Roppongi, Minato-ku. Tel. (03)3584-3262.*

The classiest karaoke bar is **Festa**, just north of the Russian Embassy on Gaien Higashi Dori, where you can eat gourmet fare and sing your heart out in private rooms. The best deal is the ¥5000 package that includes the room charge, three hours of karaoke and Japanese food. *3-5-7 Azabudai, Minato-ku. Tel. (03)5570-1500. Open 5pm to 5am. Closed Sunday and holidays.*

CULTURAL PERFORMANCES

The *Tokyo Journal*, a monthly magazine, is an excellent source of information on performing arts events. The English language newspapers also have listings.

Kabuki
KABUKI-ZA THEATER, *on Harumi Dori, just past Showa Dori. Higashi Ginza Station on the Hibiya subway line is the closest stop, but it's only about a 5-minute walk from the Ginza Station on the Ginza subway line. Ticket prices ¥2500 to ¥16,500. One act tickets ¥600 to ¥1000, depending on the length of the act. Matinee begins at 11am; evening performance at around 4:30pm. For reservations, call (03)5565-6000 at least one day in advance.*

You'll be given a reservation number; armed with your reservation number, go to the ticket office to the right of the main entrance on the day of the performance. For one-act tickets, there's a ticket window to the left of the main entrance. Tickets go on sale 15 minutes before the act begins. If you see one act and decide you want to stay for the next one, you have to go back downstairs to buy another ticket. Call the Tourist Information Office for one act schedule times.

We highly recommend that you rent earphones with English commentary that are available in the lobby. They cost ¥600 plus a ¥1000 deposit, which is refunded when you return the headset. Unfortunately, you can't get earphones with a one-act ticket. *Kabuki* is performed every month from the 1st through the 25th.

NATIONAL THEATER (Kokuritsu Gekijo), *near the Hanzomon station of the Hanzomon subway line. Tickets are ¥1500 to ¥9000. Earphones with English commentary available. 4-1 Hayabusa-cho, Chiyoda-ku. Tel. (03)3265-7411.*

The National Theater features *kabuki* performances on a regular basis. *Kabuki* there doesn't have the "downtown, down home" atmosphere of the Kabuki-za; the focus is more educational. A small gallery on the second floor displays *ukiyo-e* woodblock prints and documents pertaining to the current performance. The theater's summertime classroom series is a short lecture on *kabuki* followed by a performance. It's geared to high school students, but don't let that put you off — it's an excellent introduction to *kabuki*.

Noh

Unlike *kabuki* and *bunraku, noh* plays are staged only once with the same cast. A *noh* theater has only a handful of productions every month and tickets tend to sell out quickly.

NATIONAL NOH THEATER (Kokuritsu Noh-gakudo). *4-18-1 Sendagaya, Shibuya-ku. Tel. (03)3423-1331. Tickets generally range from ¥2100 to ¥3800.*

Tickets available at the box office and Ticket Pia and Ticket Saison agencies. Usually there are a half-dozen productions a month.

HOSHO NOH THEATER (Hosho Noh-gakudo). *1-5-9 Hongo, Bunkyo-ku. Tel. (03)3811-4843. Suidobashi Station on JR Sobu or Mita subway line. Tickets range from ¥3500 to ¥6500.*

An English summary of the play is usually available..

TESSENKAI NOH THEATER (Tessenkai Noh Gakudo Kenshujo). *4-21-29 Minami Aoyama, Minato-ku. Tel. (03)3401-2285. Exit B4 of Omotesando Station on Chiyoda, Ginza and Hanzomon subway lines.*

Turn left at top of exit. Theater is on the left, about two blocks down.

KANZE NOH THEATER (Kanze Noh Gakudo). *1-16-4 Shoto, Shibuya-ku. Tel. (03)3469-5241. 10 minute walk from Shibuya Station.*

Head to Tokyu Department Store; take the road going uphill by the entrance of Orchard Hall, around the back of the department store.

Bunraku

Bunraku Puppet Theater is performed in the small hall of the National Theater (Kokuritsu Gekijo, Shogekijo) several months a year (see Kabuki, above). The hall was specially designed for *bunraku*. If it's in town when you are, we urge you to go. Rent the English earphones.

Western Classical & Popular Music, Dance & Theater

Tokyo is on the touring map for world class artists and the listings are a virtual *Who's Who* of the music world. Japan has a great interest in Western music; Tokyo alone boasts ten resident symphony orchestras.

In the late 1980s, at the height of the bubble economy, some people went to concerts night after night paying ¥30,000 a ticket without thinking twice. Fortunately those days are long gone, but the plethora of concert halls constructed during that frenzy still remains. Now tickets are more reasonably priced. You still will have to pay top dollar for superstars. Tickets for a recent tour of New York's Metropolitan Opera featuring Luciano Pavarotti and Placido Domingo, for example, sold for ¥14,000 to ¥62,000. You won't have to fork over that much for most performances. Tickets for piano, violin or chamber music range from ¥3000 to ¥8000. The *Tokyo Journal's* listings are the best source of information in English. You can go to a Ticket PIA or Ticket Saison counter for information, but most is printed in Japanese. Some major halls are:

ORCHARD HALL, *use the Hachiko exit of Shibuya Station. Tel. (03)3477-3244.*

This is part of the Bunkamura complex, attached to Tokyu Honten Department Store in Shibuya. The hall is the home of the Tokyo Philharmonic.

SUNTORY HALL, *part of the Ark Hills complex near Roppongi. The closest subway is Kokkai Gijido-mae on the Chiyoda subway line or take bus # 1 from Shibuya Station's east side to the Ark Hills stop. Tel. (03)3584-9999.*

There are two concert halls; the acoustics in the main hall are excellent. You can buy drinks and sandwiches at the bar if you can't wait until after the concert. If we are not seeing a vocal recital, we like to sit on the seats behind the stage so we can see the conductor's facial expressions; these tickets happen to be the cheapest.

TOKYO METROPOLITAN FESTIVAL HALL (Tokyo Bunka Kaikan), *at Ueno Park; use Ueno Station, Koen (park) exit. Tel. (03) 3828-2111.*

There are two halls; the small concert hall is one of the best in Tokyo for chamber music.

NHK HALL, *use Harajuku or Shibuya Station. Tel. (03)3465-1751.*

NHK Hall accommodates over 4000 people, making it one of the Tokyo's largest halls. The acoustics are good, but we find the building uninspired.

TOKYO OPERA CITY THEATER, *Hatsudai Station on Keio line or Shinjuku Station. Tel. (03)5353-9999.*

The long-awaited opera house opened in 1997.

HAMA RIKYU ASAHI HALL, *adjacent to Asahi Shimbun (Newspaper) Building, use Shimbashi or Tsukiji Stations. Tel. (03)3351-4043.*

Good acoustics.

TOKYO GEIJUTSU GEKIJO, *part of the Tokyo Metropolitan Art Space. Use Ikebukuro Station, exit 2b. Tel. (03)5391-2111.*

TOKYO INTERNATIONAL FORUM (Tokyo Kokusai Forum), *use Yurakucho Station on the JR Yamanote line. Tel. (03)5221-9000.*

One of Tokyo's newest, has four halls.

CASALS HALL, *use Ochanomizu Station on JR Sobu line or Shin Ochanomizu on Chiyoda subway line. Tel. (03)3291-2525.*

Named to honor cellist Pablo Casals, this hall was built for chamber music concerts. The balcony seats are excellent.

KIOI-CHO HALL, *use Akasaka Mitsuke or Yotsuya Stations. Tel. (03)3237-0061.*

Built at the time of the bubble economy, the hall is over the top – marble floors and a much-too-big chandelier; the acoustics are excellent.

OJI HALL, *use Ginza Station. Tel. (03)3567-9990.*

Relatively small but perfect for piano concerts.

TSUDA HALL, *use Sendagaya Station. Tel. (03)3402-1851.*

Like Oji Hall, this is also an excellent venue for piano concerts.

KAN-I HOKEN HALL, *use Gotanda Station, located on the west side. Tel. (03)3490-5111.*

Not acoustically perfect, but offers excellent ballet, modern dance, musicals and foreign stage plays.

ART HALL AFFINIS, *use Toranomon Station on Ginza subway line, exit 3. Tel. (03)5572-4945.*

This is one of Tokyo's newest chamber music halls.

Theaters

Panasonic Globe Theater, *3-1-2 Hyakunin-cho, Shinjuku-ku. Tel. (03)3360-1151. Use Shin-Okubo Station on the JR Yamanote line.*

A copy of the English original – it's twice the size – usually presents Shakespearean plays performed by Japanese and foreign companies.

Ginza Saison Gekijo, *1-11-1 Ginza, Chuo-ku. Tel. (03)3535-0555. Use Ginza Itchome subway station.*

Come here to see Japanese and foreign stage plays.

Popular Music

Superstars like the Rolling Stones and Michael Jackson perform at the Tokyo Dome. Artists who might not attract 50,000 fans appear at the many concert halls, clubs and "live houses" that dot Tokyo. In addition to the halls listed above and Blue Note Tokyo, the following clubs are popular venues:

CLUB CITTA KAWASAKI, *use Kawasaki Station on the JR Keihin Tohoku line. Tel. (044)244-7888.*

CLUB QUATTRO, *5F, Quattro Building, 32-13 Udagawa-cho, Shibuya-ku. Tel. (03)3477-8750. From Shibuya Station's Hachiko Plaza, walk down the brick road at the huge Shibuya Hachiko crossing.*

ON AIR WEST, *on Rambling Road in Shibuya's Maruyama-cho. 2-3 Maruyama-cho, Shibuya-ku. Tel. (03)5458-4646. From Shibuya Station's Hachiko Plaza walk to Tokyu Honten Department Store and bear to the left. Turn left at Shibuya City Hotel.*

Ticket Agencies
You can reserve tickets by calling or going to a ticket agency. When making a telephone reservation, take the confirmation number to a ticket counter by the date the agent tells you. Tokyo is sprinkled with ticket counters; the agent can tell you the closest one. Ticket Pia and Ticket Saison accept credit cards.

Ticket agencies will not accept reservations on the day of a performance. You'll need to call the hall to reserve tickets and pick them up at the box office before the performance. Box offices do not accept credit cards.
- **Ticket Pia**, *Tel. (03)5237-9999*
- **Ticket Saison**, *Tel. (03)5990-9999*
- **CN Playguide**, *Tel. (03)3257-9999; (03)3257-9990* for classical music.

FLOWER ARRANGING

Classes are all in English at the following places:
OHARA SCHOOL, *5-7-17 Minami Aoyama, Minato-ku. Tel. (03)3499-1200. Three-minute walk from Omotesando Station on Ginza, Hanzomon and Chiyoda subway lines.*

Classes 10am to 12 noon, Monday, Wednesday, Thursday and Friday. ¥1500 plus about ¥2000 for flowers. Reservations required.

SOGETSU SCHOOL, *7-2-21 Akasaka, Minato-ku. Tel. (03)3408-1151. 5-minute walk from No. 4 exit Aoyama Itchome exit of Ginza and Hanzomon subway lines.*

Classes 10am to 12 noon Monday and Friday. ¥3670 including flowers. Reservations required.

IKENOBO OCHANOMIZU GAKUIN, *2-3 Kanda Surugadai, Chiyoda-ku. Tel. (03)3292-3071. 3-minute walk from Ochanomizu Station on JR Chuo and Sobu lines and Chiyoda subway line.*

Classes on Wednesday at 11am, 2pm and 4pm. ¥3700 fee includes flowers. Reservations required.

TEA CEREMONY

You can participate in a traditional Japanese tea ceremony, which is more like a meditative ritual than having tea in the Western sense.

TOKO-AN (IMPERIAL HOTEL), *4F, Main Building, 1-1-1 Uchisaiwai-cho, Chiyoda-ku. Tel. (03)3504-1111. Hibiya Station of Hibiya, Chiyoda and Toei Mita subway lines.*

Tea ceremony performed between 10am and 6pm except Sunday and holidays. Reservation required. Tea ceremony takes about 20 minutes. ¥1500.

CHOSHO-AN (HOTEL OKURA), *7F, Main Building, 2-10-4 Toranomon, Minato-ku. Tel. (03)3582-0111. Toranomon Station of Ginza subway line or Kamiyacho Station of Hibiya subway line.*

Tea ceremony performed daily, 11am to 5pm. Reservations required. Tea ceremony takes about 30 minutes. ¥1050.

SEISEI-AN (HOTEL NEW OTANI), *7F, Tower, 4-1 Kioi-cho, Chiyoda-ku, Tokyo. Tel. (03)3265-1111. Near Akasaka Mitsuke Station of Ginza and Marunouchi subway lines and Nagatacho Station of Yurakucho and Hanzomon subway lines.*

Tea ceremony performed 11am to 12 noon and 1pm to 4pm Thursday, Friday and Saturday. Reservations required for groups of five or more. Tea ceremony takes about 20 minutes. ¥1050.

CHADO KAIKAN HALL, *3-39-17 Takadanobaba, Shinjuku-ku. Tel. (03)3361-2446). From Takadanobaba Station on JR Yamanote line, walk 15 minutes or take a bus heading toward Otakibashi-shako and get off at the Takadanobaba yon(4)-chome stop.*

Tea ceremony is performed between 10:30am and 2:30pm, Monday through Thursday, but only three weeks of every month. Tea ceremony takes about one hour. ¥2000.

PUBLIC BATHS

The *sento* or public bath is a Tokyo institution that is fast disappearing. In 1968, Tokyo had 2687 public baths that served 6 million people a day, but today the number has dwindled to 1500. Many Japanese houses and apartments did not have baths, but over 90% do today. Most *sento* are local neighborhood institutions where you see people, mostly students and old people, enter carrying a plastic bucket with their soap and toiletries. For basic bath etiquette, see the sidebar on Bathing Etiquette in Chapter 6, *Planning Your Trip*.

In *shitamachi* (the old commoner's area), even today the tradition of relaxing with your neighbors is still alive. In Yanaka, for example, more than 10 *sento* (public baths) are located within a small radius.

VOLCANO WATCHING & HOT SPRINGS

Volcanoes and hot springs go together, so even Tokyo has hot springs called *onsen*. After all, Mt. Fuji is only an hour away by train. It last erupted in 1701, and although it is now dormant, it could erupt again.

The following are a few *sento* worth trying:

KOSHI NO YU and **AZABU JUBAN ONSEN**, *1-5-22 Azabu Juban, Minato-ku. Tel. (03)3401-8324. Open 3pm to 11pm. Closed Tuesday. Ground floor: ¥370; 3rd floor: ¥1300.*

On the first floor, you can soak in the same hot spring water as the *onsen* on the third floor. The old style bath has a two-story high ceiling and a mural painting. The Azabu Juban area has a lot of foreign residents so it's not unusual to see non-Japanese bathing here.

DAI NI SAKURA YU, *6-6-2 Jingu-mae, Shibuya-ku. Tel. (03)3400-5680. Open 3:30pm to 11pm. Closed Monday. Jingumae Station on the Chiyoda subway line. Use exit 4, turn around at the top of the stairs and cross Meiji Dori, take the second right (it's a narrow road). Before the road forks, turn right at the coin laundry. Turn right again. The bath is the building that looks like a temple.*

This 40-year-old building resembles a temple and is a wonderfully old-fashioned bathing experience in the midst of trendy Harajuku.

PUBLIC BATHING THE JAPANESE WAY

Public bathhouses, **sento,** *have a long history in Japan – back to the 8th century. Much more than a place to clean your body, they are community centers. Neighbors exchange news and gossip and bond with each other. Certain bath houses have been associated with the sex trade. They were called "Toruko" after the Turkish bath, but after the Turkish Embassy complained, they began to be called "Soaplands." Public baths however are legitimate, family-oriented places. Since most homes and apartments now have private baths, the remaining sento are struggling to survive in an environment of decreasing use and increasing costs. Most now have electronic massage chairs, and some have coffee bars. Soon we expect a Starbucks. You may even find a diaper changing table in the men's changing room.*

16. SPORTS & RECREATION

Since Japan perfected the art of making TVs, VCRs and other tools for couch potatoes, you may not think it would be a good place for live sports. But spectator sports like sumo, baseball, soccer, karate and judo, are thriving in Japan.

Do you find doing more exciting that watching? Hiking, skiing, cycling and mountain and rock climbing all beckon. And if it's martial arts that interest you, there could be a *dojo* in your future.

Searching for some mindless entertainment? *Pachinko* is sure to fit the bill or why not croon your heart out in a karaoke pub or box?

On your mark, get set, go.

SUMO

Sumo wrestling, the Japanese national sport, involves wrestling matches between huge, nearly naked men who can weigh as much as 500 pounds. The sport itself is very simple, but its rituals together with its simplicity make sumo a fascinating sport to watch. We know many foreigners living in Japan who are glued to the tube during an entire tournament.

SUMO LEGENDS

One former grand champion polished off six dozen bowls of noodles in one sitting.

Another once wolfed down 36 box lunches.

A champion consumed three bottles of whiskey during a night of drinking.

And then there's the story about a 440-pound wrestler who drank 38 quart bottles of beer during an all-night drinking session with his stablemates.

Sumo goes back 2000 years and is tied to Shinto religion: matches at shrines were offerings to the gods for a good harvest. To this day, bouts take place in a ring, *dohyo*, under a thatched roof resembling a shrine.

So what is sumo all about?

Before an actual bout begins, wrestlers go through a series of rituals that include throwing salt to purify the ring and staring each other down. Then they begin. The first man who steps out of the ring or touches the ground with any part of his body other than the soles of his feet, loses. If two wrestlers fall simultaneously, the first one to touch the ground loses. The *gyoji* (referee), wearing traditional, colorful robes and a tall hat, makes the final judgment and announces his decision by pointing his fan toward the winner.

Wrestlers can use any or all of more than 48 different techniques including pushing, pulling, lifting, tripping and slapping. But there are limits: for example, they cannot pull off each other's topnots or punch. Most bouts are over within a minute or so.

Known as *rikishi* (strong men), sumo wrestlers live communally in *heya* (stables). In this hierarchical arrangement, younger wrestlers defer to the upper-ranked *rikishi*, and perform menial tasks such as cleaning in addition to training. Wrestlers train from early morning until about 11am. Next they have their first of two meals of the day, gaining bulk by eating huge quantities of *chanko nabe*, a stew with meat, fish, tofu, *udon* noodles and vegetables. If you would like to visit a sumo stable to watch a training session, check for telephone numbers under Sports in the Tokyo chapter.

Tournaments last 15 days and are held six times a year: three in Tokyo and one each in Osaka, Nagoya and Fukuoka. The wrestler who wins the most bouts is the champion for that tournament.

The best seats, boxes with *tatami* mats and near the ring, are almost impossible to obtain. Companies and individuals renew their subscriptions year after year. It's easier to obtain chair seats, especially the least expensive advance sale seats at ¥3000 and the unreserved seats at ¥1500, sold each morning of a tournament. The daily seats go on sale at 9am at the box office. On weekends, holidays and during the last week of the tournament, you must go early to be assured of a ticket; on weekdays, especially early in the tournament, you can sometimes get to the box office as late as 9am or 10am and still get a ticket.

A tournament begins each day at 10am, and the lowest-ranking *rikishi* wrestle first. The really good guys don't go on until about 4pm, and the last bout always ends by 6pm. If you have an inexpensive ticket, it's perfectly acceptable to sit closer to the ring in the reserved seats until the rightful owner shows up — usually about 3pm.

Tokyo hosts three, 15-day **sumo tournaments** every year in January, May and September. NHK (Channel 1) televises the bouts every day from 4 to 6pm. NHK satellite broadcasts sumo with English explanations, but not every hotel provides satellite service. If you are in Tokyo, don't settle for watching a bout on television when you could see it live.

Sumo tournaments take place at the Sumo Stadium, formally known as the Kokugikan, at Ryogoku Station of JR Sobu line. Advance tickets go on sale at the stadium as well as at Play Guides Ticket Bureaus — branches at Isetan Department Store in Shinjuku, Seibu Department Store in Shibuya and Ikebukuro, and Kyukyodo in Ginza. The most expensive seating is on *tatami* mats near the ring. These seats come with food and souvenirs, but are almost impossible to obtain. Further back are chair seats. They cost ¥8100, ¥6100, ¥3600 and ¥2100. Standing-room tickets for ¥1500 go on sale at 9am each day of the tournament.

Weekends sell out quickly and the second week sells out before the first. Sometimes it's fairly easy to get tickets on weekdays during the first week. But if you want standing-room tickets on weekends, you have to be in line at least an hour or two before tickets go on sale.

The sumo tournament runs from 10am until 6pm; the lowest ranking wrestlers go first. The good guys don't wrestle until about 3:30pm, and most ticket holders don't come until then. You can buy an inexpensive ticket and sit down near the ring until the rightful owner of the seat claims his seat. You don't have to be embarrassed because everybody does this.

Sumo wrestlers live communally in **stables** and practice from about 6am to 11am. Some stables allow visitors to watch the practice, but you must make an appointment in advance.

Try:
- **Azumazeki Stable**, *Tel. (03)3625-0033*. This stable has a lot of Hawaiian-born wrestlers. It's near the Honjo Azumabashi Station of the Toei Asakusa subway line.
- **Tatsunami Stable**, *Tel. (03)3631-2424*. Near Ryogoku Station on the JR Sobu line.
- **Kasugano Stable**, *Tel. (03)3631-1871*. Near Ryogoku Station on the JR Sobu line.
- **Osaka**: held in Osaka Furitsu Taiiku Kaikan – March: 2nd Sunday through 4th Sunday
- **Nagoya**: Aichi Ken Taiiku-kan – July: 1st Sunday through 3rd Sunday
- **Fukuoka**: held in Fukuoka Kokusai Center Sogo Hall – November: 2nd Sunday through 4th Sunday

MARTIAL ARTS

In addition to extreme physical fitness, all the martial arts involve and emphasize rigorous mental training and discipline. For devotees, visiting

Japan provides an opportunity to see some of the top black-belt experts. You can actually participate at some of the *dojo* (training centers). For information, refer to the sports section of the Tokyo chapter. If you are in another part of the country, contact the appropriate federation for local places. Take along your training uniform, remember your techniques and try not to break any bones.

Karate

Karate originated in China, developed in Okinawa and arrived in mainland Japan in the early 20th century. Karate (empty hand) is primarily a means of self-defense. Although the empty hands are considered as weapons themselves, no other weapons are allowed. Kicking is permitted and that empty hand is used for lots of punching.

Try:

- **Japan Karate Association/International Headquarters JKA** (Nihon Karate Kyokai), *Kowa Building, 2nd Floor, 2-9-6 Shiroganedai, Minato-ku. Tel. (03)3440-1415.* Take a trial class for ¥1000 but spectators aren't allowed.

- **Goju-ryu Yoyogi Ryushinkan**,. *4-30-3 Sendagaya, Shibuya-ku. Tel. (03)3402-0123.* Near Yoyogi Station on JR Yamanote line. This school offers monthly instruction and allows spectators. Classes 3 to 5pm; 7 to 9pm Monday, Wednesday and Friday.

For more information, contact **The Japan Karate-do Federation**, *6F, No. 2 Sempaku Shinkokai Building, 1-11-2 Toranomon, Minato-ku, Tokyo. Tel. (03)3503-6640 or the International Headquarters of the Japan Karate Association, 2F, Kowa Building, 2-9-6 Shiroganedai, Minato-ku, Tokyo. Tel. (03)3440-1415.* There's no gym here, only offices.

Judo

Judo, another form of self-defense, is native to Japan and was developed from battlefield techniques — participants learn to dodge and toss their opponents. Police men and women often end up as national champions so be careful who you challenge. A trip to the **Kodokan**, judo headquarters, in Tokyo is a must for judo enthusiasts. The Kodokan offers monthly instruction and has a spectators gallery to view practice sessions. Classes run 6pm to 7:30pm Monday through Saturday.

For more information, contact **All Japan Judo Federation**, *c/o Kodokan, 1-16-30 Kasuga, Bunkyo-ku, Tokyo. Tel. (03)3818-4199.*

Nihon Budokan Budo Gakuen holds classes at the Nihon Budokan in Kitanomaru Park, 6:30pm to 7:30pm Monday, Wednesday and Friday. Spectators are welcome to watch practice sessions in this hall built for martial arts competitions in the 1964 Olympics.

Kendo

Kendo, Japan's traditional form of fencing, evolved from medieval swordsmanship. *Kendo* probably has the widest participation of any sport among Japanese school children. You'll see children on the train toting their bamboo swords to class. The All Japan Championships are held in Tokyo each December.

For more information, contact **All-Japan Kendo Federation**, *c/o Nippon Budokan, 2-3 Kitanomaru-koen, Chiyoda-ku, Tokyo. Tel. (03)3211-5804.*

Aikido

Aikido is a 20th century blend of karate, judo and *kendo*. The attackee uses the movements of the attacker to thwart the attacker himself. For more information, contact **International Aikido Federation**, *17-18 Wakamatsu-cho, Shinjuku-ku, Tokyo. Tel. (03)3203-9236.* At the same address is the **Aikido Hombu Dojo**, the gym that offers lessons on a monthly basis. Visitors are welcome to observe practice sessions.

BASEBALL - YAKYU

America's favorite pastime is also Japan's. One of the few Western sports to catch on really big, Japan is baseball crazy. While professional baseball is popular, the summertime high school championships take on almost mythical proportions.

If you are in Japan between early April and late September, attend a baseball game for an exhilarating experience. If you buy a ticket in the bleachers, you'll quickly be caught up in the local crowd's enthusiasm.

Japan has two leagues. **Central** and **Pacific**; each has six teams. The pennant winners slug it out in the Japan Series every autumn. Baseball fields are smaller than their American cousins and except for four domed stadiums at Tokyo, Nagoya, Osaka and Fukuoka, most games are played outdoors.

Teams are allowed three foreign players on their rosters — usually imports from the American baseball leagues.

Most of the teams are named after corporations, not after a town. The first time Patrice went to a game, she thought the team was named the Nippon Hams, not the Nippon Ham Fighters. The Yomiuri Giants, based in Tokyo, are everyone's favorite team and tickets are hard to get on short notice. Unless they are really hot, getting tickets for other teams is not usually a problem. Tickets are available at the stadium either in advance or at the game or through computerized ticket vendors such as Ticket Pia.

Want to keep up to date on Japanese baseball? Check out this English-language Internet site: *http://www.fsjsports.com.*

Six professional baseball teams call the metro Tokyo area home. Baseball has two leagues: the Pacific and the Central. The baseball season begins in mid-April and ends with the Japan Series in October. Tickets are usually pretty easy to obtain at the stadium or through ticket agencies except for the Yomiuri Giants, nearly everyone's favorite team. Their seats sell out well in advance. Most teams have inexpensive outfield seats for children, usually about ¥500; bleacher tickets for their mommies and daddies cost about double.

Baseball fans may want to stop at the **Baseball Hall of Fame Museum** (Yakyu Taiiku Hakubutsukan) at Tokyo Dome. ¥350. *Tel. (03)3811-3600.*

For the **Central League**:

Yomiuri Giants play at Tokyo Dome, a covered stadium, so games are never rained out. Tickets range from ¥1200 for nonreserved outfield bleachers to ¥5900 for the best seats. Tokyo Dome is a one-minute walk from Korakuen Station on the Marunouchi subway line and three-minute walk from Suidobashi Station on the JR Sobu, JR Chuo and Mita subway line. *Tel. (03)3811-2111.*

Yakult Swallows play at Jingu Stadium in Meiji Outer Garden in central Tokyo. Tickets cost between ¥1500 and ¥3900. Jingu Stadium is a five-minute walk from Gaien-mae Station on the Ginza subway line. *Tel. (03)3236-8000.*

Yokohama Bay Stars play at Yokohama Stadium. Tickets range from ¥1500 to ¥5000. Yokohama Stadium is near Kan-nai Station on the JR Negishi line. *Tel. (045)661-1251.*

For the **Pacific League**:

Nippon Ham Fighters play at Tokyo Dome. The first time Patrice went to a game, she thought the team was named the Nippon Hams, but that's the name of the company that owns them. Tickets cost ¥1500 to ¥5100. See the Yomiuri Giants listing above for transportation information. *Tel. (03)3811-2111.*

Seibu Lions play at Seibu Lions Stadium. Tickets cost ¥1500 to ¥3200. When the Lions win the pennant or the Japan Series, Seibu Department Store has a huge sale to celebrate. The stadium is at Seibu Kyujomae Station on the Seibu Ikebukuro line. *Tel. (0429)25-1151.*

Chiba Lotte Marines play at Chiba Marine Stadium. Tickets cost ¥1300 to ¥4000. The stadium is a 15-minute walk from the Kaihin Makuhari Station on the JR Keiyo line. *Tel. (043)296-8900.*

SOCCER

Soccer hit Japan big time a half-dozen years ago when the professional J. League was launched. While the initial ardor has dimmed somewhat, soccer is still popular among young people. Be ready to jump up and cheer along with the other enthusiastic fans. Japan and Korea will cohost the World Cup in 2002.

The 17 Japanese teams have both international and Japanese players. The season runs April through September.

J League is Japan's popular professional soccer league. The season runs from early April through May, then takes a break and resumes for July. After that, the championship playoffs run from August through mid-October. The Tokyo metro area has seven soccer teams. Tickets are available at Ticket Pia, *Tel. (03)5237-9999*, and Ticket Saison, *Tel. (03)3250-9911*, as well as at the stadiums. Most of the time, teams play their home games at their stadiums, but occasionally they play at the National Stadium (Kokuritsu Stadium) near Sendagaya Station on the JR Sobu line in central Tokyo. Ticket prices run between ¥2000 and ¥5000.

The Tokyo area teams are as follows:

JEF United Ichihara play at Ichihara Stadium in Chiba Prefecture. 20-minute walk from the west exit of Goi Station on the JR Uchibo line. *Tel. (0436)21-4441.*

Kashiwa Reysol play at Kashiwa Stadium in Kashiwa City. 20-minute walk from the east exit of Kashiwa Station on the Chiyoda subway line. *Tel. (0471)62-2201.*

Urawa Red Diamonds play at Komaba Stadium in Urawa City. Direct buses run from the west exit of Urawa Station on the JR line. *Tel. (048)882-8149.*

Verdy Kawasaki play at Todoroki Stadium in Kawasaki. From Musashi Kosugi Station on the Tokyu Toyoko line or JR Nambu line, take a bus from #1 or #2 bus stand heading toward Mizonokuchi and get off at Todoroki Ground Iriguchi stop. *Tel. (044)722-0303.*

Yokohama Marinos play at Mitsuzawa Stadium in Yokohama. From the west exit of Yokohama Station, take a bus from #7, 8, 9 or 11 bus stands and get off at Mitsuzawa Koen stop or walk 10 minutes from Mitsuzawa Kamicho Station on the Yokohama Shiei subway line. *Tel. (045)311-7614.*

Yokohama Flugels play at Mitsuzawa Stadium in Yokohama. See the Yokohama Marinos for directions. *Tel. (045)311-7614.*

Bellmare Hiratsuka play at Hiratsuka Stadium in Hiratsuka City. Take a shuttle bus from the north exit of Hiratsuka Station on the JR Tokaido line or from the Hon Atsugi or Isehara Stations on the Odakyu line. *Tel. (0463)33-4455.*

PACHINKO

A hybrid between one armed bandits and pinball, *pachinko* mesmerizes hundreds of thousands of Japanese every day. You can't miss *pachinko* parlors; they are everywhere — all 18,000 strong. In cities you usually find them near train stations. You'll recognize them by their flashing neon lights and their gaudy, plastic flower arrangements. When you walk by, the ringing noise is almost deafening and you'll notice that cigarette smoke clouds the room. In rural areas, *pachinko* parlors' signs light up an area for blocks like a mini-Las Vegas.

While technically not considered a form of gambling, players earn small prizes like lighter fluid flints or a certificate in exchange for *pachinko* balls. To collect their winnings, players go around the corner to a small window, which looks like a drug drop-point, and exchange these certificates for cash.

Until recently, the game, patronized mainly by students and housewives who "should" be spending their time elsewhere, had an unsavory image. Many of the parlors are owned by second or third generation Koreans resident in Japan, whose donations are one of North Korea's main sources of foreign currency. *Pachinko* parlor owners always turn up on the list of the country's biggest tax dodgers. But in the last year or two, the industry has tried to change its image. New, upscale parlors have marble floors, coffee bars and nonsmoking sections. Although still outside, their exchange windows resemble movie theater ticket windows.

Unlike pinball, there's very little skill involved other than choosing a machine that is set for a larger payoff. *Pachinko* mavens line up before a shop opens to have first choice. How do you tell which machines are best? Look for the machines that have the widest space between the pins around the big payoff hole.

So if you have an hour to kill waiting for a train, pop into a *pachinko* parlor. But keep your eye on the clock.

KARAOKE

Put a microphone in front of a normally reserved Japanese, and a transformation occurs. Soon he (or she) is belting out tunes in Japanese and often in a foreign language also.

Japan has melded technology with music to produce karaoke, a product they now export all around the world. Laser discs or the latest satellite-provided karaoke libraries provide the music and display the words on a video screen while you do the singing. Anyone can be an instant Frank Sinatra or Barbra Streisand.

In the last few years, a major transformation has occurred: karaoke bars have given way to karaoke boxes. Rather than singing in front of strangers at a pub, now you can rent a room that will seat anywhere from 2 to 50 and enjoy your own private karaoke session.

Most machines usually have a few songs in English. You have no excuse not to belt out *My Way, I Left My Heart in San Francisco, Country Road* and a sampling of Beatles tunes.

HELICOPTER RIDES

When all the chaos of the streets of Tokyo gets to you, take a night-time helicopter ride – the lights look like a work in progress. Executive Air Services offers a 15-minute ride that takes you from Urayasu, near Tokyo Disneyland, over the waterfront development area, the Rainbow Bridge, around Tokyo Tower and back for ¥14,500. Available Thursday through Sunday nights. It's best to go on Thursday or Friday because all the salarymen working late means the office buildings are aglow.

*Contact: **Executive Air Services**, 14 Chidori, Urayasu, Chiba. Tel. (0473)80-5555.*

JAPANESE ARCHERY - KYUDO

All Nippon Kyudo Federation (Zen Nihon Kyudo Renmei). *4F, Kishi Memorial Hall, 1-1-1 Jinnan, Shibuya-ku. Tel. (03)3481-2387.* Maybe it's because of stray arrows, but spectators aren't allowed at any of the schools.

SWIMMING POOLS

Tokyo Gymnasium Indoor Swimming Pool, *Tel. (03)5474-2111.* Sendagaya Station on JR Sobu line. Open 9:30am to 9pm. ¥450. Has 50 meter and 25 meter pools.

Tokyo Tatsumi International Swimming Pool, *Tel. (03)5569-5061.* 10-minute walk from Tatsumi Station on Yurakucho subway line. Open 9am to 9pm. Closed 3rd Monday. ¥450.

17. SHOPPING

Tokyo is a shopper's dream. Are you interested in state-of-the-art electronics, the latest international fashions, age-old traditional crafts? All are available. Some of our favorite places to shop are described in the following pages.

Japan's **department stores** are cultural institutions themselves. In addition to every conceivable style of clothing, the stores have extensive basement food floors where they sell prepared gourmet treats in addition to staples, meat, fish and vegetables. Most have galleries where exhibitions rival top museums. The kimono department usually has other, more affordable items like *yukata* (cotton robes), which are good mementos of Japan.

Department stores usually close about twice a month — always on the same day of the week. There isn't any pattern to their closing, and they stay open all week during the gift-giving seasons in June and December. We list the closed day after each department store, but remember, it isn't every week.

The standard opening time for department stores is 10am; they close between 7 and 8pm. Other stores usually open around the same time, sometimes 11am. Tokyo is not an early morning city. Arriving at a department store right as it opens is an unbelievable experience. Uniformed staff members stand at the entrance and bow to the first customers of the day.

Large stores will usually refund the 5% consumption tax to foreign visitors if you purchase goods over ¥10,000. Keep your passport handy; you'll need to show it.

FLEA MARKETS

We love to browse in the **flea markets**. Held at shrines, they're usually open from dawn until about 3pm. You'll find inexpensive second-hand kimono, vintage porcelain, ceramic dishes, lacquer ware, clocks, movie posters, dolls, toys and just plain junk; go early for the best selection.

MORE THAN JUST SHOPPING: JAPANESE DEPARTMENT STORES

When friends visit from abroad, we always start one day by going to a department store for its official opening ceremony, which begins at 10am sharp. Don't be late or you'll miss it! At the main entrance, you'll hear soft music playing over the loudspeaker system. Uniformed employees line up inside the entrance to the store, smiling in welcome and bowing politely. They make you feel like a VIP, which is great fun for a little while!

Japan's department stores pride themselves on being cultural as well as shopping centers. You would never expect to find an exhibition of Japanese masterpieces from the Tokyo National Museum at Macy's. But in Japan, you might find an exhibition of French Impressionists from a top museum displayed in a special gallery. Be sure to visit these galleries usually located on a top floor of most department stores; there's almost always an admission charge.

And don't miss the basement food floor! Wander around sampling delicacies to your heart's content; some stores are so generous with their free tastes that you can even forego lunch. Make sure you go to the fruit section to see ¥15,000 melons and ¥10,000 packages of cherries. Before you faint, be aware that most are bought by companies as gifts. Then go to the meat department and check out the Kobe and other premium beef selling for ¥50,000 a kilo, a mere $250 a pound. The more expensive the meat, the more marbled it is with fat. We still don't know who buys it.

Some department stores have Japanese souvenirs in a special section catering to tourists; if you are in a store that doesn't, go to the kimono department where a variety of traditional items like noren curtains or scarves are for sale – either one makes a great gift.

Antiques can be pricey, but the markets offer goods for every budget. Used silk kimono are real bargains, costing as little as ¥1000. If a kimono smells musty, one trick is to put it in a clothes dryer with a sheet of fabric softener and run it on low for a few minutes. Dealers speak a little English; some post prices and others don't. You can always ask for a discount, and you can often get a 10% reduction — sometimes more. Rain cancels flea markets.

Some good flea markets for you to visit include:
- **Togo Shrine**, 1st and 4th Sundays. Harajuku Station on Yamanote Line or Meiji Jingumae Station on Chiyoda subway line.
- **Nogi Shrine**, 2nd Sunday. Nogizaka Station on Chiyoda subway line.
- **Hanazono Shrine**, 2nd and 3rd Sundays; Shinjuku san-chome Station on Marunouchi subway line.

- **Roi Building**, 4th Thursday and Friday, Roppongi Station on Hibiya subway line.
- **Tomioka Shrine**, 1st of month and 1st Sunday. Monzen Naka-cho Station on Tozai subway line; walk east on Eitai Dori for about 3 minutes, shrine is on left.
- **Heiwajima Antique Fair** (Zenkoku Kotto Matsuri), *2F, Heiwajima Tokyo Ryutsu Center. Tel. (03)3980-8228.* Tokyo Monorail from JR Hamamatsucho Station to Ryutsu Center stop. The three-day sale is held in March, May, June, September and December and has over 200 dealers from all parts of Japan. If you can't find it here, it probably doesn't exist.

SHOPPING IN GINZA & NEIGHBORING DISTRICTS
DEPARTMENT STORES
- **Mitsukoshi**, *Ginza 4-chome intersection. Closed Monday. Tel. (03)3562-1111.*
- **Wako**, *Ginza 4-chome intersection. Closed Sunday. Tel. (03)3562-2111.*
- **Matsuya**, *One block down from Mitsukoshi. Closed Tuesday. Tel. (03)3567-1211.*
- **Matsuzakaya**, *South of Ginza 4-chome intersection. Closed Wednesday. Tel. (03)3572-1111.*
- **Hankyu**, *Near Yurakucho Station on Harumi Dori. Closed Thursday. Tel. (03)3575-2233.*
- **Seibu**, *Next to Hankyu. Closed Wednesday. Tel. (03)3286-0111.*

OTHER STORES
- **Takumi**, *8-4-2 Ginza, Chuo-ku. Tel. (03)3571-2017. Open 11am to 7pm. Closed Sunday.* Japanese folk crafts.
- **Kyukyodo**, *5-7-4 Ginza, Chuo-ku. Tel. (03)3571-4429. Open 10am to 7:30pm; 11am to 7pm on Sunday and holidays.* Sells incense, Japanese *washi* paper, tea ceremony utensils, cards and calligraphy supplies.
- **Mikimoto Pearls**, *4-5-5 Ginza, Chuo-ku. Tel. (03)3535-4611. Open 10am to 6pm. Closed Wednesday.* Japan's premier pearl shop of the company who invented the culturing process.
- **Itoya**, *2-7-15 Ginza, Chuo-ku. Tel. (03)3561-8311. Open 10am to 7pm; 10:30am to 6pm Sunday and holidays.* A large, well-stocked stationery and paper goods store — a delight for browsing.
- **Jena**, *5-6-1 Ginza, Chuo-ku. Tel. (03)3571-2980. Open 10:30am to 7:50pm; 12 noon to 6pm Sunday. Closed holidays.* A large selection of foreign books.
- **Tenshodo**, *4-3-9 Ginza, Chuo-ku. Tel. (03)3561-0021.* With a 120-year history, this shop sells the unlikely combination of toys and jewelry.

Japanese women didn't wear jewelry with kimono, only hair ornaments, so this shop was one of Japan's first to sell Western-style jewelry.

· **Yoseido Gallery**, *5-5-15 Ginza, Chuo-ku. Tel. (03)3571-1312. Open 10am to 6:30pm. Closed Sunday and holidays.* Carries a large selection of contemporary prints by Japanese artists.

· **Hayashi Kimono**, *International Arcade, 2-1-1 Yurakucho, Chiyoda-ku. Tel. (03)3501-4012. Open daily 9:30am to 6:30pm.* Hayashi has a good selection of used kimono, *happi* coats, cotton *yukata*, T-shirts and other souvenir items. It's in the International Arcade, which is under the tracks on the road on the north side of the Imperial Hotel.

SHOPPING IN NIHONBASHI

DEPARTMENT STORES

· **Mitsukoshi**, Mitsukoshi-mae Station on Ginza subway line. *Closed Monday. Tel. (03)3241-3311.*

· **Takashimaya**, At Nihonbashi Station on Ginza and Tozai subway lines. *Closed Wednesday. Tel. (03)3211-4111.*

· **Tokyu**, At Nihonbashi Station on Ginza and Tozai subway lines. *Closed Thursday. Tel. (03)3273-3111.*

OTHER STORES

· **Ozu Washi**, *2-6-3 Nihonbashi Honcho, Chuo-ku. Tel. (03)3663-8788. Open 10am to 6pm. Closed Sunday.* Ozu is a calligrapher's paradise with hundreds of papers to choose from. It also sells stationery and small paper gift items.

· **Haibara**, *2-7-6 Nihonbashi, Chuo-ku. Tel. (03)3272-3801. Open 9:30am to 5pm. Closed Sunday and holidays.* A good selection of Japanese paper craft items and stationery.

· **Heiando**, *3-10-11 Nihonbashi, Chuo-ku. Tel. (03)3770-3641. Open 10am to 6pm. Closed Sunday and holidays.* Exquisite lacquer ware.

SHOPPING IN ROPPONGI & NEIGHBORING DISTRICTS

· **Kurofune**, *7-7-4 Roppongi, Minato-ku. Tel. (03)3479-1552. Open 10am to 6pm. Closed Sunday.* Kurofune (Black Ship), run by American John Adair, has an impeccable collection of antique *tansu* chests and ceramic hibachi – many museum-quality.

· **Art Plaza Magatani**, *5-10-13 Toranomon, Minato-ku. Tel. (03)3433-6321. Open 10am to 6pm. Closed Sunday and holidays.* Magatani resembles a junk store with goods cluttering every surface, but there's a wide variety of Japanese antiques, including dolls.

- **Japan Sword**, *3-8-1 Toranomon, Minato-ku. Tel. (03)3434-4321. Open 9:30am to 6pm weekdays, 9:30am to 5pm Saturday. Closed Sunday and holidays.* This shop is more like a museum of traditional Japanese swords.
- **Axis Building**, *5-17-1 Roppongi, Minato-ku. Tel. (03)3587-2781. Most shops are closed Sunday.* This building has shops with modern designs including **Living Motif**, selling housewares; **Nuno**, selling contemporary Japanese textiles and clothes; **Kisso**, contemporary ceramics and **Bushy**, modern lacquer ware.
- **Boutique Yuya**, *6-15-2 Roppongi, Minato-ku. Tel. (03)5474-2097. Open 12 noon to 5pm or by appointment. Closed Sunday and holidays.* Stunning, one-of-a-kind contemporary clothing made from vintage kimono.
- **Blue and White**, *2-9-2 Azabu Juban, Minato-ku. Tel. (03)3451-0537. Open 10am to 6pm. Closed holidays.* Almost everything is this shop is blue and white: textiles, ceramics, paper, original clothing and other articles; you'll find some of the most creative items with a traditional feel that are available in Tokyo.
- **Hasebeya**, *1-5-24 Azabu Juban, Minato-ku. Tel. (03)3401-9998.* Carries high caliber antique *tansu* chests and decorative items.
- **Okura Oriental Art**, *3-3-14 Azabudai, Minato-ku. Tel. (03)3585-5309. Open 10am to 6pm. Closed Monday.* A good selection of *tansu* chests, porcelain and other Japanese antiques is available.
- **Kathryn Milan**, *3-1-14 Nishi Azabu, Minato-ku. Tel. (03)3408-1532. Open 10am to 6pm weekends and holidays, by appointment at other times.* Antique *tansu* chests and other items are beautifully displayed in an early 20th century house.
- **Wally Yonamine Pearls**, *4-11-8 Roppongi, Minato-ku, Tokyo. Tel. (03)3402-4001. Open 9:30am to 5:30pm. Closed Sunday and holidays.* This pearl shop is a favorite of the expat community.
- **Washikobo**, *1-8-10 Nishi-Azabu, Minato-ku. Tel. (03)3405-1841. Open 10am to 6pm. Closed Sunday and national holidays.* Filled with all kinds of Japanese paper, crafts and traditional toys from all over Japan. We can easily spend an hour browsing in this small shop. It's a great place to buy lightweight souvenirs.
- **Tolman Collection**, *2-2-18 Shiba Daimon, Minato-ku, 105. Tel. (03)3434-1300. Open 11am to 7pm. Closed Tuesday.* Housed in a former *geisha* residence, the gallery sells contemporary Japanese prints.
- **Tsukamoto**, *4-1-9 Roppongi, Minato-ku. Tel. (03)3403-3747.* An excellent selection of folk art pottery from Mashiko.
- **Tomoyo**, *Gody Building, 1F, 6-8-8 Roppongi, Minato-ku. Tel. (03)3479-1176. Open 9:30am to 6pm; until 4pm Saturday. Closed Sunday.* Original clothes and decorative items using traditional Japanese textiles.

SHOPPING IN SHIBUYA

Shibuya is actually wall-to-wall stores. There are lots of "fashion buildings" filled with small stores, an urban Japanese answer to shopping malls. Stop in Tokyu Plaza, 109 and Parco to see what they're all about.

DEPARTMENT STORES

• **Seibu**, North of Shibuya Station Hachiko Plaza. *Closed Wednesday. Tel. (03)3462-0111.*
• **Tokyu Toyoko**, At Shibuya Station. *Closed Thursday. Tel. (03)3477-3111.*
• **Tokyu Honten**, 10-minute walk west of Shibuya Station. *Closed Tuesday. Tel. (03)3477-3111.*
• **Marui**, One block down from Seibu. *Closed Wednesday. Tel. (03)3464-0101.*

OTHER STORES

• **Parco**, *15-1 Udagawa-cho, Shibuya-ku. Tel. (03)3464-5111. Open daily 10am to 8:30pm.* Chic fashion building.
• **Tokyu Hands**, *12-18 Udagawa-cho, Shibuya-ku. Tel. (03)5489-5111. Open 10am to 8pm. Closed some Wednesdays.* Don't miss the ultimate do-it-yourself shop.
• **Tower Records**, *1-22-14 Jinnan, Shibuya-ku. Tel. (03)3496-3661. Open daily 10am to 10pm.* World's largest record shop — actually, it only has CDs and tapes. The bookstore has an excellent selection of English-language books, magazines and newspapers from around the world at Tokyo's best prices.
• **Beniya**, *2-16-8 Shibuya, Shibuya-ku. Tel. (03)3400-8084. Open 10am to 7pm. Closed Thursday.* Has a good selection of Japanese and Southeast Asian folk crafts.
• **Kuroda Toen**, *B1, Metro Plaza Building. Tel. (03)3499-3225. Open 11am to 7pm. Closed Sunday and holidays.* This shop has a good selection of unusual ceramic ware.
• **Marunan**, *2-5-1 Dogenzaka, Shibuya-ku. Tel. (03)3461-2325. Open daily 10am to 8:30pm.* Large fabric store that has a good selection of Japanese fabrics in the basement.
• **Uematsu**, *2-19-15 Shibuya, Shibuya-ku. Tel. (03)3400-5556. Open 10am to 7pm. Closed 1st and 3rd Sundays.* Across the bus plaza on the east side of Shibuya Station, Uematsu carries art supplies including special brushes and inks for Japanese calligraphy and *sumi-e* painting.

SHOPPING IN HARAJUKU, OMOTESANDO & AOYAMA

Takeshita Dori caters to junior high and high school students. The shops are filled with inexpensive clothing and jewelry.

Omotesando, a wide, tree lined boulevard, was made for browsing. Cafes, fashionable clothing stores and antique shops all vie for your attention.

The extension of Omotesando south of Aoyama Dori has a high concentration of fashion-designer boutiques. The From First Building on the right side, just before the Nezu Institute of Arts, has Issey Miyake, Jurgen Lehl and Masuda (Nicole) boutiques.

Kotto Dori is the street running from Kinokuniya Supermarket to the Fuji Film Building. Although many are being run out by fashion designers' shops, there are still some art dealers along this road, including **Morita Antiques** and **Karakusa**.

Some notable stores in these districts include:

• **Oriental Bazaar**, *5-9-13 Jingumae, on Omotesando. Tel. (03)3400-3933. Open 9:30am to 6:30pm. Closed Thursday.* It's touristy, but is the best place in town for one-stop souvenir shopping. Oriental Bazaar sells antiques and new items. Look for cotton *yukata* robes, vintage kimono, ceramics, *ukiyo-e* prints and much more. Mori Silver on the second floor has some of the most reasonable prices in town for pearls.

• **Fuji Torii Co**, *6-1-10 Jingumae, Shibuya-ku. Tel. (03)3400-2777. Open 11am to 6pm, Closed Thursday.* Sells antiques, screens, scrolls, lacquer, ceramics, lamps, furniture, woodblock prints, paper crafts and traditional stationery. Next to Kiddyland on Omotesando.

• **Kiddyland**, *6-1-9 Jingumae, Shibuya-ku. Tel. (03)3409-3431. Open 10am to 8pm. Closed 3rd Tuesday.* Five floors of toys for kids of all ages. Packed on weekends.

• **Ishii Collection**, *6-3-15 Minami Aoyama, Minato-ku. Tel. (03)3468-6683. Open 10:30am to 6:30pm.* Ishii is a tiny store with antique *tansu* chests.

• **Honjo Gallery**, *Palace Aoyama Building, 6-l-6 Minami Aoyama, Minato-ku. Tel. (03)3400-0277. Open 10:30am to 5pm; 12 noon to 4pm Sunday. Closed Monday.* Honjo sells *ukiyo-e* woodblock prints and contemporary and traditional art objects.

• **Japan Traditional Craft Center**, *Plaza 246 Building, 2F, 3-1-1-Minami Aoyama, Minato-ku. Tel. (03)3403-2460. Open 10am to 6pm. Closed Thursday and December 29 through January 4.* An excellent selection of crafts from all over Japan.

The basement of the Hanae Mori Building is a center for antiques. Small shops sell Western and Japanese antiques. **Beniya** (different from the Shibuya craft shop) has a good selection of *ukiyo-e* woodblock prints; **Kikori** has antique *tansu* chests. Look also for the corner shop, **Komon Aizome Sei**, selling blue and white traditional textiles and clothing.

SHOPPING IN SHINJUKU

Shinjuku is one large shopping center with a half-dozen department stores and countless smaller shops.

DEPARTMENT STORES

- **Keio**, At Shinjuku Station's west exit. *Closed Thursday. Tel. (03)3342-2111.*
- **Odakyu**, At Shinjuku Station's west exit. *Closed Tuesday. Tel. (03)3342-1111.* Odakyu Halc has an excellent selection of furniture.
- **Mitsukoshi**, On Shinjuku Dori, east of Shinjuku Station. *Closed Monday. Tel. (03)3354-1111.*
- **Isetan**, On Shinjuku Dori, east of Shinjuku Station. *Closed Wednesday. Tel. (03)3352-1111.* Foreign Customer Service: (03)3225-2514.
- **Marui**, On Shinjuku Dori, east of Shinjuku Station. *Closed Wednesday. Tel. (03)3354-0101.*
- **Takashimaya**, In Times Square Building, south exit of Shinjuku Station. *Closed Wednesday. Tel. (03)5361-1111.*

OTHER STORES

Times Square Building, *Shinjuku South, 5-24-2 Sendagaya, Shibuya-ku.* We don't know where its name came from, but it has nothing to do with New York. It's a shopper's paradise containing Takashimaya Department Store, Kinokuniya Book Store, Tokyu Hands do-it-yourself shop, HMV Record Shop, game arcade Joyopolis, an IMAX theater, and 28 restaurants.

Discount electronic shops are **Yodobashi Camera** at Shinjuku Station west exit and **Sakuraya** on Shinjuku Dori east of Shinjuku Station.

Bingoya, *10-6 Wakamatsu-cho Shinjuku-ku. Tel. (03)3202-8778. Open 10am to 7pm. Closed Monday.* Take bus #74 towards Tokyo Joshidai from Shinjuku Station's west exit. Get off at the 8th stop, Kawada-cho. For the Japan folk craft lover, Bingoya is a dream come true. Though located at an odd place, it's worth the detour. The five-storied small building is packed with folk crafts: natural color hemp cloth, blue and white fabrics, hand-woven material from all over Japan, delicate bamboo baskets, intriguing straw work, ceramics for daily use, fascinating folk toys, hand-made paper, beautiful paper lanterns, and folk style furniture. It's easy to spend money and time. And, if you find you bought too much to carry, ship your purchases directly abroad.

SHOPPING IN ASAKUSABASHI-RYOGOKU

Asakusabashi's shops sell wrapping paper and other paper goods, Japanese dolls, toys and seasonal decorations at incredibly cheap prices.

Shimojima is the largest paper goods shop and has several stores along Edo Dori. Japanese dolls in cases for Girls' and Children's Days are the specialty of a half-dozen stores on Edo Dori including **Kyugetsu, Yoshitoku, Shugetsu** and **Kuramae Ningyo-sha**.

Some notable stores in this district include:

• **Sakura Horikiri**, *1-25-3 Yanagibashi. Taito-ku. Tel. (03)3864-1773. Open 9:30am to 5:30pm. Closed Sunday and holidays.* The shop is stocked with paper kits and paper to make attractive craft items such as sets of drawers. You can choose among 800 different papers and, if you wish, assemble the kit in the store. The staff speaks some English and there are English instructions to take home. This activity is great for a rainy day. From Asakusabashi Station, walk north on Edo Dori; turn right after Kyugetsu Doll Store and it's on far left corner of second block.

• **Glass Land Tokyo**, *3-27-8 Asakusabashi, Taito-ku. Tel. (03)5821-5115. Open 10am to 6pm.* From Asakusabashi Station, walk north on Edo Dori and turn left onto Kuramae Bashi Dori. It's three blocks down on the left. This outlet store for Sasaki Crystal offers some of the best deals in town on stemware and other glass items.

• **Ryogoku Takahashi Company**, *4-31-15 Ryogoku, Sumida-ku. Tel. (03)3631-2420.* This shop is loaded with inexpensive sumo wrestling souvenirs.

SHOPPING IN ASAKUSA

Asakusa has many shops selling traditional Japanese goods; we've listed them above under the Asakusa section in *Seeing the Sights*.

SHOPPING IN OCHANOMIZU

• **Origami Kaikan**, *1-7-14 Yushima, Taito-ku. Tel. (03)3811-4025. Open 9am to 5pm. Closed Sunday and holidays.* One of the best places for Japanese *washi* paper, Origami Kaikan sells *yuzen* paper (patterns printed on paper). It also has paper for calling cards, stationery and origami. Make sure you see the second showroom that's downstairs from the main room.

TOKYO'S SPECIALIZED MARKETS

Tokyo's shops believe in the motto "birds of a feather flock together." Here are some of the areas where similar shops cluster.

Akihabara. Dizzying array of discount electronics, computers and household appliances. Akihabara Station on JR Yamanote and JR Sobu lines.

Asakusabashi. Wrapping paper, boxes, artificial flowers, toys and Japanese dolls. Asakusabashi Station on the JR Sobu line.

Hanakawado. Shoes, shoes and more shoes. The district started by selling traditional footwear like geta and zori, but has branched out. On Edo Dori near Asakusa. Asakusa Station on Ginza subway line.

Jimbocho. New, secondhand and rare books, prints and maps. Jimbocho Station on Tozai subway line.

Kappabashi. Restaurant supply district. Come here for plastic food models, tableware, kitchen utensils, pots, uniforms and anything else the restaurant trade desires. Tawaramachi Station on the Ginza subway line.

Musashi Koyama. Covered shopping street selling inexpensive clothes, household items, toys and secondhand furniture. Musashi Koyama Station on the Mekama line – two stops from Meguro.

Nippori. Everything for sewing: fabric, notions and patterns. On Nippori Chuo Dori. Nippori Station on JR Yamanote line.

Okachimachi. Jewelry in all price ranges, including small diamond, emerald and pearl districts. Under and west of the tracks heading south from Okachimachi Station on the JR Yamanote line

Togoshi Ginza. Sells inexpensive toys, clothes and household articles. Japanese go there for bargain shopping. Togoshi Ginza Station on the Ikegami line – two stops from Gotanda Station.

Tsukiji Outer Market. Sells kitchen utensils, knives, dishes, and anything else chefs may need. Tsukiji Station on Hibiya subway line.

18. EXCURSIONS & DAY TRIPS

Sharing space with 25 million people in the greater Tokyo area makes even the most avid urbanite itch to get out of town. Fortunately, within an hour or two are charming places where you can take in gorgeous scenery, breathe fresh air and rejuvenate yourself.

While we do list some hotels and inns, most of these trips assume that your home base will be Tokyo, so refer to Chapter 12 for places to stay.

GREAT SIDE TRIPS FROM TOKYO

- *The cosmopolitan, international city of Yokohama*
- *The Great Buddha at Kamakura*
- *Hakone's hot springs and Open Air Museum*
- *MOA Museum of Art in Atami, one of Japan's finest*
- *The quiet port town of Shimoda*
- *Nikko's ornate Toshogu Shrine*
- *The quiet hot spring resort and unique "exiles cuisine" of Yunishigawa*
- *The splendid ceramics museum in Ashikaga*
- *The studio of a charming ambassador of indigo dyeing near Ashikaga*

YOKOHAMA

Just 18 kilometers south of Tokyo, **Yokohama**, Japan's second largest city, is often overlooked next to high-profile Tokyo. The delightful cosmopolitan city faces the waterfront. And, as one of the first ports to reopen to foreigners (1859) after the long period of isolation, Yokohama's engaging history begs for further exploration.

American Commodore Mathew Perry landed with his Black Ships in Yokohama in 1854, one year after he demanded the Tokugawa shogunate

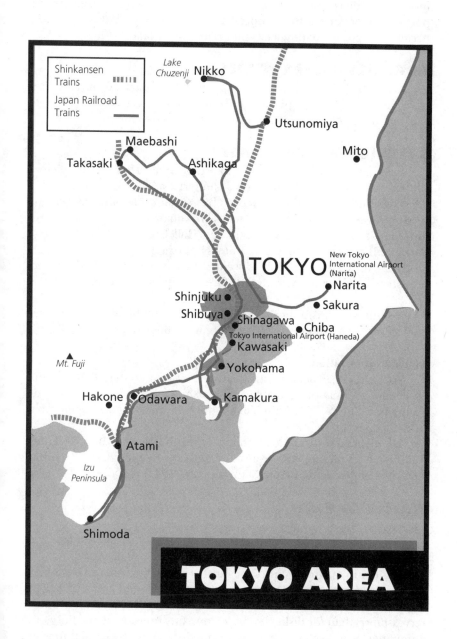

Shinkansen Trains

Japan Railroad Trains

Lake Chuzenji

Nikko

Utsunomiya

Mito

Maebashi

Takasaki

Ashikaga

TOKYO

New Tokyo International Airport (Narita)

Narita

Shinjuku

Shibuya

Sakura

Shinagawa

Chiba

Tokyo International Airport (Haneda)

Kawasaki

Mt. Fuji

Yokohama

Hakone

Odawara

Kamakura

Atami

Izu Peninsula

Shimoda

TOKYO AREA

open up Japan to trade. The shogunate complied. Yokohama soon grew into one of the largest ports in Asia and had a wild-west atmosphere. As port-of-call for American, European and Chinese ships, Yokohama soon became a very international city and remains so today.

ARRIVALS & DEPARTURES

Accessible by train from Tokyo, the trip takes a mere 30 minutes. You have the choice of the JR Keihin Tohoku line, JR Yokosuka line, JR Tokaido line, Tokyu Toyoko line and Keihin Kyuko line.

GETTING AROUND TOWN

Yokohama has excellent mass transit systems. There's a municipal subway, numerous train lines, buses and ferries.

The Blue Line, a double-decker bus system, provides convenient service for sightseeing. The route is Yokohama Station, Yokohama Museum of Art, Sakuragicho Station, City Hall, Chinatown, Harbor View Park and Bay Bridge. The return route is Bay Bridge, MYCAL Honmoku, Motomachi, Yokohama Doll Museum, Yamashita Park, Sakuragicho Station and Yokohama Station. The fare is ¥270 and a one-day pass costs ¥600.

A shuttle boat, Sea Bass, runs every 15 minutes between Yokohama Station and Yamashita Park. 10am to 6pm. ¥600.

Tourist Information

Yokohama has been an international city for so long that there is excellent information available in English. The tourist offices are at **Yokohama Station** and **Shin Yokohama Station**. Both are open daily from 10am to 6pm.

The **Central Information Office** is on the first floor of the Silk Center Building, a 15-minute walk from Kannai Station. Open 8:45am to 5pm weekdays and 8:45am to 1pm Saturdays, *Tel. (045)641-5824.*

WHERE TO EAT

Chinatown

MANCHINRO TENSHINPO *(Chinese dim sum, moderate), 156 Yamashita-cho. Tel. (045)664-4004. Open daily 10 am to 10pm.*

Manchinro has to be one of the most popular dim sum restaurants in Chinatown. Even with a reservation, you'll probably end up waiting 15 to 30 minutes. Still, it's worth the hassle for the tasty dim sum. Manchinro serves more than 70 dishes: some of our favorites are shark fin *gyoza* dumplings, scallop *gyoza*, steamed shrimp dumplings, steamed tofu with shrimp and spring rolls. For ¥3500 to ¥4000, you'll have plenty to eat.

SAIKO SHINKAN *(Chinese dim sum, inexpensive), 192 Yamashita-cho. Tel. (045)664-3155. Open 11:30am to 9pm. Closed 3rd Thursday.*
This dim sum restaurant is another favorite. We especially like mixed rice wrapped and steamed in leaves and crab meat *gyoza*. You can order a dim sum set for ¥3000.

Minato Mirai
LA VELA *(Italian, moderate), 2F, Intercontinental Hotel, 1-1-1 Minato Mirai, Nishi-ku. Tel. (045)223-2222. Open 11:30am to 2pm, until 5:30pm weekends; 5:30pm to 9:30pm.*
This is a wonderful place to eat and take in the exhilarating views of Yokohama Bay through the large picture windows. The food is authentic Italian fare. The lunchtime set (¥3200) has a salad and appetizer buffet and a dessert buffet; you select your entree.

SEEING THE SIGHTS
Negishi Station Area
Sankeien Garden. *Open daily 9am to 4:30pm. Closed December 29-31. ¥300 for outer garden and ¥300 for inner garden. From JR Negishi Station, take a bus 10 minutes to Honmoku stop. 6-minute walk. Or from JR Negishi Station, 7-minute taxi ride. Or from Yokohama Station's east exit, take bus #2 or #125 to Honmoku Sankeien mae (about 35 minutes).*
Located in a highly industrialized area, Sankeien is an oasis of rolling green hills, ponds, bridges and traditional Japanese buildings. The wealthy silk merchant Hara Tomitaro founded Sankeien in 1906. The inner garden houses an excellent collection of historic buildings moved from all over Japan. Since Japanese houses are constructed of wood without using nails, they are easily moved from place to place. The Rinshunkaku is a villa of the Tokugawa shogun. The Juto Oido is one of the few buildings remaining from Tenzui-ji Temple in Kyoto, built by Hideyoshi in 1591. At the direction of the second Tokugawa shogun, the Choshukaku was constructed in 1623 for Fushimi castle. The Yanohara house is an extremely well-preserved farmhouse. Sankeien is also famous for its flowering plants: plum, cherry, iris and water lilies and for colorful autumn foliage.

Sakuragicho Station Area
Minato Mirai 21 is a large, new futuristic development on the water complete with hotels, shopping, museums and an amusement park. A moving sidewalk whisks you — well, actually, crawls is more accurate — from JR Sakuragicho Station.
Among the park's attractions are:

Nippon Maru is a 29-sail tall ship constructed in 1930 as a training vessel. The graceful ship, as tall as a 12-storied building, is nicknamed the Swan of the Pacific. Now retired, it sits in dry dock and is open to the public. *Open 9am to 5pm. Closed Mondays and December 29-31. ¥600 (combined admission with Yokohama Maritime Museum).*

Next to the Nippon Maru is the **Yokohama Maritime Museum**, a beautifully laid-out underground museum that shows the history of the port of Yokohama from the time when Commodore Perry sailed his Black Ships and demanded Japan open trade. *Open 10am to 5pm; until 6:30 in July and August; until 4:30 in November and December. Closed Monday and December 29-31. ¥600 (combined admission with Nippon Maru).*

Yokohama Museum of Art (Yokohama Bijutsukan) houses art and photography from this century. *Tel. (045)221-0300. Open 10am to 6pm. Closed Thursday. ¥500 for permanent collection, additional charge for temporary exhibitions.*

Landmark Tower, a 70-storied skyscraper, is currently Asia's tallest building. The futuristic building looks like something from Sci-Fi movies. The 68th-floor Japanese restaurant Shikitei and Chinese restaurant Kouen both have fantastic nighttime views of the city and bay.

Cosmo World has some amusement rides left behind from the 1989 exposition. **Yokohama Gulliver Land**, under the world's largest wooden dome, sports a model of Yokohama in the 1960s and a futuristic view of the Minato Mirai project in 2010. The world's tallest **Ferris wheel** is here also. The 105-meter high wheel takes 15 minutes to go around once and offers great views from the top.

Kannai Station Area

Kanagawa Prefecture Museum of Cultural History (Kanagawa Kenritsu Rekishi Hakubutsukan). *5-60 Minaminaka Dori, Naka-ku. Tel. (045)201-0926. Open 9:30am to 5pm. Closed Monday, last Tuesday of the month and New Year's. ¥300. 8-minute walk from JR Kannai Station.*

It's a worthwhile stop just to see the fantastic 1904 Beaux Arts-style building – the oldest building extant in Yokohama, and there's an added bonus of the recently renovated museum that has excellent displays covering prehistory, the Kamakura period (the region's heyday), Edo culture, the Meiji era and modern Japan.

Yokohama Archives of History (Yokohama Kaiko Shiryokan). *3 Nihon Odori, Naka-ku. Tel. (045)201-2100. Open 9:30am to 5pm. Closed Monday and December 28 through January 4. ¥200.*

The archives, located at the site of the signing of the first friendship treaty between Japan and the US, is filled with exhibits showing Japan's encounter with the West during Yokohama's early days, the second half of the 19th century. History buffs will love it; all others should skip it.

Silk Center and Silk Museum. *1 Yamashita-cho, Naka-ku. Tel. (045)641-0841. Open 9am to 4:30pm. Closed Monday, last day of the month and New Year's. ¥300.*

Yokohama thrived on its silk industry at the turn of the century. There's a tourist information center on the first floor and a museum showing how to make silk is on the second and third floors. Buy your silk in the basement arcade.

Ishikawacho Station Area

Motomachi, accessible to Ishigawa-cho Station, catered to the foreign residents restricted to living in this area during Yokohama's early days. Today it is the city's toniest shopping district filled with boutiques, restaurants and bars. You can climb up the Bluff to **French Hill** (Furansu zaka) and **Harbor View Park** (Minato no Mieru Oka) for great views. The **Foreigner's Cemetery** (Gaijin Bochi) is a great place to wander and look at the tombstone inscriptions. *Open only Friday through Sunday in April and November, and Sunday and national holidays May through October.* The entire area has a very Western feel.

Yokohama Doll Museum (Yokohama Ningyo no Ie). *18 Yamashita-cho, Naka-ku. Tel. (045)671-9361. Open 10am to 5pm; until 7pm in July and August. Closed Monday and December 29 through January 1. ¥300. 13-minute walk from Ishikawacho Station.*

The museum has an excellent collection of dolls from all over the world. One room displays international dolls, another room Japanese. It's a delightful place for children or fans of dolls.

Yamashita Park, running along the waterfront for about one kilometer, is a great place for a stroll and some fresh sea air.

Chinatown is between Yamashita Park and Ishikawacho Station. The area is small but is packed with restaurants and shops selling Chinese goods. We've listed a couple of good restaurants under *Where to Eat*, but the best rule is to go to a place where people are standing in line.

Elsewhere in Yokohama

The **Skywalk** under the Yokohama Bay Bridge is not for the faint-hearted. An elevator carries you up to the observation deck where you walk along the Skywalk that's suspended under the bridge. At the end is the Sky Lounge where you can take in the spectacular panoramic view. When the weather is clear, you can see Mt. Fuji lording over the metropolitan area. *Tel. (045)506-0500. Open 9am to 9pm; 10am to 6pm November through March. Closed third Thursday. ¥600. The Blue Line double-decker bus stops here; from JR Sakuragicho Station, it's the last stop on the Skywalk bus.*

Yokohama Children's Science Center (Yokohama Kodomo Kagakukan). *5-2-1 Yokodai, Isogo-ku. Tel. (045)832-1166. Open 9:30am to 5pm. Closed Monday and December 28 through January 1. ¥400. Planetarium and Omnimax are each ¥600 extra. From Yokohama Station, take the JR Negishi line to Yokodai Station. 3-minute walk.*

The center puts science on a level that children can understand, and there're lots of hands-on exhibits and demonstrations about science and space. The space gym teaches about astronaut training, and the planetarium about space itself. Enjoy incredible films at the domed Omnimax theater where the seats are tilted at a 30° angle for maximum viewing pleasure.

YOKOHAMA'S THEME PARKS

Yokohama isn't all museums and parks – check out these theme parks:
WILD BLUE YOKOHAMA, *Tel. (045)511-2323. Open 10am to 9pm. ¥2900. From Tsurumi Station on JR Keihin Tohoku line, take a taxi for the 10-minute ride or the #16 bus from bus platform #5 to Heian Koko-mae bus stop.*

This indoor water park is great for older kids. Home to the longest indoor wave pool in the world, the waves change – some are good for boarding, others for swimming. The fan-shaped artificial beach even has lounge chairs. In addition to the standard beach, you'll find a waterway – a circular pool with constant current; a kiddies' lagoon – a shallow pool for infants; and a party lagoon – an outdoor pool with waterfall and water slides. And, because most of the park is under cover, you never have to worry about being rained out or sunburned. Try it on weekdays because weekends are crowded. And avoid the Japanese school holidays.

***YOKOHAMA HAKKEIJIMA SEA PARADISE**, Hakkeijima, Kanazawa-ku. Tel. (045)788-8888. Open daily 10am to 9pm but varies with the season. Aqua Museum: ¥2400. Rides: ¥300 to ¥1000. No admission charge to enter the island. Take the Keihin Kyuko line to Yokohama and change for the Seaside line to Hakkeijima. (55 minutes from Shinagawa Station).*

A new theme park on a reclaimed island, Sea Paradise has a large aquarium with dolphin, seal and sea lion shows. Their signature Sea Tube has an escalator that forms a tunnel to travel through the huge fish tank. As you ascend, fish swim all around you. For an additional fee, the island also features amusement rides. There're lots of stores and a variety of restaurants. In case you have your yacht with you, there's even a marina.

KAMAKURA

Kamakura was the shogun's capital from 1192 to 1333 and gave its name to the epoch. This small town, just a one-hour train ride south of central Tokyo, is the perfect place for a side trip. Surrounded on three sides by low mountains and on the fourth by the sea, verdant Kamakura feels a million miles from Tokyo. Most of Kamakura's residents commute to Tokyo, but the town is much more than just a suburb. It has an air of quiet greatness — over 100 temples, built in its heyday, still remain. Kamakura's most famous landmark is the **Daibutsu**, the Great Buddha, which stands 13 meters tall.

If you have at least three days in Tokyo, make sure you spend one of them in Kamakura. For those looking to stretch their legs, hiking trails in the hills link temples together. But there's also plenty to see in the flatlands.

ARRIVALS & DEPARTURES

The JR Yokosuka line leaves from Tokyo Station every 15 minutes. You can also board it at Shimbashi, Shinagawa and Yokohama Stations. The train takes about an hour from central Tokyo. Get off at Kamakura Station or Kita Kamakura Station.

Tourist Information

The **Tourist Information Office** is located in Kamakura Station and has maps and brochures in English. Open daily 9am to 6pm, *Tel. (0467)22-3350.*

WHERE TO EAT

Kamakura, a center for Zen Buddhism for hundreds of years, has many restaurants that serve vegetarian Buddhist food, *shojin ryori.* Try it in a peaceful setting. You don't have to eat only temple food. Restaurants dish up everything from French and Italian to Indian. Although most visitors to Kamakura come for the day and leave before eating dinner, some places require dinner reservations.

HISAGOTEI *(Tofu cuisine, moderate), 3-8-7 Komachi. Tel. (0467)24-1882. Open daily 11:30am to 8pm, if they don't have any reservations for dinner they close at 6pm. 15-minute walk from Kamakura Station.*

The chef, a tofu lover, prides himself on serving excellent tofu. You can get it here in every conceivable form: steamed, jellied, pureed and cooked with fish and seasonal vegetables. Located in a quiet area off Wakamiya-oji, the main drag, Hisagotei is a lovely restaurant where you can enjoy a relaxing meal while overlooking a green garden with many hydrangeas. The *Hagi-zen,* a seven course set, costs ¥5000.

MONZEN *(Buddhist vegetarian, moderate), 407 Yamanouchi. Tel.* *(0467)25-1121. Open daily 11am to 7:30pm.*

Monzen caters *shojin ryori* at Kencho-ji Temple for large annual religious rituals, so there's no question about its authenticity. A set meal consists of nine different dishes, rice and soup and costs ¥5000. We're always amazed how many different ingredients are used to create the famous Zen five tastes — sweet, sour, salty, hot and bitter; five different cooking methods — raw, simmer, fry, grill and steam; and five different colors — yellow, blue, red, white and black. Monzen serves you at tables or in Japanese rooms. No need to make a reservation.

SA-AMI *(Buddhist vegetarian, moderate), 2-4-4 Jomyoji. Tel. (0467)24-9420 Open 11am to 4pm. You can make reservations for dinner. Closed Thursday.*

Sa-ami is on the right as you approach Hokoku-ji, the Zen temple where the chef learned to prepare special Buddhist vegetarian cuisine. He selects each vegetable and carefully cuts, cooks and serves it. He uses time-consuming procedures to produce high-quality fare; it takes one night to make perfect *goma dofu* (sesame tofu). The seven course *Honzen* costs ¥4000. Order the *tenshin* set for vegetarian dim sum for ¥2000. The food is so healthy, we can't help but feel virtuous after eating here. It's best to make lunch reservations because Sa-ami is popular.

HACHINOKI *(Buddhist vegetarian, moderate), 7 Yamanouchi. Tel. (0467)22-8719. Open 11am to 5pm. Closed Monday.*

Hachinoki, which opened in the early 1960s, is one of the oldest *shojin ryori* restaurants in Kita Kamakura. The mother of the current owner was very creative with her vegetarian menus and the tradition continues. Specialties include tofu with nuts and bamboo shoots cooked in an original sauce. The restaurant has a lovely garden setting. The set course, which changes monthly, offers seven different dishes, rice and soup for ¥3000. As it tends to sell out quickly, it's best to arrive before noon. Reservations accepted only from groups of ten or more. There's also a branch just a few minutes walk from Kita Kamakura station at *350 Yamanouchi, Kamakura.*

A RICCIONE *(Italian, inexpensive to moderate), B1, Komachi Building, 2-12-30 Komachi. Tel. (0467)24-5491. Open daily 11am to 9:30pm.*

A branch of the Milan restaurant, A Riccione has delicious home-made pasta and lots of seafood. The wine list is quite extensive. Set meals begin at ¥2500.

MONTE COSTA *(Italian, inexpensive to moderate), 1-5-7 Yukinoshita. Tel. (0467)23-0808. Open 11am to 8pm. Closed Monday and 3rd Tuesday.*

This older house combines traditional Japanese and Western architecture, creating a unique ambiance. All rooms look out onto a small garden. The chef goes to the market every morning to select the freshest seafood; he recommends patrons order a la carte. We love the herb marinated seafood, ¥1500. Italian *kaiseki* course costs ¥5000. Monte Costa is rather crowded at lunchtime; it is advisable to make a reservation. The restaurant is located just off Komachi Dori.

MIYOKAWA *(Kaiseki, inexpensive), 1-16-17 Hase, Kamakura. Tel. (0467)25-5556. Open daily 11am to 9pm.*

This elegant restaurant has surprisingly inexpensive lunch fare. The most popular set meal is *Hyotan Bento* at ¥2300, a lunch presented in a lacquered, gourd-shaped container. It's a treat for the eyes. You can eat at tables or in *tatami* mat rooms. Since Miyokawa is close to the Great Buddha, it is always crowded, so it's best to make reservations.

SEEING THE SIGHTS
A First-Trip Itinerary

Kamakura has 69 temples and 20 shrines, but for a first-time visit, we think it's best to limit yourself to just a few. One itinerary is to see the **Great Buddha**, **Hase Temple** and **Tsurugaoka Hachimangu Shrine**, leaving time to walk to the water's edge as well as browse in Kamakura's many antique and craft shops.

At Kamakura Station, you can either take a taxi (about a 10-minute ride; tell the driver "Daibutsu" — Die-boot-su) or a tram. To go by tram, do not leave Kamakura Station when you get off the train. Take the Enoden tram — you'll have to turn in your train tickets at a little window and buy a new ticket to Hase Station. Take the tram three stops to Hase Station, about five minutes. We love this little tram that practically runs through the backyards of houses along the tracks.

At Hase Station, turn in your ticket and walk along the road towards the right for about four blocks until the souvenir shops end and a wooden gate is on your right. This gate is the entrance to **Kotoku-in**, which houses the **Great Buddha**.

Serene and pensive, the Great Buddha sits surrounded by the Kamakura hills. With the help of a priest, a court lady raised the funds to make a Buddha. Completed in 1243, it was destroyed in a storm not five years later. The determined lady once again raised funds and a new bronze Buddha was completed inside a large wooden hall in 1252. That building was damaged several times. Clearly the Buddha wanted to be outdoors, and in 1495 a great tidal wave swept away the wooden building. The Great Buddha has remained exposed to the elements ever since. His face gives the impression of calmness and discipline. You may notice that the statue seems ill proportioned from a distance, which is true because it was designed to be viewed from about five feet in front.

For ¥20, you can go inside the Buddha. There actually isn't much to see inside the hollow bronze figure, but you may want to try it. After all, how many other times can you go inside a Buddha? Be sure to notice the giant straw sandals hanging on the building wall next to the Buddha. These are for the Buddha in case he wants to get up and walk. To the best of our knowledge, he hasn't used them yet. *The temple is open daily from 7am to 6pm; until 5pm October through March. ¥200.*

As you exit the temple, turn left and walk along the street leading back to the tram. Turn right two blocks down; after one block, this road dead ends at the entrance gate of **Hase Kannon Temple**. Pass through a small garden with pond and climb the stairs to reach the main area of the temple. Hase's origins date to the 8th century and the eleven-faced Kannon statue is believed to predate the temple. It stands 9.3 meters and is Japan's tallest wooden statue. To the right of the main hall is an octagonal prayer wheel; one turn is supposed to be as good as reading the sutras in the hall.

Since you've climbed up all the stairs, walk over to the area with tables. From this vantage point you have a good view of the sea that's often dotted with windsurfers. There's a small snack bar where you can get noodles and sweets.

On the grounds of the temple you can't help noticing hundreds and hundreds of small statues, many with small bibs, toys and pinwheels. These are Jizo, the guardian of children, and are placed to pacify the spirits of children never born because of miscarriage and abortion. *Hase Kannon Temple is open 8am to 5pm. ¥300.*

Leave the temple and walk back to the main street; turn right and you will reach the Enoden tram that will take you back to Kamakura. If you want to see the beach, the same street will lead you toward Yuigahama Beach. Waikiki it isn't, but being one of the closest beaches to Tokyo means it's unbearably crowded with sunseekers and windsurfers in summer, especially on weekends. On sunny winter days, it's a lovely place to feel the warmth of the sun.

Retrace your steps to the tram to Kamakura Station.

At Kamakura station, use the east exit, the one on the right side of the station. As you exit to a large plaza with lots of buses, on the left there's a small street called **Komachi Dori**. Just before you come to Komachi Dori is **Toshimaya**, a shop usually crowded with Japanese buying their famous dove-shaped cookies, a mandatory souvenir from Kamakura. The smallest packet costs ¥450. Walk along Komachi Dori past antique and craft stores, tucked among other shops. It's also packed with restaurants, both traditional and modern, and lots of coffee shops where you can rest your tired feet.

Along this road, on the left is **Mon**, a comfortable coffee shop displaying works by local artists; **Yamago** selling bamboo craft items; and **Shato**, a tiny store stuffed with colorful Japanese *washi* paper and crafts.

On the right past Shato is **Takahashi**, which sells bamboo baskets, garden gates and wooden garden tools.

When the stores along the road give way to greenery, turn right and you will reach the entrance to **Tsurugaoka Hachimangu Shrine**, founded by the Minamoto clan in 1063. Pass through the vermilion gate and you will reach a red drum-shaped bridge. In the old days, only the shogun was allowed to cross it. But you don't have to try negotiating the bridge's steep slopes because it's flanked by two flat bridges — how did the shogun do it?

When shogun Minamoto Yoritomo's wife, Hojo Masako, was pregnant, he ordered a grand boulevard constructed so the new prince could arrive in style for his blessing at the shrine. The large avenue, **Wakamiya Oji** (Young Prince Avenue), leads from the sea to the shrine. The median is planted with cherry trees and azaleas and is a favorite flower viewing place for Japanese.

Yoritomo's wife Masako was one of the most powerful women in Japanese history. Her husband and two sons died before her, so she and her father ran the country.

IN THE QUIET COURTYARD OF TSURUGAOKA HACHIMANGU SHRINE

Dramatic events in Japanese history occurred in the shrine's courtyard – the area where there's a covered dance platform and steep, stone steps leading to Tsurugaoka Hachimangu Shrine's main buildings. The shogun Minamoto Yoritomo turned against his half-brother Yoshitsune, who wasted no time fleeing. Yoritomo captured his brother's lover, Shizuka, a beauty famed for her dancing. He ordered her to dance for him, and she defiantly performed a dance praising her lover. Yoritomo was so angered that he ordered her killed, but his wife Masako interceded to spare Shizuka's life.

As you climb the steps, on your left is a huge ginko tree that also played an important role in history. In 1219 the third Kamakura shogun was assassinated there by a disgruntled nephew who was hiding behind the tree. There were no heirs; the Kamakura shogunate ended! Power passed from the Minamoto to the Hojo clan and Kamakura remained the capital. In the autumn the tree's golden colors brighten up the area.

In contrast to the spacious lower grounds, the actual shrine buildings at the top of the steps are crowded together and not worth much time. However, there are two museums on the shrine's lower grounds worth visiting.

The first is the **Kanagawa Museum of Modern Art** (Kanagawa Kenritsu Kindai Bijutsukan), which was designed by a Japanese disciple of Le Corbusier. The museum holds Japanese and international contemporary art exhibits. *Tel. (0467)22-5000. Open 9:30am to 4:30pm. Closed Monday. ¥800.*

The **Treasure House** (Kokuhokan) is on the opposite side of the shrine's grounds. A stop here is a must for anyone interested in Kamakura-era art; it houses sculptures and paintings, many belonging to the temples scattered around Kamakura. The sculpture of this era was dynamic and vigorous. *Tel. (0467)22-0753. Open 9am to 4pm. Closed Monday. ¥150.*

As you walk down Wakamiya Oji, stop to browse in the shops selling the local specialty, Kamakura *bori* (carved lacquer ware). Turn right at Kamakura Station to catch the train to Tokyo.

Overachiever's Itinerary — An Alternative Walking Tour

If you are filled with energy and want to see lots of temples, get an early start and take the JR Yokosuka train to Kita Kamakura Station, one stop before Kamakura. Near the station are three quiet temples:

Engaku-ji Temple is one of Kamakura's five great Zen temples. It goes back to 1282 and was built for the souls of the soldiers killed during Kublai Khan's invasion. Today it is only a shadow of its former self and most of the buildings are recent reconstructions. The large wooden gate, built in 1780, gives some hint of its former grandeur. The grounds are large with many subtemples, so allow yourself 30 to 60 minutes if you want to get a good feel for a Zen temple. The tiny Chinese-style Sharidan was built in 1285 and houses a relic from the Buddha. The wood joinery is simply fantastic. *Open 8am to 5:30pm; until 4pm in winter. ¥200.*

Tokei-ji Temple, founded in the 13th century, was known as the divorce temple. It was a Buddhist nunnery where women could seek refuge from abusive husbands. A man could divorce his wife by just writing a letter to her, but a woman did not have a similar right. After residing at Tokei-ji for three years, a woman was divorced. It was a sanctuary until the end of the Edo period. The narrow, stone steps leading to the temple gate lead to a small quiet garden. We can't ever visit without imagining those women who must have run up those steps knowing they would be safe if they reached the top. Today, women visit to pray to rid themselves of persistent unsuitable suitors and to find Mr. Right. *Open 8:30 daily am to 5pm; until 4pm November through February. ¥50 for the garden, ¥300 for the Treasure House.*

Meigetsu-in is also known as the Hydrangea temple because there are thousands of flowers that bloom in June. Masses of pink, blue, purple and white hydrangeas line the stone steps leading to the gate and to the garden. The bamboo groves accentuate the beauty of the flowers in the garden. There are also thousands of people who come to see them. If you want to see the temple at the height of its beauty, try to arrive early in the morning. At other times of the year, the temple is practically deserted. *Open daily 9 am to 4:30pm. ¥300.*

Walk along the main road for about 15 minutes from Kita Kamakura Station and you'll reach **Kencho-ji Temple**, the first and grandest of Kamakura's five great Zen temples and founded in 1253. The extensive grounds have many subtemples scattered about. To enjoy a lovely Japanese garden, go to Hojo, the abbot's quarters, which is the last of the main buildings in a straight line from the main gate, itself the finest wooden structure in Kamakura. Take off your shoes and walk along the wooden balcony that leads to the garden; its design is attributed to the priest Muso Kokushi who designed Tenryu-ji Temple in Kyoto. This garden incorporates bushes and trees and a pond. If you are full of energy, climb up the narrow, 245 steps and walk until you reach the peak of the hill. It's an exercise that Zen priests must have done for centuries; the breezes at the top feel so refreshing. *Open 8:30am to 4:30pm. ¥300.*

Leave Kencho-ji and continue to walk along the main road — it's busy and noisy, but there is no other way. In about 10 minutes you'll reach the upper part of **Tsurugaoka Hachimangu Shrine**, which is described in our first walking tour.

From the shrine, walk down wide Wakamiya Oji or Komachi Dori, which runs parallel and is the road to the right. When you reach Kamakura Station, catch the Enoden tram or take a taxi to the Great Buddha, following the course set out in the first walking tour.

Zeni-arai Benten & Hokoku-ji Temple
A couple of other favorite places in Kamakura are the following:

In the hills to the west of Hachimangu Shrine lies **Zeni-arai Benten**, a small, colorful shrine tucked in a mountain grotto. It's very popular with Japanese because it's believed that money washed there will double in value. There are even baskets to make the process easier. Yen or foreign money can be washed; next time we're going to try credit cards.

Hokoku-ji Temple was built at the end of the Kamakura period. The temple's bamboo garden, the ground covered by fallen bamboo leaves, is a little off-the-beaten path but a beautiful place to visit. We love to watch the rays of sunlight streaming through the thick foliage. You can sit and have a cup of tea in the serene setting. *From Kamakura Station take the #4 Keihin Kyuko bus. Get off at Jomyo-ji and walk for about five minutes. Open 9am to 4pm. ¥200.*

SHOPPING

Komachi Dori and **Wakamiya Oji** have shops selling antiques, bamboo crafts, Japanese paper and Kamakura *bori*, local lacquer ware.

Serious collectors of Japanese art should make an appointment to visit **House of Antiques**, a beautifully converted farmhouse, which is a store selling screens, furniture and other Japanese antiques. *Phone Mr. Takishita at (0467)43-1441. 5-15-5 Kajiwara, Kamakura.*

HAKONE & MT. FUJI

A mere hour southwest of Tokyo, **Hakone** is the city's playground. Tokyo's urban sprawl suddenly stops at the mountains. Tokyoites go there to breathe clean air and get back in touch with nature. The resort area has something for everyone: hiking, boating, hot springs, golfing, art museums and splendid views of **Mt. Fuji**.

You can make Hakone a one-day trip, but start early to get the most out of your day. If you can spare the time, Hakone is a good place to stay overnight to see what a Japanese hot spring area is all about.

ARRIVALS & DEPARTURES

Hakone is a large area covering many mountains and towns. The most convenient gateway is the town of **Hakone Yumoto**.

The fastest way to get to Hakone, and the recommended route for rail pass holders, is to take the JR *Kodama* (local) shinkansen train from Tokyo Station to Odawara, about 30 minutes, and change for the Odakyu private rail line to Hakone Yumoto, 10 minutes. The less expensive Tokaido local train takes 1 hour and 30 minutes from Tokyo Station to Odawara.

If you aren't using a rail pass, the best way to Hakone is to take the private Odakyu train line from Shinjuku Station to Hakone Yumoto. The Romance Car (their name, not ours) is an all-reserved-seat express that takes 1 hour 25 minutes to Hakone Yumoto. The Odakyu express to Odawara takes 90 minutes; then it's another 10 minutes to Hakone Yumoto; some of the trains go all the way through to Hakone Yumoto.

One word of warning: Traffic on Hakone's narrow mountain roads often backs up on weekends and holidays. If you have the choice of taking a bus or train, opt for the train. We have inched along in buses for hours; it sure is frustrating. If you have the option, go midweek.

Hakone Free Pass

If you plan to travel around the Hakone area, purchase the **Hakone Free Pass** or the **Hakone Weekday Pass** available at Odakyu train ticket offices and through travel agents. Even if you are going to Hakone for only one day, you won't have to buy separate tickets for all the different conveyances. If you plan to go to Hakone and only spend time at Hakone Yumoto, you don't need to buy the pass.

The Free Pass is good for travel for three days on Odakyu trains, the Hakone Tozan Railway, the Sounzan cable car, the Hakone Ropeway, the boat on Lake Ashinoko and Hakone Tozan buses. The Weekday Pass is good for two days of travel Monday through Friday on these same modes of transportation. JR rail pass holders should buy the Hakone pass to start in Odawara: the Free Pass costs ¥4050 and the Weekday Pass ¥3340. If you are starting your travel from Shinjuku Station, the Free Pass costs ¥5400 and the Weekday Pass ¥4600; each includes round-trip transportation on the Odakyu line from Shinjuku Station. The Odakyu's Romance Car surcharge is an additional ¥850 each way. Free Pass and Weekday Pass holders are entitled to small admission discounts at many museums.

Tourist Information
The **Hakone Tourist Information Office** is about one block from Hakone Yumoto Station. Go out the exit onto the plaza and walk up the main road; Tourist Information is on the left, next to the Fire Station. Open daily 8:30am to 5pm, *Tel. (0460)5-7111*. They have a lot of information in English and have English-speaking staff members.

WHERE TO STAY

Virtually all hotels and inns in the Hakone area have hot springs. Hakone's terrain was created by volcanic eruptions and hot spring villages are scattered around a fairly large area. To really enjoy the place, try to stay at one that has a *rotemburo* open air bath.

NARAYA RYOKAN, *162 Miyanoshita, Hakone, Ashigarashimo-gun, Kanagawa, 250-0404. Tel. (0460)2-2411, Fax (0460)2-6231. Rates from ¥28,000 per person with two meals. Credit cards.*

This elegant Japanese *ryokan* in a beautiful and spacious garden setting is in perfect harmony with the surrounding mountains. And if that wasn't enough, the *kaiseki* food is a real treat. The 20-room inn goes back several hundred years, but the current buildings were built about a century ago. The hotel has a loyal following of dignitaries and ordinary people who come back again and again.

FUJIYA HOTEL, *359 Miyanoshita, Hakone, Ashigarashimo-gun, Kanagawa, 250-0404. Tel. (0460)2-2211, Fax (0460)2-2210. Twins from ¥20,000. Ask for their special rate for foreigners, currently a twin is $118. Credit cards.*

The Fujiya was the first Western-style hotel built in Japan and is a hybrid of Japanese and Western architectural styles. If you like faded glory, Fujiya is for you. The hotel shows its age, which is what we find charming about it. The dining room is from the 1930s and is a pleasant place to have lunch or dinner. The rooms have Japanese details like coffered ceilings and *shoji* screens; the old fashioned furniture may remind you of your grandmother's. We find Fujiya, nestled in the side of a mountain, a pleasant getaway.

ICHINOYU, *90 Tonosawa, Hakone, Ashigarashimo-gun, Kanagawa, 250-0315. Tel. (0460)5-5331, Fax (0460)5-5335. From ¥16,000 per person with two meals. Credit cards.*

Ichinoyu is a rambling wooden inn along the river's edge. The current buildings are about 100 years old but the inn itself, Hakone's oldest, goes back over 350 years. They are very proud that the shogun paid them a visit. It's a delightful, unpretentious old inn.

TAMAKI, *1300 Gora, Hakone, Ashigarashimo-gun, Kanagawa, 250-0408. Tel. (0460)2-3103, Fax (0460)2-3104. From ¥15,000 per person with two meals. Credit cards. 4-minute walk from Gora Station.*

A large red Japanese umbrella greets you at the entrance, rain or shine. Tamaki is a small Japanese inn with only 12 rooms. The proprietress gives her personal attention to the guests. The garden has huge mountain cherry trees. The inn pays attention to small details: at the outdoor bath, the bamboo baskets for clothes match the bamboo roof. The homestyle *kaiseki* cooking tops off your stay.

MOTO HAKONE GUEST HOUSE, *103 Moto-Hakone, Hakone, Ashigarashimo-gun, Kanagawa, 250-0522. Tel. (0460)3-7880, Fax (0460)4-6578. Singles ¥5000. Twins ¥10,000. Member of the Japanese Inn Group and Welcome Inn Reservation Center.*

This centrally located small inn is close to Lake Ashinoko in Moto Hakone. With only five rooms, it's like staying in someone's home. The Japanese-style accommodations are simple, but good value for the economy-minded traveler.

FUJI HAKONE GUEST HOUSE, *912 Sengokuhara, Hakone, Ashigarashimo, Kanagawa, 250-0631. Tel. (0460)4-6577, Fax (0460)4-6578. Singles from ¥5000. Twins from ¥10,000. Credit cards. Member of Japanese Inn Group and Welcome Inn Reservation Center.*

The Fuji Hakone Guest House is a little far off-the-beaten track, but is a comfortable Japanese-style inn. It's a small house set back from the road and is a good budget choice.

WHERE TO EAT

HATSUHANA *(Noodles, inexpensive), Yumoto. Tel. (0460)5-8287. Open 10am to 7pm. Closed Tuesday.*

Located at the foot of Yumoto Bridge, Hatsuhana is one of Hakone's most famous *soba* shops. The specialty is *soba* with grated mountain potatoes. It's so popular that 20 kilos of mountain potatoes are used each day. *Seiro soba* costs ¥900; *yamakake soba* ¥950.

SHIKAJAYA *(Tofu cuisine. inexpensive), 6-minute walk from Yumoto Station. Tel. (0460)5-5751. Open 11am to 2:30pm. Closed Thursday.*

Shikajaya's specialty is tofu, and it's so good, they serve Soun-ji Temple monks. All food is freshly cooked after you order. *Shika-tenshin,* the most popular set, consists of tofu steak with *miso* sauce, rice and soup, ¥2300; a set with more dishes is ¥3200.

JURAKU *(Tempura, inexpensive), Miyanoshita. Tel. (0460)2-2318. Open 11am to 9pm. Closed 1st and 3rd Mondays.*

Juraku, a Miyanoshita *tempura* shop, is close to Hakone Shrine and the Fujiya Hotel. *Tendon* costs ¥1000, *Tempura teishoku* set is ¥1800.

PICKOT *(Bakery, inexpensive), Miyanoshita. Tel. (0460) 2-2211. Open daily 10:30am to 5:30pm.*

This bakery is located just in front of Fujiya Hotel and sells the Fujiya Hotel's famous bread. Pick up some bread and sandwiches for a quick lunch.

SEEING THE SIGHTS

Hakone's transportation system lends itself to taking a circular route that covers a number of terrains and sights as well as lots of different modes of transportation: train, cable car, ropeway, boat and bus. You can do this route in one day if you leave Tokyo by 8am, but you will not have time to see all the museums listed.

From Hakone Yumoto, take the **Hakone Tozan Railway**. This little train has switchbacks to negotiate the steep mountain slopes; it takes 50 minutes to go 15 kilometers. The motorman runs from one end of the train to the other every time there's a switchback. As the train passes through the deeply forested areas, it almost touches hydrangeas, azaleas and other flowering bushes along the tracks.

The Hakone Tozan Railway's Miyanoshita Station is convenient to the **Fujiya Hotel**, Japan's first Western-style hotel and built in 1878. You can eat lunch in the wood-paneled, 1930s dining room; it's like stepping back in time. Across the street from the hotel are several Japanese antique shops, a holdover from the days when most of the visitors were foreigners. One is S.M. Shiba; it's been serving foreign visitors for over 100 years.

Miyanoshita also offers a wonderful outdoor hot spring bath, **Shizenkan**, where you soak on the side of a hill in a heavily wooded area overlooking the river gorge. It's a little difficult to locate. As you come out the driveway of the Fujiya Hotel, turn left onto the main road. Just after the road forks you stay to the right; the entrance path is beyond a small parking lot. *Tel. (0460)2-0265. Open 10am to 8pm. ¥2500. Since they limit the* *number of bathers, you must make a reservation on weekends, and it's advised on weekdays.*

Continue on the train to the Chokoku no Mori stop. Slightly up the hill to the left of the station is the **Hakone Open Air Museum** (Chokoku no Mori) — a wonderful mountaintop site that blends beautiful natural scenery with modern sculpture. This museum alone is worth a trip to Hakone. Works by Rodin, Moore, Miro, Calder, Debuffet, Brancusi and other 20th century masters grace the lawns, and there's an entire Henry Moore area. Pavilions house sculptures not suited for outdoor exposure, and there's a playground where kids can touch and play on sculptures. The Picasso pavilion displays oil paintings, sculptures, tiles and plates, demonstrating Picasso's versatility and energy. *Tel. (0460)2-1161. Open 9am to 5pm, March through October; until 4pm November through February. ¥1500.*

Return to the train station and ride one stop to Gora, the end of the line. Take the cable car to Koen-kami Station. The **Hakone Art Museum** is just a two-minute walk. This museum, a sister to the MOA Museum in Atami, is devoted to Japanese ceramics and tea ceremony wares. The collections of prehistoric Jomon pottery as well as Bizen pottery are impressive. Although small, the beautifully landscaped Japanese-style Shinsenkyo Garden has maple trees, a bamboo grove and a teahouse. The garden's ground is covered with soft moss. *Tel. (0460)2-2623. Open 9am to 4pm. Closed Thursday. ¥800.*

Take the cable car to the top of the mountain, Sounzan. The nearby **Hakone Sounzan Art Museum** houses the unlikely combination of Henry Moore prints and Chinese porcelain. *Open 9am to 5pm; until 4pm November through March. Closed Tuesday. ¥1000.*

At Sounzan, board the Hakone Ropeway for a tummy-wrenching ride over a large gorge. It's not for those who have a fear of heights. Get off at **Owakudani**, literally "large boiling hell," where the terrain resembles a moonscape. Hakone has a long history of volcanic eruptions and the last eruption occurred here. The air is heavy with the sulfuric stench that's reminiscent of rotten eggs, and you'll wonder what suddenly happened to the verdant forest. There's a short, walking trail through the surreal landscape. You can also buy eggs that have been boiled in the gurgling hot spring water. Local lore says eating one will extend your life for seven years. The Natural Science Museum is a good place to take the kids; you can see a volcanic eruption on film. *Tel. (0460)4-9149. Open 9am to 4:30pm; until 4pm December through February. ¥400.*

Continue on the ropeway down the mountain to **Lake Ashinoko**. If you're lucky, you'll be able to see the elusive Mt. Fuji from the gondola as you come down the mountain. At the lake, board the tacky faux pirate ship. Despite the touristy kitsch of your conveyance, it's a lovely cruise

HOT SPRING BATHING IN HAKONE YUMOTO

Even if you come to Yumoto just for the day, top off your trip with an outdoor hot spring bath; Yumoto offers several open to the public. It's best to bring your own towel, but if you don't have one, you can buy a small, thin one similar to a kitchen towel, at the front desk for about ¥200.

__Kappa Tengoku__ is on the hill above Hakone Yumoto Station. Exit into the small plaza where taxis line up and take the small road under the tracks. Immediately turn right and walk up the steep hill; Kappa is on the left. Kappa Tengoku is an older place with a stone outdoor bath set among trees. Tel. (0460)5-6121. Open 10am to 10pm. ¥700.

__Yuzo__ has a large indoor bath and a small outdoor bath. It's pleasant but since it's on the main drag, the outdoor bath doesn't have views of nature. From Hakone Yumoto Station, walk up the main street. Yuzo is several blocks up on the right; the Ebisu bridge bears off to the left and in front of Yuzo, a small street comes out at a sharp angle on the right. Yuzo does not have a sign marked in English. The building is white stucco and has diagonal tiles on the ground floor. Its restaurant serves reasonably priced Japanese meals. You can also stay there; rooms cost ¥15,000 per person with two meals. The bath is open 10am to 9pm. Closed Wednesday. ¥1300.

__Tenzan__ has two separate baths; to the right is a newer wooden bath that's half indoors and half outdoors, and to the left is a rock bath entirely outdoors plus four other baths. Tenzan is very popular on weekends so it's best to come first thing in the morning. Tenzan's restaurant serves shabu-shabu for ¥2300 and tenzanyaki (teppanyaki) for ¥1800 on the first floor. The second floor has less expensive noodles and snack foods. Tenzan is about a 15-minute walk from Hakone Yumoto Station, near the Oku Yumoto Iriguchi bus stop. Tel. (0460)5-7446. Open daily 9am to 10pm. The admission policy is a little tricky. It costs ¥900 to enter either the baths on the right or the ones on the left. If you want to try them both, pay an additional ¥200.

across the large Lake Ashinoko, which is surrounded by mountains. On the left shore of the lake, the red *torii* gate in the water belongs to Hakone Shrine. This gate is one of the most photographed sights in Hakone; don't be surprised when the cameras start clicking. Get off the boat at Hakone Machi.

Near Hakone Machi is the **Hakone Checkpoint** (Hakone Sekisho), a replica of the building that stood there during the Edo period when people's right to travel was severely restricted by the shogunate. This spot was a major barrier on the Tokaido Road that linked Edo (Tokyo) to Kyoto. Since mountains were on all sides, it was difficult and dangerous to get off the road. The shogunate especially wanted to be sure that wives and children of feudal lords required to live in Edo, essentially as hostages, didn't sneak home. The checkpoint dates to 1619. The adjacent exhibition hall shows the history of the Tokaido Road. *Open 9am to 4:30pm; until 4pm December through February. ¥200.*

Along the lake beyond the checkpoint are several hundred cryptomeria trees planted by the shogunate in 1618. If the weather cooperates, this is one of the best places to photograph Mt. Fuji.

From Moto Hakone, take the Tozan bus back to Hakone Yumoto. The main road in town is lined with shops selling crafts, sweets and pickles.

Other Sights

Hatajuku Yosegi Hall (Hatajuku Yosegi Kaikan). A specialty of Hakone is *yosegi,* a wood inlaid mosaic made into all sorts of objects like boxes, chests and bookmarks. Every shop in Hakone sells them, but at Yosegi Hall you can see the process. *Yosegi* make an unusual souvenir. *Tel. (0460)5-8170. Open 9am to 5pm. Closed at New Year's. Free admission. Hatajuku bus stop.*

Amazake Jaya, near Yosegi Hall, is a rustic country-style place good for a drink and rest. The specialty is *amazake,* a nonalcoholic offshoot of *sake* rice wine.

Yutopia. The name is a play on words. *Yu* is Japanese for hot water. And it does provide the ultimate bathing experience. Yutopia is a bathing theme park. There's an herb bath, a coffee bath, a waterfall bath, a foot-massage bath, a *sake* rice wine bath, a lavender-scented bath, and a large swimming pool filled with hot spring water. Altogether, there are twenty different baths and pools. Wear a bathing suit. Rent a bath towel for ¥200. *Tel. (0460)2-4111. Open 9am to 6:30pm. ¥2600. From Hakone Yumoto take the Tozan train to Kowakudani or bus to Kowaki-en.*

Kowaki-en Kodomo no Mura. Adjacent to Yutopia is a recreation center for children. It has go carts, a swimming pool, a skating rink, a maze and more. *Tel. (0460)2-4111. Open daily 9am to 5pm. ¥900 for adults and ¥700 for children.* In the same complex is a large, impersonal hotel, Kowaki-en, where you may find it convenient to stay if you want to spend time at Yutopia and Kodomo no Mura. *Telephone number is the same; fax: (0460)2-4123. Rates are per person with two meals: from ¥11,000 for Japanese room, ¥16,000 for Western room.*

SHOPPING

Hakone is filled with shops selling *yosegi* inlaid wooden boxes and other crafts. One especially nice shop is **Taichido** in Hakone Yumoto; it sells wooden *daruma* dolls, the roly-poly dolls that evolved from a priest who meditated so long his legs and arms atrophied. *Tel. (0460)5-7051. Open 9am to 5pm.*

EXCURSIONS & DAY TRIPS
CLIMBING MOUNT FUJI

The Japanese have an expression: Everyone must climb **Mt. Fuji** once, but only a fool would do it twice.

Long the symbol of Japan, the 3,776 meter Mt. Fuji is the country's tallest peak. A Shinto shrine graces the summit of the dormant volcano. Mt. Fuji, or *Fuji-san* as the Japanese call it, first erupted 8,000 years ago. The most recent eruption was in the early 18th century.

The graceful mountain, beautiful to view from afar, changes with the seasons and may be one reason why the Japanese glory in seasonal variety. Fuji in winter is blanketed with snow, and in summer, the mountain takes on a bluish hue. The date of the first snowfall in September is an eagerly waited event reported on TV and in newspapers.

Mt. Fuji has different profiles. The view from the Pacific Ocean is considered the front. This view is the one you see from the *shinkansen* train from Tokyo to Kyoto. Some people prefer the opposite view.

Despite Fuji-san's distant beauty, the climb up it isn't at all attractive. Volcanic ash covers much of the terrain. But it's worth the climb for the spectacular view from the summit. The mountain isn't an especially difficult climb — every year some octogenarians do it — but you need to be physically fit.

The mountain has rest areas called stations, and today a road goes up to the fifth station. After that, you're on your own. The most popular hiking trail leaves from the fifth station and takes from five to seven hours to reach the peak.

Many people try to reach the peak in the early morning to see the breathtaking sunrise. One way to do this is to climb most of the way early in the day and spend the night at a mountain hut. Then you get up at about 3am to finish the climb. An alternative is to start your climb at around 9pm and climb all night. You should reach the peak before sunrise.

The climbing season runs from July 1 to August 31. The 25 mountain huts are open only during this period. Before and after, the danger of a heavy snowfall is too great although, out of season, some hearty types do climb up with skis attached to their backs.

Make sure you have good hiking boots, a long-sleeved shirt and pants, rain gear, a flashlight, plenty of water and warm clothing including a jacket — even if it's warm at the fifth station, you still can get snow at the top.

A favorite souvenir is a walking stick bought at the fifth station for ¥1000 and stamped at every station on your way up. Another is to buy a can of Mt. Fuji summit air.

A few words of warning: the mountain huts are simple with *futon* mattresses placed on the floor. No one is turned away, so you may have less than one *futon* to yourself. Also, Mt. Fuji is very crowded, especially on weekends. Be prepared to be part of an endless line snaking its way toward the summit.

Getting to Fuji

By bus: Kawaguchiko is the jumping off place to reach Mt. Fuji's fifth station. Buses to Kawaguchiko run frequently from platform #50 at the Shinjuku Highway Bus Terminal across the street from Keio Department Store at the west exit of Shinjuku Station. Fare ¥1700 one way.

By train: Take the JR Chuo line to Otsuki where you change to the Fuji Kyuko line. The trip takes 2 hours to 2 hours 30 minutes, depending on which train you are on. The fare is ¥4000 for limited express trains and ¥2370 for rapid trains. If you have a rail pass, you have to pay the fare on the private Fuji Kyuko line: ¥1110.

From Kawaguchiko to the fifth station, called Fuji-san gogome, there are six buses a day and more on weekends. Fare ¥1700 one way.

Direct bus from Tokyo's Shinjuku Station to the fifth station operates daily between July 10 and August 31 and on weekends and holidays from September 1 through November 23. The trip takes 2 hours 30 minutes; there are only three buses a day. Reservations are required. Contact Fuji Kyuko Reservation Center, *Tel. (03)3374-2221*. Travel agents can also book seats.

ATAMI

A hot spring seaside resort town on the Izu Peninsula, **Atami** is only 45 minutes south of Tokyo Station by *shinkansen* train. It has an excellent museum of Japanese art, the MOA Museum, and a fantastic Japanese inn, Horai. But besides these, the city is entirely skippable.

Tokyoites used to visit a once quiet Atami for the mild winter weather. But, in the late 1950s, large nondescript hotels and condos began to be built, ruining the natural beauty of the area. You'll find *pachinko* parlors, bars and red-light districts. Many of the numerous inns and hotels cater to the peculiarly Japanese practice of company overnight outings when all the employees eat, drink and sing karaoke as part of the bonding ritual. These outings are regarded as one of the required annual events, like Christmas parties in America.

ARRIVALS & DEPARTURES

The *Kodama* (local) shinkansen train runs from Tokyo Station to Atami and takes 45 minutes. If you are using a rail pass, this train is the best way. The *Odoriko* and Super View *Odoriko* limited expresses from Tokyo or Shinjuku Stations cost nearly the same as the shinkansen but take 1 hour 15 minutes. The Super View trains have extra large windows on the side facing the sea. The least expensive alternative is the Acty train that runs from Tokyo or Shinagawa Stations and takes 1 hour 30 minutes.

WHERE TO STAY

Atami has a fabulous top-of-the-line Japanese inn, Horai. If this isn't what you are looking for, we recommend that you don't spend the night in Atami. The hotels are right on top of each other, huge concrete boxes with little to recommend them. Hakone is not far away or you can head for Shimoda, at the tip of the Izu peninsula.

HORAI, *750 Izusan, Atami, Shizuoka, 413-0002. Tel. (0557)80-5151, Fax (0557)80-0205. From ¥41,000 per person with two meals. Credit cards.*

Horai is an elegant Japanese inn on a hill overlooking Sagami Bay. With only 16 rooms, including five separate cottages, guests are pampered in fine style. The outdoor hot spring bath, protected by a wooden roof, offers a wonderful view of the sea. For more information, see Horai in Chapter 11, our Best Places to Stay.

SEEING THE SIGHTS

The main reason to visit Atami is to see the **MOA Museum of Art** (MOA Bijutsukan). It's a monument to an egomaniac, Okada Mokichi, who founded a religion based on the premise that man can best discover his spiritual self when surrounded by beautiful objects. And surround himself he did. In the 1940s, Okada bought up masterpieces of Japanese and Chinese art and later built a monument to house them that combines technology and art. MOA stands for Mokichi Okada Association (Okada is the family name). The whole thing sounds like a great tax dodge, but the collection and setting are superb.

From Atami Station, take a bus from platform #4 or taxi to the museum; either will take under 10 minutes. Built on a hillside, you enter the museum from the lowest level. Humongously long escalators, actually 203 meters long, take you up the mountain until you reach a strange circular hall where a laser show is seen periodically throughout the day.

Continue up another escalator until you reach the Henry Moore Plaza where the outdoor Moore statue is on a bluff; take in the great views of the sea. The beautifully designed main hall of the museum has floor-to-ceiling windows designed to take in the exhilarating view.

The museum itself has many superb works of Japanese art including the Rimpa school artist Ogata Korin's 18th century *Red and White Plum Blossoms*. To preserve the delicate screen, it is only on display from the end of January until the end of February, the same time the plum trees blossom. On display year round is Nonomura Ninsei's elegant *Wisteria Design Tea Jar*. The extensive collection also has paintings, calligraphy and sculpture and exquisite Chinese Sung Dynasty celadon ceramics. The museum also has a small collection of Western paintings that includes a Rembrandt and a few Monets.

Okada was a tea connoisseur and the museum has lots of tea utensils as well as a replica of Hideyoshi's gaudy, golden teahouse. On the extensive museum grounds is a replica of Ogata Korin's Kyoto home and teahouse and a restaurant serving *kaiseki* cuisine using food grown on the MOA's organic farm. *Tel. (0557)84-2511. Open 9am to 5pm. Closed Thursday and at New Year's. ¥1500.*

If you visit the museum in February and are inspired by Korin's magnificent Plum Blossom screen, you can go to **Atami Plum Garden** (Atami Baien), on a nearby hill, to see hundreds of plum blossoms. Atami's mild climate means plums start blooming as early as December.

SHIMODA

South of Tokyo, near the tip of the Izu Peninsula is the historic town of **Shimoda**. It's of special interest to Western visitors because in 1854, **Commodore Matthew Perry** arrived with his American Black Ships and negotiated with Japanese officials to open Japan to trade after a two-hundred year period of isolation. Shimoda was one of the first two ports open to foreigners. The first American consul, Townsend Harris, established his residence here in 1856.

Shimoda also has hot springs and many buildings with an attractive old style of architecture called *namako-kabe,* diamond shaped black tiles outlined with white plaster.

ARRIVALS & DEPARTURES

The JR limited express *Odoriko* train and the Super View *Odoriko* train take 2 hours 25 minutes to reach Shimoda from Tokyo or Shinjuku Station. The Super View has large windows and costs more; it is an all-reserved-seat train. You can also take the Izu Kyuko Railway from Atami and Ito City.

Tourist Information

Near Izukyu Shimoda Station, Shimoda's **tourist information office** has lots of information in English. *Tel. (0558)22-1531.*

WHERE TO STAY

KOMURASAKI, *1-5-30 Nishi Hongo, Shimoda, Shizuoka, 415-0036. Tel. (0558)22-2126, Fax (0558)22-2127. ¥35,000 per person with two meals. Diners Club and Amex.*

Our friends who recommended this tiny charming inn wanted to keep it a secret. Komurasaki has only five rooms all facing the well-kept Japanese garden. Each room has a *rotemburo* (an outdoor hot spring bath) on the balcony for private bathing. In the bathroom there's also a wooden bath tub from which you can admire the garden through the large windows. The owner, a charming and friendly woman, is attentive to the needs of her guests. It's only three minutes from Shimoda Station, but the owner is happy to pick you up if you telephone.

ISHIBASHI RYOKAN, *185-1 Rendai-ji, Shimoda, Shizuoka, 415-0031. Tel. (0558)22-2222, Fax (0558)22-2121. From ¥15,000 per person with two meals. Credit cards.*

Ishibashi *Ryokan* has spa facilities such as whirlpool and steam baths plus an outdoor bath.

KANAYA RYOKAN, *114-2 Kouchi, Shimoda, Shizuoka, 415-0011. Tel. (0558)22-0325, Fax (0558)23-6078. From ¥15,000 per person with two meals. No credit cards.*

Kanaya has the largest bath tub in the Izu Peninsula, and there are a lot of bath tubs in Izu! The wooden tub is 15 meters by 5 meters.

MINSHUKU HAJI, *708 Sotoura, Shimoda, Shizuoka, 415-0000. Tel. (0558)22-2597, Fax (0558)22-1064. From ¥7000 per person with two meals. No credit cards. Member of Welcome Inn Reservation Center.*

Haji, a simple inn located in a beach area called Sotoura, is run by a man who speaks English. It's a ten-minute bus ride from Shimoda Station.

WHERE TO EAT

Fish is what you eat in Shimoda, fish so fresh it probably was swimming in the morning.

NAKAGAWA *(Japanese, inexpensive,. 1-12-17 Shimoda. Tel. (0558)22-0310. Open 11am to 9pm. 10-minute walk from Shimoda Station.*

This restaurant, decorated with rustic folk art, has a very friendly staff. Fish is the specialty. The *tempura teishoku* (¥1500) is delicious as is the deep fried *kinmedai karaage* (tasty red snapper), ¥1200.

KIYUU *(Japanese, inexpensive), Renjaku-cho Dori. Tel. (0558)22-8698. Open 11am to 9pm. 5-minute walk from the station.*

The proprietors tell us that their fish is the freshest in Shimoda, but we are wondering who is counting the nano-seconds. The *sashimi teishoku* sets cost ¥1300 and ¥1600, and yes, the fish is delicious. If you want your fish cooked, try the *tempura teishoku*, ¥1500. *Omakase* set (chef's special) is ¥3000.

SEEING THE SIGHTS

Shimoda is a small town where most of the sights can be reached on foot.

To see what these feared Black Ships are all about, you can take a 20-minute ride on a replica of Perry's boat, the **Susquehanna**. Given the size of today's aircraft carriers, it's hard to believe that this ship could have evoked such panic. *Boats depart between 9:30am and 3:30pm. ¥900.*

Gyokusen-ji Temple is where American consul Townsend Harris and his translator Henry Heusken lived in 1856–7. The site reverted to a Zen temple after Harris left. A hall on the temple's grounds displays documents in English and Japanese. You'll also find a sign erected in Japanese and English to commemorate the first cow killed to be eaten in Japan; it was for Harris' consumption.

Ryosen-ji Temple is where Commodore Perry negotiated with officials of the Tokugawa shogunate to arrange the US Peace Treaty signed in 1854. The treasure hall houses documents about this period. Nearby Choraku-ji Temple is where the Japan-America Peace Treaty ratifications were exchanged and the Japan-Russia Peace Treaty was signed in 1854.

Hofuku-ji Temple is where the courtesan Tojin Okichi is buried. Assigned to be Harris' attendant in 1857, she was dismissed after three days because of a skin ailment. Chastised for being rejected by a foreign barbarian, she lived out her days in shame. Okichi committed suicide in 1890. The temple displays Okichi's personal effects. *Open daily 8am to 5pm. ¥300.*

Anchokuro is the restaurant Okichi established in 1882; it is in business today as a *sushi* shop. The second floor rooms are preserved and some of Okichi's belongings are on display. *Open 10am to 8pm. ¥200.*

Zushu Shimoda History Museum is a well-designed museum with attractive exhibits chronicling Shimoda's past. It's a must for history buffs. *Tel. (0558)23-2500. Open 8:30am to 5pm. ¥820.*

For a change of pace from all this history, head to the **Shimoda Floating Aquarium** (Shimoda Kaichu Suizokkan), a ten-minute bus ride from Shimoda Station. The aquarium floats so you can see fish swimming in their native habitats. The aquarium also features dolphin shows and feeding sessions. A limited number of people can touch or swim with the dolphins and pilot whales. *Tel. (0558)22-3567. Open daily 9am to 5pm. Closed December 6-10. ¥1700.*

NIKKO

One of Japan's most famous architectural monuments, **Toshogu Shrine**, is in **Nikko**, a small town in the mountains that's a two-hour train ride northwest of Tokyo. The shrine, so ornate you think it can't be possibly be Japanese, is the mausoleum of Tokugawa Ieyasu, the 16th century unifier who founded the Tokugawa shogunate that ruled for 260 years.

But Nikko offers much more than just this shrine. The surrounding mountains offer walking and hiking; Lake Chuzenji is popular for water sports; and Yumoto has hot springs and skiing. Nikko is a popular summer retreat with temperatures lower than Tokyo's. Emperor Taisho, the grandfather of the present emperor, had a villa in Nikko.

If you get an early start and only visit the Toshogu Shrine area, you can make a day trip to Nikko. But if you want to go up into the mountains, you need to stay overnight.

ARRIVALS & DEPARTURES

The easiest and least expensive way to Nikko is via the private Tobu line from Asakusa Station in northeastern Tokyo. The limited express trains take 1 hour 55 minutes; all seats are reserved (¥2530). For half the price, you can take the *kyuko* (express) train that takes 15 minutes longer (¥1270). The only catch on the express is you have to make sure you sit in the front two cars because some trains divide at Shimo Imaichi Station, the stop before Nikko Station.

To take advantage of your JR rail pass, take the Tohoku shinkansen train from Tokyo or Ueno Station to Utsunomiya (50 minutes). Change for the Nikko line for the 45 minute ride to JR Nikko Station. Note that JR and Nikko Tobu Stations are a few minutes walk from each other.

Tourist Information

Stop at the tourist information window in the Nikko Tobu Station to pick up maps and English-language brochures, *Tel. (0288)53-4511.*

WHERE TO STAY

KANAYA HOTEL, *1300 Kami-hatsuishi-machi, Nikko, Tochigi, 321-1401. Tel. (0288)54-0001, Fax (0288)53-2487. Twins from ¥18,000. Doubles from ¥22,000. Credit cards.*

This classic hotel was one of the first Western hotels in Japan. The rooms blend Japanese and Western architecture. While it is showing its age, Kanaya is a good choice if you want to stay in a hotel with a lot of character. Perched up on a hill above the Shinkyo Sacred Bridge, Kanaya has fantastic views of the mountains.

MORI-NO-HOTEL, *2551 Yumoto, Nikko. Tochigi, 321-1662. Tel. (0288)62-2338, Fax (0288)62-2477. ¥16,000 per person with two meals. Credit cards.*
Located in the midst of a forest, Mori-no-Hotel is an ideal place to relax after a busy day in Nikko. It's 50 minutes by bus from Nikko but worth the trip for a quiet getaway. A fire is lit in the lobby fireplace every evening; even in summer Oku-Nikko (Inner Nikko) becomes cool in the evening. The rooms are Japanese-style.

NIKKO ASTOREA HOTEL, *Kotoku Onsen Nikko, Tochigi, 321-1400. Tel. (0288)55-0585, Fax (0288)55-0731. From ¥14,000 per person with two meals. Credit cards.*
This hotel is a favorite retreat when we feel the need to escape from Tokyo. We like to come here any time of year: when the new leaves turn the hills bright green; when the mountains provide welcome relief from the summer heat; when autumn colors brighten the forest and when snow falls on us in the outdoor bath after a day of cross-country skiing. The wooden lodge's open lobby with floor-to-ceiling windows offers great views of the mountains. The staff is friendly and helpful, and meals are served in the first floor dining room. Choose between Japanese- and Western-style accommodations. The hotel has a large indoor hot spring bath and a wonderful stone outdoor bath.

TURTLE INN NIKKO, *2-16 Takumi-cho, Nikko, Tochigi, 321. Tel. (0288)53-3168, Fax (0288)53-3883. From ¥3900 per person without meals. Credit cards. Member of Japanese Inn Group and Welcome Inn Reservation Center.*

HOTORI-AN, *8-28 Takumi-cho, Nikko, Tochigi, 321-1433. Tel. (0288)53-3663, Fax (0288)53-3883. From ¥5200 per person without meals. Credit cards. Member of Japanese Inn Group and Welcome Inn Reservation Center.*
Turtle Inn and Hotori-an, just down the street from each other, are run by the same friendly people and either is a good budget inn choice. Opened in 1994, Hotori-an is newer and all 11 rooms have private baths. One room is Western style, and the rest are Japanese style. Turtle Inn also has 11 rooms: five Japanese style and six Western style. Only three rooms here have private baths. You can have Japanese or Western dinner and breakfast served on Mashiko folk pottery. Hotori-an also has a small gallery of Mashiko pottery. The inns are only a 10-minute walk from Toshogu Shrine.

WHERE TO EAT

GYOSHINTEI *(Buddhist vegetarian, moderate), 2339-1 Sannai, Nikko. Tel. (0288)53-3751. Open 11am to 7pm. Closed Thursday.*
Housed in a simple Japanese building behind the stone building Meiji no Yakata restaurant, Gyoshintei serves Buddhist vegetarian food. The main dining room, where you sit on *tatami* mats, looks out over the

garden. The specialty is *yuba* (soy milk skin), a delicate food cooked in broth, with fresh vegetables. *Kushizen* set costs ¥3500, *honzen* set ¥5000. *Kaiseki* meals are available for ¥5000 and ¥8000. The restaurant is rather small so it's best to make reservations.

NIKKO KANAYA HOTEL (*Western, moderate*), *1300 Kami-hatsuishi, Nikko. Tel. (0288)54-0001. Open 12 noon to 3pm; 6pm to 7:30pm.*

The main dining room of the Kanaya Hotel is a charming old-fashioned room. The house specialty is trout, but other Western dishes are also served. Located on the hill behind Shinkyo Bridge, it's a convenient lunch place. The lunch set costs ¥3500 and consists of an appetizer, grilled rainbow trout — a Nikko specialty — dessert and coffee.

MASUDAYA (*Japanese, moderate*), *439 Ichiyamachi, Nikko. Tel. (0288)54-2151. Open 11am to 2pm, or earlier if they run out of the day's food. Closed Thursday.*

Masudaya specializes in *yuba*, the curd that collects on the top of boiling soy milk. The delicate food is much more delicious than it sounds. Masudaya serves some of the best *yuba* in Nikko. The lunch set (¥4100 at a Western table) includes *yuba* soup, *yuba sashimi*, fried fish and other *yuba* dishes. If you sit on *tatami* mats, the set costs ¥5500 and includes dessert. Masudaya is open only for lunch and reservations are a necessity. It's located on the left side of the main road, about half way between Nikko Tobu Station and Shinkyo Bridge.

SEEING THE SIGHTS

As you exit Nikko Tobu train station, either take a bus from platform 1, 2 or 3 in front of Nikko Tobu Station to the Shinkyo Bridge stop or walk up the main road (toward the right as you exit the station) for about 20 minutes until you reach the Shinkyo Bridge.

Shinkyo Bridge is a gently arched, red wooden bridge over the Daiya River; it marks the entrance to the shrine's grounds. In the old days, only shoguns and imperial messengers crossed the bridge.

Follow the long sloping walkway called Omotesando, and you'll soon reach a large courtyard with temple buildings. Here you can buy a set of tickets for ¥900 for admission to Toshogu Shrine, Rinno-ji Temple and Futarasan Shrine.

The first temple you see is **Rinno-ji**, a Buddhist temple with a long history that stretches back to 766. The main hall is called the Sanbutsudo (Three Buddha Hall) and houses three huge gilded statues of Buddhist deities. The hall's architecture is unusual in that the low stone floor in front of the statues allows visitors to stand right in front of them. You need to walk around to the right side of the building to go down the stairs for a close-up view.

The close proximity of Rinno-ji, a Buddhist temple, and Toshogu, a Shinto shrine, illustrates that the two religions have had a long and close relationship over the past thousand years. When Buddhism was persecuted in the late 19th century, special dispensation was given to Nikko so the temples there did not experience anywhere near the destruction of many others.

Continue up Omotesando and you'll reach the Sennin Ichidan (1000 people stone stairs); these ten broad steps were as far as commoners could venture. The over 8-meter granite *torii* gate is Japan's largest stone *torii*. You have arrived at Toshogu Shrine.

Toshogu Shrine has put Nikko on the map. Tokugawa Iemitsu, the third shogun, built the Shinto shrine in 1636 to deify his grandfather, Ieyasu, founder of the shogunate that ruled Japan from 1603 until 1868. The arts favored by the 16th century great unifiers and 17th century shoguns were bold and brash, a big change from the monochrome Zen Buddhist art that preceded it. These guys had power and money and used it to create huge monuments. Iemitsu brought together the best artists and craftsmen in the land to create the flamboyant shrine.

To the left of the *torii* gate is a five-storied pagoda. Wait, you may be thinking, this is a Shinto shrine and pagodas belong in Buddhist temples. Well, this pagoda shows how intertwined the two religions were. After you enter the gate, this area contains the **Sacred Storehouses**. The **Sacred Stable** is on the left; it has the famous carving of monkeys: hear no evil, speak no evil, see no evil.

Climb up the steps to the next terrace; the many stone lanterns you see were donated by feudal lords all over Japan. The huge revolving bronze lantern is from Holland, the only European country with which Japan maintained diplomatic relations. The Tokugawa family crest is upside down, but being foreigners, they got away with that error. If a feudal lord had made that mistake, it might have cost him his life. All the way on the left is the **Honjido**, dedicated to the 12 gods of war. On the ceiling is an enormous painting of a dragon. If you clap your hands at the marked spot, you can hear the dragon roar.

At the top of the stairs to the upper terrace is the famed **Yomei Mon Gate**. Lavishly decorated with over 400 carvings, no place on the entire surface is unadorned. The gate's nickname is Higurashi no Mon, Sunset Gate, because you can become so engrossed in looking at it, the whole day will pass. You'll find birds, flowers, dragons, Chinese sages and so much more.

TOO PERFECT?

The artisans who made the Yomei Mon Gate were so impressed with their work that they thought if they made the gate too perfect, the gods would be jealous. So they made one flaw: the geometrical pattern is upside down on the far left pillar. It's called the evil-averting pillar. It must have worked because the shrine has stood for 350 years.

A small **Karamon** (Chinese gate) leads to the inner courtyard. You can remove your shoes and enter the **Honden**, main hall. You pass through the **Haiden** where a mirror represents the deity of Tokugawa, then through a passageway called Ishi-no-ma to enter the main hall.

The eastern side of the inner courtyard has the **Sakashita-mon Gate**, beyond which are the stairs leading to Ieyasu's tomb. On the lintel is the famous statue of the **Nemuri Neko**, the sleeping cat. She is sleeping so peacefully even the steady click of cameras doesn't awaken her. It's rumored that she comes down at night to rid the shrine of mice.

Climb the simple stone stairs to the top of the hill to **Ieyasu's tomb**. All around the tall cryptomeria trees lend a sacred air to the site. The unadorned tomb is such a contrast to all the ornateness down below; we really get the impression that Ieyasu is in a truly peaceful state. And well he should be. When he died at the age of 74, he had accomplished what he set out to do. Not only did he manage to rule Japan, but he also put in place an administrative structure that enabled his heirs to rule for 260 years.

You need to go back down all the steps and retrace your path to the exit of Toshogu Shrine. Rather than walking down the broad Omotesando, turn right and walk along the path lined with stone lanterns. You'll come to **Futarasan Shrine**, constructed by Ieyasu's son, Hidetada. To the left of the main hall is a pleasant garden; its simplicity is a respite from the highly decorated Toshogu Shrine.

Beyond Futarasan Shrine is **Daiyuin**, the mausoleum of Iemitsu, the third Tokugawa shogun and Toshogu's builder. Unlike the Shinto shrine built for his grandfather, Iemitsu's own tomb is purely Buddhist.

From there you can return to the main street and either catch a bus to go into the mountains or return to the train station.

Lake Chuzenji, Kotoku & Yumoto

The road from Nikko to Lake Chuzenji is called Iroha Slope — the equivalent of ABC slope because each hairpin turn is named after one of the 48 sounds in the old Japanese alphabet. You can catch a bus from

Nikko Tobu Station or on the main road that runs in front of Toshogu Shrine.

The lakeside area is a popular place for Japanese to vacation, and the Kegon waterfall is on the itinerary of every tour group. We honestly don't think it's worth the effort. The streets around the lake are filled with tacky souvenir stands and the waterfall is modest; you can take an elevator to its base if you feel like it. Unless you cannot survive without pedaling a swan boat around the lake, continue on to **Kotoku** and **Yumoto**.

Yumoto and Kotoku are on a plateau surrounded by mountains. The small hot spring town of Yumoto has lots of inns. It also has the honor of having Japan's first ski slope; the hill is modest but popular with people looking for a convenient ski slope. Walk around the small **Lake Yunoko**, which means hot water lake — you can feel the warmth of the lake fed by hot springs. It's especially pleasant in autumn when the foliage puts on a show.

Kotoku, one of our favorite Tokyo getaways, features meadows framed by mountains and peaceful birch forests. During the winter, cross-country ski trails criss cross the terrain. The Astorea Hotel is a comfortable lodge.

The surrounding mountains and plains have lots of hiking trails, something for every level. **Senjogahara** is a marsh where you can saunter along on wooden walkways. Surrounded by volcanic mountains, it was once a lake. During the summer the marsh is filled with wildflowers.

YUNISHIGAWA ONSEN

Deep in the mountains, this unassuming remote hot spring village northwest of Nikko has a surprising history.

In 1185, the Genji clan annihilated its rivals, the **Heike**, but some Heike managed to flee. The victorious Genji went on to establish the Kamakura shogunate, but their need for vengeance was so strong, they searched to eradicate the surviving Heike, some of whom fled to the Nikko area. The Heike felt they were safe — this was 500 years before Toshogu Shrine was built and Nikko was like being in remote Alaska — nothing was there.

But, when a son was born to the leader of the Heike, the group celebrated by using a kimono to make a carp banner, long a boy's symbol. The noise of the chickens the Heike kept also gave away their positions. Genji warriors discovered and killed about half the exiles. The surviving Heike fled farther north and ended up in Yunishigawa. To this day residents of Yunishigawa neither raise chickens nor fly the carp banner on Boys' Day.

The Heike had lived the high life in Kyoto and even married into the imperial family, so primitive living in a harsh mountain hamlet was a major step down. To bolster their spirits, the young Heike women prepared feasts of mountain vegetable stew, grilled deer, bear meat and river fish. Yunishigawa is today famous for its "exiles cuisine" cooked over an open hearth.

Four hundred years ago, the discovery of hot springs in Yunishigawa put the village on the map. The Heike have been hoteliers ever since. Yunishigawa is famous for its outdoor baths along the banks of the river. You can soak year round, looking at snow, brilliant red autumn foliage, or green hillsides. When we visited Yunishigawa in February, the snow was piled ten feet high.

ARRIVALS & DEPARTURES

Yunishigawa can be combined with a trip to Nikko. Spend the morning at Toshogu Shrine in Nikko. After lunch take the Tobu train from Nikko to Kinugawa Onsen. You will have to change trains in Shimo Imaichi Station, the first stop. At Kinugawa Onsen Station, switch to the train to Yunishigawa Station. Board the Tobu bus to Yunishigawa. 25 minutes, ¥880. The buses meet the train.

To travel to Yunishigawa directly from Tokyo's Asakusa Station, take the Tobu line express train to Yunishigawa Onsen, about three hours. There are eight trains a day. Board the Tobu bus for the 25-minute ride to Yunishigawa.

WHERE TO STAY

HONKE BANKYU RYOKAN, *Yunishigawa Onsen, Tochigi, 321-2601. Tel. (0288)98-0011, Fax (0288)98-0666. Rates from ¥18,000 per person with two meals. Credit cards.*

This older inn is a real treat. Each of the 30 Japanese-style guest rooms is decorated in a rustic fashion; some of the rooms have their own hearth for cooking Heike cuisine and all have wooden bath tubs. They also have a large outdoor wooden bath overlooking the river. Honke Bankyu is famous for its food. With a family descended from the original group of exiles, they should know what Yunishigawa cuisine is all about.

YAMASHIROYA GRAND HOTEL, *Yunishigawa Onsen, Tochigi, 321-2601. Tel. (0288)98-0311, Fax (0288)98-0733. Rates from ¥6500 per person with breakfast. Credit cards.*

This simple hotel on the water in the central part of the village is a good budget choice. The outdoor bath overlooks the river. If you wish to have dinner, it's available for ¥3000, ¥5000 and ¥10,000.

SEEING THE SIGHTS

Yunishigawa is easily seen on foot. The real attractions are the baths, the unusual food, the terrific scenery and the good hiking, but you can get a dose of history at the following places:

In the center of town is the **Exiles Folklore Museum**, a tiny, one-room place that resembles a cluttered attic. It's easy to dismiss it entirely until you realize that many of the objects are over one thousand years old. *Tel. (0288)98-0432. ¥300.*

Up the road is **Heike Village** (Heike no Sato), a group of seven traditional thatched-roof buildings with displays of how the Heike lived. Craftsmen demonstrate carving bowls and ladles, one way the Heike supported themselves. Other buildings have Heike costumes and furnishings. *Tel. (0288)98-0126. Open 8:30am to 5pm; 9am to 4:30 December through March. ¥500.*

ASHIKAGA

Ashikaga, north of Tokyo, has a fabulous museum of Japanese porcelain, a must for ceramics aficionados. It also has a wonderful indigo dyer who welcomes visitors and gladly gives explanations in English. These two attributes alone make for a worthwhile getaway. But we have more for you. One of the most charming country hot spring inns is about an hour and a half from Ashikaga. All three combine to make a memorable off-the-beaten-path side trip.

ARRIVALS & DEPARTURES

The Tobu train Isezaki line provides service to Ashikaga from Tokyo's Asakusa Station. The limited express takes 70 minutes, costs ¥2100 and runs every hour. The semiexpress takes almost two hours and costs ¥940.

WHERE TO STAY

CHUJIKAN, *2036 Fuegashima, Miyagi-mura, Seta-gun, Gunma, 371-1100. Tel. (0272)83-3015, Fax (0272)83-7522. From ¥10,000 per person with two meals. Credit cards.*

We enjoyed our stay at Chujikan so much that we've included it in our Best Places to Stay in Chapter 11. The inn was recently reconstructed in a traditional Japanese rural style. The lobby is like a farmhouse; you step up from the entrance area into a small, sunny room with an *irori* hearth. All 13 rooms are Japanese style and have private toilets and sinks. But the real winner is the stone outdoor bath that overlooks a river ravine and waterfall. The men's and women's baths are side by side, separated by a bamboo fence. In the evening, the waterfall is illuminated. The food is country-style home cooking served in a Japanese-style central dining room. The cheerful cook explains each dish she is serving. Staying at Chujikan is like taking a step back in time.

From Ashikaga Station (or Omata Station if you are coming from Sei Ai Kobo), take the JR Ryomo line to Maebashi, about 45 minutes. Take a shuttle bus from Maebashi Station to Chuo Maebashi Station and take the Jomo Dentetsu train to Ogo Station (15 minutes). From there catch a bus to Akagi Jinja Shrine (25 minutes). As you get off, call the hotel from the public phone and you'll be picked up. Taxi from Maebashi Station takes 45 minutes and costs about ¥5000. A taxi from Ogo Station takes 20 minutes and costs ¥3000.

SEEING THE SIGHTS

Kurita Museum, *1542 Komaba-cho, Ashikaga, Tochigi. Tel. (0284)91-1026. Open daily 9:30am to 5pm; until 6pm on Sunday and holidays. Closed December 29-31. ¥1550. 15- minute taxi ride from Tobu Ashikaga Station, fare is ¥2500 to ¥3000. From JR Tomita Station on JR Ryomo line, 10-minute walk. On the way back you can wait for a bus to the station or ask the information desk to call a taxi.*

Located on a hilly 660 acres of pine woods, the dozen buildings were designed by architect Taniguchi Yoshiro and reflect the traditional Japanese aesthetic of subdued beauty. The collection of Imari and Nabeshima ceramics is the largest in the world. Nabeshima ware is unequaled for its subtle colors; Imari's designs are famous the world over. One building houses the highly prized, ornately embellished porcelains that decorate European castles and manor houses. Another has the more subdued Nabeshima and Imari ware made for Japanese feudal lords and other wealthy individuals. Every time we go back, they seem to have added a new building.

The museum's works were collected by a businessman, Kurita Hideo. As the hometown boy who made good, he decided to establish the museum in Ashikaga. Our only gripe is every building has a gift shop, and the one at the entrance is probably half the length of a football field.

Sei Ai Kobo, *897-1 Omata-cho, Ashikaga, Tochigi. Tel. (0284)62-1531.*

This workshop is the showroom of Mr. Okawa, an energetic seventy-something man who has to be Japan's best ambassador for indigo dyeing. Mr. Okawa is happy to demonstrate the natural dyeing process, and he does so in good English learned at technical school. For ¥1000 you can dye a handkerchief: by folding and tying it, you can make an original design. You'll wash out your creation in the small stream running behind Mr. Okawa's workshop, the same place where he rinses all his works. The showroom is filled with his handiwork: scarves, shawls, *noren* curtains, clothing and more, all deep blue indigo color. Our favorite are indigo silk socks with five toes that are supposed to prevent athlete's foot. Unfortunately, the one-sized socks were too small for our husbands, so we are now their proud owners.

From the Tobu Ashikaga and JR Ashikaga train stations, a taxi to Mr. Okawa's workshop costs about ¥4500. A less expensive way is to take the bus from Tobu Ashikaga Station heading to Kiryu Tenjin machi and get off at Omata Station. From there it's a few minutes by taxi or a 10-minute walk.

If you use JR trains, take the JR Tohoku Honsen line from Ueno Station to Oyama Station — rapid trains take about one hour; and switch to the JR Ryomo line to Omata Station — a 45-minute ride. It's a few minutes by taxi or a 10-minute walk.

INDIGO BLUES

*The all-natural **indigo dyeing process** is disappearing in Japan. Fortunately, dedicated dyers like Mr. Okawa work hard to preserve the art.*

Indigo is a bush grown in Shikoku, an island in Western Japan. In the autumn, the leaves are picked and placed in a jar to decompose for several months. Then sake rice wine and sugar are added to start the long fermentation process. The dye is a living organism and needs to be fed sake and stirred daily to keep it alive.

The pot of dye doesn't look like much – a green, oozy liquid. Indigo needs oxygen to bring out the color, so when cloth comes out of the pot it looks greenish, but within a few seconds, exposure to air changes the color to its characteristic blue color.

19. PRACTICAL INFORMATION

CHURCHES

All of the following churches have services in English:
- **Franciscan Chapel Center** (Catholic), *4-2-37 Roppongi, Minato-ku. Tel. (03)3401-2141.*
- **St. Alban's Church** (Anglican/Episcopal), *3-6-25 Shiba Koen, Minato-ku. Tel. (03)3431-8534.*
- **St. Anselm's Benedictine Church** (Roman Catholic), *4-6-22 Kamiosaki, Shinagawa-ku. Tel. (03)3491-6966.*
- **St. Paul's International Lutheran Church**, *1-2-32 Fujimi, Chiyoda-ku. Tel. (03)3261-3740.*
- **Tokyo Baptist Church**, *9-2 Hachiyama-cho, Shibuya-ku. Tel. (03)3461-8425.*
- **Tokyo Union Church** (Interdenominational), *5-7-7 Jingumae, Shibuya-ku. Tel. (03)3400-0047.*

ESSENTIAL PHONE NUMBERS
- **Tourist Information Center**, *Tel. (03)3201-3331.*
- **JR East InfoLine**, *Tel. (03)3423-0111.* 10am to 6pm weekdays. Information on JR trains all over Japan.
- **Tokyo English Life Line**, *Tel. (03)5721-4347.* 9am to 4pm; 7pm to 11pm daily. Personal crisis counseling.
- **Japan Helpline**, toll free *Tel. 0120-461-997.* 24 hours. Offers advice and assistance.
- **NTT Information Service in English** (telephone directory assistance), *Tel. (03)5295-1010.* 9am to 5pm weekdays.
- **Police**, *Tel. 110*
- **Fire & Ambulance**, *Tel. 119*

HEALTH

There are doctors who serve the English-speaking community. In an medical emergency, it's best to contact the front desk of your hotel. Call 119 for an ambulance.

- **Tokyo Medical and Surgical Clinic**, *No. 32 Mori Building, 3-4-30 Shiba Koen, Minato-ku. Tel. (03)3436-3028.* Across from Tokyo Tower. All doctors are English speaking. Clinic has a doctor on call 24 hours for emergencies.
- **St. Luke's Hospital**, *9-1 Akashicho, Chuo-ku. Tel. (03)3541-5151.* Has a long history of serving the foreign community.
- **Japan Helpline** is a 24-hour toll free service. They will assist you to find a doctor or hospital in a medical emergency. *Tel. 0120-461-997.*
- Pharmacies with English-speaking staff: **American Pharmacy**, *Hibiya Park Building, 1-8-1 Yurakucho, Chiyoda-ku, Tokyo. Tel. (03)3271-4034.* Open daily 9:30am to 7pm; **Tokyo Medical and Surgical Clinic Pharmacy**, *No. 32 Mori Building, 3-4-30 Shiba Koen, Minato-ku. Tel. (03)3434-5817.* Open 9am to 5:30pm, until 1pm on Saturday. Closed Sunday; **National Supermarket Pharmacy**, *4-5-2 Minami Azabu, Minato-ku. Tel. (03)3442-3181.* Open daily 9:30am to 6:30pm.
- For a Shiatsu massage, try: **Namikoshi Shiatsu**, *3F, Dai Nana Seiko Building, 5-5-9 Akasaka, Minato-ku.* ¥6500 for a one-hour massage. Basic English spoken; popular with foreigners.
- For acupuncture, try: **Edward Acupuncture Clinic**, *Coop Sangenjaya 301, 2-17-12 Sangenjaya, Setagaya-ku. Tel. (03)3418-8989.* Englishman Edward Obaidley trained in Japan; and **Baba Kaiseido Acupuncture Office**, *2-4-5-305 Shiba Daimon, Minato-ku. Tel. (03)3432-0260.* English spoken.

LIBRARIES

- **National Diet Library**, *1-10-1 Nagatacho, Chiyoda-ku. Tel. (03)3581-2331.* The largest collection of books in Japan, the Diet Library is open to anyone over 20 years old. Books may not be checked out.
- **Tokyo Metropolitan Central Library**, *5-7-13 Minami Azabu, Minato-ku. Tel. (03)3442-8451.* A research library (books may not be checked out).
- **JETRO Library**, *2-2-5 Toranomon, Minato-ku. Tel. (03)3582-5549. Open 9:30am to 4:30pm, Monday through Friday. Closed 3rd Tuesday.* Focuses on economic and trade publications.
- **Japan Foundation Library**, *20F, Ark Mori Building, 1-12-32 Akasaka, Minato-ku. Tel. (03)5562-3527.* This library has an extensive collection of English-language books on Japan. Only non-Japanese residents may borrow books.
- **American Center Library**, *11F, ABC Building, 2-6-3 Shiba Koen, Minato-ku. Tel. (03)3436-0901.* Run by the US Government, the collection focuses on the US and has a large selection of American magazines. Only Japanese may borrow books.

- **British Council Library**, *1-2 Kagurazaka, Shinjuku-ku. Tel. (03)3235-8031*. Publications on the UK are the focus. Annual membership fee ¥3500.
- **World Magazine Gallery**, *3-13-10 Ginza, Chuo-ku. Tel. (03)3545-7227. Open 10am to 7pm. Closed Monday*. You'll find over 100 magazines that you can read on the premises or in the adjacent coffee shop. You can't borrow them, but they have copy machines. Walk down the street to the right of Kabuki-za Theater for two blocks. Magazine House is on the 2nd floor of the eight-storied pink and gray striped building.

POST OFFICE

- **Central Post Office**, *just south of Tokyo Station*, has a 24-hour counter.

20. GLOSSARY

COMMON JAPANESE TERMS

Bento: Lunch box – when ordered at a restaurant, can be an extensive meal

Daimyo: Feudal lord

Dori: Street or avenue

Futon: Thin mattress put on tatami mats

Geisha: Female entertainer

Haiku: Seventeen syllable poem

Happi: Short jacket worn at festivals

Honmaru: The central area of a castle where the keep stands

Irori: Open hearth

Jinja: Shinto shrine

Kaiseki: Formal Japanese cuisine

Kimono: Traditional Japanese garment

Koen: Public park

Mikoshi: Portable Shinto shrines used in festivals

Minshuku: Small family-run inns

Ninja: An Edo period spy

Noren: Short curtain hung in doorways

Onsen: Hot springs

Oshibori: Wet towel offered at restaurants

Origami: Folding paper craft

Otemon: Main gate of a castle

Pachinko: Pinball-like game

Post town: Towns which served as stopping points for Edo period travelers

Rotemburo: Outdoor bath, spa

Ryokan: Japanese inn

Shiatsu massage: Traditional Japanese massage using acupressure

Shogun: Military governors who ruled Japan from late 12th century until 1868

Shogunate: The government of the shogun
Shoji: Sliding doors with translucent paper panels
Tabi: One-toed socks
Tatami: Woven rice straw mats placed on the floor in traditional Japanese rooms
Teishoku: Set meal
Tokonoma: Alcove in traditional Japanese room where art and a flower arrangement are placed
Ukiyo-e: Edo period woodblock prints
Washi: Hand-made Japanese paper
Yukata: Casual cotton kimono

COMMON JAPANESE SUFFIXES

-san: Mountain (Mt. Fuji is Fuji-san)
-san: Mr., Mrs., or Ms. (Mr. Yamada is Yamada-san)
-dera: Buddhist temple (Kiyomizu Temple is Kiyomizu-dera)
-ji: Buddhist temple (Nanzen Temple is Nanzen-ji)
-jo: Castle (Himeji Castle is Himeji-jo)
-bashi: Bridge (Nihon Bridge is Nihonbashi)
-ko: Lake (Lake Biwa is Biwako)

INDEX

THINGS CHANGE!

Phone numbers, prices, addresses, quality of food, etc, all change. If you come across any new information, we'd appreciate hearing from you. No item is too small! Drop us an e-mail note at: Jopenroad@aol.com, or write us at:

Tokyo Guide
*Open Road Publishing, P.O. Box 284
Cold Spring Harbor, NY 11724*

OPEN ROAD PUBLISHING

U.S.A.

Colorado Guide, $16.95
Hawaii Guide, $17.95
Arizona Guide, $16.95
Texas Guide, $16.95
New Mexico Guide, $14.95
Disneyworld & Orlando Theme Parks, $13.95
Boston Guide, $13.95
Las Vegas Guide, $13.95
San Francisco Guide, $14.95
California Wine Country Guide, $12.95
America's Cheap Sleeps, $16.95
America's Grand Hotels, $14.95
America's Most Charming Towns &
   Villages, $16.95
Florida Golf Guide, $16.95
Golf Courses of the Southwest, $14.95
Washington DC Ethnic Restaurant
   Guide, $9.95

MIDDLE EAST/AFRICA

Israel Guide, $17.95
Jerusalem Guide, $13.95
Egypt Guide, $17.95
Kenya Guide, $18.95

UNIQUE TRAVEL

New Year's Eve 1999!, $16.95
The World's Most Intimate Cruises, $17.95
Celebrity Weddings & Honeymoon
   Getaways, $16.95
CDC's Complete Guide to Healthy
   Travel, $14.95

SMART HANDBOOKS

The Smart Runner's Handbook, $9.95
The Smart Home Buyer's
   Handbook, $16.95

CENTRAL AMERICA & CARIBBEAN

Caribbean Guide, $19.95
Caribbean With Kids, $14.95
Central America Guide, $17.95
Costa Rica Guide, $17.95
Belize Guide, $16.95
Honduras & Bay Islands Guide, $15.95
Guatemala Guide, $17.95
Southern Mexico & Yucatan Guide, $14.95
Bermuda Guide, $14.95
Bahamas Guide, $13.95

EUROPE

London Guide, $14.95
Rome & Southern Italy Guide, $14.95
Paris Guide, $13.95
Moscow Guide, $15.95
Prague Guide, $14.95
France Guide, $16.95
Portugal Guide, $16.95
Ireland Guide, $16.95
Spain Guide, $18.95
Italy Guide, $19.95
Holland Guide, $15.95
Austria Guide, $15.95
Czech & Slovak Republics Guide, $16.95
Greek Islands Guide, $16.95
Turkey Guide, $17.95

ASIA

Tokyo Guide, $14.95
Japan Guide, $19.95
Tahiti & French Polynesia Guide, $17.95
China Guide, $18.95
Hong Kong & Macau Guide, $13.95
Vietnam Guide, $14.95
Thailand Guide, $17.95
Philippines Guide, $16.95

To order any Open Road book, send us a check or money order for the price of the book(s) plus $3.00 shipping and handling for domestic orders, to: **Open Road Publishing, PO Box 284, Cold Spring Harbor, NY 11724**